THE CRITICS

LEHMAN ENGEL

★   ★   ★   ★

The Critics

★   ★   ★   ★

Macmillan Publishing Co., Inc.

NEW YORK

Macmillan Publishing Co., Inc.
866 Third Avenue, New York, N.Y. 10022
Collier Macmillan Canada, Ltd.

Library of Congress Cataloging in Publication Data

Engel, Lehman, 1910–
  The critics.
  Includes index.
  1. Dramatic criticism—United States—History.
I. Title.
PN1707.E5   792′.015   76-10829
ISBN 0-02-536060-4

FIRST PRINTING 1976

Printed in the United States of America

What O'Neill has succeeded in doing in *The Great God Brown* . . . is obviously more important than what he has not succeeded in doing.

—BROOKS ATKINSON

Nostalgia has become a semi-permanent part of the American psyche, and why not? Nostalgia is nature's way of telling you the road to Utopia is blocked straight ahead, so swing around and try the back road through the past.

—MACK KROLL

It has one or two show-stoppers but practically no show-advancers.

—GEORGE OPPENHEIMER

Why is the best British humor so clearly superior to ours? Partly because it is more satirical, which is to say it is about something, not just sealed off in a vacuum.

—JOHN SIMON

Contents

ACKNOWLEDGMENTS xi

INTRODUCTION xiii

1 Cerberus: The Three New York Dailies 1

2 Walter Kerr 77

3 A Summary of Some Earlier Critics 94

4 Two Elder Statesmen 102

5 Peripheral Newspapers 115

6 Magazines 146

7 Some Critics Outside New York 225

8 Et Resurrexit 290

9 Conclusion 306

INDEX 321

ACKNOWLEDGMENTS

The author wishes to acknowledge the invaluable assistance of many people who helped to make this book possible. These include many of the critics and reviewers who supplied me with copies of their own work.

I am grateful to Dan Sullivan for calling attention to a number of critical works, to Robert Eason for research in the work of John Rosenfield, to Robert Joseph, Ray Roberts, James Neyland, Norma Grossman and the late Arthur Kober for the loan of material; to Lorraine Steurer; and to Robert Bishop for his invaluable work in preparing the manuscript, as well as to many others who encouraged me to embark on this enterprise.

Introduction

Like it or not, the critic has a responsibility to the theater without which he would not be a reviewer. It would therefore seem important to the theater and to everyone connected with it, even if only empathically, that he keep in mind his obligation to make certain that what he has to say inflicts the least damage possible on the theater.

To be sure, the daily theater reviewer is in the position of being "damned if you do and damned if you don't." If he writes well of a show that is found less than praiseworthy by many people who attend because of his praise, he is loathed. Similarly, if he pans a show that is, perhaps in spite of obvious weaknesses, enjoyed by one segment of the public—given sufficient time to discover it for itself— he is the object of derision. Both situations are amply illustrated in the following pages.

I personally did not enjoy *Same Time, Next Year* (a hit) or *Pacific Overtures* (not a hit) but I would encourage (and for reasons very different from a reviewer's) the theatergoer potentially interested in one or the other (not the *same* playgoer) to see the one I felt he would be most likely to enjoy.

The question of absolute critical taste belongs, in my opinion, to the critic who has the necessary background and experience to warrant his being considered an authority and who is given the time and space for sober consideration in his journal. The daily reviewer certainly has neither the time nor the space for careful consideration, yet the lack of these very things produces the conditions that make his opinion important: immediacy and instant decision-making for good or bad. He is the Dow Jones of the theater and it is rare when his judgment, justified or not, fails to coincide with, or to cause the end or the beginning of, a show's life-span.

This book is chiefly concerned with the daily reviewer who, because of his immediate decision and the enormity of his audience, wields much greater power than the critic. If I seem unusually brutal toward him at times, I hope the reader will bear with me. I don't think I have levelled any charges against anyone that have not been amply substantiated by his own words. And what matters most to me, and hopefully to the reader, is the theater itself, which too often suffers needlessly as a result of carelessness, personal proclivities, and an attempt on the part of certain reviewers to attract attention through irony and ridicule. Ridicule is not to be confused, as it too frequently is, with criticism.

One of the most destructive concomitants of daily reviewing is the compulsion to comment on every single element of a new show. For example, I attended the opening of *Fiddler on the Roof*, and as I was going up the aisle after the final curtain, arm-in-arm with a happy, somewhat tearful but enthusiastic audience, someone asked how I liked the music. I was taken aback at the question, since my being a professional musician had not funneled my attention solely to the music and so I had only a slight memory of it; in fact, I had only a slight recollection of any of the single elements because I had surrendered myself that first time to the total experience of the show. Yet most of the pleased reviewers had affixed at least one adjective to the show itself, to the director, the choreographer, several principal players (especially to Zero Mostel, the star), the scenic designer, the lighting, the lyrics, music, libretto, and so on.

From a purely personal point of view, heightened by decades of creative theatrical involvement as well as theatergoing, I had been too engrossed by the show as a whole to do anything resembling umpire-like score-keeping. I don't think I am less intelligent than any of the reviewers or even less experienced at evaluating what I see; but I would have been powerless to tick off the credits, one by one. Indeed, I believe anyone capable of doing just that must of necessity fail to grasp the sum total, which is the main point. Because of my initial inability to deal with the separate elements, I had to return to *Fiddler* numerous times and force myself to suffer disengagement from the whole in order to examine its parts.

Since theater is experience, it is wasteful that many a reviewer wards it off by standing outside the presentation to tally its faults and virtues, often missing the show's whole point. For a theater experience is not generated by any one or two good or poor elements, but is the sum of them all.

I am not suggesting that the experience of feeling should rule out thought; but I do suggest that in the theater, feeling is *first*. It seems to me that when any show fails to provide enough feeling—happy or sad—to engross an audience, it fails. And if it fails, the reviewers' thoughtful examination is essential in trying to determine the precise reasons for its failure. These conclusions are important to the writer, the director, and the producer, as well as to the audience.

But the critics—especially the three whose reviews appear daily—do indeed, with a few notable exceptions, wield the power to persuade or dissuade the theatergoing brave, and I propose to examine what they say and how they say it. Their words, and the way they use them, have definite effects on the public and, therefore, on the theater itself.

As for television theater reviews, it is my opinion that being oral, they have little impact on the fate of shows. If they are favorable and therefore useful to the producer in his follow-up advertisements, they seem more important in print. But the voices of the TV reviewers are heard at random times during the late-evening news programs, and locating their lean spots requires patience and a special interest on the part of the viewer. Since most of them are on the air during the same time-span, hearing more than one is a matter of chance. The largest number of tube-observers either are not at home or not awake during their telecasts, and what is said by the reviewer is heard so *en passant* by those who are watching that it is remembered merely as a simple plus or minus. It is doubtful that these reviews have the power to lengthen or abbreviate the run of a show.

For the most part, I will *not* be writing about *critics*. What we read daily are pieces by journalist-reviewers who have a job to perform within a restricted time. Their judgments are swift and personal, the result of reaction rather than consideration. They have a commercial obligation to their employers and to their readers who are potential ticket-buyers.

Dr. Jack Watson, retired dean of the Cincinnati College-Conservatory of Music, writes that criticism is a "partial biography of the critic himself," and Stephen Pepper, head of the Department of Philosophy at the University of California in Berkeley, said, "If you like one artist and I like another, that is a psychologically interesting difference between us."

Since I subscribe to each of these observations, I must also believe that, in effect, each critic exposes himself in his reviews. He displays his limitations as well as his knowledge, his highly personal preferences, and so on. The latter *might* be acceptable were it not for the fact that these preferences automatically become "Supreme Court" edicts: When Nero's thumb points upward, the gladiator's life is spared; thumb down, he is slain.

Among New York drama critics there are tiresome repetitions of a purely personal nature. As criticism they are not only unacceptable, but immoral, in view of the disastrous effects they usually have. One of the most destructive elements to be found at the core of too many reviews is anger. Anger is an animal reaction generated by any of several quite different causes. Some of these reactions are common and normal to most human beings, even if they are unproductive and somewhat self-destructive.

I believe, however, that when a play, performance, musical score, scenery, or direction is poor but nonetheless sincere, critical anger against it should be replaced by at least peripheral analysis and reason. For by coolly pointing out the faults which he sincerely believes exist, the critic is rendering a service to those who create as well as to those who observe. He is then assuming the roles of guide and teacher, and these can never be truly effective if they incriminate rather than advise. Critical anger reveals the critic's own fears, and though he is destroying what he is reacting against, he is also revealing his own psyche—a course that he had best forgo.

It is my feeling, although producers who might conceivably benefit from it would become its strongest opponents, that reviewers should not report on new productions until several weeks after an unofficial opening. Such an idea is in line with extensive previewing and was most successfully applied in the case of *A Chorus Line,* which played to wildly enthusiastic audiences four or five weeks before the reviewers were invited to see it.

Perhaps (as will be discussed a little more fully later) critics who want to be helpful might refrain altogether from filing *any* review of a new show about which they felt negatively: poor word-of-mouth alone would then be entirely responsible for the show's failure.

In any event, all reviewers must surely be aware that there are many different "publics" and that one conceivably fascinated by a Marlowe play might despise *Hello, Dolly!* or vice versa. With this kind of awareness it seems to me possible that—without resorting to perjury or incriminating the reviewer himself—reviews might be slanted toward the general group that would find satisfaction in a particular presentation.

In the end, it is the tone and accent of a review that usually affects the theater piece under consideration. In addition to guidance by reviewers, a number of well-known factors determine to a great extent the theatergoing of the many publics. So the reviewers, or "critics," as too many of these writers are called, have a serious responsibility —not, unfortunately, always wisely employed—toward those people whose attendance at the theater is encouraged or deterred by what is written in the daily press.

Many reviewers possess the qualities which would allow them to become critics—if they had sufficient time and space. But as matters stand today—matters not altogether of their own making—reviewers are thermometers that advise either going out or staying snugly at home. It is this aspect of theater reviewing that the following pages will attempt to pinpoint.

THE CRITICS

Cerberus:
The Three New York Dailies

CLIVE BARNES

BETWEEN BROOKS ATKINSON's retirement in 1960 and Clive Barnes' takeover in 1967, *The New York Times* employed three main reviewers. Howard Taubman, who had graduated from music critic to drama, held the post from 1960 to 1966; Stanley Kauffman took over next for a brief period, followed by Walter Kerr. (During the tenures of these writers, dramatic criticism was also supplied by Dan Sullivan, Mel Gussow, Lewis Funke, and others.) Kerr wrote daily reviews for more than a year, then concentrated on writing Sunday essays after Barnes arrived on the scene.

Clive Barnes contends that he possesses little, if any, power. ". . . critics [don't] close shows, not really," he says. ". . . producers and playwrights are the people who close shows."

The New York Times, for which Barnes is the leading theater and dance critic, enjoys a daily circulation of nearly 878,000. This wide reading audience automatically gives Barnes first-magnitude power and automatically makes his contention that he possesses little, if any, power, false. Further, Barnes is being evasive in shifting the blame for being closers of shows from critics (particularly himself, because of the enormity of his power), to producers and playwrights. Obviously what he suggests is that only bad plays and poor productions make bad shows; he ignores the fact that critical displeasure can and does frequently precipitate the end of a show's run, despite its merits and potential interest.

Later, in the same interview in which he made the foregoing statements, Barnes complains, "If I were to think in those terms [that he had the power to close shows], it might be disturbing." It seems to me that the workers who lose their jobs when a show folds, the producer who had perhaps given two years of his life getting the production onto the stage, and the backers who made the production possible have a more realistic reason than Barnes to be "disturbed."

Every drama critic of *The New York Times* has always possessed the power to close shows. Formerly—in the good old days of Brooks Atkinson and, later, of Walter Kerr, when he was a daily reviewer—the royal power worked both ways, which is to say that those gentlemen also could, and frequently did, sustain a show's life because of their enthusiasm. Today, Mr. Barnes' enthusiasm has been so frequently misdirected that he has forfeited the life-giving power he inherited. But with the clicking of his typewriter, he can still effectively chop off the head of a show.

In this connection, the following exchange is relevant here. The views expressed are from taped conversations between Mr. Barnes and unidentified questioners made by the *Dramatists Guild Quarterly*.

BARNES: I have tried to make the reviews rather more personal, tried to remove the sense of judgment in them. I said once, and I believe it, if the drama critic of the *Times* must stand on his head in public to stop people from taking him so seriously, that's a valuable duty for him to do. Critics don't want power, they want influence, and there is a big difference. But it is really the producers who give the critics power.

Q: How is that?

BARNES: The producers are continually making the public aware of the critics' judgment in advertisements and other public statements. As soon as you have full-page advertisements shouting about "unanimous raves," you immediately put yourself into a vulnerable position when you have unanimous pans.

Remember, the real box-office power is word of mouth.

When a play opens on Monday and the reviews come out on Tuesday, at that moment the word of mouth is almost entirely the critics, and the *Times* is the most important. But that power has already eroded, and what people are saying becomes most important.

If the producers were ready to nurse certain shows, if they showed more faith in their product, I think they could often do a lot better.

Word-of-mouth advertising has always been an important factor in the life of a show. However, given today's practices, there is no time for it to germinate between the time the show opens and the time the reviews appear. And if the reviews are poor, the producer needs much more than "faith" to keep the show running. The dollar layout each week is enormous, and with no assurance that his struggle will in the end succeed, any producer who attempts to raise and spend money, in the hope that the time he is buying will engender a sufficient amount of positive public response, is probably throwing good money after bad. More often, a critic's favorable review of a show whose central idea fails to interest a large segment of the public will close after a briefer-than-calculated run because of negative word-of-mouth reactions. (". . . critics can get people into the theater for a certain time, but they can't keep them coming.") But again, only time can create the hopeful situation and a poor press allows no time.

I must also disagree with Barnes' contention that "there is a big difference" between "influence," which he favors, and "power," with which he wants no traffic. An adverse opinion of a show published in *The New York Times* will "influence" audiences not to attend. Is this not "power"? Aren't influence and power synonymous in this case?

Clive Barnes usually composes interesting, readable reviews. His background is serviceable and his judgment—when it is clearly one-directional (which it usually is not)—is frequently fair. However, his inconsistencies are legion and I believe he suffers from an acute fear of being thought old.* In a frantic effort to forestall such an allegation he plunges headlong into see-how-mod-I-am waters to prove that he is on the side of the young angels and the sometimes menacing minorities. He may have some admirable motives, but I have carefully studied his writings and think much of what he says is misplaced, harmful, and decidedly unfair.

Admittedly, any reviewer who wants to encourage good theater must be troubled when he has to write about an unfinished, possibly amateurish though promising work. However, when he misleads creative people and audiences by employing an identical vocabulary to describe both the best and the most immature, his ambiguity cannot fail to have destructive consequences for all—the less accomplished, the more professional, and the audiences. Also, because Barnes has deafeningly trumpeted so many double- and triple-standard proclamations in behalf of less-than-accomplished

---

*Long after I had reached this conclusion, I read the following Barnes statement: ". . . people who consider themselves in the avant-garde think I am a fuddy-duddy."

efforts, he has sacrificed a significant part of his own inherited status as both critic and power. You can cry "Wolf!" only so many times before listeners start turning off their hearing aids.

To illustrate my point, let's look at the way Mr. Barnes deals with black-theater productions. Most of the favorable things he says about *What the Wine-Sellers Buy* by Ron Milner seem to be excuses for something that fails to meet a higher standard. This apologetic optimism is seldom found in Barnes' reviews of nonethnic plays:

"It is an interesting play and deserves a wider circulation. . . ."

"It is a pretty simple, even sentimental story, but what raises it above the level of daytime television is Mr. Milner's way with language and his observation of character."

"The acting had an idiomatic zest to it." (The worst actors in the world can have an "idiomatic zest.")

"Mr. Williams is cool and brilliant, like a refrigerated diamond." (This is one of Mr. Barnes' many ambiguous metaphors. But "brilliant" in his vocabulary also applies to Laurence Olivier, Zero Mostel, Eugene O'Neill, and many others, and would therefore equate Mr. Dick A. Williams with those who dwell in the highest galaxy.)

"Mr. Milner's play is very worthy of attention . . . will be applauded by many."

Ending this review are patent cop-outs that are misleading to the uninitiated reader. Does Barnes feel that he is performing a service to the playwright, his reading public, and to himself?

There is similar pussyfooting about *Black Sunlight* by Al Davis:

"Mr. Davis' play does present a credible picture. . . ." (Does?)

". . . where Mr. Davis and his director, Kris Keiser, have been successful is in catching something of the African atmosphere."

". . . an idealism occasionally unfulfilled was captured in this stiff but not uninteresting play."

A play that is *not* uninteresting is interesting. Isn't "occasionally unfulfilled" a vague and meaningless qualification indicating that only under these conditions would Mr. Barnes refuse to be more direct?

And what do remarks like "catching something of the African atmosphere" mean? Would a Rhodesian or a Ugandan think so, or only an American? Puccini did *not* catch an American atmosphere in *The Girl of the Golden West*, although possibly Italians thought he had. And while the chorus of priestesses in *Aïda* might have been thought "Egyptian" by the Italians of the composer's day, this was surely not true of the Egyptians. To me this sort of assessment is meaningless and therefore better left unsaid.

Mr. Barnes goes on:

"The playwright gains from public appraisal, and the audience gets yet another glimpse of all those young black playwrights on the move."

Are *"all"* those young black playwrights" talented? If we can't be specific about who is talented and "on the move," these packed-in-cotton phrases are created solely because the playwrights are black. This is discrimination of the most arrant kind, unfruitful for anybody and misleading to everyone.

Writing about *My Sister, My Sister* by Ray Aranha, Barnes says in his final paragraph: *"My Sister, My Sister* is strong and demanding theater. It is not perfect, but it is certainly a striking psychological sketch for a family portrait."

The play, in truth, was neither strong nor demanding. To describe it as "not perfect" is to patronize and confuse, and calling it a "striking psychological sketch" recalls *Equus, Who's Afraid of Virginia Woolf?* and any play by Pinter, Storey, Ionesco, or even Beckett. Is it helpful to lead the author of *My Sister, My Sister* to believe that his play belongs in such distinguished company?

Billy Noname, a musical (book by W. W. Mackey, music and lyrics by Johnny Brandon), elicited the following comments from Barnes: "Growing up black is the subject . . . The musical itself is a strange piece of work that had me in fluctuating moods of approval and uncertainty throughout the evening."

It's odd that Barnes didn't experience "fluctuating moods of approval and uncertainty" when he saw *Henry, Sweet Henry; Maggie Flynn; Billy; Look to the Lilies; Hogan's Goat; Georgy; Dear World; F. Jasmine Addams; Minnie's Boys; Her First Roman; How Now Dow Jones;* and many other musicals about which he drew definite and adverse conclusions. But *Billy Noname* was somehow a "strange piece of work." Its "sincerity is undeniable, but its clarity and significance are more in question." I can state, without any qualifications, that all the other musicals listed above were also "sincere." All lacked "clarity" and "significance." Why was it so difficult for Barnes to be positive about *Billy Noname?*

"One dance, starring Charles Moore as a returning GI on V-J Day, was exceptional; but all in all this is the best choreography we have seen in the musical theater for some time."

It is impossible of course to know what duration of time Barnes has in mind. A day? A week? A decade? However *Billy Noname* opened on Monday evening, March 2, 1970. During the six months prior to that date, there was choreography in other productions by Peter Gennaro, Alvin Ailey, Onna White, Jacques D'Amboise, and Howard Joffrey, to name but a few; but the dances in *Billy Noname*, according to Barnes, were "the best . . . we have seen in the musical theater for some time."

The River Niger by Joseph A. Walker "is big, wide and deep. It is one of the best black plays . . ." said Barnes. Is it desirable to *segregate* works of art: Michelangelo was one of the best Italian sculptors, Picasso one of the best Spanish painters, Tennessee Williams one of the best Southern white playwrights, and so on?

Barnes *offends* the movement of black theater because he deludes many of the playwrights into thinking themselves more accomplished than they actually are. (Most are new and as yet inexperienced.) He inhibits attendance by making their plays seem more "special," which some of them are not. And he is being unfair to the rest of the theater by basing his reviews on criteria different from those by which he judges nonethnic productions.

Black theater is not the only one considered ethnic, and Barnes employed a similar soft pedal when he encountered a dreadful musical called *Ari*, thought to be Jewish because of its subject matter. Like the black plays, it was militant.

Barnes, at the outset of his review, says that Leon Uris' *Exodus* was popular as a novel and a film, neither of which he read or saw, but "it was clearly within its own terms of reference highly successful."

No doubt. Factual, if nonessential to the review of *Ari*, the son of *Exodus*:

"Mr. Uris is trying to write a serious musical and, indeed, it must be one of the least lighthearted musicals in Broadway history, which is a kind of record. . . . But seriousness is not always a substitute for art . . ."

"Naturally enough, *Exodus* starts with a strong story . . ."

Why is starting with a strong story natural? The beginning of this review is an exercise in foot-shuffling, coughing, clearing of throat, sharpening of pencils, going to the bathroom, or perhaps whistling with the lights out.

"Apart from the initial situation of the story itself and a couple of songs by Walt Smith, almost everything else about *Exodus* is faulty."

"Sometimes the musical is extraordinarily difficult to follow."

"I suspect that the story will be most appreciated by people who have already read the book—but, after all, there must be enough of these around."

Why is Barnes so apologetic with his remarks that "about everything else . . . is faulty" and "sometimes the musical is extraordinarily difficult to follow"? Doesn't his statement, "the story will be appreciated . . . ," sound like an attempt at appeasement? Of course, there are many people who have read the book; but how can this have anything to do with the enjoyment of the show? It is not as though they were seeing an opera in Italian or a play in Yiddish.

Finally, halfway down the second column, Barnes says something definite and clearly adverse:

"The dialogue . . . is about as bright as a grimy windowpane, and a further aid to the show's soporific nature is provided by Mr. Uris' lyrics, which are banal and clumsy . . . it is a lackluster score."

After that, the floodgates open. But why did it take so long in this "ethnic" (as a matter of fact, it wasn't ethnic) show? It was about a Jewish struggle, which does not qualify it for a stained-glass window in a Tel-Aviv synagogue.

In a sense, this method of complimenting the unfinished, the promising, the possible, or the probable (at best, a guessing game) is the one employed by parents in connection with young children who have recited a jingle or played "Chopsticks" on the piano. When applied to adults, with the harmless living-room applause translated into print in the leading journal of a metropolis, harm is done to everyone. And latent within this formula, there lurks the evil (probably unconscious) that comes from being patronizing.

Now, bearing in mind Barnes' largely apologetic and qualified observations about less-than-first-class material, look at the direct comments he makes about shows that were nonethnic, professional, and the work of more practiced talents:

Cabaret (revisited): "It is not among my favorite musicals."

Loot: "You will either hate *Loot* or like it a lot. But don't take your Aunt Mildred—especially if she has just died." (This latter was the last sentence of the review.)

Indians: "Mr. Kopit had a startlingly good concept, which went slightly but disastrously awry."

Cry for Us All: "It was called *Cry for Us All*. I found myself crying only for Mr. Alford [the author of the play]." (In first paragaraph.)

Dear World: "*Dear World*—Dear Heavens!—Dear tickets: that in telegraphese seems to be my message for the Mark Hellinger Theatre . . ." (First sentence.)

Follies: ". . . is the kind of musical that should have its cast album out on 78s." (In first paragraph).

Godspell: ". . . a certain atmosphere of amateurism that is pleasant enough to encounter almost anywhere but in the professional theatre." (Why should this off-Broadway theater be considered more professional than the others offering ethnic plays?)

Maggie Flynn: "Whatever it is that has happened to the musical is not likely to be put right by *Maggie Flynn*." (First sentence.)

Henry, Sweet Henry: "Whatever it is that happened to the American musical is not likely to be put right by *Henry, Sweet Henry*."

Minnie's Boys (music by Larry Grossman and lyrics by Hal Hacka-day): "It would probably be unfair to characterize the music as gross and hack . . ."

Pippin: "The book is feeble and the music bland, yet the show runs like a racehorse."

Georgy: "Whatever it is that is wrong with *Georgy* . . . is wrong for too long." (First sentence.)

The Fig Leaves Are Falling: ". . . there is nothing much wrong with *The Fig Leaves Are Falling* . . . that a new book, new lyrics, new settings, new direction, new choreography, and a partially new cast would not quite possibly put right." (First paragraph.)

Hair: "I think it is simply that it is so likeable." (In first paragraph).

Irrefutably, these excerpts and many others are "judgments" and they are at odds with the *Times'* reviewer's following remarks:*

"[The function of a critic] is [to serve as] a link between the artist and the audience. Obviously, part of the job involves an act of judgment, but I think those who consider the judgment the most important element of his function are wrong."

Despite Mr. Barnes' thoughts to the contrary, one must discount his conclusion.

Q: Have you been made to feel that your function as a critic is to sell tickets?

BARNES: A lot of *you* think that is my function. I refuse to accept it. Although it would be utterly unrealistic of me to adopt the completely pure attitude . . .

Whether he accepts it or not is beside the point: *The New York Times'* reviewer's judgment (conclusion) in fact helps to sell or to prevent the sale of tickets.

I should like next to consider Barnes' review of *Company* (book

*From a discussion between Barnes and an anonymous questioner taped by the *Dramatists Guild Quarterly*.

by George Furth, music and lyrics by Stephen Sondheim, produced and directed by Harold Prince, designed by Boris Aronson), which opened April 26, 1970. Barnes' review, a detailed account of which follows, consisted of confusion, bias, error, and inconsistency.

Paragraphs 1 and 2 are about New York City (pencil- or knife-sharpening) and are never specifically related to the show; hence twenty lines of nonrelevance start the review of a show by a composer-lyricist and producer-director of unique importance in today's theater.

Paragraph 3 continues: ". . . about which I have some personal reservations . . . deserves to be a hit in a lean season . . . will be particularly popular with tourists, especially those from Vladivostok [this refers to the opening sentence about New York] and West-chester who will get the kind of insight into New York's jungle that you perceive in the survival-kit information provided by *New York* magazine. Indeed, if you like *New York* magazine, you will probably love *Company*."

Paragraph 4 gives the credits and says the show "is about the joys and pains of married love in New York City. Particularly the pains."

In relating *Company's* plot (in Paragraph 5), Barnes groups "five apparently *childless* and *seemingly unemployed* couples [author's italics] . . ."

Paragraph 6 refers to the leading character's three girl friends: "One of them is vulgar enough actually to work for a living. She is an airline stewardess, but luckily takes her hat off in bed."

Writing of Sondheim's music in Paragraph 7, Barnes observes: "It is the kind of music that makes me say: 'Oh, yeah?' rather than 'Gee whiz!' but I readily concede that many people will consider its sheer musical literacy as offsetting all other considerations."

In a discussion of Mr. Furth's book (Paragraph 8), Barnes says "it is a strange mixture of lines almost witty enough to be memorable and other phrases that more decorously might have been left on the road."

In Paragraph 9, the critic calls the characters (with a single exception) "trivial, shallow, worthless, and horrid"—"just the kind . . . you expend hours each day trying to escape from."

Paragraph 10 relates to the same "undesirable" people.

Paragraph 11 faults the play's structure, saying it lacks "a variety of pace and character" and the problem is left to the director "to impose a satisfactory unity on the show. This Mr. Prince has not done . . ."

Regarding Boris Aronson's set (Paragraph 12): "It is all in a tasteful shade of perspex, and looks better than it sounds."

Paragraph 13 refers to Michael Bennett's choreography: "[It] has genuine vitality, and it is one of the major joys of the show."

In Paragraph 14 he expressed his dislike of Dean Jones who first played the lead in *Company* but was replaced after a short time by Larry Kert, who was far superior. The other members of the cast are mentioned as "all fine."

A musical that "deserves to be a hit in a lean season" is clearly not thought well of by the reviewer. *Company* was not popular with tourists who generally disliked it because of its newness. The reference to *New York* magazine has nothing to do with *Company* and is a not-very-indirect slap at John Simon, *New York* magazine's reviewer.

Barnes was so eager to cast this show aside that he failed to listen carefully. How can couples be "seemingly unemployed" just because the audience does not see them at work? If they were poor, they wouldn't live in penthouses and would be concerned with their financial woes. These they must not have.

In Act One, David says:

"This is everything, huh? No. *This* is everything. I got my wife, my kids, a home."

And in Act Two, Peter says:

"I mean I've got responsibilities . . . Susan and the kids to take care of."

The couples, then, are not "childless."

Barnes' resentment—and I cannot understand resentment in *any* critic—of *Company* is everywhere evident. It takes the form of a wisecrack in referring to the airline stewardess who is "vulgar enough actually to work for a living" and "luckily takes her hat off in bed."

A reviewer who writes in this flip style about a musical that—like it or not—is seriously trying to go somewhere new, is being reckless with the theater itself.

In describing Sondheim's music as " 'Oh, yeah?' rather than 'Gee whiz!' " Barnes is being snide.

In calling all but one of the characters "trivial, shallow, worthless, and horrid," it would seem that Barnes missed the entire point. Are the characters not similar in these respects to those in *The Seagull* and *King Lear*? And as for their being "the kind . . . you expend hours . . . trying to escape from," I should like to pose a question: Wouldn't anyone in his right mind want to escape from most of the characters in the plays by O'Neill, Pinter, Ibsen, Albee, or Williams? I wouldn't relish entertaining the Macbeths, either— or Beethoven or Wagner for that matter.

The observation that "Boris Aronson's set . . . looks better than it sounds" is arrogant. Isn't it supposed to?

In his appreciation of Michael Bennett's choreography as "one of the major joys of the show," Barnes is slyly expressing his loathing for the rest of *Company*, since in the two-and-a-half-hour show, there is only one solo dance that lasts perhaps five minutes and a staged musical number ("dance" is not a correct appellation).

Barnes' final paragraph is given in its entirety:

"I was antagonized by the slickness, the obviousness, of *Company*. But I stress that I really believe a lot of people are going to love it. Don't let me put you off. Between ourselves, I had reservations about *West Side Story*."

And again, from the *Dramatists Guild Quarterly's* taped conversations with Barnes:

Q: Do you feel you should encourage the play that tried something more difficult and succeeded less than the play which succeeded more in a lesser intention?

BARNES: The answer is yes.

So Barnes' review of *Company*, a truly significant show, especially in this period of transition, is indecisive about its most important elements and generally discouraging to the ticket buyer. In this case, *did* he "encourage the play that tried something more difficult"?

And now about Barnes and *Hair*.

"So new, so fresh and so unassuming, even in its pretensions."

In paragraph 2 he says: "When *Hair* started its long-term joust against Broadway's world of Sigmund Romberg . . . ," and goes on to say of the music that it "came across with a kind of acid-rock, powerhouse lyricism . . . brilliant lyrics!"

While it is possible that Barnes' approval of the "Yip-Yip-Hooray roaring boys" may be sincere, his approbation is another manifestation of his fear of being thought a "fuddy-duddy."

Is it possible that anything can be "unassuming, even in its pretentiousness"? This is either meaningless or precious, but in any case, it is certainly confusing.

In referring to a "long-term joust against Broadway's world of Sigmund Romberg . . ." Barnes disregards the composers who broke away from the Romberg school to create our most important musical theater era. Surely he is aware that the Broadway musical was advancing in a new direction while Romberg was still writing. Romberg's last show, *My Romance* in 1948, was a failure; but more than twenty years before that Kern, Rodgers, Porter, Gershwin, Schwartz, Styne, Weill, Berlin, Rome, Blitzstein, Arlen, Lane, and later Bernstein and Sondheim, had already left Romberg to history and had "advanced" in an orderly and meaningful manner. And while their music had grown, their contributions had also advanced the musical theater.

Hair was indeed an explosion that made a loud noise. Its music did not advance theater or theater music, and like all rockets it eventually fizzled out, removing itself and its impotent descendants forever from the theater where it had never belonged in the first place. *Hair* and its progeny underwrote the ailing record industry by appealing to the kids who never noticed its failings as a theatrical piece because they had never attended the theater.

Next, Barnes heard the music of *Hair* "with a kind of acid-rock, powerhouse lyricism." Doesn't lyricism connote lilt, expressiveness, and consonance? How, then, can anyone reconcile it with acid-rock and powerhouse?

As for "brilliant lyrics"—!!

"Aquarius," the best in the long, long series of songs, has a juvenile jingle for lyrics. "Manchester's" key line is: "And I believe that Gawd believes in Claude" [the singer of the song].

"Manhattan"* is largely a catalogue of any and everything. So is "Colored Spade," which has such a hitherto unthought-of couplet: "Watermelon/Hominy Grits."

"Sodomy" ends with "Masturbation can be fun. . . ." What precedes this "fresh" humor is a catalogue of sexual nomenclature.

"Ain't Got No" is breathtakingly brilliant—it consists of eighteen "Ain't Got No's," each followed by another formless, leading-nowhere catalogue of nouns from "home" to "mind."

"I Got Life" has fifty-seven lines beginning with the first two of these words, each line again ending with a single word—first, family; then relatives; then parts of the body.

The lyrics of the other songs in *Hair* are equally "brilliant."

Barnes, in the same review, prescribes a panacea that no other book-writers in trouble had better take to heart:

"Now the authors of the dowdy book—and brilliant lyrics—have done a very brave thing. They have in effect done away with it altogether." Then he continues: "The theme, such as it is, concerns a dropout who freaks in, but the attitudes are those of protest or alienation. As the hero says at one point: 'I want to eat mushrooms. I want to sleep in the sun.'

"These attitudes will annoy many people, but as long as Thoreau is part of America's heritage, others will respond to this musical that marches to a different drummer."

*Cheeky title. Remember the lyrics to the song of the same name by one Lorenz Hart? "Brilliant lyrics," anyone?

Is it possible that those two sophomoric lines would remind anyone of Thoreau? Besides, they are such an infinitesimal part of *Hair* as to be scarcely noticed. They have nothing in common with the rest of the language in this show. And Thoreau?

This is not criticism, but an effort to justify a feeling. Mr. Barnes simply liked *Hair* and he was at pains to substantiate his position. What he came up with is as far removed from the realities of *Hair* as scampi is from chocolate candy.

We see what Sondheim-Furth-Prince got for seriously trying in *Company*, what *Hair* got out of knowing absolutely nothing (followed, predictably, by the inevitable debacle of two of its writers' second try, *Dude*). Now let us see what, in Barnes' opinion, merits genuine glee.

Let's begin with two shows, *Promenade* and *The Journey of Snow White*, by Al Carmines; then like a crab, go backward, and try to lay out some of the ingredients Barnes espouses as concomitants of successful musicals.

Promenade has music by Al Carmines, and book and lyrics by Maria Irene Fornes. This is no book in any conventional sense. Indeed it comes close to being no book in any unconventional sense. There is a kind of theme running through the work—the confrontation between goodies and baddies. . . .

The *Candide*-like episodes are strung together loosely, and the atmosphere is more one of wry irony than social satire. But it is the music and lyrics that count. And these add up magnificently.

There may be those who will question the slightness of the story line, but there will be more, many, many more who will glory in the show's dexterity, wit and compassion. Miss Fornes's lyrics, like her book, seem to have a sweetly irrelevant relevance. There is a Dada zaniness here that creeps up on you where you least expect it, and a topsy-turvy Brechtian morality that is most attractive.

At times the book and lyrics are perhaps coy—but always with a certain knowingness that prevents the coyness from becoming cloying. And a very cool madness is everywhere—extravagant, wild and diverting.

Mr. Carmines writes music like other people doodle. It cascades out of him in all shapes, sizes and styles. He is devastatingly eclectic, a veritable Autolycus of melodies. He can write you a twenties tune or a thirties tune, give a touch of Friml, a dash of Gershwin, a little Puccini even, spiced with Noël Coward, faced with Kurt Weill and Jacques Brel. Mr. Carmines is not so much a composer as a computer bank. Yet strangely enough these sweet, happy and inexhaustible pastiches all come out with the Carmines signature. Timeless, relaxed and melodious, his music always suggests, exquisitely, your favorite song being sung in the next room. . . . . .

To recap: "no book," "kind of theme," "*Candide*-like episodes strung together loosely," "slightness of the story line," "irrelevant relevance," "topsy-turvy Brechtian morality that is most attractive," "perhaps coy," "cool madness," "[Carmines' music] cascades out of him in all shapes, sizes and styles." Then Barnes identifies this music of a thousand faces: "twenties tune," "thirties tune," "a touch of Friml, a dash of Gershwin, a little Puccini even [why not?], spiced with Noël Coward, faced with Kurt Weill and Jacques Brel."

This is a perfect description of music by an amateur. It's what every artist has to learn *not* to do. It's as easy to do as sitting on a piano stool, which is exactly what Mr. Carmines does.

Then compare Barnes' reaction to Carmines' *The Journey of Snow White*, nearly two years and several shows after *Promenade:*

Al Carmines is the kind of artist who joins rather than merges. . . . It [the show] is delightful, like eating pistachio ice cream to the sound of cornets.

Mr. Carmines has produced both the libretto and the music, and is offering some happy insights into the Snow White myth. Mr. Carmines is so subject to influence that you might think he confuses the role of the artist with elective office, and is attempting to please everyone. But this is to misunderstand his method and his talents.

He is not one of those artists who cannibalize influences and merge them into their own artistic personalities. Rather he is a frankly eclectic artist whose extreme originality depends to a large extent upon the things he puts together. . . .

The music varies from Puccini, to Donizetti, a little Gilbert and Sullivan, a touch of church music, a shade of Gershwin, a few phrases of Mahler, not to mention Wagner, Mozart and others too numerous to hear. Yet it is happy, and the lyrics have wit and dexterity.

In the celebrated interview in the *Drama Review*, Barnes says that one of the functions of the critic is to "offer insights to the reader." This is certainly a very important point. That being the case, however, who is going to offer insights into what Barnes writes?

"Confuses the role of the artist with elective office." What has an artist to do with elective office? And who says Mr. Carmines is an artist? He hardly qualifies as such from Barnes' description of his musical style-in-a-blender. An artist invariably creates a style that is peculiarly his own. By putting together that list of musical styles, Barnes places Carmines in a category in which one would expect to find a demented chef or the *Macbeth* witches.

Carmines' success is as much a result of Barnes' raving as is the plague of rock musicals which we have endured for nearly a decade. None of these belonged in the theater which their writers never learned how to use. (More recently, Barnes "announced" that rock in the theater has had it; but that smacks somewhat of *The Sorcerer's Apprentice*.)

In his review of *Promenade* Barnes said of Carmines: "He is devastatingly eclectic." This is high praise, indeed, and Barnes makes similar comments about Carmines' other music. However, ponder Barnes' inconsistency when writing of other composers' scores in the following shows:

Henry, Sweet Henry: "The main trouble is with the music and lyrics by Bob Merrill, which are feeble. . . . For Mr. Merrill to write a musical like this is tantamount to Karlheinz Stockhausen's trying to compose in the style of Mendelssohn. It doesn't work."

Jesus Christ Superstar: "The music itself is extraordinarily eclectic. It runs so many gamuts it almost becomes a musical cart." (Recall Barnes' delight with Carmines' writing tunes reminiscent of the twenties or thirties with a touch of Friml, Gershwin, Puccini, Coward, Weill, etc.). The *precise* difference here is that Carmines is "*devastatingly* eclectic" (good) while the score of *Jesus Christ Superstar* is "*extraordinarily* eclectic" (bad).

1776: "For the music it would have been easy for Mr. Edwards to have produced a pastiche of Revolutionary tunes, but this he has studiously avoided."

Barnes writes aphorisms about the needs of the musicals. These, as the following excerpts show, waver like the lines on a seismograph:

Maggie Flynn: "I am very square about musicals and feel that the most important thing about them is the music."

Minnie's Boys: "It has a generally undistinguished score, but a couple of decent enough numbers, and a certain feel for its period, a certain kind of show business vitality."

F. Jasmine Addams: "The first essential of a musical adaptation is for it to add something to the play adapted."

Pippin: ". . . the book is feeble and the music bland, yet the show moves like a racehorse. It was probably Mr. Fosse's night. . . ."

Red, White and Maddox: "Yet despite failings, believe me, *Red, White and Maddox* is fun in the first place, and significant in the second. Who needs a third place?" (N.B. Barnes is enthusiastic about Act One; Act Two "goes too far." The music was never even *mentioned*.)

Promises, Promises: "Also it is a 'new musical' that does, for once, seem entitled to call itself 'new.' To an extent the new element is to be found in the book, for although ancestors can be found for the story . . . the intimacy of the piece is fresh. . . . Even more, there is the best of music; this is the first musical where you go out feeling rhythms rather than humming tunes."

The following represent Barnes' confusions in the matter of musical style which is Aye at several points and Nay at others:

George M!: "And at least the audience went out, for the first time this season, humming the music, even if most of it was more than 50 years old."

On the Town (revival): ". . . and while some of the glory has doubtless departed, there were moments of brightness if not incandescence. Perhaps—could it be?*—New York has changed. Certainly music has." (The music of *George M!* certainly hasn't.)

Gigi: "That the show . . . for all its incidental sparkle, never quite takes off in the manner of a *My Fair Lady* is partly a matter of changing taste."

The Pajama Game (revival): ". . . yet the music still stands—especially in elevators . . ."

Dames at Sea: ". . . a little gem of a musical. . . . It is the kind of blithe nostalgia for the glimpse rather than the remembrance of things past that informs *Dames at Sea*, giving a youthful air, making a pastiche without a middle-aged sag."

No, No, Nanette: "It is music to hum, and particularly music to dance to." (Of course after 50 years of the music, you hum it. And there's not a tap-dancer inhabitant of a single cemetery who hasn't danced to it.)

Let us next look at Clive Barnes wearing scholarly and philosophical vestments:

Henry, Sweet Henry: "I suspect that, in musicals, characters are not shaded, nor do they interplay."

Her First Roman: "There is an enormous difference in speed, timing, and even basic nature between a serious play and a musical."

How Now Dow Jones: "But if you have not got a strong book or a strong score, any musical is in trouble."

*A "smarty" quote from *West Side Story*.

Now—Barnes on Aspirations, or Thanatopsis:

Pippin: "It is, I felt, a trite and uninteresting story with aspirations to a seriousness it never for one moment fulfills. It is a commonplace set to rock music, and I must say I found most of the music somewhat characterless. . . ."

Zorba: "In total, *Zorba* is not as good as its aspirations. . . ."

Cabaret: ". . . is markedly one of those shows where its apparent aspirations are the very worst enemies of its evident achievements."

Follies: ". . . obviously everyone concerned here is determined to treat the musical comedy seriously as an art form, and such aspiration should be encouraged."

A Barnes Bouquet of Misunderstandings:

Cry for Us All: "Never in the history of the theater, with the possible exception of *West Side Story*, has there been a successful musical comedy or operetta on a truly tragic theme."

That sentence is packed with equivocating words such as "successful," "musical comedy," and "truly tragic," and Barnes could argue that any or all of the shows in the following list fail to qualify. However at the risk of inciting arguments, I suggest that the following musicals, although not comedies, were successful in dealing with tragic themes: *Fiddler on the Roof, Carousel, Godspell, Jesus Christ Superstar, Man of La Mancha, Cabaret.*

Barnes said of *No, No, Nanette:* "Youmans specialized in short musical phrases."

Not true. In "Tea for Two" the song is based on three-note motifs. Motifs are *not* phrases. Youmans' phrases are four or eight bars in length, which is normal and usual.

How's That, Barnes? Department

And Miss Reardon Drinks a Little: ". . . is nearly better than it is. But not quite nearly enough. . . ."

A Midsummer Night's Dream: "Only the text is sacred, to be illuminated, or like some baby child, cosseted, and once in a while cuffed behind the ear, to show a proper religious irreverence."

Hedda Gabler: ". . . must be one of the most flawless plays ever written. . . . There is only one unbelievable coincidence. . . ."

A Doll's House: " . . . acid tests of great acting as infallible and as merciless as litmus paper."

How the Other Half Loves: "Phil Silvers, who has overnight learned how to play comedy rather than television, . . ."

(Notes on Silvers' career: Started at age fourteen in *Gus Edwards' Revue* (1925); was with Minsky's Burlesque from 1934 to 1939)

Broadway Shows: *Yokel Boy* (1939)
                High Button Shoes (1947)
                Top Banana (1951)
                Do Re Mi (1960)
                (Toured with USO during World War II)

Films: (Appeared in twenty-one, from 1941 to 1968.)

Front Page: "There are many bad bad plays, a few good bad plays, and just one or two positively great bad plays."

Morning, Noon and Night: "I had never before encountered an electric violin and can hardly wait to tell Isaac Stern about it." (End of review.)

Forty Carats: "Ideally, I suppose, the lighthearted, feather-brained French boulevard comedy should be as light and as feathery as a soufflé—as delicately flavored as a crêpe suzette. *Forty Carats* . . . has rather more of the consistency of an omelette and the flavor of a buckwheat pancake. People who like omelettes and buckwheat pancakes—and both certainly have their admirable uses—will find it a well-made dish, missing only something in frivolity."

The Moths: ". . . the best plays are those that are either good or bad. Then the critic can rave or rant, the damn fool critical ritual is completed, and the producer knows whether he is rich or poor. . . .* Of course I like a bad play more than most people like a good play, and could not function were this not so. . . . No, it is not a good play."

The Grass Harp: "The new musical . . . is unpretentious—understandably unpretentious. It is based on the novel and play by Truman Capote that were both folksy and fey. The musical is also folksy and fey, insofar as it has any real character at all, for it is the kind of show that it is almost as difficult to dislike as to like."

Maggie Flynn: ". . . based on an idea by John Flaxman. Mr. Flaxman's idea, as I see it, was to set *The Sound of Music* played blackface against the background of the New Year Draft Riots of 1863. It was a strong idea."

Billy: "If the book is unfair to Melville, the music and lyrics positively insult his genius. They are like graffiti on the wall of litera-

---

*Doesn't this refute Barnes' claim that he doesn't have the power to close a show? And, by the way, whatever does he mean?

ture. I feel pity for the perpetrators, Ron Dante and Gene Allan, for I presume they can have no conception of what they have done. . . . I am sure that both these young men can do better work—and I am certain they must—so I hope they will not take it too personally when I say that *Billy* is a perfect axiom that nothing kills a show so effectively as lack of talent."

Why Hanna's Skirt Won't Stay Down: "The dialogue is deliberately weak, like underbrewed tea."

Waiting for Godot: "Surely Beckett himself doesn't know who Godot is, or else he would have introduced him to us, I imagine."

Lenny Bruce: "If Mr. Bruce had lived, does anyone imagine that he would be doing his same old routine? He would have moved on somewhere."

Minnie's Boys: "At a time when almost every Broadway musical is an adaptation of something else, an original show, based on nothing but itself, is instantly appealing."

Ours is no special time in history for adapting libretti from works in other media: it has always been a fact of the musical theater, operetta, and opera. But was *Minnie's Boys,* based on the lives of the Marx Brothers, not based on something? And in any case this promising opening sentence is the prelude to a poor review for a poor show that terminated disastrously.

Two Gentlemen of Verona: "At times the poetry sounds ironic (which is fun enough), but most of the time it seems perfectly natural, which perhaps shows that there is rarely anything wrong with a musical book that a little blank verse might not put right." (All writers in trouble take note.)

A Breeze from the Gulf: "The play has been staged by John Going and it is difficult to object to his work when he has produced three really thrilling, old-style grandstand performances. But he does let play and actors proceed along at too remorseless a level and too even a tone. If the play needs reworking, then also some of Mr. Going's direction needs reconsideration."

Barnes' Crystal Ball Department

Salvation: "Perhaps the producer, David Black, might one day reseat the house with some of the profits from the show's first couple of years." (*Salvation* ran just over six months.)

Mod Donna: ". . . it is one of the most pertinent and stimulating offerings it [New York Shakespeare Festival] has so far given us in

the three-year history of the Public Theater on Lafayette Street."
(Closed after 48 performances.)

Room Service (revival): "When I consider most new plays, I thank
God for old ones. Of course, new plays are vital to the theater, but
it must also be remembered that if you have not actually seen a
play, then it is new to you. . . . *Room Service* . . . is that rare animal,
a totally sustained farce, and although it is some 40 years old, it
bears its age lightly . . . it should by every right in the book win over
the town once more." (Closed after 24 performances.)

Promenade: "If you want my advice, go to the box-office of the new
Promenade Theatre . . . as soon as practicable." (Closed after 32
weeks.)

In a review of the Hartford Stage Company's production of *Room
Service* (May 17, 1975), Barnes had the following to say of the play:

"*Room Service* has simply got to be one of the flimsiest of Broadway comedies ever to be a hit—and yet somehow both on stage and
in that zany Marx Brothers film, it always makes it on the seat of its
pants."

Barnes' Hates

1776: "Although personally I felt that the settings by Jo Mielziner
were very disappointing and old-fashioned. . . ."

Look to the Lilies: ". . . deplorably frowsy settings provided by the
veteran Jo Mielziner . . . would moreover have gained quite a lot
from the delicately suggestive kind of versions a designer such as
Ming Cho Lee might have provided."

Georgy: ". . . but Jo Mielziner's rather repressing scenery, which
kept on folding in and out like a child's dollhouse, left a somewhat foggy impression on the spirit."

In Praise of Love: "This has been handsomely designed by Jo Mielziner in his most opulently lavish mood and looks more like Park
Avenue, New York, than Islington, London."

In response to a question regarding interest in news of the theater
by readers outside New York, Barnes said, "They do want to be informed of what's happening about theater, not just all over the
country, but all over the world."

Information is one thing. A *New York Times* critic's review of a
play in London or Washington or Toronto that may be coming, or
perhaps has been announced as definitely coming to Broadway, is

another. And a reprint of a review of such a play, written by a critic other than the New York critic, is still something else.

My personal opinion is that it is immoral for New York critics to send in reviews of foreign or out-of-town showings. Too often the local critic changes his mind about such shows after they are brought to New York. And in many instances the show may have come to New York *because* the critic was initially favorable.

Another exchange between anonymous interrogators and Mr. Barnes, reported in the *Dramatists Guild Quarterly*, is relative to foreign–New York reviewing:

BARNES: If a London play is going to be done in New York, the producer can say, "I don't want you to see this play," and I won't. If he says, "I want you to see the play if you like, but please don't write about it," that is what I will do. Or he can say, "Go see the play and write about it if you want to." I can't see why this is not legitimate. [Perhaps the play has not been optioned for New York pending Barnes' review.]

Q: Mr. Barnes, you function in the New York arena. Why doesn't the *Times* allow its man in London to cover that play? You are the man who is going to review that play here in New York when it arrives, and if you have already announced that the play is bad and that you don't like it, the playwright doesn't have a chance, does he?

BARNES: Look at it this way, I am doing nothing that every other New York critic hasn't traditionally done. [Traditionally, murder, rape, robbery, and other crimes have also been committed.]

Other considerations are involved in reviewing a foreign or out-of-town play. A cast change in the New York production of a London show, for example, will invite comparisons, often to the detriment of the local version, and no critic can suddenly become so innocent as to be uninfluenced by this contrast.

In addition—and we must face this unfortunate fact—many shows that interest or amuse audiences and help Broadway to continue working, won't bear a second watching. If the critic has enjoyed it at a first viewing in London and then has been disappointed on seeing it a second time, his report can be devastatingly discouraging.*

I will not enumerate the specific examples of these unfortunate occurrences, but none of them *could* happen if local critics printed no opinions about shows until they are seen in New York. It would even be preferable if these shows were eschewed everywhere *but* New York.

---

*Martin Gottfried was apoplectic about *Equus* in London, and bored by *Sherlock Holmes* there. He had a complete change of heart about both when he saw them in New York.

Barnes' inconsistencies within a single review have been pointed out again and again but they continue. One is to be observed in his November 22, 1974 review of *Saturday Sunday Monday*. In the first section of the review, Barnes plays culinary hopscotch:

". . . diverting little slice of salami . . ."

"It is the only play I have ever encountered that occasionally smells better than it sounds."

"It has merits beyond the olfactory."

"I liked the play this side of idolatry—a good way this side. It is beautifully done—or should I say beautifully cooked?—and I unswervingly recommend it."

Reading every word of the review compounds the confusion. I would *guess* that Barnes did not like the play but he is so catsy-mousey about saying so that it is difficult to be certain. And after all there is that phrase, ". . . I unswervingly recommend it."

Qui sait?

Very much a propos of the preceding excerpts, I quote a further exchange from the *Dramatists Guild Quarterly* interview with Barnes:

Q: Reviewing Julius Epstein's *But Seriously*, you found it necessary to say that he wrote *Casablanca*, which proves that movies are not written. . . .

BARNES: Can I say that one of the difficulties of the first night, and I think this is true of any critic, is that sometimes we write things we regret the next morning. That was possibly one of them. I intended it as a light-hearted joke. Perhaps the author didn't take it that way. I'm sorry, it wasn't meant to be . . .

Q: By the time you finished your lighthearted joke, the play was dead.

Q: In your review of *Lovely Ladies, Kind Gentlemen* you saw fit to mention that John Patrick wrote such epics as *Suzie Wong*. He also wrote one of the best American plays ever written, the brilliant *The Hasty Heart*, and one wonders why you didn't say, "It's a shame that John Patrick who wrote *The Hasty Heart* is mixed up in this." One wonders, What kind of cynical attitude, what lack of knowledge am I up against?

BARNES: But I don't think you should take jokes to indicate a lack of knowledge.

Barnes has the ability to write interestingly. Nevertheless, one seldom knows exactly what he thinks or recommends or condemns. When he exhibits genuine enthusiam, he is apt to spew out adjectives that, though certainly heartwarming to the people involved in the particular production, are unsupported by argument. What we are given resembles an orgasm more than a substantiated judgment.

Barnes wrote of the recent revival of O'Neill's *A Moon for the*

Misbegotten with unbridled praise, especially welcome in the light
of Martin Gottfried's senseless put-down. However Barnes gave
little if any reason for his eruption.

Again in the revival of *Long Day's Journey into Night*, Barnes,
overwhelmed by O'Neill, goes off like a Roman candle with superlatives that, being unsubstantiated, are meaningless.

". . . greatest . . ."

". . . staging that is heartfelt, authentic, and thrilling."

". . . glorious highlights of many a season."

". . . towering achievement."

"O'Neill . . . dares to reveal characters painfully, accurately, like
a surgeon with a scalpel, like a poet with a phrase."

Does a surgeon "reveal characters . . . with a scalpel" no matter
how "painfully" he uses it? Of course Barnes' idea is lurking there
somewhere darkly, but clearer explanations of O'Neill's method of
character revelation are possible.

In the same earlier quoted interviews, Barnes said, "I think the
analysis of a play is much more important than the judgment of a
play."

This point is certainly valid, but the critic does not act in accord-
ance with what he says. Nearly everything Barnes had to say about
A Moon for the Misbegotten and *Long Day's Journey into Night*
was judgment. It was incalculably helpful to the two plays' successes
but it said nothing more than what might have been said by any
fairly educated theatergoer with a *feeling* of satisfaction. One of Mr.
Barnes' obligations as the most influential theater critic—probably
the most influential in the world—is to (in his own words) "offer
insights to the reader."

On occasion, Barnes demonstrates his ability to do so. In his review of Neil Simon's *The Gingerbread Lady*, he fulfilled all of his
avowed critical obligations. It is a serious review which has some
cogent things to say about the author's past and present, and it
deals analytically with the characters and the actors. Some excerpts
follow:

One of the most interesting aspects of Mr. Simon's work has been its
apparent heartlessness. You always felt that his characters would die with
a jaunty wisecrack stuck into their mouth's like a Groucho cigar. In *The
Gingerbread Lady* they do. . . .

In *The Gingerbread Lady*, Mr. Simon has written his first determinedly
serious play. It is not serious because of its theme or subject matter, but
because of its heroine, a self-destructive, nymphomaniac alcoholic. The
portrait is not particularly original or unusual—a battered lady talking with

the flip-flippancy of Manhattan's walking wounded poised perhaps for a moment's air before what will probably be the final gulp. . . .

For all its manic-depressive emotional mayhem, the theater party ladies will be relieved to know that Mr. Simon's play is as funny as ever—the customary avalanche of hilarity and landslide of pure unbuttoned joy. This time, however, drunks in the theater parties will feel compelled to seek assistance from Alcoholics Anonymous and the rest of the audience will need a stiff drink. Mr. Simon is a funny, funny man—with tears running down his cheek, most of them genuine. . . .

Mr. Simon's humor has always been contrived. Characters talk to themselves in his plays—they even tell jokes to themselves. The laughs are superbly gift-wrapped, but not always completely revealing. . . . What mattered was the superb verbal fancy, the really incredibly funny jokes that were both at the same time truthful and artificial.

Truthful because they had the edge of wit and were always based on common sense; artificial because they made everyone talk alike, act alike. They were more like puppet fantasy projections of the playwright himself. In *The Last of the Red-Hot Lovers* Mr. Simon started to move from his earlier pattern—here in *The Gingerbread Lady* he has broken through. The wit is self-pitying, self-destructive and self-depreciating—and it has enabled him to create a larger-than-life and yet still credible human being. A woman with incurable honesty and incurable weakness, who hides behind jokes that would make her a fortune as a scriptwriter, and threshes away at the world around with the feeble defiance of a landed and bruised fish. . . .

It is not the kind of play where you laugh till it hurts—merely it hurts till you laugh.

Maureen Stapleton as the battered, baffled lush thrush has probably the part of her career and she is quite wonderful. The baritone note of outrage in her voice, the friendly despair of her manner, the fierce anxiety, yet even fiercer pride, of her attitude, all combine in a portrait of a memorable lady. Childlike, innocent, confused, sly but trusting—Miss Stapleton plays her game of solitaire with no card unturned. . . .

But this is a remarkable and moving dialogue between a great actress and a playwright who has suddenly discovered the way to express the emptiness beneath the smart remark and the shy compassion that can be smothered by a wisecrack. There was perhaps not too much for the director to do other than act as umpire for the encounter. Robert Moore umpired impeccably. . . .

I am grateful to Barnes for drawing attention to the too-seldom-expressed idea that "it [anything] is not serious because of its theme or subject matter, but because of . . . whatever it is that stimulates the author to create a thoughtful sober work." The "seriousness" is not negated by its comedic qualities—an all-too-frequent confusion.

Also in this notice, Barnes employs a minimum of storytelling. Readers need only know this or that small part of a show's situation on which the reviewer is to base his own thesis.

Although I rarely agree with Clive Barnes (which is beside the point), I admire his sometime courage to dissent in the face of predictable success. Even here, he can be confused. Take the case of *Jesus Christ Superstar*. His notice begins:

Nothing could convince me that any show that has sold two-and-one-half million copies of its album before the opening night is anything like all bad. But I must also confess to experiencing some disappointment when *Jesus Christ Superstar* opened at the Mark Hellinger Theatre last night.

There is ambiguity here, for Barnes seems to imply that the recording preceding the show was part of some *plan* as a preproduction release. The truth is, the recording was done independently; and though it indeed marked the debut of the project, the *production* as a show was only a hope, and its fulfillment took place more than a year later.

Barnes properly connects the production of the story of Jesus Christ with big business but unfortunately adds ". . . it is apparent that this midcult version of the Passion story is seriously and sincerely intended."

There could hardly be a greater presumption. Even before I saw *Jesus Christ Superstar,* I thought it smelled highly of the supermarket. When I saw the same opening night performance that Barnes saw, that opinion was doubly strengthened, though I admired some parts of the show.

Barnes does point out the atrocious language of the show—the attempt to impart to words too well-known classically ordinary phraseology such as "God forgive them! They don't know what they are doing."

Then Barnes takes a swipe at the eclecticism of the music. (Remember Carmines' blessed, hallowed eclecticism?) Although I was in despair because of this element in *Jesus Christ Superstar*, I am bothered more by Barnes' unalloyed admiration of the identical fault in Carmines.

Barnes next considers the very essence of the show and its director. This part of his review is truly explicit:

There is a certain vulgarity here typical of an age that takes a peculiar delight in painting mustaches on the *Mona Lisa* and demonstrating that every great man was a regular guy at heart. . . .

Most of the music is pleasant, although unmemorable. . . . It is, unhappily, neither innovative nor original.

The music does have the bustling merit of vitality, which is what has made its records sell, and what Tom O'Horgan has seized upon in his monumentally ingenious staging. Ever since his beginning at La Mama, Mr. O'Horgan has tried to startle us. Once he startled us with small things, now he startles us with big things. This time, the things got too big.

There were too many purely decorative effects, artistic excrescences dreamed up by the director and his designers, Robin Wagner and Randy Barcelo, that seemed intended to make us gasp and our blood run cold. The stage is full of platforms, carriages descend from the heavens, and even the stars over Gethsemane are captured in a blue plastic box. The total effect is brilliant but cheap—like the Christmas decorations of a chic Fifth Avenue store.

It is unfortunate that the sound equipment—which sounded rather blurred, incidentally—involved the use of hand mikes, which, while dressed up as pieces of rope, and occasionally handed around from actor to actor like holy chalices, remained unmistakably mikes—not least when Jesus jumps up dramatically to seize one, in the approved TV-spectacular manner.

For me, the real disappointment came not in the music—which is better than run-of-the-mill Broadway and the best score for an English musical in years—but in the conception. There is a coyness in its contemporaneity, a sneaky pleasure in the boldness of its anachronisms, a special, undefined air of smugness in its daring. Christ is updated, but hardly, I felt, renewed.

I believe in Barnes' sincerity, in his honorable motives in trying to help new writers, new projects, and ethnic theater. I believe that at the present time, he is battling to help save what remains of Broadway. But this campaign—perhaps little better than a year old—is too late. His double-standard reviewing (raves for many rank amateurs versus intolerance for much that was "professional" if less than the best in the commercial theater) has by now helped to weaken the commercial theater and weakened Barnes' status. He has, like a Pied Piper, misled—albeit with good intentions—too many as-yet-unqualified writers and performers into feeling that they had arrived, whereas what they deserved was honest encouragement to inspire them to learn and become more than they actually were.

Barnes' enthusiasms and overextended activity have produced cavalier reviews that have harmed the theater, and no matter how unintentionally, he has misled audiences. He has not fulfilled his obligations as the most influential critic, an automatic position belonging to the first reviewer of *The New York Times*, to "offer [as in his own stated opinion] insights to the reader," and his opinions are too seldom explained. The destruction he has wrought has been nearly complete, and resurrection requires more faith than most of us possess.

DOUGLAS WATT

The New York *Daily News* has the largest circulation of any newspaper: 2,120,549 daily and 2,933,182 Sunday. In size, format, and character it is a tabloid, which Webster defines as "condensed" and "characterized by sensationalism." In quoting Webster I am in no way denigrating the *Daily News*; rather I'm attempting to classify it.

The *New York Times* has two and a half times as much news coverage as the *Daily News*, twelve times as much financial news, one quarter as many racing charts, and no comics, of which the *News* has the equivalent of one and a quarter pages. The *News* has no daily book reviews, little theater advertising, and gives half as much space to reviews of theater and concerts as the *Times*.

The general advertising is twice as great in the *Times*, whose advertisers, in general, represent more expensive and more prestigious businesses than those in the *News*. There is a small overlap.

Although the *News* has twice the number of readers as the *Times*, a large number of these purchase less expensive wardrobes, jewelry, and other items; are less interested in finance, books, and theater; and more interested in horse racing, photographs, betting, comic strips, horoscopes, and chit-chat columns.

It follows that the drama critic of the *News* must appeal to a simpler audience—perhaps, on average, a less intellectual one. What he writes needs to be clear and direct, and not overlong. He may hope to entice some of his readers into occasional theatergoing. But judging by the infinitely smaller number of theater ads, producers must feel that advertising in the *News* yields few customers.

Nevertheless, all producers take advantage of the *News*' drama critic's favorable reviews by publishing quotes in their large *Times* ads. If this appears to be a contradiction of sorts, it is.

Many New Yorkers read both the *Times* and the *News*, and all people vitally interested in the theater read both critics, who are the two out of three New York newspaper critics whose opinions are most important to any theater production. The *News*' reviewer, Douglas Watt, is as different from the *Times*' Clive Barnes as possible. Watt is unpretentious and has no axes to grind. He is no philosopher—real or self-appointed—and no essayist. He is self-effacing and never cantankerous. When he writes about theater, theater is his topic. He makes no effort to amuse through cleverness at the expense of others, nor does he strive to attract a sycophantic public. He is perfect for his reading public and helpful to the theater in general because of his clarity, simplicity, and directness. One has no need to ponder his meaning.

On November 25, 1974, a new black musical opened off-Broadway—*The Prodigal Sister*. It had music by the talented young black composer Micki Grant, whose work was stimulating in *Don't Bother Me, I Can't Cope*. However, *The Prodigal Sister* seems to have achieved less.

For the sake of comparison, let's first look at the way Clive Barnes began his review:

"Artlessness is one of the most difficult qualities to capture on stage. It either emerges looking cute, coy, or both. And yet artlessness, it seems to me, is exactly the word to describe the new black musical, *The Prodigal Sister*, which opened last night at the Theater de Lys."

The first sentence puts one on guard. Watch out! Barnes is going to build a defensive argument. However the paragraph ends without his making any decision: We are left without any rebuttal to "cute, coy or both."

Most of Barnes' last paragraph follows:

"This is by no means a slick and glossy Broadway musical or even an Off Broadway musical with aspirations in such a direction—and its good nature and fervor seem to stand somewhere between a black block party and a revival meeting. There is a simple joyousness here that is thoroughly engaging. If you enjoyed *Don't Bother Me, I Can't Cope*, I am sure you will also enjoy *The Prodigal Sister*."

Now it seems clear enough that Barnes means to be favorable (he has just established the merits of cast and production). Midway, in referring to Miss Grant's music, he says that its "easy-on-the-ear mixture of rhythm with blues is not unusually imaginative, but, like the Rod Rodgers choreography, it is consistently fluent."

Now here's the Douglas Watt review of *The Prodigal Sister*, which begins:

"The fifteen performers in *The Prodigal Sister*, an all-black musical that opened last night at the Theatre De Lys, are ready, willing and able. But the writers have left them high and dry.

"Shouting and singing for joy and jiving don't mean a thing unless you've got something to sing about. And the book and songs that the ladies J. E. Franklin (author, co-lyricist) and Micki Grant (music, co-lyricist) have provided are too simple-minded to keep even the least demanding audience entertained for the hour-and-a-half it takes *The Prodigal Sister* to unwind.

"Intended to be as innocent and heartwarming as, say, *Purlie* or *Don't Play Us Cheap*, it looks and sounds merely awkward, for it doesn't have anything to say."

Later:

"Miss Grant's music, which was such a stimulating part of *Don't Bother Me, I Can't Cope*, can't even work up much excitement in its hand-clapping, gospel interludes."

And finally:

"The small combo alongside the stage seems able enough but has the monotonous habit of repeating a riff over and over beneath snatches of dialogue.

."But there were lots of things I didn't understand about *The Prodigal Sister*, especially how it got there in the first place."

There is no doubt in anyone's mind about how Watt feels about this musical. Barnes, on the other hand, refused to commit himself.

Barnes wrote a similarly Janus-like notice for the recent *Saturday Sunday Monday*, and therefore it was a pleasure to read the final Watt statement about this play:

". . . but everything about it, both characters and situations, is stock material, so that even as a genre play it is terribly thin stuff. A Rossini score would have helped, though."

No one should or does agree wholeheartedly with the opinions of anyone else—friend, foe, or reviewer. However, it is good to find a reviewer whose communication is crystal clear. Here, for example, are Watt's observations on several productions:

"Pippin is a musical of enormous style and I hail it. Staged by Bob Fosse within an inch of its life, last night's arrival at the Imperial survives—nay, triumphs—by reason of its grace, humor, imagination and, yes, its very cleverness. . . . *Pippin* is extraordinary musical theater."

Wild and Wonderful: "Seldom have I returned for the second half of a musical with such reluctance as I felt last night . . ."

Two Gentlemen of Verona: "As we all knew it would, when it shimmered its delights on Central Park audiences this summer, the musical *Two Gentlemen of Verona* has come to Broadway. And now joy is rampant on the stage of the St. James . . ."

Gigi: "When Alfred Drake, fleet of foot and smooth as silk [watch out!] is telling us, 'I'm Glad I'm Not Young Anymore,' or when the entrancing Maria Karnilova is kicking up her heels in 'The Night They Invented Champagne,' or . . . better yet . . . when the two of them are beautifully underplaying that fetching duet, 'I Remember It Well,' the new show called *Gigi* is all it should be."

It is not necessary for any theatergoer to read on. That the rest of Watt's review is not really favorable comes as no surprise.

"Sextet, an intimate musical that opened last night at the Bijou, is so frail a thing and so pathetically eager to be liked, that one must regard it more with pity than outright displeasure."

"Over Here!, a garish World War II home-front musical that opened

at the Shubert last night, has nothing more on its dizzy mind than the fond and gently mocking evocation of the largely synthetic entertainment of the period. That's shameless. But thanks to its prevailing good nature and liveliness, it manages to be reasonably diverting."

Watt's attitude toward ethnic theater is also direct. He is not indulgent, as is Barnes, nor does he have the time, the audience, or the inclination to be as analytical as Kerr. But he is truthful and he behaves toward new playwrights as he does toward the established ones. Is any other way fair? I doubt it. To attempt to transform promise and talent into genius and vintage product by the turn of a phrase is to mislead, because it would be, if successful, only a trick. In the end everything would be as it was.

Watt does not employ double-standards. The following excerpts are from, first, his reviews of black experimental plays and then from *Ari,* mentioned in this connection only because Clive Barnes began to treat it as a sacred passage straight out of the Torah.

The River Niger (March 29, 1973): "The play, a loosely-organized affair with too many subplots, too many didactic moments, and a weakly melodramatic ending, somehow holds together by reason of Walker's gift for pungent dialogue and its sheer vitality, both in writing and performance. . . . *The River Niger* works best as domestic comedy-drama, without the melodramatic overtones. It's much too long, and its focus could be sharper. But it is the work of a forceful and talented writer and Broadway is the richer for it."

The Great MacDaddy (March 19, 1974): *"The Great MacDaddy,* which got the Negro Ensemble Company season off to a late start last night at the St. Marks Playhouse, is an ambitious but incoherent 'musical odyssey,' an unsuccessful attempt to apply an African story-telling style to black American history.

"The combination of Paul Carter Harrison's episodic script and Coleridge-Taylor Perkinson's music has the virtue of exploiting the singing, dancing, and acting talents of a large and talented company. In spite of engaging moments, though, the evening is undramatic, and seems to go nowhere."

What the Wine-Sellers Buy (February 15, 1974): ". . . the story is essentially a trite one, and it is stretched over three acts only with difficulty. . . . At times, it seems little more than an Andy Hardy story with a '70s look. And the fact that it all is obviously true to life in outline doesn't prevent it from seeming contrived on the stage. . . . It's a lively piece of theater by a writer of promise, but it's too obvious for its own good."

My Sister, My Sister (May 1, 1974): "A bewilderingly layered black family drama called *My Sister, My Sister* temporarily restored the Little Theater, a once attractive playhouse grown unbelievably shabby, to the legit ranks last night.

"Though Ray Aranha's two-act play appears simple enough on the surface, and is even fairly simple-minded in its treatment of individual scenes, it shifts back and forth in time so frequently that it dissipates meaning, loses whatever small impact it might have had and very quickly becomes a bore.

"In a blundering attempt to adopt a poetic stance, the author has sacrificed credibility. Only in individual scenes, usually quarrelsome and not terribly interesting, is there a feeling of reality. It must be admitted, too, that there are moments, very few, when a sense of poignancy is almost within reach.

"Paul Weidner has staged *My Sister, My Sister* matter-of-factly in a dull set by Lawrence King. But then they, as well as the actors, must have found themselves baffled by this play. It goes nowhere, really, or else gets wherever it is going before it has hardly begun. Somewhere buried inside its strange structure there is an ache, a loss of innocence, that the author has evidently felt very strongly but has gone to great lengths to obscure."

The Black Terror (November 11, 1971): "*The Black Terror*, which opened at the New York Shakespeare Festival's Other Stage last night, is a wordy and contrived first play and as melodramatic as its title might suggest. Yet it is not without its interest. . . . Though the play, if it can truly be called one, is largely a rather monotonous polemic, Wesley comes close to an entertaining idea in the figures of the reluctant assassin, and a defiant young woman, a zealous revolutionary, who has been instructed to live with him, possibly to keep his morale up, but who at first rejects all his physical advances.

"Wesley shows promise but he needs a good deal of self-discipline and he might begin by restraining himself from using four-letter words in such abundance that they lose whatever effect they might have."

Ari (January 16, 1971): "It couldn't have been easy but the makers of last night's *Ari* have managed to take one of modern history's most stirring achievements, the formation of the state of Israel, and convert it into a humorless and numbingly dull musical. . . . As if Uris' book, with its soap-opera romance thrown in, wasn't bad enough, he has also contributed the show's pedestrian song lyrics. And the composer, Walt Smith, has been of absolutely no help, having provided a score that would have sounded tired and even dated in the days of *The Desert Song*. . . . It's all rather infuriating when you consider the thrilling source material and the cheap use that has been made of it.

"Because everything is so wrong about *Ari* everybody suffers. Lucia Victor's staging looks plodding, Talley Beatty's two dance scenes seem dragged in, and Robert Randolph's scenery appears cumbersome.

"Finally, of course, a subject as awesome as this is scarcely fitting material for the frivolities of the Broadway musical form. On the other hand, a laugh or two wouldn't have hurt."

These opinions are honest and clear. For the new writers, they should be far from discouraging. Watt praises the author of *The River Niger* while pointing out some of the weaknesses of the play. He says that the author of *What the Wine-Sellers Buy* has "promise," and he found *The Black Terror* "not without interest." He found no merit in *The Great MacDaddy, My Sister, My Sister,* or *Ari.*

Many new writers boil over with things to say. For that matter, so does everyone standing in a line at a supermarket. But that fact alone does not guarantee their saying it interestingly enough to engage an audience for an evening. Creating a play or a show presupposes that the author has talent and skill. When a new writer's work is propelled onto a stage before he has acquired sufficient technique to warrant its being there, the fault is the producer's for being overindulgent and lacking in judgment and taste. The playwright then is seen prematurely, unfairly, and at a great disadvantage. Watt does not indulge such writers or himself in the wasteful exercise of offering false praise.

For an example of Watt's comprehension, spelled out in simple terms, look at his review of *Company.* There is no ambivalence and no fuzziness. He had a happy experience which he is able to share with his readers:

"Let's hear it for *Company,* the newest and slickest thing in town. As smooth as the steel-and-glass buildings of midtown Manhattan and as jumpy as an alley cat, it is Broadway's first musical treatment of nerve ends.

"Dean Jones, who has the central part, is a bachelor whose closest friends include three girls and five married couples. At the beginning and end, he is being given a surprise party by the pairs on his 35th birthday. In between, he remembers troublesome scenes with all of them and at the finish decides that marriage is—well, go see for yourself.

"Brilliance is all in this show. George Furth's book is diamond-sharp, funny and chilling both. But Stephen Sondheim's songs, while equally scintillating, shine through time and again with a welcome and essential warmth. They make the evening. And interestingly, though Sondheim obviously has been listening to the sounds of today, he wisely favors his own which apply perfectly to the 30-ish crowd onstage.

"Actually, there are only 14 up there (four offstage female voices join in on some of the songs). They move through a fascinating Boris Aronson setting of aluminum-and-plastic rectangles, including a few working elevators, that enclose us inescapably in this new city of ours.

"The cast is splendid. Everybody in it, but especially the women, has big moments. Listen to Elaine Stritch, a rich three-times-married, deep in her cups, rise from a discotheque table to sing an abrasive 'The Ladies Who Lunch.' Watch Donna McKechnie dance a lonely bacchanal. Hear Pamela Myers, the most forthright girl in New York City, bounce her voice against the back wall as she sings, in 'Another Hundred People,' about all the daily arrivals here and their mixings.

"Or delight in the inventiveness of choreographer, Michael Bennett's vaudevillian staging of a mountingly effective coupling of a soft-shoe number and martial one for the entire company. 'You Could Drive a Person Crazy,' by the trio of girl friends, is a joy. And let's not overlook the engaging hero, Jones, in his final 'Being Alive.'

"Others to cherish are Susan Browning, an adorable brunette airline stewardess, a fly-by-night companion whose next stop is Barcelona; Barbara Barrie's playful karate-trained wife; Beth Howland's wedding-shy Amy, and Tari Ralston's pot-happy Jenny. I was fond of all the rest, too.

"Harold Prince, who is also the producer, has staged the book with sharp skill. Jonathan's Tunick's sparkling orchestrations are of immense help. And the orchestra, under Harold Hastings, is first-rate.

"How nice to have another New York show, and such an adroit one."

This account is unpretentious. It does not claim to have found hidden meanings. Calling *Company* "Broadway's first musical treatment of nerve ends," Watt struck upon an appropriate metaphor. Had he been more technical he would have communicated less of his own experience to his readers and they, in turn, would have comprehended less. Of its kind, this, I believe, is ideal theatrical reportage.

Watt is by no means always satisfied; but the causes of his displeasure are usually pinpointed and never hostile. Other critics have said they believed that one of their jobs was to offer "insights to the reader." Watt does just that and in a very forthright way. Many people, for example, felt unsatisfied with the short-lived *Mack & Mabel*, and Watt was able to translate the cause of their feelings:

"*Mack & Mabel*, which came to the Majestic last night, is an amiable fool of a musical so desperately anxious to tickle our funny-bones and touch our hearts that it succeeds in doing neither. I spent the evening feeling sorry for it.

"It's really a shame, because everything about *Mack & Mabel* is designed to please, with the unfortunate exception of the book and songs. The admirable Robert Preston, who plays Mack Sennett, is as vigorous and winning a leading man as ever, and the equally prognathic Bernadette Peters, who is cast as Mabel Normand, is a cute and appealing leading lady. Furthermore, Gower Champion, who has staged the entire show, has pulled out all the stops in what is, in addition, an excellently-designed production.

"The truth probably is that Sennett and Miss Normand were not especially interesting people in themselves, and the emerging movie business had, as we all know, a great deal more to offer than a pie in the face."

About *Absurd Person Singular*, Watt said:

"A mildly entertaining farce generating the most amusement in its middle act continued our British theater season last night when Alan Ayckbourn's *Absurd Person Singular* bowed at the Music Box with an all-star cast of six.

"The astonishingly prolific Ayckbourn (since *Singular*, which is still running in London, an Ayckbourn triology has opened and been followed by two other evenings of comedy) is familiarly referred to as the British Neil Simon. But I think this is underrating Simon greatly, for Ayckbourn is more a concocter of ridiculous situations than a master of witty dialogue. . . .

"But there's very little substance, and not quite enough invention to carry the whole evening. Every now and then, Ayckbourn's daffy caricatures of suburban Britishers suggest figures in an achingly empty landscape, but I don't think that's exactly what he has in mind."

The National Health: "If you enjoy smartly turned hospital humor and lighthearted dancing on the grave, you're likely to have a high old time of it at *The National Health*, which last night began a new subscription season at the nonprofit Circle in the Square/Joseph E.

Levine Theater. And why not, for British playwright Peter Nichols is in fine spirits in this facile comedy creation of a couple of years ago.

"I imagine both Nichols and New Haven's Long Wharf Theater, whose entertaining production this is, would like us to take *The National Health* a bit more seriously than that, to look upon it as an ironic comment on the impersonal treatment accorded life and death in a hospital, in this case one of England's state-owned institutions.

"But observing the goings-on in this men's ward, so suitably designed by Virginia Dancy Webb, I was struck by what a comparatively pleasant and companionable place it was, even with its occasional visits by an officious matron who simply breezed through the place on perfunctory inspection tours. The patients, though the less-handicapped ones were understandably bored, were free to behave pretty much as they wished, even to smoking, and the nurses seemed an agreeable lot. . . .

"I can't consider *The National Health* as much more than a comedy in unfunny surroundings. But I found it enjoyable, and welcomed the fact that a place could be found in our theater for such a play, and one with so large a cast.

"Meanwhile, carry on, Pete."

Occasionally—on Sunday—Watt writes a piece which is not directly connected with a theatrical opening. The following fairly brief one—quoted in its entirety—does more to clarify the rock-in-the-theater issue than any other I have read on the same subject:

"A veteran Broadway composer with a new project in hand remarked the other day that he and some of his colleagues were approaching their work with some concern. They're worried over the recent and increasing outcries that the trouble with the new musicals is that they don't reflect 'the music of our time,' meaning rock.

"They needn't worry. Lack of verse is their only problem.

"The Broadway musical theater needs invigoration, true. But the one important thing wrong with it in recent seasons has been, with very few exceptions, the absence of a truly gifted theater composer. Inspiration makes its own rules.

"Rock is, at most, just one music of our time. Actually, it's not a musical form at all, but an apparatus, a hard-sell means of presenting blues, ballads, old standards, classical themes or anything else you care to mention.

"For what it's worth, we might draw attention to the fact that the enduring fame of the Beatles rests largely on the songwriting ability of John Lennon (words) and Paul McCartney (music), whose most successful pieces ('Michelle,' 'Yesterday,' 'Eleanor Rigby,' and the rest) break down when removed from the Beatles' apparatus, into conventional song form.

"A show composer must obviously reserve the right to choose his own musical form for the story in front of him. If he's worth anything, he creates his own standards."

Despite his mild manner, Watt nevertheless does not nearly always agree with his colleagues on the other daily papers. I would like to show some of these differences, which I find reasoned and sensible, although several adverse reviews flew in the face of easily predictable success.

First to be considered is the 1973 revival of *Candide,* which continued successfully through 1975. From Watt's point of view, both the virtues and the faults of this production are spelled out, and it is obvious that the writer is truly familiar with Bernstein's distinguished score:

"No. I hate to have to say it, but no. After our having waited all these years for a dazzling new approach to Leonard Bernstein's *Candide,* the Chelsea Theatre of Brooklyn has gone to a good deal of trouble to amuse us with a bustling new, and abbreviated, version of the comic operetta. But it just doesn't work.

"The Chelsea's fourth-story loft theater at the Brooklyn Academy of Music, where I went to Wednesday's matinee, has been ingeniously made over into stained-wood 'environment' for actors and spectators—a tinker-toy arrangement of ramps, steep flights of steps, stiff-backed benches, pits, small stages here and there, nooks for groupings of costumed members of the small orchestra, and platforms (with foam rubber cushions) for customers' legs to dangle from.

"Being part of the show, and forced to swivel your head this way and that, isn't the most comfortable way to attend the theater; still, a playpen of this sort has the appeal of novelty, especially for the younger element.

"But although this version of a show that is necessarily static, due to the nature of its episodic story, gains an artificial momentum, it does so at the expense of its greatest single asset, the Bernstein score. . . .

"Along with the thin and scattered orchestral accompaniment, there is an emphasis on performers who can sing a bit rather than singers who can act a bit. In almost every way, including the omission of the jolly quartet 'What's the Use?' (the gambling scene has been dropped), Bernstein is slighted.

"Furthermore, though this excessively campy production may keep you craning your neck in expectation for its hour-and-three-quarters duration, your only laughs, if any, will be nervous ones.

"For I am finally forced to admit two things: one, that while Candide's ordeals are entertaining on the printed page, they are merely repetitious on the stage; and two, that it is never good practice to kid a kidder, particularly one who, like Voltaire, has a chip on his shoulder.

"For sheer virtuosity, I can think of no Broadway score to match *Candide*, which skips from Rossini to Ravel with all sorts of stops in between. And since it's a shame to do without it, perhaps concert presentations (with full orchestra, of course) are in order from now on."

A Breeze from the Gulf was an unsuccessful play, but it contained interesting elements. Ruth Ford's performance was generally admired and most of the press was indulgent toward the play while finding it unsatisfying.

The following excerpts from Watt's review makes these points. They are clearly stated, reasoned, and without animosity:

"Some eloquent performing by Ruth Ford as she gathers up bits and pieces of a role, nice work by her teammates Scott McKay and Robert Drivas, and a few telling scenes do not succeed in making a convincing play of Mart Crowley's *A Breeze from the Gulf*, which came to the Eastside Playhouse last night.

"It is like a series of connected notes, some of them extremely moving, for a play the author either couldn't or wouldn't write, or perhaps has yet to. Strongly autobiographical in flavor, it skims almost guiltily across 15 years in the life of an unfortunate Mississippi family of Irish-American Catholics—father, mother and son.

"There are moments in *A Breeze from the Gulf* as compelling as anything on our stages, and Miss Ford is tremendous. But Crowley has not found the true play that lurks somewhere in this sketchy set of 1950–65 memoirs."

In his review of *Gigi* (the first few phrases were quoted earlier), Watt writes in an exemplary fashion about a show he could not admire. He begins by detailing some of the show's virtues, then step by step, points out its faults. I quote all of Watt's notice:

"When Alfred Drake, fleet of foot and smooth as silk, is telling us 'I'm Glad I'm Not Young Anymore,' or when the entrancing Maria Karnilova is kicking up her heels in 'The Night They Invented Champagne,' or . . . better yet . . . when the two of them are beautifully underplaying that fetching duet 'I Remember It Well,' the new show called *Gigi* is all it should be. But for too much of the time last night's arrival at the Uris merely struggles to evoke once more the chic and rapture of the Lerner-Loewe film classic.

"The trouble seems to lie with the tremulous Gigi herself and with her surprised and somewhat reluctant lover, the jaded Gaston; in other words, with the very heart of Colette's little story which, having been a film, a play and then that stunning film musical, is now bent on rounding out its career as a stage show.

"The unhappy fact is that neither the Gigi, Karin Wolfe, who seems a competent performer, nor the Gaston, Daniel Massey, an able enough actor, possesses an ounce of charm. And charm is everything here.

"So the show, or as much of it as possible, has been thrown to Drake, who plays Gaston's suave womanizer of an uncle.

"Drake, bearded and with his hair darkened and gray-tipped, is ever ready to sweep us up into those lovely old songs and a few new ones as well. Miss Karnilova as Gigi's grandmother and the redoubtable Agnes Moorehead, playing Gigi's rich retired courtesan of an aunt, match him in authority.

"About the songs: most of the good ones remain, but in order to make this into a full-scale Broadway musical, Lerner and Loewe have felt obliged to write five new ones, and though Lerner's lyrics are deft enough, Loewe's music seems unable to rise to the occasion. 'Paris Is Paris Again' is attractive, but the others are fairly weak.

"An unfortunate exception is 'The Contract,' a quartet dominated by Miss Moorehead and a lawyer, expertly played and sung by George Gaynes, as they haggle over the terms of Gigi's anticipated liaison with Gaston. This extra emphasis on the business arrangements, clear enough in the film, seems a bit out of place.

"In fact, a good deal of this *Gigi* seems out of place, for although Oliver Smith's lavish scenery depicts Parisian exteriors and interiors, and Oliver Messel's handsome costumes are intended to add to the illusion, it is often a musical that appears anxious to get to Jones Beach.

"Joseph Hardy has staged the play smoothly and Onna White has provided engaging dances. A lissome blonde named Sandahl Bergman does well enough as the featured dancer (she also plays Gaston's discarded mistress), though, as I've suggested, Miss Karnilova has only to twinkle a toe to win the dance prize.

"*Gigi* which was performed for Edwin Lester's Los Angeles and San Francisco subscribers last summer and then played St. Louis, Detroit and Toronto before being installed here by Saint-Subber, offers a pleasant and, of course, tuneful evening. But the magic and, more particularly, Paris have all but disappeared."

In contrast to this is Martin Gottfried's tirade that is sharply personal and less factual, and hence should be dismissed as the product of an unsound, even clinical, indisposition. While other parts of his review are quoted in the chapter on Gottfried, I should like to reproduce his opening paragraph here:

"The movie *Gigi* was a cynical if successful capitalization on the success of *My Fair Lady*—an imitation in terms of both story and music designed to turn a profit even before the film rights to *My Fair Lady* itself were sold. To then convert the movie *Gigi* into a stage musical only compounds the cynicism into a double copy. It is indicative of the current depressing attitude toward the musical theater as a marketplace for packaged versions of established properties."

Cynical, shmynical! Almost without exception, all operas and musicals are "packaged versions of established properties." That is a fact that should not be surprising or upsetting to any reviewer. An original libretto is seldom to be found and a *successful* original one—never. This may change with time, and I hope it will, but screams will not be a proper substitute for plotting a new and arduous course.

It is Watt's *attitude* in the face of obvious failure that is contrasted here with Gottfried's rage.

Veronica's Room was a promising show that went nowhere. Watt makes this point at once but in an understanding and respectful tone, without sacrificing clear expression of his dissatisfaction. It must have been obvious to everyone in the audience on opening night that the play was not working. There was an air of high expectation at the outset, which is normal when an audience hopes to be horrified or shocked or surprised at performances of a new "thriller." This expectation plummeted as the evening wore on. There was a feeling of disappointment and under such circumstances, one is sorry for the author, the actors, and the producer. Everyone connected with the project will lose and the audience and the reviewers must know it. Why then raise such a fuss? Watt didn't:

"In the first of the two short acts that make up *Veronica's Room*, which came to the Music Box last night, Ira Levin has a pretty slick thriller going for him, and we're all eyes and ears. But in the second act, he's got to work his and our way out of the puzzle and he can't. Not satisfactorily, anyway. . . .

". . . the play falls apart before our eyes with Levin's last desperate bursts of invention, and we've guessed where it's leading (nowhere, really) before Levin has seemed to.

"Too bad, too, because the dialogue is crisp and the acting and direction are smart, indeed. But once he brings up incest, and moves on to some Jamesian suggestions of latent evil, Levin begins to lose the game, and with it, us. Good try, though."

Although all reviewers admired Christopher Plummer and disliked the musical based on *Cyrano de Bergerac*—a project frequently attempted, but which always fails, and in my opinion, one impossible of success—Douglas Watt's disapproval was perceptive and somewhat different from that of his colleagues. His feeling about the causes of failure and about Plummer are interesting and reasonably explained in the following excerpts:

"Since Edmond Rostand's *Cyrano de Bergerac* is all flourish, anyway—a masterpiece of flourish, if you will—it seems rather unnecessary to deck it out with musical flourishes. Yet that is just what has been done in *Cyrano,* which opened last night at the Palace, and the result is an awesomely silly musical. . . .

"The songs add parody to a play with parodistic elements of its own but one, I should add, that can be vastly enjoyable on its own terms. And as deft a Cyrano as Christopher Plummer, the star, is, the songs continually rob his characterization of stature so that one almost wishes the producers had gone all out and gotten a comedian on the order of a younger Jimmy Durante to play it.

"Only at times is Plummer permitted to convey the flavor of the play on its own terms, most notably in his excellent account during the balcony scene. He is so satisfying here that even when the music begins to underscore the scene and the Roxane (now Roxana, possibly because the composer opted for it) leans forward to rhapsodize in a dopey ballad called 'You Have Made Me Love,' the audience remains engrossed.

"Even so, it's a long evening and, as I have said, a silly one, though probably not silly enough to make it truly worthwhile."

A revival of *A Streetcar Named Desire* (1973) was successful. Watt's remarks about Rosemary Harris and James Farentino are cogent, and his feeling about Ellis Rabb's treatment of the staging is precisely explained. Even with objections, this review concluded, "Reservations aside, this is certainly a *Streetcar* worth seeing."

His other comments follow:

"It is difficult for one who recalls the shattering impact of the original production to be satisfied with those that have succeeded it. But although this one has its weaknesses, some endemic to the house itself, it is nevertheless remarkably persuasive. Above all, we are ever aware of the beauty and strength of the writing. . . .

"Rosemary Harris, one of our best actresses, is Blanche DuBois.

Miss Harris is uncommonly skillful in the role, and at times utterly lovely. Her approach to the role is whimsical. She is especially fine in Blanche's humorous moments. Miss Harris' cool seductiveness, however, keeps her just outside the character, hovering over it like a hummingbird, and Blanche's vulnerability, the part of her that tears at us, is absent. Miss Harris' is an excellently studied characterization, but it doesn't move us very much.

"James Farentino is a sound Stanley—vigorous, filled with animal force, and easy in the part. There is some final thrust, call it presence, missing in his performance, but it is very effective, all the same. . . .

"Rabb's use of the full stage is mistaken, I think. Instead of lending atmosphere to the play, it detracts from its tight center. Glimpsing the street scenes behind the set (ball playing, strolling, etc.) only seemed like watching unoccupied extras amusing themselves backstage; they might just as well have been playing pinochle. The Beaumont itself is not exactly conducive to total absorption in an intimate drama such as this."

Watt's review of *Seesaw* made its most important point (that it was two shows instead of one) plainly and reasonably. While the other reviewers were by no means thoroughly satisfied, Watt made it unquestionable that there were enjoyable elements, the main points being that the drama extracted from the original play, *Two for the Seesaw*, was effective and the music-dance portions were also delightful, but. . . .

This review is simple and communicative. The reader is made to feel that despite incurable faults, the show, the performers, and the direction are attractive:

"In *Seesaw*, which opened at the Uris last night, an intimate, bittersweet comedy and a big, brassy musical seem to exist side by side, independent of one another. Both shows have great points in their favor, but they never truly become one—two ends of a seesaw, if you like. . . .

"But the evening tugs most strongly at us in those tiny apartment cutouts (there are two now, his and hers) in which Gittel and Jerry ardently love and separate. . . .

"The city's principal representative here is an incredibly tall, gangling, personable fellow with large, clog-shod feet, named Tommy Tune. He is a tap dancer and stops the show leading a rhythmic, balloon-filled number set to the words of a statute Jerry is memorizing for a New York bar exam. The number has been beautifully staged and is enhanced by Ann Roth's festive costumes. . . .

"In lyricist Dorothy Fields, who goes all the way back to 'I Can't Give You Anything but Love,' and composer Cy Coleman, who goes back to, well, 'Witchcraft' and other hits, the Broadway theater has one of the most skilled teams. *Seesaw* may not represent the pair in such lively form as *Sweet Charity* did, but they've supplied the evening with several attractive numbers, among them 'Welcome to Holiday Inn,' 'He's Good for Me,' and 'I'm Way Ahead.' And, of course, the aforementioned 'We've Got It.'

"In *Seesaw*, you get two shows for the price of one. Both are entertaining, but I would have settled for the one with Miss Lee and Howard and perhaps a few songs. There are such things as intimate musicals."

Status Quo Vadis was a disaster. And again I should like to compare excerpts from Martin Gottfried's review with sections from Douglas Watt's. Both are adverse. Gottfried's review is unnecessarily vicious (everyone agreed that the show was poor), whereas Watt's is neither patronizing nor cruel. One senses personal jealousy in the former and normal annoyance in the latter.

Here is Gottfried's first paragraph and part of his final one:

"I know of at least two superb plays by proven, serious American playwrights that cannot get commercial productions because they call for 17 actors, but the amateurish, shallow, obvious and ultimately tasteless *Status Quo Vadis* can get a Broadway production despite its cast of 22. This is infuriating and it is the only thing about this show at the Brooks Atkinson Theatre that can draw an emotional response. *Status Quo Vadis* is an incompetently written, blandly directed, and terribly performed play, dealing superficially with a trite subject, and that is the best you can say about it. . . .

"But it is the author-director who is exclusively to blame—to blame for choosing a superobvious premise; to blame for following wherever it leads; to blame for being incapable of doing even that; to blame for letting his script wander into irrelevancies; to blame for the bizarre and sneaky sexual sublayer; to blame for contributing to the disastrous amateurism of today's Broadway; to blame for wasting so much money when other, valid work is going undone."

Mr. Watt's opening paragraph, a later one, and the last:

"In *Status Quo Vadis*, last night's play at the Atkinson, Donald Driver, who both wrote and directed it, has seized on a trite theme and enthusiastically presented it in a dated theatrical style. It is as if, say, he had unwittingly invented a ball-point pen and designed it like a fountain pen. . . .

"So Driver has tried to have it both ways by presenting a morality tale as if it were a joke but bitter on the inside. He has staged it brightly and efficiently on his own terms and his cast serves him ably. The dialogue is snappily entertaining at times and here and there produces an effective scene. But to what purpose?

"*Status Quo Vadis* is a play on which a great deal of care has been expended for no visible reason at all."

Douglas Watt was the principal dissenter in the case of a smash hit, *Same Time, Next Year*. I would like to quote from his Sunday essay (July 13, 1975), which appeared several months after the show's successful opening. In these excerpts, Watt sets forth his very reasonable point of view without ever losing his cool. He also refrains from making the show unattractive to the general theatergoer, although there is a built-in, if unstated, warning to those of us who would not, and did not, care for a show of this genre.

"There is, thank heavens, no such thing as a surefire formula for a theatrical work, either play or musical, for the stage cannot be merchandised, or, to put it less euphemistically, shoved down the public's throat, the way movies or television shows are. The merchandising goes on, of course, in the form of advertising, publicity and subtle preparation of people's attitudes toward a future attraction and its stars; but no matter how much these doubtless important considerations count for, a theater piece depends ultimately on that simplest form of communication, word of mouth. All the promotion in the world can't save a show audiences don't take to and tell friends about, though a worthless film may earn back its cost and then some through fancy exploitation. The theater isn't exactly pure, but I'm afraid it's as near as we can come to purity in the entertainment world, being, among other things, a far more democratic institution than the world of fine music. . . .

"If, though, there is anything resembling a promising formula for the stage, it is to be found in the comedy—in a single setting and for two, three or at most four characters—in which man's rosiest romantic fantasies are realized. Man's and woman's, I should say, for in a society in which women are finally succeeding in their long quest for equal rights it would be folly to present the subject entirely from the man's viewpoint.

"The root idea is the roll in the hay with no harmful after effects, the assignation without tears, the extramarital affair minus bruises either emotional or physical. It may be that young couples today, with their indifference toward the institution of marriage and with their group gropings, have already arrived at this blissful state, though I have my doubts. But for those older couples, or even younger ones with stricter upbringings who enjoy the theater, there is obviously a marvelous source of vicarious pleasure, of wish fulfillment, in observing strangers who make it in the night, or afternoon ('But in the Morning, No,' as Cole Porter titled his courtly duet for Ethel Merman and Bert Lahr in *DuBarry Was a Lady*).

"Such a work is *Same Time, Next Year*, the two-character smash of last season that should be with us for at least a couple of seasons to come. . . .

"Dream dust, all, and only the ability to succumb to their un-likelihood is needed, along with slick writing and appealing per-formances, to carry an audience over the rainbow. In *Same Time, Next Year*, you've got to believe in, and root for, a 25-year (thus far) romance in which the participants, both happily wed to others, meet clandestinely for one weekend every year. Naughty but nice people, never spoiling the setup by, say, one's rushing impetuously to the other's side during the off season for an irresistible extra roll in the hay. Actually, you'd rather imagine that after 25 years, or even 20 or 15, provided they managed to get by with this stuff that long, both parties would begin inventing excuses to avoid that long haul to an upstate cabin for one more damned weekend. . . .

"The formula, which in *Same Time* and *6 Rms* cleverly avoids the necessity of taking sides and the accompanying misgivings by reshaping the eternal triangle into a flexible rectangle, is really air-tight. As a formula. The rest is easy, requiring only a skilled comedy writer, a sensitive producer, two irresistible performers, a shrewd director, the right theater and lots of money. Even then, though, you can't be sure. . . ."

Each reviewer, by setting his own style, determines his own ob-ligations. Critical tantrums demand justification. Philosophical dis-course requires orderly elucidation, time, and space. Pretentious peroration needs rationalization. Of these three, philosophical dis-course is the only commendable one. But time limitations put this out of reach of the daily reviewer. There is only one other pos-sibility and that is Douglas Watt's unpretentious directness which dares to celebrate without apology when he feels celebration is in order, and indicates clear displeasure, without any ridicule, when that course seems appropriate.

MARTIN GOTTFRIED

Martin Gottfried is offensive because he demonstrates again and again that his knowledge is limited, his judgments swim in repeti-tious generalities, and he is given to fits of rage, often detonated by invented, nonexistent causes.

Language generalities are only one of Gottfried's many faults, and his misuse of words is deplorable. His opinions are expressed with a positiveness that allows no equivocation, yet he frequently changes them drastically after having already caused irrevocable harm. He never assumes personal blame for these changes but chalks them up to a variety of other reasons. He issues edicts on many things about which he is not qualified to make judgments, whereas it is not incumbent upon him to comment on anything about which he cannot be certain. Nobody knows everything. The question is whether Gottfried knows anything. Certainly he has not learned that under certain circumstances silence is platinum.

In what follows I will say nothing of him that is not substantiated by his writings.

After seeing *Equus* in London, Gottfried was enraged. He found nothing to like about it. Following much frothing at the pen, he wrote:

"What all of this fake artistic production has to do with the play is hard to understand until you realize Shaffer's problems as a playwright. He is a talented, sensitive naturalist who wants to write stylized plays; he is inclined toward stories that understand master-slave homosexuals, especially intellectuals and brutes, but is reluctant to be open about it."

Well, now! On what *fact* does Dr. Gottfried base this condemnation? Nothing resembling the inclination imputed to Peter Shaffer by Gottfried is to be found in *Five Finger Exercise, Black Comedy, The Royal Hunt of the Sun*, or any of Shaffer's other plays, and Gottfried's outrage has caused him to lose whatever perspective he might have had.

If one could agree at all with this diatribe, one must still ask if it is permissible for a critic to act in a doctoral manner and fault a playwright for being "reluctant to be open about" anything personal. Should a playwright have to go into Gottfried's confessional or be condemned as a wanderer from the faith? It seems to me that it is the audience's and the reviewer's business to evaluate whatever it is that the author presents on the stage and not to behave like Hercule Poirot trying to uncover or invent personal "evidence" that is not included in the drama. Is Gottfried trying the play or the author? The answer seems obvious, although Gottfried takes a similar position again and again with many other writers of other plays.

Finally in the same angry review, Gottfried wrote of the "unforgettably vulgar music." Except for some brief movie music, *there is no music in* Equus! He willed it, and willed it to be "unforgettably vulgar." *Mais elle n'existe pas;* there are only sound effects. Music has pitch, harmony (stated or implied), rhythm, cadence, and form.

But this is not the end of Gottfried's outpourings concerning *Equus*. For the play came to Broadway, where it is a smash hit despite some ultrasophisticates who fault its psychological thesis. What they overlook is that *Equus* is a rare theatrical experience, and an initial failure to come to grips with this fact is like soliciting a historian to pronounce *Antony and Cleopatra, Caesar and Cleopatra* or Schiller's *Mary Stuart* poor plays because they are historically inaccurate.

However, *Equus* in New York elicited *another* review by Martin Gottfried. The last sentence says something about all of it: "The result is breathtaking." (He also again discovers a nonexistent homosexual quality.)

The article begins: "The interaction between a written play and its production is so significant that the same script can be gray one night and brilliant another. Though this is no dazzling insight, the experience is invariably startling. In London, *Equus* was a trite social drama, unconvincingly disguised as an artistic work. Last night at the Plymouth Theater, it was a simply devastating experience. The difference was simply the power of a basic conception, an energizing production and an inspired company outweighing an essentially trite and occasionally weird idea. At London's National Theatre, the play's thought smothered its strength. Here, the muscle wins out, and in that it curiously reflects the play's very idea.

"It was Hopkins who was largely responsible for the difference in production effectiveness. In London, Alec McCowen played the psychiatrist with character detail that obscured the emotion in the man. Hopkins brings an interior fire in its own way parallel to the boy's outer one. He also adds an honesty to the play's sexual character by including subtle homosexual qualities—the holding of a cigaret, a touch of bitchiness, a gesture, a speech mannerism.

"Dexter's staging, while dynamically pressurized on the whole, is of course most flamboyant in his choreography of the horses—they bring chills whenever they appear—and they are the key to his raising [sic!] the small play, through ritual, to epic size. The result is breathtaking."

Martin Gottfried seems to know nothing about human nature, since the reader does not live who would not cheer him if, in this review of *Equus*—which was a complete turnabout of his previous notice—he could have brought himself to say that he had originally made an error in judgment, that what he saw in New York made him realize he had been wrong. But no. Instead, he tries to attribute his dramatic change of heart to production differences and Anthony Hopkins' performance.

I saw both the London and New York productions, and to say that the British version "was a trite social drama, unconvincingly disguised as an artistic work" offers no explanation for Gottfried's about-face. The production in each city was identical—identically directed, identically written, and so on. It was "a simply devastating experience" in both cities.

"At London's National Theatre, the play's thought smothered its strength. Here, the muscle wins out, and in that it curiously reflects the play's very idea."

Is it possible that thought can smother strength? Oh, yes: "The pen is mightier than the sword." Now another cliché has had its day.

Mr. Gottfried reads homosexuality into this play as he does in so many others in which it does not exist. But that is Gottfried's problem, not *Equus'*. Gottfried, however, ought to change his record; the tune has become tiresome.

I should next like to quote four reviews of three recent productions.

Henry Fonda as Clarence Darrow (April 28, 1974):
Barnes (*Times*): "I urge everyone, man, woman and child, interested in justice and America to see this play. For that matter, I urge everyone interested in consummate acting and the ultimate in courtroom dramas to see it. It is just plain wonderful."

Watts (*Post*): "What a master of his profession the modest Henry Fonda is!"

Watt (*Daily News*): "Fonda's enormous skill and easy command of a stage never desert him in this one-man show . . ."

Gottfried (*Women's Wear Daily*): "He is a personality rather than an actor. It is Fonda people want to see—not Fonda convincingly playing a character . . . it is only Fonda he can play. . . . I skipped the second half myself, certain that you didn't really have to be there."

A Moon for the Misbegotten (December 31, 1973):
Barnes (*Times*): ". . . one of the great plays of the 20th Century. . . . Ben Edwards has provided a very open and free setting, and his lighting, so absolutely essential to this diurnal travel of the day, is carefully sensitive to the mood and occasion. . . . Mr. Quintero plays his cards unerringly. . . . [Colleen Dewhurst] spoke O'Neill as if it were being spoken for the first time. . . ."

Watt (*Daily News*): "With the stunning revival of *A Moon for the*

Misbegotten . . . Eugene O'Neill's last completed play comes into its own, revealing itself as the radiant and deeply affecting work it is."

Watts (*Post*): ". . . brilliant production. . . . [Colleen Dewhurst] is just right for it. . . . superb performance in a fascinating and deeply moving drama. . . . Jason Robards . . . is perfect."

Gottfried (*Women's Wear Daily*): ". . . shameless use of the past reputations of its director and actors, rather than their present talents. . . . This production is partly a drama version of the current, cheap vogue for old musicals cast with old stars. . . . commercial. . . . First produced in 1943, it closed on the road, beside which it should have been buried. . . . staging is listless. . . . skimpy farmhouse set hardly used . . . the producer is so cynical."

The Iceman Cometh (December 12, 1973):
Barnes (*Times*): "He [O'Neill] wrote long plays, but never carelessly. His plays were long because the best of them are essentially plays of theme rather than exposition."

Watt (*Daily News*): ". . . absorbing revival of an enthralling play."

Gottfried (*Women's Wear Daily*): "Technically, *The Iceman Cometh* is a mess. It takes five hours to tell a story that needs only five minutes . . . the play's disorganization, its lack of definite characters and failure to coordinate them, its adolescent philosophizing, its general sprawl . . . monstrous, clumsy play."

Sextet (March 4, 1974):
Barnes (*Times*): "*Sextet* is not the worst musical we have seen this season—it is not a disgrace. But it lacks intellectual assurance and emotional worldliness—the two qualities it sought hardest to exhibit."

Watts (*Post*): "It is an amiable and quite agreeable little show, with some attractive songs by Lawrence Hurwit, and it is certainly painless, although I am sadly forced to doubt that its pleasant qualities are likely to set Broadway on fire."

Watt (*Daily News*): ". . . is so frail a thing and so pathetically eager to be liked, that one must regard it more with pity than outright displeasure."

Gottfried (*Women's Wear Daily*): ". . . mostly terrific musical. . . . Lawrence Hurwit's score is a marvelous mix of satire and original material, special both ways, containing technique with melody and theatrical flair. . . . Goldsmith's lyrics are marred only occasionally by a lapse in techniques or content, but are otherwise excellent. . . . My only complaint about the direction, really, is its disinterest in dance. . . . I am so mainly taken with this clever and straight and musical and funny and unusual and fine show."

As the foregoing reveals, in each case Gottfried disagreed with the other daily reviewers. It's as though he had seen entirely different shows.

Disagreement among reviewers is neither new nor deplorable, except when it is baseless. Gottfried's reasons for his opposing opinions are rarely comprehensible, and to this failing are added his arrogance in the face of his general ignorance (to be demonstrated later) and his poor, poor journalism.

His description of *Sextet* as "containing technique with melody and theatrical flair" is a grammatical hodgepodge. And to say that "my only complaint about the direction . . . is its disinterest in dance" is tantamount to saying that "my one complaint about Molière is that his plays contain no songs." Should anyone bewail the absence of something that was never intended to be there in the first place?

Gottfried's sardonic and supercilious opening sentence in his *Darrow* notice was this: "If I told you that the name of the play was *Clarence Darrow* and that it was a one-man show starring Henry Fonda, would you really have to go to the Helen Hayes Theater or even read this review to find out what it is like? That's what it is like."

Many plays have had titles that have communicated an advance sense of tastelessness. Among them, selected at random from an A index, were *Achilles Had a Heel, Alibi Jim, All Wet, The Altar of Friendship,* and *All Kinds of Giants* (all flops). But when did the name of a *man* as the title of a play, even if it were played as a solo performance, warrant such sarcasm? Does Gottfried have a similar reaction to *Macbeth, Hamlet, King Lear,* and *Julius Caesar?*

Recently Roy Dotrice concluded a triumphant second visit to Broadway in a one-man show, *Brief Lives;* and I recall that John Gielgud, a few seasons back, glowed brilliantly without assistance in *The Ages of Man.* By what divine right does Gottfried hold up to ridicule a sincere performance which he approached with acknowledged prejudice? But Gottfried with utter complacence, wrote, "That's what it is like." It was an unconscionable, irresponsible gesture, unbecoming to a man entrusted with the position of interpreting what he sees (or, in this case, what he only partially saw) to his readers.

Gottfried has five strings to his bow that he twangs repeatedly:

He uses "commercial" as though it were a dirty word; too often regards the physical setting(s) of a production as being "money-saving" or "skimpy" (both of which concern making and spending money); points out what is out of fashion in the theater; reveals a fear of imitating the past; and loves to sermonize.

To illustrate, in his review of *A Moon for the Misbegotten,* he accuses the production of being "a commercial package," objects to the "skimpy" farmhouse set, and says ". . . this is a manufactured attempt to imitate that past" (meaning Quintero's, Robards' and Dewhurst's).

Now here are the opening paragraph and a few excerpts from Gottfried's *New York Post* review (September 19, 1974) of *Naomi Court* by Michael Sawyer:

"Theater styles come and go, but the only enduring value is quality. If a play is good, it is good. If it is exciting or involving or upsetting or frightening or funny or whatever it means to be, then it makes no difference whether, as in the case of *Naomi Court,* it is naturalistic when naturalism is out of style. Despite the past credits of its author, which promise little, and despite some flaws, Michael Sawyer's play is what the theater is all about. It is a gut experience—tense, unnerving, unexpected and not without deep feeling."

There can be little doubt from the above that Gottfried is master of the cliché deeply integrated in spurious sermonizing. "Theater styles come and go but the only enduring value is quality."

Isn't this a broad generalization? (In Shakespeare, the poetry, philosophy, drama, and comedy, among other elements—possess "quality." In Molière, the "enduring value" emanates from farce, satire, wit.)

"If it is exciting . . . then it makes no difference whether . . . it is naturalistic when naturalism is out of style. . . .

"We try to idealize our lives in our dreams, but never manage to fool ourselves. The dreams end up the same as realities because we have created both. . . .

". . . a Pinter influence is potent, the lady is indeed too close to Williams, her fiancé's romanticism is somewhat overdone and this half of the play skates perilously close to maudlin. The second act is padded and the hustler's cruelty grows repetitious, etc. . . . These flaws exist, but the play transcends them. . . .

". . . working on an unfortunately shabby set . . ."

The penultimate sentence: "It is a play to see, all right."

Except in matters of clothing, "out of style" is inapplicable when the time element is a mere decade or two.

For instance, in the long view of history, there is a negligible stylistic difference between the compositions of Karl Phillip Emanuel

Bach and his father, the great Johann Sebastian Bach. Nevertheless the father's work was dismissed for a long period after he died while that of his son was thought to be great and new. I do not believe in any consideration of what must be construed as "fashion" in matters of art. Critics who persist in using such labels invariably arrive at an impasse when something "new" turns out to be, in reality, something quite "old." Art nouveau, neoclassicism, neoromanticism, art deco, and so forth, are only a few of the art styles that might fittingly be described as "new-old."

"Dreams end up the same as realities" is not only an appallingly clumsy sentence, but it is unrelated to dramatic criticism. It is also fraudulent. Gottfried's efforts at impersonating psychiatrist, philosopher, and critic are hollow and infantile. There are more things in heaven and earth than he has dreamed of. After employing such words as "overdone," "maudlin," and "repetitious," and stating that "these flaws exist," Gottfried finally recommends the play.

The following are from other Gottfried reviews:

". . . is her usual impeccable self . . ."

". . . actors do very well for themselves."

"It looks great."

". . . superb performances . . . unsurpassed anywhere."

". . . the entire production had a style and purpose of its own."

". . . seemed absolutely right."

"The kids are tremendous."

"The score keeps moving, but with a somewhat undistinguished shuffle."

"The staging . . . is clearly intended to take Broadway by storm but seems to have got the wrong weather forecast."

"The difficulty of the play is in the writing."

". . . so atrocious that it is almost appealing."

". . . is not the worst play of this Broadway season so far."

". . . lighting is honest and direct."

". . . magnificent performances . . . wonderful sets and costumes . . ."

". . . did as well as could have been expected."

". . . being an allegory or something of the kind . . ."

". . . confused and self-conscious . . ." (used six times in one review!)

Again, these are just words. The only conclusions a reader might, with effort, reach is that the writer approves or disapproves. And could anyone hold in any esteem the opinions of a reviewer who resorts to such general qualifications as "very well," "great," "superb," "unsurpassed," et cetera, et cetera, et cetera? These emissions are thoughtless. Because they are nonspecific, they tell us nothing.

They communicate no sense of the reviewer's experience nor do they give any supportive basis for his judgment. If Gottfried were less pretentious and confined his remarks to a reviewer's service without wave-making as a critic, supportive rescuing would be less essential.

From *Fashion* (*Women's Wear Daily*, February 20, 1974): "The Pippin-Brown score is likewise gay, once more a tour down Broadway's memory lane, mimicking one show tune style after another and providing us with the season's second imitation of 'Mame,' a song that was itself an imitation. Brown's lyrics are equally campy ('Up on your feet . . . three to get ready'), and yet he and Pippin have come up with a score that is as catchy and bright as any in the Gershwin-to-Jerry Herman vernacular. That's a wide range to say the least, and yet there aren't that many good composers in it, especially today. . . ."

"Catchy" and "to say the least" are campier than anything in Brown's lyrics. Then there is the comment on the comment: "That's a wide range . . . and yet there aren't that many good composers in it, especially today."

Is this a qualified observation on good composers? At *my* last count, there were hundreds.

From *Candide* (*Women's Wear Daily*, March 13, 1974): "Commercial theater gives one tremendous motivation—it is for the money, it is no fooling, one cannot fall back on subsidy or subscription audiences—and it is this motivation that will drive a grown-up theater-maker to work that surpasses the most admirable of noncommercial work. It is why only Broadway shows seem to be exciting."

Part of this harangue was better said in a childhood jingle:

> "One for the money
> Two for the show . . ."

And this time, Martin Gottfried finds "commercial" useful.

But to continue:

"Prince's ability to work initially with a choreographer—Patricia Birch—is unique and tremendous. . . . While there is little dance as such in *Candide*, there is a great deal of dance movement and musical staging, both of which are far more consequential to a musical's musicality than a dance number. Ms. Birch's work is terrific."

First, "unique and tremendous" have no significance without considerable explication. Prince's "ability to work . . . with a choreographer" could only be marvelled at by one who knows nothing about Prince or the theater. I know of no director staging a musical in which there is dancing who has not worked with a choreographer, and Prince has done it before when he staged *She Loves Me* (choreographer: Carol Haney); *Baker Street* (choreographer: Lee Becker

Theodore); *Cabaret* (choreographer: Ronald Field); *Zorba* (choreographer: Ronald Field); *Company* (choreographer: Michael Bennett); *Follies* (choreographer *and* co-director: Michael Bennett).

There is a great mishmash of intention in "little dance as such" and "great deal of dance movement and musical staging, both of which are far more consequential to a musical's musicality than a dance number."

"Dance movement" is "dance" but not necessarily "*a* dance," which denotes choreography in a rounded form: beginning, middle and end—dance movement cast in a form. But "dance movement and musical staging" in no way affect a 'musical's musicality." They might very well affect the visual presentation of musical numbers. However "musicality" and "staging" are as different and unrelated as cardboard and caviar.

Moreover, this entire mess has no precise definition. For example, a good dance (the "Beach Ballet" in *Carousel,* the dream lampoon in *Fiddler on the Roof,* the dance in the gym in *West Side Story,* for starters) added immeasurably to the total effect of these musical shows. And musical staging is an integral necessity in *all* musicals, whether accomplished successfully or not.

Finally, again, in this section we have those words: "tremendous," "consequential," and "terrific."

Continuing with Gottfried's review of *Candide:* "First written as operetta satire, it no longer seems so when the show is not produced as operetta satire. The score is so superb, though, that it always came through as great music, as well as great theater music, and it still does. . . . Hershy Kay's lucid orchestrations have been bloated by the additional musicians stupidly required by the musicians' union, and they now sound a little muddy but quite delightful."

Nevertheless, *Candide* was and is operetta satire. As a great dramatist-poet once said: "Seems, madam! Nay, it is." Surely the Bernstein score deserves better comprehension from a reviewer than "so superb" and "great." These are Gottfried's stamps on nearly everything he likes, regardless of style or quality.

As for Hershy Kay's orchestrations, they are either "lucid" or "bloated"—not both. I also suspect that the additional musicians had little to do with the "stupidity" of the musicians' union: The theater simply was larger. Mr. Gottfried's opinion that the orchestrations "have been bloated" is only one amateur's opinion and there is where "stupidity" lies. Although I myself noticed no basic difference in orchestration, a conversation with Hershy Kay assures me that there were basically no changes. The addition of players chiefly allowed the work of one man to be shared (alternately) by two, in most cases.

Here Gottfried is at odds with himself, since in his initial review of *Candide* when it opened at Brooklyn's Chelsea Theatre Center, he said: "In fact, Kay did a great job, staying true to the music's sophistication while creating a whole different sound for it, ranging from woodwind and string quartet to triple pianos, one of which I think was electrified [*sic*]."

It should have been obvious that when such a small combo was moved to a much larger theater, the orchestration necessarily had to be enlarged. This enlargement need not result in "bloat."

From *Death of a Salesman* (revival) (*Women's Wear Daily*, November 5, 1974), two excerpts:

"Although it is fashionable to dismiss Miller as a holdover from the Depression's social realists, like most fashionable thinking, that is thoughtless. He has been too adept with metaphor, too imaginative with reality levels, too successful at extending contemporary situations into universal themes and too graceful a writer to by any means be written off as a junior Odets and minor Ibsenite [I think he means Ibsen]. . . .

"The play has too many other provocative qualities to deal with in a brief criticism—its deft use of metaphors such as travelling and selling; its concept of a man being exhausted in both senses of the word; its treatment of love and the need for it; the unsentimental depth of its feelings."

First of all, just who at this moment and in this article is "dismissing" Miller? Who is writing him off? Since the reader is not given the cause and source of these references, their mention here —apparently as part of an argument—is unnecessary.

And the writing—"exhausted in both senses of the word"! What precisely does Gottfried mean? Also, ". . . too adept with metaphor" and "too imaginative with reality levels" are so vague as to suggest that Gottfried is talking to himself.

Regarding fashion and Miller, I should like to quote from William Hazlitt's essay (circa 1827):

Fashion constantly begins and ends in the two things it abhors most, singularity and vulgarity. It is the perpetual setting up and then disowning a certain standard of taste, elegance, and refinement, which has no other foundation or authority than that it is the prevailing distraction of the moment, which was yesterday ridiculous from its being new, and tomorrow will be odious from its being common.

Why is Gottfried so conscious of fashion?

From *The Sirens* (*Women's Wear Daily*, May 3, 1974): "The legacy of American bigotry is so complex that it is still impossible to discuss the work of black playwrights without racial references, although that should be the only way to discuss art (or any) work. At a time when theaters are so desperate to prove their liberalism and atone for past sins they will do amateur work if the author is black, the remarkably gifted and growing Richard Wesley could probably have his grade school notebooks produced if he wanted to.

"Wesley is classy enough to be above these seekers, but I think the demand for his work may have misled them into thinking unfinished work is finished and lesser work is better. . . .

"Wesley's writing, needless to say, is regularly gorgeous, and his poetic treatment of the black vernacular is exquisite, but he has just got to discipline his work; he has got to go it alone. He is too good for less."

While Gottfried's point about production of gifted work by black playwrights is incontrovertibly correct, his writing is atrocious. How can he be taken seriously when, it would appear, his resources as a grammarian include "classy," "needless to say," "regularly gorgeous," "go it alone"? Nobody's writing can be described as "regularly gorgeous." "Needless to say" and "go it alone" can be found too often both in the horrendous melodramas of the turn of the century and in the advice-to-the-lovelorn columns. They are not among the tools of a contemporary writer and they are meaningless when employed by a reviewer.

Gottfried's review of *Going Through Changes* by Richard Wesley (*Women's Wear Daily*, February 4, 1974): The opening sermon— "These days, it's great to be a playwright. If there is any problem, it's in choosing among all the theaters that want to do your plays—the white liberal ones, the rich professional ones, the poor dedicated ones; there is a problem in coping with pressures to 'write black' instead of writing what comes to mind; in being sure you are wanted for your talent rather than your race; in being criticized as simply a playwright rather than a black playwright. But if these are problems, they are nice ones to have."

I doubt that Gottfried is naive, but his confusion is evident. He cannot honestly mean "If there is any problem, it's in choosing among all the theaters that want to do your plays." Does he really *believe* there is such a profusion of theaters wanting to produce Mr. Wesley's (or most authors') plays that he has a choice? I don't know a single playwright—red, black, green, or purple—who is in a position to choose "among all the theaters that want to do" his plays.

"*Going Through Changes* should not be forced into a staged-reading style, with the company seated at the rear, rising to play their scenes in non-sets. Perhaps budgetary problems forced this, and hopefully a subsequent production will be dealt with on a scenic basis, giving Wesley the necessary challenge of making his play work as full-fledged theater. God knows these plays deserve it—they are simply exquisite."

What Gottfried was trying to say when he wrote "hopefully a subsequent production will be dealt with on a scenic basis . . ." was that "hopefully a subsequent production employing scenery . . ."

A scenic production is not what provides a challenge to a play's working. Often times, a play is destroyed by too much production or one that is inappropriate. The scenic production and the dancing girls gave *The Black Crook* (1866) its success but then everyone knew from the beginning that there was no play. *The Cradle Will Rock* (1938) worked electrifyingly well when it appeared sans everything except Blitzstein's opus.

Revival of *The Pajama Game* (*Women's Wear Daily*, December 10, 1973): "The first good musical of the season is the revival of *The Pajama Game*. . . . It is not only an incorporably [*sic*!] better-made and more entertaining show than what else has come along so far, but, though 20 years older, it is fresher and less old-fashioned. Its basic material is good—a score remarkably consistent for melody and charm with a book that may be silly but is at least adult and well made—and the craftsmanship of its assembly is a nasty reminder of how far downhill the technique of musical-making has slid since the Fifties."

And how can a book that is silly be adult and well made? And "the craftsmanship of its assembly" is *not* "a nasty reminder of how far downhill the technique of musical-making has slid since the Fifties."

A knowledgeable reviewer should be able to detect the fact that *The Pajama Game* has—first of all—no second-act book! George Abbott, master showman, has put together an entire act of production numbers, most of which relate to nothing and to nobody important in the book. Sandwiched between these are a number of feeble attempts to keep the characters and plot alive chiefly by interjecting scenes involving the two principals who otherwise could possibly be forgotten.

But Act Two also contains, besides the "I'll Never Be Jealous Again" ballet, the production numbers "Steam Heat," "Hernando's Hideaway," "Think of the Time I Save," and "Seven and a Half Cents," the last a finale in which boy and girl are (surprise!) at last united.

Further, *The Pajama Game* is one example of George Abbott's invention known as the "crossover"; this is a scene, song, parade, or whatever that takes place before a traveller curtain while the scenery behind it is being changed. That device served us long and well *at that time*, twenty years ago, and for a reviewer to observe that in *Pajama Game* the "craftsmanship of its assembly is a nasty reminder of how far downhill the technique of musical-making has slid" is an indication that he is unaware of musical-production evolution. In more recent times the crossover has been eliminated in favor of *no* scene changes, *no* waits, *no* water-treading. Examples: *Fiddler on the Roof* demonstrates the process as it was growing out of the older method, while *Pippin, Sweet Charity, Company, Zorba, Follies, A Little Night Music,* and even *Hair* are into the new.

"Frankly, I came to the show with skepticism. Rock music has struck such terror in the hearts of musical producers that they don't know what the public wants (the answer: simply a good show, whatever the kind of music). Broadway economics has only intensified the problem. As a result, many of today's musicals are cynical packages, hoping to recoup on tour before facing the lions (audiences as well as critics) in New York. This is what *The Pajama Game* revival appeared to be, especially with its interracial casting that seemed more a commercial exploitation than a sensible idea."

If what the public wants is "simply a good show, whatever the kind of music," then there need be no mention of music in a musical show; it apparently does not matter to Mr. Gottfried.

About "many of today's musicals are cynical packages, hoping to recoup on tour before facing the lions . . .": Is there something peculiar about a producer's wanting "to recoup on tour. . . ."? If he succeeds there might be more musicals on Broadway. Today's risk level makes the chance of raising the necessary capital nearly impossible.

There is another confusion here—not wholly assignable to Gottfried. The long pre-Broadway tour is certainly aimed at recoupment. But no one ever mentions in this connection the productions of new shows at the Long Wharf Theater in New Haven, Connecticut; the Goodspeed Opera House, East Haddam, Connecticut; the Los Angeles Civic Light Opera; Arena Stage, Washington; and other out-of-New York theaters. Such a practice is also wise and careful: Producers have a chance to see and evaluate shows before involving themselves in more expensive productions and costlier rehearsal periods. Both methods hopefully avoid financial catastrophe. Neither assures Broadway success. But the need to avoid as much risk as possible is increasingly pressing.

The next sentence commences with a singular pronoun which, in this muddle, must refer to the plural "cynical packages": "This is what *The Pajama Game* revival appeared to be, especially with its interracial casting that seemed more a commercial exploitation than a sensible idea."

There he goes again with his dirty word "commercial". In defense of this "interracial casting" another reviewer wrote that the romantic conflict between the man (the factory foreman) and the girl (the union leader) was so thin that by adding the racial element, the conflict was strengthened.

Mr. Gottfried's suspicious nature goes berserk when he is confronted with anything he can attribute to "commercialism".

Now he withdraws his racial objection:

"Instead, the show seems no revival at all and the racial mix has added a depth to its story—as a matter of fact, this *Pajama Game* makes more sense on racial matters than most of the recent plays that mean to. Yet, the script has been only barely changed to acknowledge the black-white romance (the girl says, 'It wouldn't work . . . there's a little thing called racial prejudice,' and the guy replies, 'You mean you won't go out with us Polacks?')"

Now we are really confused! ". . . the racial mix has added a depth to its story . . ." versus the earlier paragraph: ". . . cynical packages. . . . This is what *The Pajama Game* revival appeared to be, especially with its interracial casting . . ."

Would the reader like to close his eyes and play Eeny, Meeny, Miny, Mo?

"This hardly makes the show's book a major literary or social work, but then the show is only meant as entertainment and that it provides in abundance. The story about union problems in a Midwest pajama factory remains a pretext for musical numbers, many of them hopelessly irrelevant, but it is hard to quibble when the music is so catchy and doesn't sound dated at all, even with the original Don Walker orchestrations. Needless to say, one shouldn't be surprised that the show works—considering that the original was co-directed by Jerome Robbins and choreographed by Bob Fosse. The omission of Robbins' name on the program is inexcusable, since everything seems copied from the original; but at least Fosse is given his credit and of course this was the show which introduced his trademarks—small groups, angular, eccentric, and with derbies if possible. Fosse's 'Steam Heat' is still a show-stopper."

"The show is only meant as entertainment." So were *Maggie Flynn; Buttrio Square; Georgy; Henry, Sweet Henry; Minnie's Boys; Molly;* and many other failures, but no one excused their shortcomings on such grounds.

As far as "the music is so catchy" is concerned, one would have to have been stone-deaf these past twenty-odd years since *The Pa-*

jama Game first opened, not to have become thoroughly familiar
with the music. By now, the music of *Pelléas* and *Wozzeck* (in part)
have also become "catchy."

Again, it is apparent that Martin Gottfried is in high-dudgeon over
the omission of Jerome Robbins' name from the program. Though
I have no specific knowledge of *Pajama Game,* I have had enough
experience to know that originally there had to be something *con-
tractual* about the use of Robbins' name, and in this revival—
probably because Robbins did not choose to work on the show
again— he was no longer involved in any way.

I'm also certain that Bob Fosse is amused by Gottfried's analysis
of his trademark—"small groups, angular, eccentric, and with derbies
if possible." "Eccentric" is an old-fashioned term for a type (not
style) of dancing employed by writers whose knowledge of dance
was so limited that what they referred to was neither ballet nor
modern.

Martin Gottfried or anyone else can *like* or even *love* the music
of *The Pajama Game* but you'd have to be deaf not to identify the
music with the fifties (no disgrace—but true).

"The rest may not be quite that brilliant but it is invariably
cheerful. George Abbott, who co-directed the original with Robbins,
has staged this version as if it were still 1954, smartly oblivious to
technical progress (he is still afraid to change scenery in full
view). . . ."

From the review of *Charley's Aunt* at Niagara-on-the-Lake, Ontario,
Canada (*Women's Wear Daily,* June 5, 1974):

After mentioning that many people enjoy this play and that
"many critics don't even bother to review it," Gottfried said: "Some
people would say this proves it is bad and others would say this
proves it is good."

And other people get *paid* for writing deep thoughts like that?

"Maurice Strike's sets are perfectly handsome in the style of a
Victorian greeting card [*sic!*] and the overall presentation is artistic
rather than commercial."

Greeting cards are not commercial?

"It is virtually a ballet and it is masterful. His direction is also
quite wonderful with romance."

Sounds like a high school-girl's love letter. This is followed here
and there with petite phrases and comments such as "extremely
uneven"; "simply excellent"; "perfectly all right"; "probably make
a career of that which, given her talent, she shouldn't"; and "Others
in the cast range, I'm afraid, from satisfactory to novice."

In a book he wrote in 1963–1969, Gottfried said: "For all its bravado about sex, the theater is still so shy about it that there is all but an outright denial that it even exists."*

Anyone with any awareness would have sensed in 1963 that attitudes toward sex would change. Now that they have, what has the theater derived thereby? Some box offices have shown an increased profit, but as far as theatrical artistry or "growth" is concerned, there has not been one whit of improvement. Why does Gottfried consider it such a virtue to exhibit on stage the rather everyday acts with which we are all familiar? Must we see *everything?* Shakespeare thought it unnecessary in *Romeo and Juliet* to show the marriage ceremony of the lovers and instead veered away from the obvious with a simple speech from Friar Laurence that ended the scene:

> Come, come with me, and we will make short work;
> For, by your leaves, you shall not stay alone
> Till Holy Church incorporate two in one.*

Gottfried undergoes typewriter hysterics at the scarcity of new playwrights. He dismisses the older, developed ones. But when he witnesses something genuinely brave and new (not commercial) such as Albee's *Box-Mao-Box* (1968) he concludes his review with:

"The truth is, though, that whatever the form, he seems as careless and as pompous as ever—perhaps too pompous to be true and perhaps too careless to ever finish his work."

I never read programs but I understood within two minutes that Albee's play was constructed along the lines of a musical "theme with variations." I relaxed and enjoyed.

So, now, does Martin Gottfried want new things or is he unable to recognize them when he sees them?

Gottfried's list of the "just tremendous" includes *House of Flowers, Semi-Detached, A Murderer Among Us, Dynamite Tonight, Macbird, Saturday Night, Viet Rock, To Bury a Cousin, The Rimers of Eldritch, Hooray! It's a Glorious Day. . . .* And All That.

One man's taste is most people's poison.

Man of La Mancha (*Women's Wear Daily,* 1965): "Nevertheless, Mitch Leigh wrote a very fine Spanishy [*sic*!] score and was lucky to have oboe, bassoon, flamenco guitar, and all sorts of nice things orchestrated into it by Neil Warner. Someday there will be a terrific Spanish musical. . . ."

Opening Nights (New York: Putnam, 1963).
*Act 11, Scene 6.

What does Gottfried mean by "lucky"? The instrumentation of a show is a matter discussed at length, prior to rehearsals by composer and orchestrator, and sometimes the musical director. So "luck" plays no part in the choice of instrumentation. I suggest that "a terrific Spanish musical" must come from Spain.

". . . the collapse of Broadway's frontline dramatists [Williams, Miller, Inge] and the collapse of the idea of 'drama' along with them."*

In 1966, he had written: ". . . the middle-aged American playwrights are in serious trouble and our theater is suffering because of it. Look at Broadway drama and you will see nothing—a retired Lillian Hellman, an uncertain Arthur Miller, a bewildered Tennessee Williams, a defeated (dead) William Inge."

Mr. Gottfried attempts to discredit each and has his arguments neatly based on each author's having written a play less good than his impressive earlier best. This, for Gottfried, automatically signals "The End"!

It seems never to have occurred to Martin Gottfried that all true artists are conditioned, stimulated, inhibited, or in a great many other ways affected by the world in which they live. In an important way, it is this very effect—for good or ill—that makes artists of them: They truly represent their lives and times.

The young generation of American playwrights in 1955 were victims of three blazing catastrophes: the Depression years that began in 1929 and hung blindingly in the air for another decade, World War II, which was followed almost immediately by the destructive House Un-American Activities Committee which (until Watergate in the '70s), presented the Greatest Show on Earth, starring Senator Joseph McCarthy. Beginning in 1947, the committee pillaged, burned, deprived, and destroyed—sometimes only by insinuation—everybody it chose to attack.

And why does the then-younger generation of writers over which Gottfried has read savage benedictions *seem* to have perished? It is my own feeling that Gottfried has no idea of the world and the artist. Having survived the war (the first), these writers, as young people had to undergo the painful Depression. This made the majority of them militant and they wrote aggressively and with passion about the kind of life they were forced to endure. Even the more poetic Tennessee Williams, although he dealt with the emotional problems of "special" people, obliquely assigned their predicaments to the insensitive universe. Lillian Hellman, Arthur

*Gottfried, *Opening Nights.*

Miller, Sidney Kingsley, Clifford Odets, Irwin Shaw, and Arthur
Laurents were more direct, and most of them became personally
terrorized by the senseless and destructive capers of the House Un-
American Activities Committee (1947–1955). Even the few who
were not directly charged had reason to fear that they might become involved and the playwrighting response resulted in silence
for the majority. At the start of this devastation, Hellman was forty-
two; Williams, thirty-three; Miller, thirty-two; Laurents, twenty-
nine; Shaw, thirty-four; Odets, forty-one; and Kingsley, forty-one.

Two of these marched ahead. Williams went on with his personal
poetic plays that at least outwardly held no cudgels. Arthur Miller
walked straight on, with *The Crucible* (1953) and *A View from the
Bridge* (1955), both of which shouted strong battle cries in the face
of the committee.

But the toll is what Martin Gottfried fails utterly to take into
account. The trials and the fear of trials, the harassment that these
writers endured—nightmares that came unheralded and meaning-
lessly both day and night and again and again, had debilitating effects on all of them and on others of their generation. What came
afterward—that is, after the scars had become ineradicable—was
largely without teeth. Mingled with fear was disillusionment brought
on by the savagery of a reckless witch hunt that easily surpassed
any other in American history.

No playwright who endured these holocausts—the last one in
particular—can be sanely evaluated without these facts of their
lives being taken into account. The burial of talented people before their deaths is as unreasonably savage as anything else they
survived except that, in this case—the case of Mr. Martin Gottfried
—the evaluation is so reckless and its source so insignificant that
one can only try to shrug it off as offensive, insensitive, and ignorant.

It is fascinating to compare Gottfried in 1966—positive and without a trace of humanity or a vestige of understanding of what art
or the artist is really about—with Gottfried in 1975.

As we have seen, at the earlier time he had written:
". . . the middle-aged American playwrights are in serious trouble
. . . an uncertain Arthur Miller. . . ."

But in 1975 after the revival of *Death of a Salesman*, here is what
he had to say:
". . . most important of all, let Miller see for himself, the depth and
humanity of which he was capable in 1949 and which must still
lie within him."

Perhaps Gottfried is developing.

In the same piece—a long essay that appeared a week after the
revival opening, he went on:

". . . it is difficult to comprehend anyone ever having dismissed it as merely a Depression liberal's attack on the capitalist system."
". . . it is only amusing to recall criticism of it as being a work of old-fashioned naturalism."

Gottfried has done it again. It's as though he were in the middle of an argument, only who is arguing and about what? And why recall it here and now? These adverse opinions of *Death of a Salesman* to which he alludes did not represent any general trend at the time of the play's premiere. Did this reviewer *invent* them so that St. George Gottfried could whip out his good broadsword and head up a new crusade? I know of no reviewer as conscious of "fashion" as Gottfried and it was in his 1974 review of the same play (quoted earlier) that he wrote:
"Although it is fashionable to dismiss Miller as a holdover from the Depression's social realists, like most fashionable thinking, that is thoughtless."

Bravo! Was this fashionable criticism uttered by anyone of importance in any important place? If not, why make so much of it?

From *A Theater Divided:**

West Side Story: ". . . instead of a story proceeding with regular interruptions in a dance, a song, a production number, constructed according to the old standards of musical staging, the work developed as an entity. Music never began or ended, dances were not separate 'numbers.' Instead, all movement was choreographic and music was continuous, winding in and out of the dialogue."

It's one thing to admire *West Side Story* and another to be factually incorrect. Every song in it ends. Every dance ends. G. Schirmer, Inc. published the vocal score. I suggest that Mr. Gottfried have a look.

The impression Mr. Gottfried got of "winding in and out of the dialogue" is due to underscoring that began in musicals about 1940 with *Pal Joey* and has been employed in all good musicals to date (earlier it was practiced in operettas such as *The Desert Song* and *The Student Prince*). And *no* show—old or new—is "constructed according to the old standards of musical staging." *Construction* of any work and its subsequent *staging* represent two different phases in the birth of a work.

The Magic Show (*Women's Wear Daily*, May 30, 1974): "I never met anyone who didn't love magicians, and yet, for some peculiar

---

*Martin Gottfried, *A Theater Divided: A Study of the Postwar American Stage* (Boston: Little, Brown, 1968).

reason, they seem to be a dying breed. You don't see them on television or in nightclubs, and I think the reason lies with old-time
producers and television executives who simply toss them on the
garbage heap with other vaudeville acts—contortionists, ventrilo-
quists, tap dancers, acrobats, and jugglers. They're all dismissed as
corny.

"Now some of them are, of course, corny, though I'll love a good
juggler at any time."

(He used "corny" six times in this review!)

"But magic itself was never corny; it was always amazing. And, of
course, it is especially related to the young rock scene, which has
so many connections to fantasy and hallucination."

". . . most terrific magician I've ever seen . . ."

"[tricks] are fantastic and incredible."

"I am amazed even after I have been told how a trick works."

"I just couldn't believe my eyes."

". . . the show is still his doing an act."

"It should have been a free-flowing hallucination."

(Re songs): ". . . some folky . . ."

". . . amplified to death."

"I could watch the tricks all night."

Again we find Gottfried as an "inventor" of pseudophilosophical
aphorisms with a spewing out of adjectives that have no basic asso-
ciation with *The Magic Show*. They could apply to anything he
liked but he tells his readers nothing except his personal reactions:

"I'll love a good juggler at any time. . . . Most terrific magician
I've ever seen. . . . I am amazed. . . . I just couldn't believe my eyes.
. . . I could watch the tricks all night."

For such comments to have interest or validity, the reader would
have to be a close friend of the writer's or Mr. Gottfried would need
to have distinguished professional credentials that would endow
his blanket personal endorsement with special significance.

Again, the enthusiasm is unsupported and it conveys nothing but
Gottfried's personal ecstasy.

"Amazing," "terrific," "fantastic," "incredible"—his judgment
without his reasoning.

What he has reference to is never described. After reading Gottfried's review, we know no more than before about *The Magic Show*

—only about Gottfried, and do we care? He might as well tell us about his bathroom joys.

Anyone—especially a reviewer—who continually hurls reckless and angry accusations against any group or individual without some thoughtful investigation should be turned out to pasture. In this case:

"You don't see them [magicians] on television or in nightclubs, and I think the reason lies with old-time producers and television executives who simply toss them on the garbage heap with other vaudeville acts. . . ."

Don Quixote is again tilting at windmills. The "old-time producers" never employed magicians, at least not on Broadway (how would they have?). Magicians were employed in vaudeville and saloons. It was neither television executives nor old-time producers who put an end to vaudeville; instead it was the public that was surfeited with programs that had become stereotyped. Occasionally the vaudeville components had been programmed in the elaborate revues but these were also bankrupted by a bored public.

Nightclubs (as Gottfried suggested) from time to time also incorporated magic acts but discontinued them when it became apparent that patrons did not come to see this sort of thing or else had seen the same thing again and again. And finally, the big nightclubs also passed into history.

In the earliest days of television, before that medium had even begun to discover its own personality and differences from other media, variety shows were employed for video airing. During this period and for perhaps a decade, these vaudeville components enjoyed a temporary revival. Once again it was the public that became bored. Viewers had accepted the old fare for a time only because they were captivated by the new medium and not by what it programmed. Once the sheer novelty of pictures-at-home had worn off, the material presented was subjected to more serious scrutiny. The television directors, producers (all young men, by the way), and cameramen were evolving hitherto undiscovered techniques, finding ways of coping with material that was independent of the stage, and when these problems were resolved, the too well-known vaudeville elements were once again discarded.

If one understands anything about history and evolution, one unfailing fact emerges: Nearly every element enjoys a period of popularity, then passes into a period of arrest. Time passes—and after twenty, thirty, or many more years during which these elements lie dormant, they are resurrected and once more take on a shining new brilliance, especially for newer generations that had not enjoyed the earlier experience. Successful revival, however, comes only after a period of silence and usually when someone belonging to the new generation discovers and is able to present the old in a fresh new style. This is what Doug Henning accomplished so delightfully in *The Magic Show*.

The entire process of magicians falling out of favor was a perfectly natural manifestation of evolution: the fault of no one but rather the inevitable cleansing effect of time. The heyday of the various magicians—Kellar, Thurston, Herrmann, Albrini, to name but a few—occurred from about 1890 to, roughly, 1926, when Houdini, probably the most famous of them all, died. They went out of style; the public tired of them. Gottfried's observation that magic "is especially related to the young rock scene, which has so many connections to fantasy and hallucination" suggests only one connection: drugs.

Gigi (*Women's Wear Daily*, November 24, 1973): ". . . was a cynical if successful capitalization on the success of *My Fair Lady* . . . designed to turn a profit . . ."

". . . shabby opulence of the set . . ."

". . . makes it seem a touring revival at that."

"[Lerner and Loewe's] reputation is based, really, on only *My Fair Lady*."

"Loewe . . . away from the theater . . . has frankly grown rusty."

"American style story and Viennese-style music."

"Alfred Drake suppresses his usual ham to the extent of limiting it to enough for Thanksgiving dinner, as opposed to his usual supply for all major holidays, plus sandwiches."

". . . his French pronunciations and dialect are self-conscious and supercilious."

"Oliver Smith's physical production is a skimpy and often sloppy attempt at Cecil Beaton elegance."

"Onna White's choreography . . . is elegant and precisely danced."

There was no secret about *Gigi's* longish tour prior to Broadway, but Gottfried seems to harbor some grudge against the very idea. *No, No, Nanette* did the same thing originally in 1924 and 1925 and by the time it reached Broadway, its celebrated tunes had even then—without radio, TV, and with but few recordings—become old friends.

As for Lerner and Loewe's reputation being "based, really, on only *My Fair Lady*," it is Mr. Gottfried who is cynical. Didn't Lerner and Loewe write *Brigadoon*, a giant success that became a musical theater staple; *Paint Your Wagon*, which contained many fine songs; the delightful film version of *Gigi* (remember?); and *Camelot*, which also contains an exceptionally good score? *Only My Fair Lady?*

It is reckless of any reviewer to label Frederick Loewe as "frankly grown rusty" because he has not wanted to write a new score for some time. Such a statement is easy to make but its factuality will depend on any or everything that hopefully may follow. A critic should only bury the dead.

The reviewer's attempt at wit at the expense of Alfred Drake is labored and puerile. I doubt if anyone else thought that Drake was "hammy" in *Oklahoma!* or *Kiss Me Kate*. If he was not, then "usual" doesn't apply.

Gottfried's trouble is that he has a limited vocabulary and sets down the first word that occurs to him. I don't think he actually *means* "hammy," but it is perhaps Drake's swagger, bravado, and sense of stylish flourish that Gottfried finds difficult to describe.

His definition of Oliver Smith's physical production as "skimpy" must have made the producers hysterical, since its lavishness was extremely costly. Further, Oliver Smith need make "no attempt at Cecil Beaton elegance." The elegance attempted to represent the Paris of Smith, and Smith requires no middleman.

Saying that "Onna White's choreography . . . is . . . precisely danced" conjures up a vision of the Rockettes. Surely there is more to be said of dancing than that.

According to its producer Edwin Lester, "*Gigi* has earned back 40 to 45 percent of its investment. . . . It can well earn enough in subsidiary playing [stock and amateur] to repay its investors."

I add this from a letter addressed to me, to relieve Mr. Gottfried of any feeling of guilt that there *might* have been a profit.

Raisin (*Women's Wear Daily*, October 19, 1973): "[*Raisin*] is simply, in show business terms, a 'property'—an attempt to capitalize on the familiar title of a successful play, and still another ugly attempt by Robert Nemiroff [the producer and co-author] to profiteer on the talent of his late ex-wife, Ms. Hansberry."

This is a total lie invented by a warped mind. The composer and lyricist, Judd Woldin and Robert Brittan, have been members of my BMI Musical Theatre Workshops for about a decade. During that period, they worked from synopses of their own making on two or three musical shows. (Among these was that hot commercial property *Jonah*.) One day, they asked my opinion about musicalizing *Raisin in the Sun* which they had just read and fallen in love with. Contrary to what Mr. Gottfried wrote—"A musical cannot be made of a work that is not essentially musical. The original material must have an inherent musical mood, a rhythm, whether in its story, its setting or its characters"—it was my considered and practiced opinion that *Raisin in the Sun* offered highly potential musical opportunities. It provided many moods (love, hatred, desire, frustration, and many others) which I thought most appropriate for musical treatment. There was much to sing about. I have no idea of what *aufgeblasen* treasure lies buried in Mr. Gottfried's "must have . . . a rhythm" (perhaps table-tapping at a séance?), but in my fairly wide experience it has no meaning whatsoever.

Woldin and Brittan worked hard and long on their project, listened to and applied the criticism they received to their very sincere work-in-progress, and after much writing and rewriting sought out Robert Nemiroff strictly because he held the rights to the use of Ms. Hansberry's play. (Nothing sinister about any of this.)

Though Mr. Nemiroff withheld outright permission, he wanted to work with the composer and lyricist on the musical adaptation of the play. Literally years—possibly four or five—passed, during which Fred Coe at one point held an option. Then things looked discouraging and my boys (with families to support) were working at nothing but *Raisin*.

When everything appeared to be most hopeless, the Arena Stage in Washington agreed to try out the musical. It was a great success there, so much so that after Richard Coe raved about it in the *Washington Post*, Clive Barnes of the *Times* went down to see it and also wrote glowingly of it. On the basis of this review, plus the unqualified Washington success, Nemiroff was able to raise the money necessary for the New York production.

Raisin was restaged for the proscenium theater. It played to more glowing notices in Philadelphia and then opened on Broadway to positive reviews. Unfortunately, it has made no profit in New York.

So much for Mr. Gottfried's groundless and irresponsible presumptions about "an attempt to capitalize" and "still another ugly attempt by Robert Nemiroff to profiteer. . . ."

The rest of the Gottfried review is opinion. He says of the composer: "Woldin has not even managed to write a black score." This remark displays Mr. Gottfried at his nadir. Did Richard Rodgers, who is no more Siamese than Woldin is black, write a Siamese score for *The King and I*? Did Richard Strauss write a Greek score for *Elektra*? Did Puccini write an American score for *The Girl of the Golden West*? Did Mozart or Rossini write Spanish scores for *The Marriage of Figaro* and *The Barber of Seville*? The list of negatives is endless and includes all of the greatest writers for musical theater.

Mr. Martin Gottfried is nonfactual, nonthinking, and a lazy journalist for failing to find out simple facts before hurling reckless calumnies.

I should next like to quote briefly a few Gottfriedisms, selected at random:

Neil Simon's *God's Favorite:*

"More important, it isn't funny. Simon's name on a program does not promise a deep play, or a religious one, but it does promise a funny one."

Later:

". . . suggested that perhaps Simon was going to return to his strength —humor—and stop trying in shallow ways to be profound."

While I was also dissatisfied with *God's Favorite,* I recognize the right of any playwright to try to break out of a mold, to disregard his prior associations and the repeated easier commercial successes he has had in them. I think it is presumptuous of a reviewer to be derisive of an author's attempt to be somebody he hasn't tried being heretofore. What Gottfried is espousing is a version of type-casting. Going along with Gottfried's failure to honor a rightful effort—regardless of its having misfired *this time*—Bert Lahr could not have played the lead in *Waiting for Godot* and the author of *Hamlet* should not have written *The Comedy of Errors.*

London Assurance (Dion Boucicault): ". . . the only explanation I can conceive for its British success is a nostalgic feeling the audiences there may have felt for a bygone era."

I am puzzled that Gottfried thinks the English could only have a "nostalgic feeling" in it. In fact, I found nothing more nostalgic about it than I would have at a performance of *The Rivals* or *Twelfth Night* or *Sherlock Holmes.* Enjoyment requires no categorizing.

And then at the end of his piece, Gottfried found so much effort "expended on a self-conscious and cute production of a play to which everyone involved was condescending and in an altered version at that."

I thought that no actor was condescending but, to the contrary, all clearly understood the style appropriate to playing this kind of period farce.

The "altered version" needs no apology. *London Assurance,* for all the pleasure it gave many people and most other reviewers, is not a sacred cow. Indeed it has many faults, and the practice of reviving less-than-perfect old plays which can be made to work by cutting and altering is in no way new. For instance, Orson Welles did an unforgettable *Shoemaker's Holiday* (Dekker) and Burt Sheve-love did a *No, No, Nanette,* and had these been absolutely faithful to the originals they would have been bloody bores.

I myself was "faithful" to *The Desert Song,* but neither Mr. Gott-fried nor any other New York reviewer gave anyone connected with that production E for Effort. In this same connection, I would like to quote from Mr. Gottfried's December 16, 1973, review of *The Widowing of Mrs. Holyrod* by D. H. Lawrence:

". . . her remorse at the end seems a rationalization and is utterly unsatisfying as theater or logic. Having done such a magnificent job staging the play, the best I have seen from the talented Brown, I can only regret that he hadn't thought of the obvious solution: to make her remorse a nasty self-deception, tragic in her victimization by the brutal husband even after his death. Perhaps Brown thought of it but could not fit the script to this interpretation. In any case, he did the play as the author intended, and I believe he made a mistake."

Consistent point of view? Boucicault's work is frowned on "in an altered version," whereas with Lawrence's "Brown . . . did the play as the author intended, and I believe he made a mistake."

As You Like It (National Theatre of Great Britain): "On the simple level of sense, all-male casting makes this confusing plot into a confounding one. . . ."

"Was Williams denying the production's homosexuality?"

"It is also entirely without the spirit of Shakespeare."

All-male, or male and female, the exchange of sexual identities in *As You Like It* is certainly confusing. But homosexuality? Per-haps in Mr. Gottfried's mind, where it seems to dwell inordinately.

But what most of us saw on the opening night of *As You Like It* in no way suggested homosexuality (nor is it suggested in Strauss' opera *Der Rosenkavalier*). It was clear that the "girls" were male and never did they become, as Gottfried stated, "drag queens." (What does Gottfried think of Princeton's traditional Triangle shows?)

Lastly, for a reviewer to say that a production is "also entirely without the spirit of Shakespeare" requires something more than a bald statement. It needs support and particularized examples of failure. Gottfried's saying so does not make it so.

Love for Love (dull or not) has always been a staple in the United States. It is played frequently in regional and college theaters. It was done on Broadway (no secret) in the following years:

1925 (March), with Walter Abel, Edgar Stehli, E. J. Ballentine, Adrienne Morrison, Rosalind Fuller, etc.

1925 (September), with Henry O'Neill, Clarence Derwent, Margaret Douglass, Eva Balfour, etc.

1940, with Thomas Chalmers, Bobby Clark, Cornelia Otis Skinner, Violet Hemming, Peggy Wood, Dorothy Gish, Leo G. Carroll, Romney Brent, Walter Hampden, Dudley Digges, etc., with sets by Robert Edmond Jones.

1947, with John Gielgud, Cyril Ritchard, Adrienne Allen, Donald Bain, Pamela Brown, and Robert Flemyng.

It is a fact, then, that *Love for Love* did not take "about 300 years to be mounted here."

Of late Gottfried has been writing long serious pieces in the weekend editions of the *New York Post*. One of these (June 1975) expostulated on Bob Fosse (in itself a worthwhile enterprise) apropos of *Chicago*. The article was highly complimentary and attempted to trace Fosse's artistic development, his talent, his accomplishments. Good. But these four columns are as filled with inaccuracies, sloppy thinking, and half-truths as are all the other things Gottfried has written.

His first theme, occupying a third of the piece, touched on musicals of the past that "belonged to star composers or performers (a Rodgers and Hammerstein show, an Ethel Merman show, and so forth): ". . . musicals had grown too complex and expensive to simply be a performer's vehicle or a series of set-ups for song-and-dance numbers."

It is one thing to admire Bob Fosse and quite another to dismiss the work of authors (composers, lyricists, librettists) of a musical show as creating "a series of set-ups for song-and-dance numbers" for which the theater has "grown too complex and expensive . . ."

Here is where we get into the difference between what *is* and what *seems to be*. The best musicals of Rodgers, Loesser, Lerner-Loewe, Sondheim, Bernstein—and earlier, Kern—are so well-made, so filled with first-class creativity, that the "star-director" could be an asset if not a necessity. However, the shows *existed*, and star-directors (not mentioned by Gottfried) such as Abbott, Logan, Burrows, Hart, and others helped to transfer what already existed on paper onto the stage.

It is when the show has *not* existed—a most important fact ignored by Gottfried—that the star-directors have nearly made us believe that it did. How? By speed, wit, visual tricks, and an overall sense of style and movement that *almost* succeeded in blinding us to the poverty of the material.

This is a not inconsiderable accomplishment, but Gottfried's long article does not take into account that in the end, it is the show (its idea, theme, verbal and vocal content) that is of prime importance in the musical theater. And this content is a great deal more than "a series of set-ups for song and dance numbers."

The well-made show (setting aside for the moment the production) continues on and on for years being remounted successfully again and again by second-, third-, and fifth-rate directors, still managing to communicate whatever the show means to communicate to audiences the world over.

It is doubtful whether *without* Fosse's accomplishments in *Chicago*, there would have been a show (the same was true of *Pippin*).

As for musicals having "grown too complex and expensive to simply be a performer's vehicle," again, this is inaccurate. *Irene* was not a good show. It earned a good profit because of Debbie Reynolds and some "standard" songs. *Lorelei* was not a good show, but it did well because of Carol Channing. A number of other not-very-good shows that cannot be cited as models of first-rate musicals were sending trucks to banks daily for years because of the glamorous or "interesting" treatment they received at the hands of "star-directors." Most of these also boasted stars with considerable box-office appeal: Carol Channing, Barbra Streisand, Angela Lansbury, Mary Martin, and others.

Robbins, one of the great star-directors working in various capacities on *West Side Story* and *Fiddler on the Roof*, also performed magic; he also directed much of the creative work in preparing the latter show. And these productions not only had a star-director, but one also had a score by Bernstein and Sondheim, and the other, a score by Bock and Harnick. In both cases the scores (music and lyrics) worked immeasurably to *become* important elements of the shows, but both scores afterward emerged apart from the productions as substantial entities. Both shows (and others besides) are far more than a "series of set-ups for song and dance numbers."

To *say* what Gottfried never got around to saying: The star-director is especially important when the content of the show is too weak to stand nakedly and successfully without the addition of overpowering, pulsating, distracting, speedy visual decoration.

These all-important omissions in Gottfried's thinking—the well-created show need not rely on the mesmerism of the "star-director" —is only one of the half-thought-out points in the piece in question:

It is an idiotic fact of life that stage directors want to go on to movies. Sculptors do not feel that they have to succeed as composers. Lawyers do not feel unfulfilled until they are doctors.

How thoughtless can a writer be? Isn't it obvious to everyone except, obviously, to Martin Gottfried that directing a stage show and a movie is still *directing* even if the media is altered? But sculptor–composer and lawyer–doctor—well, what went wrong with Gottfried's thinking? Or was this an unwise attempt at humor?

Most directors *do* want to go on to the movies but their reasons are not necessarily always the same. Michael Bennett conceived, choreographed, and directed *A Chorus Line*. He wants to see his brainchild done on the screen the way he visualizes it, just as he first visualized and brought it to the stage. He does not want it tampered with. Jerome Robbins functioned in these identical capacities in *West Side Story*. He tried to see it translated to film, but gave up because he lacked the legal authority to do it as he wished. So he quit. No one in his right mind would contend that the film was as successful artistically as the stage production.

Then there is the matter of money. Is there anything wrong with making that extra sum for a few months' extra work?

Again, Gottfried cannot seem to resist what seems to be a personal necessity to discuss homosexual versus heterosexual. He mentions it as often as a man with a sore or aching back who finds the need to refer to his ailment even when the conversation is about cooking. Gottfried introduces the subject in relation to Fosse and *Chicago*. He finds that musicals are dominated by homosexuals who nevertheless "do *not* treat women as (a) objects of ridicule or (b) objects of worship." That makes it appear that God's in His heaven, so why expend (and out of left field) three long paragraphs on the subject? He tried to justify it in order to point out Fosse's "treatment of women in *Chicago* or *Pippin*, costumed, choreographed, and treated to celebrate their physical, sexual grandeur."

Where? How? I wonder if anyone else thought there was anything particularly sexual about the women in *Chicago*. Gwen Verdon has always communicated great personal warmth and Chita Rivera has the sharpness and energy of a tigress. I think I am not denigrating either of these ladies if I question Gottfried's reading of Fosse's "celebrating their physical, sexual grandeur." (I suspect that both think this is a funny idea.)

In a sense Gottfried himself, in the same article, negates this idea when he writes, "There is no heart to it [*Chicago*], that's true, and it is more impressive than thrilling."

Does anyone reconcile this statement (which, I think is very true), with celebrating physical sexual grandeur? For grandeur is undoubtedly thrilling whether it is heard in a Mass, seen while watching a mountain peak at sunset, or felt in an orgasm. And if there is no

heart, I fail to understand the sexual, the "celebrating" the woman-
liness (warmth) of it.

Bravo Fosse! But with the best of intentions Gottfried does not
really comprehend.

Someone said to me recently, "Don't write off Martin Gottfried.
He is young [born 1933] and full of enthusiasm."

Gottfried should receive no special dispensation for being young.
(And, by the way, is forty-three young?) All of us have experienced
youth—some to advantage. His enthusiasm, if expressed forcefully,
is nevertheless usually dark. He is impatient, and in making his
impatience known, what seems to emerge is intense frustration,
and even that is ambivalent. He sneers because one play is tampered
with and complains because another has not been. He is seized with
an idea—currently the one about star-directors—as the answer to an
expensive and ailing theater. But he fails to take into account that
knowledgeable creative writers have had no need of guides to lead
them out of the labyrinth and that star-directors, even those working successfully with inconsequential material, are, in the end,
not helping anything except the commercial aspects of the theater
of which Gottfried is profoundly contemptuous—even when they
function for the good.

Second, Gottfried indicates a sense of discovery in writing of
star-directors, when in fact they have always existed, especially in
periods when creativity was especially low. David Belasco is a
particularly apt example. *The Heart of Maryland* (1895) ran for 240
performances; *The Darling of the Gods* (1902), 182; and *The Return
of Peter Grimm* (1911), 231.

Third, star-directors have sometimes done much more than Gottfried seems to be aware of. In at least two cases that I know of, such
a director—long before rehearsals—was active with librettists, composers, and lyricists, and without this creative direction, two of his
biggest hit shows would have been far less than they became by the
time of their official unveiling. In both cases, what he caused the
writers to accomplish was far more valuable to the projects than
what he created on the stage.

Gottfried's hot displeasure at anything he can term "commercial"
is, like all of his other fixations, intensely personal. He has hurled
the "commercial" epithet at *A Moon for the Misbegotten*, *Pajama
Game* (revival), *Gigi*, and *Raisin*; but *Charley's Aunt*, he said, was
"artistic rather than commercial," and in the *Candide* revival "the
commercial theater gives one tremendous motivation." He repri-
mands Neil Simon for *God's Favorite* by admonishing him to "stop
trying in shallow ways to be profound," and condemns Edward
Albee in *Box-Mao-Box* for being "too careless to ever finish his

work." In short, Gottfried rails at "commercialism," then extols *Candide* as a good product of it, and faults Albee and Simon for trying to do something less certain of commercial success.

If "commercial" makes Gottfried cringe with horror, he ought then to genuflect before such gifts from the commercial theater as the musicals *Oklahoma!, Carousel, The King and I, My Fair Lady, West Side Story, Fiddler on the Roof, Guys and Dolls, The Most Happy Fella, Company, Gypsy, A Little Night Music,* and *Cabaret*— all somewhat better examples of musicals than any others Gottfried could name; and in plays, the productions of works by Pinter, Storey, Miller, Albee, Hellman, Williams, plus Shakespeare, Molière, Feydeau, and many more.

He invented homosexuality for *Equus*; the recent all-male production of *As You Like It*; Williams' *Out Cry*; the score, and especially the lyrics, of *Fashion*; and speaks of homosexuality at length in discussing Bob Fosse's "heterosexual" direction in *Chicago* as opposed to more-often-encountered "homosexual direction."

His suspicions concerning commercial and homosexual elements are equalled only by his consciousness of fashion.

Above all other considerations, the reviewer who is continually moved to anger and irritation automatically removes himself from the category of a thinking individual. The job of the reviewer is to think, interpret, and write, and Gottfried cannot file the slightest claim to being able to do any of these. His arrogance, ignorance, pretentiousness, and suspicious nature describe the Beckmesser (of *Die Meistersinger*)—a fool lacking humanity and talent.

In addition, no competent reviewer feels compelled to express an opinion on any subject if he is not knowledgeable about it. Least of all is he expected or required to make predictions, but Gottfried rushes right in where both angels and knowledgeable musical minds fear to tread.

In his highly favorable review of *A Chorus Line,* when he gets around to writing about the music, he says: "His [Marvin Hamlisch's] music serves the production, varying in styles for each number."

This demonstrates Gottfried's failure to understand musical style. It is homogeneous in this score.

Further: "Of course there are also complete songs, some of them quite fine, but they can never be separated from the show itself."

The oracle at Delphi couldn't possibly make such a prediction, for prediction it is. No music publisher, Broadway composer, director, or any other *experienced* musical person could or would speak with such definiteness about something that may or may not come as a result of the music's exposure. It is quite possible that one or two songs from the score of *A Chorus Line* could become "separated" and popular. Perhaps not. But the point is that no one—and especially Gottfried—*knows*. So why does he feel called upon to foretell the future? Ignorance and inexperience are the only possible reasons.

The disproportionate amount of space given here to Mr. Martin Gottfried—who has been referred to as "the illiterate John Simon"—is based on the author's feeling that Gottfried's position as a member (though in actuality the least influential) of New York's daily triumvirate of reviewers is outrageous, harmful, and indefensible.

2

Walter Kerr

WALTER KERR, like Harold Clurman, is a theater man. Both have taught and directed theater. As a daily reviewer for the unfortunately defunct *New York Herald Tribune* and, later, *The New York Times*, Kerr's influence was enormous. During those years his opinions were not only significant to commerce in the theater, but were scholarly and stimulating to the serious-minded reader.

Unfortunately, Kerr became what was at first expected to be a "second voice" by writing reviews of the week's shows in the *Sunday Times* when Clive Barnes assumed the daily assignments. In terms of the calendar alone, Kerr's new voice was many times removed from second place: shows that opened after Wednesday were read in Kerr's space ten days or so afterward. The votes cast by the daily writers of *The New York Times*, the *Daily News* and the *New York Post* had already determined the fates of shows. Those that had gotten all bad notices were closed before Kerr's voice was heard and his always-interesting point of view became an echo that was significant to the serious-minded but he was powerless to resuscitate an already cold carcass. However, if the show had been thought to be good and Kerr also thought favorably of it, his Sunday essay helped to strengthen its life.

In this chapter I am concerned with Kerr's method and style. Consider the following:

"There are at least six things that will interest you in *Sweet Charity*—the dances, the scenery, the songs, Gwen Verdon, Gwen Verdon and Gwen Verdon."

"Harold Pinter's *The Homecoming* consists of a single situation that the author refuses to dramatize until he has dragged us all, aching, through a halfdrugged dream."

"Everyone who has ever liked a performance of *The Merry Wives of Windsor*, or even half-liked one, has probably spent the next day or two apologizing to himself and his friends for his kindly excess."

"God takes care of babies, drunks and good directors." (*Promises, Promises*) .

"If you go to *Big Time Buck White*, which you might profitably do, don't go looking for drama, or psychodrama, or group therapy."

"Seeing Arthur Kopit's *Indians* is like seeing a three-ring circus on the night after the principal aerialist has been killed in a fall."

"I hope Off-Broadway isn't going to take over musical comedy (it has other things to do), but the move may be necessary." (*Your Own Thing*)

"We know what happiness is, the songs and the cartoon books have told us. But what about unhappiness?" (*Awake and Sing*)

"One's responses to a rock musical like *Salvation* are apt to be as random as the Rorschach blot that is moving about in front of you onstage."

"The difficulty with Ibsen today is that we must try to take two separate things seriously, the playwright's ideas and the playwright's playwriting." (*A Doll's House*)

"Is there a more characteristic Tennessee Williams effect than the one that occurs, noisily but helplessly, halfway through the second act of *Cat on a Hot Tin Roof*?"

"The special genius of American musical comedy doesn't lie in its stars, though God knows that Ethel Merman and Mary Martin and Bobby Clark and Victor Moore have had a thumping great deal to do with it." (*Gypsy*)

"There is supposed to be something called a 'strictly commercial entertainment,' and I think *Kismet* is it."

These sequences selected at random will illustrate one of Walter Kerr's special skills: The opening sentences grab the reader's interest and make him want to read on. They have a quality (some of these selections are from daily reviews and some from Sunday essays) which appears to be less reportorial than most other reviewers' works. They are bright and they promise an interesting discussion. They are reasonable, not vindictive, and they take us inside the matter to be discussed without bothering us at the outset with statistical listings of when and where and who, although these important pieces of information will eventually turn up.

What Kerr does superbly is draw the reader into the experience that he had, causing the reader to relive with considerable vividness this same excitement or ennui. He seldom relates a plot but instead aims at pinpointing the show's theme, how it is presented, and the manner in which the various collaborators carry out their assignments. His conclusions are substantiated and clearly expressed. The reader is often made interested in seeing even some of the shows he does not favor. Having seen the show, the theatergoer may concur or not with the reviewer's analysis and argument, but he will find in Kerr's presentation an unbiased fairness and a reasonable and developed point of view. Most of the time Kerr's tone is selfless and unimpassioned.

Since theater by purpose is communication and by nature experience, it follows that what is successfully communicated from the stage will envelop the onlooker as experience. After that, both the onlooker and the reviewer—if they have succumbed to an experience—may come to at least one conclusion: He enjoyed being "compelled," or, not being forced to participate, he was bored.

After that, the onlooker and the reviewer will attempt to discover the reasons that might have created, or failed to create, an experience. Here is where, after thoughtful reasoning, achievement or failure can be assigned by the critic, not as vindicator or sentencer, but as interpreter.

Walter Kerr assumes this role authoritatively and without animus. In his reviews he conveys the experience, presents his interpretation, and supplies his readers with conclusions as opposed to baseless enthusiasms or subjective condemnation.

In his review of Jean-Claude van Italie's *America Hurrah* (November 7, 1966) Kerr *interprets* graphically what he has seen and felt in the theater. Writing as though the show had been given in Hungarian and his readers understand only English, Kerr provides a clear translation. There is no rehash of plot. But he begins with: "I think you'll be neglecting a whisper in the wind if you don't look in on *America Hurrah.*" And his final sentence says: "And the author is someone to be watched, and wished well."

Both sentences are clarion-clear. There is no hugger-muggery: we know exactly what the writer thought!

Between those sentences, we are treated to two paragraphs:

"A pretty girl—a girl with a strong sense of obligation—leaves the accident [Kerr has described it] to go on to a party. She would like to tell everyone at the party about the accident, though no one will listen. Above all, she would like to apologize for being late. No accident is enough to make a person late for a party.

"Slowly, subtly and with a sense of having been slapped in the face, we do grasp that it is the girl herself who has been killed and that she is apologizing for having been killed at so inopportune a moment. The dead must never be inconveniently dead. Not in America, not just now."

The style of this show which is unlike that of most other shows is understood, and in *specifics.* A feeling about the evening is provided. The reviewer admired what he saw, and it is left up to me to decide whether I will or will not attend; however, I am made to be interested.

In Kerr's review of *Cabaret* (November 21, 1966), the reader's curiosity is again aroused. The first paragraph says that it "is a stunning musical with one wild wrong note. I think you'd be wise to go and argue about that startling slip later."

Much later we learn that Kerr's exception concerns the casting of Jill Haworth as Sally Bowles and we are given reasons for his dissatisfaction. The review ends with: "The style is there, though, driven like glistening nails into the musical numbers, and I think you'll find they make up for what's missing."

The reading public is told to see *Cabaret* in spite of—in the opinion of the reviewer—a single imperfection, and Kerr imparts his own sense of admiration and enthusiasm for the show and its other performers.

The closest he comes to spelling out the plot—a too-common practice among reviewers and one which I find unnecessarily boring—is when he writes:

"The story line is willing to embrace everything from Jew-baiting to abortion. But it has elected to wrap its arms around all that was troubling and all that was intolerable with a demonic grin, an insidious slink, and the painted-on charm that keeps revelers up until after midnight making false faces at the hangman."

This tells me something of the *essence* of *Cabaret* without subjecting me to a detailed recital of its plot.

There are other razor-sharp bits, relevant, specific, and admirably set down:

"We have come for the floor show, we are all at tables tonight, and anything we learn of life during the evening is going to be learned through the tipsy, tinkling, angular vision of sleek rouged-up clowns, who inhabit a world that rains silver. . . .

"This marionette's-eye view of a time and place in our lives that was brassy, wanton, carefree and doomed to crumble is brilliantly conceived. . . .

"Master of Ceremonies Joel Grey bursts from the darkness like a tracer bullet, singing us a welcome that has something of the old 'Blue Angel' in it, something of Kurt Weill, and something of all the patent-leather nightclub tunes that ever seduced us into feeling friendly toward sleek entertainers who twirled canes as they worked. Mr. Grey is cheerful, charming, soulless and conspiratorially wicked. In a pink vest, with sunburst eyes gleaming out of a cold-cream face, he is the silencer of bad dreams, the gleeful puppet of pretended joy, sin on a string.

"No matter what is happening during the evening, he is available to make light of it, make sport of it, make macabre gaiety of it.

"Miss Lenya has never been better, or if she has been, I don't believe it. Suitor Jack Gilford, with just enough hair left to cross his forehead with spitcurls and gamely spinning his partner in spite of clear signs of vertigo, makes his first-act wrap-up, a rapid-fire comic turn called 'Meeskite,' one of the treasures of the occasion."

These are only samples from a review which takes the reader to the heart of the show. Kerr communicates what he feels, without railing at the show, at his readers or at the theater. He enlightens us because he pinpoints his experience.

I should next like to quote an entire Kerr review. It is not what Broadway would call a "money" notice since it is not wholly favorable. However, it is reasonable (even if one does not always agree), interesting, provocative, and informative. It has a substantial intellectual basis. It is a "daily" review of *The Homecoming* (January 6, 1967). Here it was essential for Kerr to sketch out briefly something of the plot in order to comment on the play's philosophy and feeling.

"Harold Pinter's *The Homecoming* consists of a single situation that the author refuses to dramatize until he has dragged us all, aching, through a half-drugged dream.

"The situation, when it *is* arrived at, is interesting in the way that Pinter's numbed fantasies are almost always interesting. A Doctor of Philosophy who actually teaches philosophy returns with his wife to the family home in North London, a home that looks like an emptied-out wing of the British Museum gone thoroughly to seed. (The few pieces of furniture are lonely in this cavern, the molding along the walls breaks off and gives up before it can reach the doorways, the carpet could be made of cement.)

"A father and two brothers take one look at the wife and mistake (or do not mistake) her for a whore. She is silent, poised, leggy, self-contained. In due time the family decides that they would rather like to have a whore around, whatever about her husband and about the three children she has left behind in America. She might very well be kept available in a room at the top of the steep, forbidding staircase, and she could always pay her own keep by renting herself out a few nights a week.

"They put the proposition to her, matter-of-factly, after she has obliged them by moving into a trance-like dance with one of the brothers, brushing unfinished kisses across his lips and then obligingly draping herself to another brother's needs across a cold and impersonal sofa.

"It is at this point that Mr. Pinter's most curious and most characteristic abilities as a diviner of unspecified demons come effectively into play. We are in an unconventional situation, and of course we know that. But our habits of mind—our compulsive attempts to try to deal with the world by slide rule—still continue to function, stubbornly. We expect even so bizarre a crisis to provoke logical responses: the husband will be humiliated or outraged, the wife will prove herself either a genuine wife or a genuine whore, and so on. We have the probabilities all ready in our heads.

"But Mr. Pinter is not interested in the rational probabilities of the moment. He is interested in what *might* happen if our controlling expectations were suddenly junked, if flesh and heart and moving bone were freed from preconditioning and allowed simply to behave, existentially. The world might go another way—a surprising and ultimately unexplained way—if it went its own way, indifferent to philosophers.

"Just how the tangle at the Music Box rearranges itself I won't say, because saying nails down what is meant to continue as movement. It's enough to report that for approximately 20 minutes during the final third of *The Homecoming* the erratic energies onstage display their own naked authority by forcing us to accept the unpredictable as though it were the natural shape of things.

"During this time Vivien Merchant, as the wife who is as hardheaded as she is enigmatic, coolly and with great reserve points out that her legs move, her underwear moves with her, her lips move. ('Perhaps the fact that they move is more significant than the words that come through them.') Husband Michael Craig draws on his donnish pipe with opaque detachment ('I won't be lost in it'), father Paul Rogers leers through sucked-in teeth that seem to have been borrowed from Bert Lahr, and poltergeist Ian Holm grins maliciously at the thought of all the tables that can be turned. The performing is cagey, studied, bristling with overtones. (A good half of Mr. Pinter's suspense invariably comes from the question that sticks in our heads: 'What are these people *not* mentioning?').

"Until the final moments of the evening, however, the playwright is simply cheating us, draining away our interest with his deliberate delay. He has no more vital material to offer here then he had, say, in the very much shorter *A Slight Ache,* to which *The Homecoming* bears a strong resemblance.

"But he is determined that we shall have two hours worth of improvisational feinting, and it leads him into a good bit of coy teasing giggly echoes of Ionesco ('You liked Venice, didn't you? You had a good week. I mean, I took you there. I can speak Italian') and calculated incidental violence that is without cumulative effect (the father spits at one son, rams another in the gut, canes his own paraffin-coated dullard of a brother).

"Because none of this is of any growing importance to the ultimate confrontation, *everything* must seem to have its own arbitrary and artificial importance: the clink of a sugar lump on a saucer, the stiff, ritual crossing of trousered legs, the huddled lighting of four cigars, the effortful pronunciation of so much as a single word.

"Holding too much back for too long, the play comes to seem afflicted by an arthritic mind and tongue, and while Peter Hall has directed the visiting members of England's Royal Shakespeare Company to make sleep-walking and strangled speech constitute a theatrical effect in and for itself, we are not engrossed by the eternal hesitation waltz but seriously put off by it. The play agonizes over finding its starting point, and we share the prolonged agony without being certain that the conundrum is approaching a real core.

"Mr. Pinter is one of the most naturally gifted dramatists to have come out of England since the war. I think he is making the mistake, just now, of supposing that the elusive kernel of impulse that will do for a 40-minute play will serve just as handily, and just as suspensefully, for an all-day outing. *The Homecoming,* to put the matter as simply as possible, needs a second situation: We could easily take an additional act if the author would only scrap the interminable first. The tide must come in at least twice if we are to be fascinated so long by the shoreline."

This review made me want to see Pinter's play which I found stimulating and the first act more interesting than Mr. Kerr did.

But I feel that Mr. Kerr's appraisal was fair and provocative and his point of view was reasonably substantiated. More important was the fact that Kerr described an unusual experience, one so rare as not to be missed in the theater of our time. Had this play contained as little style, feeling, and substance as most contemporary plays, Kerr would have been stimulated to think and write less.

Here are some passages from some particularly appropriate Kerr reviews:

On *Sherry!* a quick-faded musical based on *The Man Who Came to Dinner:* "The trouble with the old jokes is that you remember them. The trouble with the new ones is that no one ever will . . . why must every line be delivered with a fresh charge of dynamite, as though it ought to—and *had* to rock the back walls? . . . When you deal with good old plays, you've got to be kind to them. They tire. . . . But most of the evening at the Alvin is an exercise in subtraction. The farce solidity of the old play is thinned out by wandering about, searching for songs and scenery."

On *Star-Spangled Girl:* "Neil Simon, your friendly neighborhood gagman, hasn't had an idea for a play this season, but he's gone ahead and written one anyway. . . .

"But not having an idea always tends to produce certain kinds of jokes, and to produce them in overabundance. For one thing, it produces the Joke with its Toes Turned In, which is to say the joke that meets itself coming and going because it has nowhere else to look. 'Will you take this job or won't you?' screams employer Perkins at a reluctant Connie Stevens, 'Because if you don't want it, I'll take it because I need the money!' The words are eating their own tails, you might say. This sort of double-crostic comic fencing finally gets right down to 'Why don't you answer my questions?', 'Why don't you question my answers?' and Mr. Simon is really too good a craftsman to force himself to such idle non-invention.

"There is also the Canceled Stamp jest, the hysterical exchange that contradicts itself in mid-flight. 'Will you look, will you just look at that girl?' shrills Mr. Benjamin from his perch at a telescope. 'All right,' murmurs Mr. Perkins, ambling over, 'Get away, I'm looking,' is Mr. Benjamin's quick riposte. The play, at such times, is moving neither hither nor yon; lines are simply wiping one another out. . . .

"But because there is no genuinely comic issue to set the two gentlemen at sword's point—it's karate they get down to, actually—and because there is no particular connection between the bulldog patriotism of the girl next door and the off-again, on-again, love affairs of the underfinanced young editors, the author is compelled to press these various dodges into service.

"Sometimes they are nimbly enough handled, and Mr. Simon can do wonders—now and again—with casually tossed-off fantasies that pop up from nowhere and whistle as they go by. . . .

"*Star-Spangled Girl* is sheer improvisation, like a man humming in the bathtub. But Lord, it does need a second chorus."

This is a witty review of a witless play, but it is not angry. It does not hurl invectives. While it says some unhappy things about Neil Simon, it does not castigate him. The points in opposition are made, one by one, and supported. The cool-tempered method is effective, and why should it be necessary to scowl at a play that is far less than a masterpiece? One does not scream at the work of the immature or the untalented. If screaming is ever in order, it should be directed at the talented and the accomplished for presenting us with unfinished or less than masterful achievements. Kerr's review, further, has some enlightening things to say about the nature of comedy and it points out incisively how comedy can be used to its own detriment when it attempts to pinch-hit for ideas. It also says "Mr. Simon is really too good a craftsman . . ."

This is explicit, kind, non-angry and witty if also adverse.

In sharp contrast to the *Times'* daily critic, Clive Barnes, Walter Kerr treats *all* theater in the same manner. When he encounters ethnic theater, and new striving playwrights, instead of lavishing unwarranted praise on them misleadingly or scolding them because of their inexperience, Kerr helpfully analyzes their work, details their faults, offers constructive suggestions, and displays patience with defects.

Following are excerpts from *Sunday Times* reviews of three black plays: *What the Wine-Sellers Buy*, *The Great MacDaddy* and *The River Niger*.

"If you have ever gone to any of the summertime festivals of street plays—exceedingly simple moralities in which Virtue and Vice contend for the souls of ghetto youngsters—you will recognize Ron Milner's *What the Wine-Sellers Buy* right off. Its bones are the bones of all such exhortations to 'stay clean,' its neighborhood pieties, its warnings the very same warnings. . . .

"At what point does a slogan stop being a slogan and begin to dissolve into the ambiguity and abrupt candor and restless complexity we're willing to call art? There are three or four suddenly hushed moments in Mr. Milner's play when we can very nearly hear the metamorphosis taking place, the evening gliding upward

into felt personal truths that are not necessarily suitable for pla-
cards. . . .

"As Mr. Milner goes on with his work, he will do well to let
impulse interrupt him oftener, let people speak for themselves instead of steadily saluting the evening's cause. He has a certain gift
for decoration, even when it is being applied to the all-too-
obvious. . . .

"Graham Greene once remarked that it was no more than a single
step from the medieval morality play—with, perhaps, a central
figure named Ambition—to *Macbeth*. But it is the step that makes
all the difference, so great a difference that by the time we get to
Macbeth it is no longer possible to say precisely where the most
urgent ambition lies.

"*What the Wine-Sellers Buy* hasn't made the step. Though it
comes teasingly close a few times. In the service of virtue, a theatrical vice wins. The characters haven't freedom enough to act for
themselves."

"Paul Carter Harrison's *The Great MacDaddy*, instead of working to
a preordained pattern, takes off from a question-mark, steps deftly
and dancingly into an unidentified desert, flutters along on any
wind that will pick it up, curves all the way home again—half classical Odyssey, half black Peer Gynt—without having bothered to
explain its multiple, high-hearted truancies. Shapeless as it is, it's
more fun.

"No use trying to chart it. As one of its more cheerful strays remarks, 'You're going to lose track, but track isn't everything.' Onto
the road, then . . . wherever the road leads.

"It doesn't lead to cohesion, or anything like it, but it challenges
dramatist Harrison to make each successive stage in the hegira
generate its own instant interest. A surprising number of these
improvisations do. . . .

"Some adventures are over-long, some overly familiar; there are
times when you feel you are listening to a play in a foreign language,
yours.

"But Mr. Harrison is interested in mystery and often capable of
making it work for him: a hand waving in the gray dawn, a freight
screeching by, a dancer doing a spinstep around her own body and
incredibly jacknifing her knees above her own shoulders (Dyane
Harvey, and who is she?), a talking scarecrow that held a 6-year-old
sitting near me rapt, initiating him into the peculiar magic of
theater. Scatterbrained and tatterdemalion, maybe; but talented."

"*The River Niger*, now being performed by the Negro Ensemble
Company, is one of the most curious experiences I have ever had in

the theater. Joseph Walker's dialogue is exemplary, knife-sharp when adrenalin is meant to flow and gently rhetorical whenever the father of a Harlem family remembers that he meant to be a poet. Douglas Turner Ward's intensely personal direction of his performers is both supple and vigorous, moving them from gang violence to boozy midnight philosophizing without ever tripping over a transition. Almost all of the performances, including Mr. Ward's own as the painter-fighter-poet who never found a battlefield, are detailed, honest, varied. And the play as a whole has no dramatic tension at all.

"It is all there and it won't move. What the author needs—it is an odd request to make—is precisely the sort of directorial master-mind we used to affect to despise, the fellow who guides a playwright in reshaping, or just shaping, the play proper. Mr. Walker can write his scenes. . . .

"But the scenes tag along after one another; they don't push. Where one invasion of the household by friends bent on revolution would do, three exist; where one amusing instance of secret tippling in the back kitchen would tell us all we need to know, we are given four, or five. The circuitousness defeats our expectations, pulls the play apart. We are eager, for instance, to discover how Mr. Ward will react to the news of his wife's illness. We do, eventually, find out, in a powerfully designed moment: Mr. Ward makes a great thrashing curve through the apartment before hurling himself cursing to the floor. But so much intervenes between our first curiosity and its ultimate satisfaction that we have lost the curiosity and are in the process of losing our satisfaction as well.

"The urgency that comes of compression is not yet among the author's bag of tricks—it's more than a trick, it's a tightrope that becomes a lifeline—and it would be a shame to continue to lose so much that is good through mere wanderlust. Compression isn't simply a matter of time: though the play is indeed overlong, cutting 40 minutes wouldn't change its thrust. It is a thrust itself that is missing, the sense that walls are closing in steadily, that we are breathing harder every minute and must soon explode or be crushed. A play must gather to a stop and we've got to see the stop coming. This one could—and more or less does—stop anywhere, content to offer us quality in passing rather than a confined passion on the rise."

These constructive reviews are appreciative of good ideas while recommending more skillful craftsmanship. All are hopeful of stronger, clearer future creativity from the playwrights. Nowhere are there extravagant claims for good where only promise exists.

This attitude should be helpful to these writers, avoids complacency and advises knowingly. Whether this advice of Kerr's comes too late after Barnes' earlier and more enthusiastic caroling, and whether or not the authors wish to believe in Barnes because he offers more approval than Kerr, is a moot question and its answer can be— human nature being what it is—wastefully tragic.

Most reviewers thought very highly of *Man of La Mancha* and it subsequently enjoyed great international success. However, Walter Kerr's review—presented here in part—lies, I believe, nearer the truth.

" 'I hope to add some measure of grace to the world' is Don Quixote's simple answer to those who question his absurd valor, and while librettist Dale Wasserman cannot be said to have added any grace to Cervantes' world, director Albert Marre has performed some such service for the stage of the ANTA Washington Square Theater. . . .

"But just as a director must take responsibility for making proper use of the stage he inherits, so librettist and composer must account in full for the materials they invade. If they cannot do *Don Quixote* altogether—which they cannot—then they are honor-bound to add an ingredient that will make so much shoplifting worthwhile.

"There isn't much honor, I'm afraid, in reducing the Knight of La Mancha's out-of-kilter idealism to the business of having him exclaim 'Ho! A young innocent approaches!' while the closest possible thing to a belly-dancer writhes near. There is less honor in pursuing the already out-of-breath jest. When the dancer places Quixote's hand upon her breast instead of her heart, the old warrior remarks that 'Such is her innocence she doesn't even know where her heart is.' Whereupon Sancho Panza adds, 'Or even how many she has.' Come, come, now, Cervantes was earthy, but he was not Willie Howard.

"Not that the language tries often for humor. Most of it is mock-literary straight, with occasional nods to rather more recent constructions. Mitch Leigh's music and Joe Darion's lyrics are generally straight-faced, too, devoting themselves to reporting on the Don's worried relatives ('I'm Only Thinking of Him') or a tavern wench's bafflement that she should be treated as a princess ('What Does He Want of Me?'). The lyrical 'Dulcinea' is certainly an attractive tune, there is response to a real dramatic need in Sancho Panza's sung defense of his woolgathering master ('I Iike him, I really like him. Tear off my fingernails one by one, I like him'), and the billowing 'Quest' song is highly serviceable as a finale. There is something essentially vulgar, however, about hearing the inspired madman promise to 'reach for an unreachable star, beat an unbeatable foe.' Cervantes' rough landscape has been planted with pretty ordinary posies. . . .

"The physical production makes everything seem possible; the diminishment of Cervantes puts everything right back in doubt."

There is nothing diabolical about audiences enjoying whatever it is they enjoy. Hugo von Hofmannsthal, in a letter to his composer Richard Strauss, wrote: "The public is never wholly wrong." Although I concur with this observation, I do know that many flawed baubles have existed in all ages and have enjoyed great success at the time because the public enjoyed them, although their basic qualities were so weak and evaporable that eventually they faded into oblivion. The best works have a way of lingering on through the centuries, and continue—often uninterruptedly—to delight those who think as well as those who don't. A perfect example of such a work is John Gay's *The Beggar's Opera* (1728).

William Hazlitt, the great English critic, encountered *The Beggar's Opera* in 1813—nearly a century after its premiere—and wrote:

The play itself is among the most popular of our dramas, and one which the public are always glad to have some new excuse for seeing acted again. Its merits are peculiarly its own. It not only delights, but instructs us, without our knowing how, and though it is at first view equally offensive to good taste and common decency. The materials, indeed, of which it is composed, the scenes, characters, and incidents, are in general of the lowest and most disgusting kind; but the author, by the sentiments and reflections which he has put into the mouths of highwaymen, turnkeys, their wives and daughters, has converted the motley group into a set of fine gentlemen and ladies, satirists and philosophers. What is still more extraordinary, he has effected this transformation without once violating probability, or "o'erstepping the modesty of nature." In fact, Gay has in this instance turned the tables on the critics; and by the assumed license of the mock-heroic style, has enabled himself to *do justice to nature*, that is to give all the force, truth, and locality of real feeling to the thoughts and expressions, without being called to the bar of false taste, and affected delicacy. . . .

In my opinion Kerr's disillusionment with *Man of La Mancha* and Hazlitt's pinpointed penetrating insight into *The Beggar's Opera* have much in common.

There was a revival of *The Time of Your Life* in November of 1969 which Walter Kerr wrote about in his Sunday piece. I should like to quote from this for two reasons. First, I have the impression that Kerr opened my own eyes to the essential weaknesses of the play and what had only subconsciously bothered me was made clear. Secondly, this review is an object-lesson in fairness. After Kerr outlines the characters, he immediately indicates that he recognizes "an outline has no tone. . . ." He also closes his piece with the suggestion that the audience will enjoy the play. Small excerpts from a lengthy essay follow.

"If Joe hates himself and the cop hates his job and the girl hates having grown up to drinking, no one else on the premises is really any better off. The dancing comedian cannot, by his own admission, get a laugh. The intelligent longshoreman cannot avoid becoming involved in a strike. The piano player is beat up, the society slummers are embarrassingly routed, Kit Carson is a fraud until he becomes something better than that, a murderer. Maybe there's some hope for the young innocent and his nice whore, running off to take a job riding a truck together. On the evidence offered, it would be a surprise if they survived the first turnpike.

"Sounds almost like Artaud, doesn't it? It's not, naturally. An outline has no tone, whereas Saroyan's tone is omnipresent, and it is soft and friendly. In fact, you could say that if Saroyan is sentimental about the likableness of people he's equally sentimental about the doom they are heading for. Even pessimism can be sentimental, since sentimentality is simply an excess of emotion in relation to the evidence offered. Pity can be too much as a pat on the head can be too much. Perhaps there's a shade too much of both here, for this slightly later and more ascetic age. But always remember: The author himself turned down at least one of the prizes he was offered. Maybe he was the realist.

"Never mind. My point this morning is that we think of Saroyan as incorruptibly sunny, whereas *The Time of Your Life* is really all about the day the last sun went down. There isn't any tomorrow in it for anybody—maybe the bartender, but will he have customers? —and instead of being a poem in praise of the green lawns of M-G-M and the high hopes of Mickey Rooney, it is much more nearly the matrix for all of the doomsday plays that have followed.

"It is more fun than most of them. But it does not promise more than most of them. We probably should remind ourselves, now that we are in the business of reminding, that Mr. Saroyan's earlier and quite beautiful play, *My Heart's in the Highlands*, ended with everybody either dead or dispossessed, and with a small boy—nothing like Mickey Rooney—wandering homeless down the streets while he says to his despairing father, 'I'm not mentioning any names, Pa, but something's wrong somewhere. . . .'

"I think you'll enjoy the evening, whatever you make of an author who spent so much time calling hello, out there, without getting any answer he could be sure of."

Kerr as general essayist (when he is not holding forth on newly opened shows) is thoughtful, stimulating, original, and readable. In his "Essay on Shakespeare" in *Horizon* Magazine, 1960, he advances an ingenious theory relating Shylock to the *commedia dell'arte* Pantalone. In his book *Tragedy and Comedy** Kerr examines these two basic elements of all theater in detail and makes enlightening deductions.

The story of the bond appears in very early folklore, when the holder of the bond was not yet a Jew, but the atmosphere of the legends is essentially melodramatic. The Jew, the bond, the passionate love for a lady of Belmont, the lady's disguise in a court of law, and the forfeited betrothal ring are found in combination as early as 1378, in Fiorentino's *Il Pecorone;* but a translation of this work was probably not available to Shakespeare, and he is thought to have picked up the outline by hearsay, without a specific tone attached. The commercial popularity of Marlowe's *Jew of Malta* may have induced Shakespeare to write his play; but the play he wrote and the Jew he created bear only the most superficial resemblance to Marlowe's savage inventions.

These sources, which Shakespeare may have carved up and recombined in his characteristic fashion, might very well lead us to a violent Jew, a voracious Jew—but not to any comic Jew that Thomas Pope is apt to have played. Was there no familiar image, no elderly, moneygrubbing, fantastically funny fellow, *anywhere* in the Elizabethan storehouse to help set Shakespeare in motion and the rest of us on a likely scent?

There was such an image, just such a fellow. His name was Pantalone, and he appeared endlessly, with many droll variations but with a few indispensable comic trademarks, in the improvised performances of the Italian *commedia dell'arte.* (The players improvised from standard scenarios, many of which survive.) That Shakespeare and his associates knew Pantalone and his retinue is quite clear. *Commedia* troupes began visiting London as early as 1574.

Who was he, what was he like? To begin with, he was a merchant of Venice. He was old, wealthy, and had his fortune tied up in shipping. When one of his cargoes was destroyed by storm or pirates, he tore his beard and spat into the sea in impotent rage. He was a miser.

"All his life long," as Pierre Louis Duchartre reconstructs him for us, "he has been engaged in trade, and he has become so sensitive to the value of money that he is an abject slave to it." His precious ducats are eternally on his mind. He is swifty suspicious, sure that someone is going to swindle him. To help save ducats, he starves his servants. His hungry valet frequently threatens to leave him. The old father of the hungry valet sometimes comes to intercede for his son. The valet invariably mimics his master's speech, behind his back.

Pantalone has a daughter, with whom he is severe. She is an ingenue in love, eager for marriage, more eager still to be out of her father's tyrannically run household. Secretly she makes arrangements to meet her lover,

*New York: Simon & Schuster, 1967.

usually by means of letters smuggled out by the friendly, conniving servant. When the chance comes, she elopes, often taking a supply of ducats along with her. Pantalone boils in rage, driven nearly out of his wits by his daughter's behavior. Others are delighted to see him so beset, he is such a "skinflint" and the "calamity-howler."

At the last, Pantalone is the butt of the joke—robbed of his ducats, deceived by his daughter, the sputtering, breast-beating, hair-tearing victim of his own greed.

He carries, of course, a large purse at his belt. He also carries a sizable dagger. He is quick to draw and brandish the dagger when outraged, which is rather often; somehow or other, though, he is never permitted to use it. Vocally, to take a cue directly from Shakespeare, "his big manly voice, turning again toward childish treble, pipes and whistles in his sound." This shrill, shuffling, furiously gesticulating patriarch is only an inch or two shy of senility. For clothing, he wears a long black cloak, a rounded black cap, and either soft slippers or Turkish sandals. He has a prominent hooked nose.

While it is unlikely now that anyone will ever be able to *prove* that Shakespeare took his Shylock from his memory of Pantalone, the catalogue of similarities is too striking to be dismissed.

Before concluding this section on Walter Kerr, I should like to quote from one of his Sunday essays.

From *The Era of the Cutie Closes* (*Sunday Times*, May 21, 1967):
"Plays can be damaged or encouraged by notices, but not controlled by them. Plays don't live on print, they live on what people think of them, say about them, or imagine them to be. The picture in the prospective playgoer's head is finally decisive, and it is composed of many things: stars, story, personal inclination, personal prejudice, scandal, hearsay, adroit promotion, the passionate insistence of friends, the need to know, the way the photographs look. Any combination can act as a drag or a snowball; the notices get there first, but they are forgotten in six weeks, provided the show lives to see six weeks. . . .

"I think that gradually, maybe sluggishly for a while, but finally and out of sheer desperation, the audience is going to take over. We're at a time of radical change in the order of things theatrical, a time when old habits and superstitions and handouts and lazinesses must perforce come to an end. The legend of 'the power of the critics' cannot survive. . . .

"Surreptitiously, the shift is already under way—and has been since the beginning of the preview system. The preview system— by means of which a show is able to work itself over for days or weeks or even months by giving public performances from which only critics are excluded—would never have been possible, and would not now be continuing, if a surprisingly sizable segment of the public hadn't discovered that it was fun to risk encounter with the uncertified and/or uncondemned. . . .

"What the reviewer really needs to let his own heart free is some assurance that other folk are doing exactly what he does: going to the theater, exulting in the theater, berating the theater. With liveliness about him, he finds himself at complete liberty. If the whole town's talking, who needs watch his tongue?

"Yes, the reviewer hopes to win the argument, if he can swing it. But first there must be an argument. On the day when the audience takes over—if it does—the air will be cleared, the subject up for grabs, everybody welcome and no holds barred. Perversely, the reviewer will not mourn any arbitrary influence he may lose; he will be the merrier for it, perhaps the more malicious for it, because he can huff and puff at his pleasure knowing the building won't fall down.

"Hasten the day."

Much later in this book—and eight years later in time—Kerr returns triumphantly to this idea after the opening of *A Chorus Line* (1975).

Kerr's essays and reviews make distinguished contributions to the theater. They spy into hidden but significant corners, criticizing on the one hand, imparting a feeling of hopefulness on the other. They are written by a man of background and taste who loves the theater as though it were his favorite, if sometimes backward, child. He understands it, is patient, and tries to be helpful by interpreting its sometime peccadilloes.

Too bad he is only on Sundays.

3

A Summary of Some Earlier Critics

FROM THE EARLIEST theatrical performances, there have been critics. Nor has this inevitability been confined to any place or time. The Greek playwrights spawned intelligent interpreters. In England where there have been great authors, great critics have flourished —and *some* critics have been loquaciously present at every event. By 1757, the *London Chronicle* was publishing daily reviews. At that time, although the pieces were unsigned, the writer was careful to appear as inoffensive as possible.

The playwright-novelist Oliver Goldsmith wrote reviews beginning in 1759. The late 1700s produced one of the all-time critical greats, William Hazlitt (1778–1830). In *The Misanthrope* (1666) Molière found understanding laughter from his audiences when he made fun of critics.

In 1779, Richard Brinsley Sheridan obviously relied on the existence of some common feeling about reviewers when he wrote his celebrated lampoon *The Critic* that satirized every nuance of the professional commentator. The piece is understandable and applicable today.

The nineteenth century saw William Archer, George Bernard Shaw, Ivor Brown, Max Beerbohm, and James Agate.

94

In the burgeoning United States where there were theatrical productions, there were inevitably those to comment on them in print. The first American musical, *The Archers* (1796) by William Dunlap and Benjamin Carr, "interested" the reviewer because it was "by one of our countrymen." In a notice that appeared after the second performance, the writer observed:

"We were pleased at the first presentation. We then believed it possessed intrinsic merit to recommend it to public support; and our favorable impressions have not been diminished."

Later, he reproved the audience for failing to give it "due support."

New American plays of the same period also received encouraging reviews and were usually greeted enthusiastically by the audiences.

Among our early *signed* critics were Edgar Allan Poe and Walt Whitman. The former wrote for the *Broadway Journal*, circa 1845, the latter for the *Brooklyn Eagle*, circa 1846. Their writing was stilted. Although Poe was definitely acrimonious about Anna Cora Mowatt's *Fashion* (1845), he was apologetic to the author because of her femininity! He wrote that Sheridan's *The School for Scandal* "was comparatively good in its day, but it would be positively bad at the present day. . . ."

In another article Poe said that "the Elizabethan theater should be abandoned" and Boucicault's *London Assurance* was the "most inane and utterly despicable of all modern comedies." If one subscribed to the theory of reincarnation, it would be possible to conclude that Martin Gottfried once inhabited the form of Edgar Allan Poe.

Walt Whitman also attacked Shakespeare, ending a piece with ". . . a style supremely grand of the sort, but in my opinion stopping short of the grandest sort, at any rate for fulfilling and satisfying modern and scientific and democratically American purposes."

Whitman decried the "star system" (1847) and regarded *Uncle Tom's Cabin* as having "pernicious abolition sympathies"! (This was in 1854, eleven years prior to the outbreak of the Civil War.) This anger toward the play's theme was somewhat two-facedly tempered by the author's deep apologies to Harriet Beecher Stowe.

By far the most elegant snob and the best critic, the most vivid writer, and most sentient observer was Henry James (1843–1916). Unlike Poe, James admired *The School for Scandal*. He wrote detailed descriptions of New York, London, and Paris theaters and their audiences, recording great social changes. In a piece on London:

"Plays and actors are perpetually talked about, private theatricals are incessant, and members of the dramatic profession are 'received' without restriction. They appear in society, and the people of society appear on the stage. . . ."

He disliked Ellen Terry and Henry Irving and wrote lengthy analyses, full of admiration amounting nearly to worship, about Bernhardt (although he added: ". . . it cannot in the least be said that she is a consummate actress . . ."), Modjeska, Salvini, Coquelin, and Duse. Essays about the last four are composed in monumental detail. He also wrote often and lengthily about criticism itself.

William Dean Howells wrote for *Harper's New Monthly Magazine,* circa 1886. Howells was known also as a playwright. He was especially taken with the work of Edward Harrigan (Harrigan and Hart), who enjoyed great popularity as author, director, producer, and star. In an essay, Howells wrote:

"The comedies of Edward Harrigan are, in fact, much decenter than the comedies of William Shakespeare. They are like Shakespeare's plays, like Molière's plays, in being the work of a dramatist who is at the same time a manager and an actor. . . ."

At a somewhat later time, George Jean Nathan (1882–1958), who wrote for Henry L. Mencken's *American Mercury,* ascended the critical throne in New York where he was considered infallible, an iconoclast, and a brave intellectual to be admired and feared. Today in retrospect, this reputation appears almost pathetically inapplicable because it is so foolish and so misplaced. The emperor indeed had no clothes!

Reading Nathan today, one can only wonder at the ambience which seemed to have surrounded him. This brave bellower was filled with racial prejudice. He was deaf to music, finding only pernicious things to say of Harold Arlen among others. He made sport of defenseless performers whose faces he objected to.

Of Leonard Bernstein's music for *On the Town* (Bernstein's first Broadway show) he said: "Bernstein's music, while occasionally not without some intrinsic merit, more frequently strains with patent discomfort for popularity."

In the same review: "The ballet phases of the show, contrived by Mr. [Jerome] Robbins, in one or two instances display symptoms of imagination, but the stage is overburdened with them and before the evening is done one is sorry one ever made remarks about the Tiller Girls."

Nathan adored O'Neill and often wrote with blind enthusiasm in his defense. In a *Strange Interlude* essay, he maintained ". . . what is argued against O'Neill's asides and soliloquies, may just as logically be argued against Shakespeare."

His fame as a feminophile led to his thinking that Loretta Young was the most significant actress to have been created by Hollywood.

Looking back on Nathan's diatribes of nearly half a century ago, it is my feeling that he was no critic but a sophomoric harlequin who used barbs that seemed witty, brilliant and vandalic at the time, but today are a pathetic waste of newsprint.

Harold Clurman recently (1975) wrote of Nathan's mentor, Mencken, who seemed to be the cat's whiskers to Clurman at the age of twenty. Clurman, once attracted by his wonderfully cocky irreverence wrote: ". . . his attitudinizing, now strikes me as adolescent. His is a largely foolish iconoclasm. . . . Apart from his wittily turned formulations and epithets of dissent he has today little substantial value."

H. T. Parker, circa 1930, writing in the *Boston Evening Transcript* (Mr. J. Brooks Atkinson's guide through Hades) was simple and astute. He was analytically-minded and never scornful.

Alexander Woollcott (1887–1943) was drama critic on *The New York Times*, circa 1920. Contrary to Woollcott's conspicuous reputation for "barbed epithets," he was a sober and thoughtful writer.

Of Walter Hampden's *Hamlet*, he concluded: "You could not possibly be bored by [it] but probably your heart would not be greatly wrung by it either." This could have been laughable, but fifty-five years later the reader receives the message.

On the other side of his nature, Woolcott wrote about Florence Reed in *The Shanghai Gesture* (1926) and concluded ". . . for she had made no more than half the descent of the winding staircase than a gust of approval swept the house—presumably because she had got that far without falling down."

Stark Young (1881–1963) was one of the most sensitive critics *The New York Times* ever had although his stay on this daily was limited to about one year. Eric Bentley wrote of him: ". . . a passionate, spontaneous being taken with whatever deserves to be loved in nature and art and people, a spirited eagerness, and receptiveness, and fullness."

Young usually wrote in specifics. The following tells us of Pauline Lord in *They Knew What They Wanted*:

"Pauline Lord gave one of those instances of her work at its best that glorifies and makes pitiful the whole art of acting. Her playing last night had that shy pathos and intensity that we saw in her *Launzi* last year. She is an actress that, when she finds a part within her range, had in that part a range and perfection at the top of all the realism in our theatre. Last night she never missed a shading or a point; she had always a wonderful, frail power in the scene, and throughout her entire performance a kind of beautiful, poignant

accuracy. And last but not least, her playing with the rest of the
company was admirable and to be recommended all over town."

His review of *The Student Prince* is a model of critical writing,
for Young was filled with enthusiasm for it *despite* his recognition
of a poor book and worse comedy material.

Robert Benchley (1889–1945) wrote criticism for *The New Yorker*.
He was thought of as a "humorist" but was in part gentle. Today
his thoughts, opinions, and humor are buried under many layers
of dust. He "understood" Kern's songs in *Show Boat* after the show's
revival in 1932—five years after its original production. He spoke
of the "missing heartbeats in Mr. Kern's music" of *Roberta* ("Yester-
days" and "Smoke Gets in Your Eyes" are in the score). As to
Porgy and Bess, he preferred the original play (minus Gershwin's
score). In covering Cole Porter's *Jubilee* he remarked, "The lyrics
which Mr. Cole Porter has devised, with an eye to pleasing perhaps
eighteen people, are negligible in market value." Of the music,
Benchley wrote: "He has hidden his most valuable tunes in incidental choruses. . . ."

The fact is that *Jubilee* contained "Why Shouldn't I?" "When
Love Comes Your Way," "Begin the Beguine" and "Just One of
Those Things" and not one of these is mentioned in Benchley's
notice!

John Mason Brown (1900–1969) was an excellent critic who wrote
for two of New York's leading newspapers in addition to *Theatre
Arts Monthly* and *Saturday Review*. Of the theater of the depression
day (Odets, Irwin Shaw, and many others) he wrote: "Ideology has
replaced aesthetics," and "Dogmas are noisier than doubts; intolerance can yell down tolerance any day." (This latter is also unfortunately applicable to some critics.)

After describing the "new, huge, long-overlooked audience,"
Brown remarked of the new dramatists:

"Their first objective has not been entertainment. They have
turned their backs on escape. . . . They have devoted themselves
to the interests and the worries, the grudges and the simplicities,
the grievances and the hopes of this new public."

"They were provocative when they were angry. They became important when they learned to laugh."

(A brilliant summation of a talented and noisily bleak if highly
creative period in American history.)

During the thirty-five years from 1925 to 1960, Brooks Atkinson
was principal drama critic for *The New York Times*. These years

witnessed the development of some of the most important American playwrights, the transition from drawing-room comedy to serious drama, and the coming-of-age of the American musical theater. The era had almost all of the Gershwin, Porter, Berlin, Schwartz, Rome, Arlen, and Styne musicals—plus *all* of Rodgers with Hart as well as Rodgers with Hammerstein. Then there were Bernstein and Sondheim. New York saw—largely through the Theatre Guild—the best foreign plays: Shaw, Molnar, Pirandello, Giraudoux, Capek, Toller—and the "new" Anderson, Sherwood, Howard, Behrman, Barry; later there were Saroyan, Ardrey, Kingsley, Odets, Irwin Shaw, Williams, Hellman, Miller, Inge, and more. It was a rich period, much of which now—fifty, forty, thirty years afterward—still remains alive and, in differing ways, important.

Brooks Atkinson was the chief interpreter of these distinguished people and the events they spawned. He was helpful to them and to their audiences. His was a position of enormous responsibility and he shouldered it modestly and with understanding.

Atkinson was consistent, seldom ruffled, sometimes shocked, never inflexible. His style and vocabulary were simple, his writing clear and meaningful. His reading public trusted him and he lived up to that trust. Space to show him here as a reviewer is limited but I should be remiss if I failed to quote briefly from several of his pieces.

On Eugene O'Neill's *The Great God Brown* (1926): "What Mr. O'Neill has succeeded in doing in *The Great God Brown* . . . is obviously more important than what he has not succeeded in doing. He has not made himself clear. But he has placed within the reach of the stage finer shades of beauty, some delicate nuances of truth and more passionate qualities of emotion than we can discover in any other single modern play." (The beginning of the review.) This was early O'Neill, presented off-Broadway.

The last sentence of a "modern dress" revival of *The Taming of the Shrew* (1927) with Mary Ellis and Basil Sydney: ". . . the amusement of the moment is matched by our consciousness of the trick."

On the use of the "aside" in *Strange Interlude* (1928): "When the 'aside' merely elaborates the spoken thought it deadens the action until *Strange Interlude* looks like a slow-motion picture. And one irreverently suspects that there may be an even deeper thought unexpressed than the nickel-weekly jargon that Mr. O'Neill offers as thinking. Sometimes the 'aside' is pure anti-climax after the speaking. When the 'aside' shows contrast, and when it releases a smoldering passion that cannot burn in the normal dialogue, it is impregnated with the very stuff of drama. Even the pedant would not dispute its legitimacy, as no one disputed it in the entire history of drama until the naturalistic technique of the well-built play laid a deadly hand on playwrighting early in the century. Mr. O'Neill has restored the 'aside' without giving it an entirely new meaning. He has not, one suspects, always used it wisely."

On Philip Barry's *Hotel Universe* (1930): "Froth gleaming with humor is a nobler invention than muddy-mettled prescribing for the soul."

On Moss Hart and George S. Kaufman's *Once in a Lifetime* (1930): "Through all this higgledy-piggledy burlesque the authors scurry rapidly and maliciously, putting a poison barb on their lines. Mr. Kaufman has not only directed the performance skillfully, but he also makes his stage début as Lawrence Vail, the transplanted playwright. It is a part written less fantastically than the play, and Mr. Kaufman, who was doubtless unnerved last evening by the long salute of applause that greeted his appearance, had little fantasy to give them. By the time of his second appearance in the last act he had recovered.

"It is all swift, shrieking and lethal. It is merciless and fairly comprehensive. If the fun lags a little during the middle sketches, it is only because the first act is so hilariously compact and because the best scenes all the way through are so outrageously fantastic."

In writing of Gershwin's *Girl Crazy* (1930), Atkinson dwelt more on the composer-lyricist contributions than the vagaries of the book. His review of Noël Coward's *Private Lives* (1931), starring Gertrude Lawrence, Laurence Olivier, Jill Esmond, and the author, Atkinson concluded: "Noël Coward's talent for little things remains unimpaired. In *Private Lives,* in which he appeared . . . he has nothing to say, and manages to say it with competent agility for three acts. . . . If Mr. Coward's talent were the least bit clumsy, there would be no comedy at all."

Gershwin's *Of Thee I Sing* (1931), the first Pulitzer Prize-winning musical, was a big hit. Atkinson admired music, lyrics, and production, but faulted the book: "The book is long and complicated, heavily freighted with slanders and gibes: and before the evening is over you feel that it is becoming synthetic and unwieldy." This paragraph accurately describes why this celebrated musical is incapable of successful revival.

Atkinson's perceptiveness, his understanding and his gentleness are well known. It would be desirable to quote much more at great length if space permitted. However, in closing I should like to point out Brooks Atkinson's sharp musical instincts by quoting a section of his review of Menotti's opera *The Consul* (1950):

"And what of the inherent quality of the music per se? One cannot think of it, in the first place, as music in a category by itself. This is an opera made of inseparable strands of speech, song, action, scene. Technically, Mr. Menotti has the whole operatic vocabulary of the romantic and modern composers at his disposal. He can write in the most simple, direct, melodic manner. Or he can go contrapuntal, or use at will polytonality, cross rhythms, the most varied orchestration. He knows how to make a few strings chant requiem in the most modern way, and he knows how to rumble with kettle drumsticks on the lowest tones of the piano to make the effect of escaping gas and impending doom.

"A modern, originally conceived, and wonderfully integrated opera triumphed."

Atkinson rendered invaluable service to the American theater during thirty-five important years. He is missed.

4

Two Elder Statesmen

BOTH RICHARD WATTS, JR. and George Oppenheimer have worked at reviewing in New York for many years. Watts has had the longest continuing career in our time of any writer in the reviewing stand. In 1924, at age twenty-six, he began as film critic on the *New York Herald Tribune* and shifted to theater criticism on the same paper in 1936 for a six-year period. In 1946, he became drama critic on the *New York Post* where he still contributes a weekly column, having, this season been followed as daily reviewer by Martin Gottfried.

Oppenheimer, born in 1900, attended Williams College and Harvard, and served in both world wars. He wrote *Here Today*, produced in 1932, and, with Arthur Kober, *A Mighty Man Is He* in 1960. He is the author-editor of *The Passionate Playgoer* and author of *A View from the Sixties*. He was author or co-author of thirty-five film scenarios and was nominated for an Oscar in 1942 for his screenplay, *The War Against Mrs. Hadley*. He also wrote the TV pilot (CBS) for the *Topper* series and, subsequently, twenty-nine segments. He has been drama critic for *Newsday* from 1955 until his shift this year to the position of contributor of Sunday essays.

Watts' manner may best be described as gentle. He is informed, a lover of the theater, a celebrated admirer of female pulchritude, and a standard-bearer for what he deems to possess quality.

Oppenheimer is a "gentleman reviewer." Despite a healthy sense of humor, he is invariably fair in his judgments and never traumatic. His Sunday essays in *Newsday* (circulation 404,000) are marked by genial wit and are without irony.

RICHARD WATTS, JR.

Watts' articles have usually been qualified by "I believe," "in my opinion," "I still can't understand," "to me" and similar extenuations. His pieces are almost invariably divided into four parts: a clear opening opinion, a detailing of the plot, opinions about play and performers, and a concluding sentence advising the reader to go or not to go.

His tone is never abrasive and even his adverse comments— seldom complex—are delivered in gentle tones. Often he seems to apologize for sounding disapproving.

In a 1966 weekend piece, Watts wrote about critics:

"It may be difficult to believe, but there are actually a few playwrights, stage directors, actors and producers who, when in an especially benevolent mood, will reluctantly admit that the reviewers know just a little about the quality of plays. But you won't find even the most wildly generous of them granting that we have the slightest grain of understanding about the other elements of the practical theater. It isn't merely the actors who will tell you we are utterly ignorant on the subject of acting or directors who insist we are hopelessly lost when discussing direction. The opinion is painfully close to unanimous.

"Could they be right about it? In the face of such unflattering unanimity of agreement, I'll make one concession. Since reviewers are at least technically writing men, it is inevitable that our primary interest is in the use of words and we are rightly or wrongly most sure of ourselves when contemplating how they are employed by another writing man, the playwright. Then also, we are to a considerable extent aware that our judgment of acting and direction has a large element of guesswork in it. It could hardly be otherwise if we haven't read the script.

"It would be, I suspect, beyond the capacity of either the experienced director or seasoned actor to say with absolute certainty how the praise or blame should be apportioned. For the reviewer, who probably has never served in either capacity, it is doubly difficult, unless he is covering a play with which he is already familiar. But, since it is the effect of a production or a performance that is important, rather than the technique employed to bring it about, I think it is possible for us to render approximate justice to all the factors involved in the work."

Obviously this statement is honest, but it is doubtful that many of Mr. Watts' colleagues would admit that "our judgment of acting and direction has a large element of guesswork in it." Nevertheless, it is often true. However, it is also incontrovertible that it is "the effect of a production or a performance that is important, rather than the technique employed to bring it about."

Watts' statement of opinion is usually brief, and I will quote in no particular sequence extracts from his notices.

1967: "A curious sort of warfare seemed to be taking place on the stage of the Alvin Theater last night. A musical comedy called *Sherry!* appeared to be in frequent combat with the celebrated play by George S. Kaufman and Moss Hart upon which it was based, and there were occasional victories scored by both sides. But, while the result was fairly entertaining, the attempt to reconcile the two aspects failed, I thought, to emphasize the best in either version. . . .

"*Sherry!* seemed to me pleasant but disappointing."

1972: "For sheer, joyous fun, shared in by audience and actors alike, it would be hard to match the musical version of *Two Gentlemen of Verona*. The free adaptation by Galt MacDermot, John Guare and Mel Shapiro, which was done in Central Park this past summer by Joseph Papp's New York Shakespeare Festival, opened on Broadway last night at the St. James Theater, and it provided an evening that is completely delightful in spirit, gaiety, tunefulness and imagination.

"*Two Gentlemen of Verona* is one of the least known and most forgettable of all the Bard's plays, and all I remembered about it was that it was the comedy in which Shakespeare brought in a dog. The dog, I am happy to say, is still there. Being so unmemorable, it is just the sort of thing which encourages a liberated treatment, and the adapters have wisely cut loose and used only its characters and background for their wild and wonderful lark. . . .

"Everything combines to make the musical *Two Gentlemen of Verona* a triumph."

These two segments will serve to establish Watts' general method and style. The following are excerpts from reviews of *Sweet Charity,* which Watts admired and *A Moon for the Misbegotten.* He had a single reservation about *Sweet Charity,* however, which he expresses as a kind of mild disappointment, forgives it, and hopes to be forgiven for having quibbled.

1966: "In addition to being a glowing performer, Gwen Verdon is so endearing on the stage that you long for even the character she happens to be playing to find happiness. The final stroke of ill luck that befalls the loveable, foolish heroine of *Sweet Charity* casts rather a pall over the ending of her new vehicle, but it is one of the few complaints I have against the brightly imaginative musical comedy, which opened Saturday night at the gaily refurbished Palace Theater.

"Next to Miss Verdon, the most exciting feature of *Sweet Charity* is Bob Fosse's brilliant choreography. Against the background of Robert Randolph's attractive setting, Mr. Fosse has staged a series of wonderfully humorous and exhilarating dance numbers. I would cite in particular the hilariously realistic and disillusioned one about a group of bored hostesses lined up for customers in a cheap dance hall, as well as another in which the dedicated members of a cult of overaged youth offer their "Rhythm of Life" ritual in the Rhythm of Life Church.

"But Mr. Fosse is up to all sorts of unusual things in his manipulations, and they usually involve Miss Verdon. Charity, the dance-hall girl with a heart of gold but no judgment of men, meets her great crush when they are trapped in a stalled elevator, and he is suffering from claustrophobia. Later they are loftily imprisoned in a swing high in midair. Then there is the time when Charity is thrust into a closet from which she has to watch her movie idol make love.

"In Fellini's early film called *Nights of Cabiria*, the source of *Sweet Charity*, the heroine, I am told, had a more explicit profession than dance-hall hostess but was equally brave and cheerful through her career of unbroken disasters. The stage adaptation has been made by Neil Simon, and, while it lacks the freshness of wit and humor he delighted us with in *Barefoot in the Park* and *The Odd Couple*, it is a serviceable springboard for the pleasant music and lyrics of Cy Coleman and Dorothy Fields and the brilliance of Miss Verdon and Mr. Fosse.

"Yet I am inescapably brought back to my original quibble. It is an integral part of Miss Verdon's tremendous appeal that she makes the luckless heroine important to you. If *Sweet Charity* were intended as a slice of life, her eventual fate would have been in the proper ironic mood. But, since it is a cheerful, festive musical comedy, I would have preferred a little cheating on her behalf, and the honesty of the ending seemed a let-down rather than an artistic virtue."

1973: "It is a shame Eugene O'Neill didn't live to see the brilliant production of his *A Moon for the Misbegotten*, which opened Saturday night at the Morosco Theater. He never succeeded in finding an actress physically suited to the role of his large and powerful-looking Josie Hogan. Now the demanding part is being played by the brilliant Colleen Dewhurst who is just right for it and is giving a superb performance in a fascinating and deeply moving drama.

"It is a basically tragic play, and yet it should put to rest the belief that O'Neill lacked a sense of humor. In fact, the first half is largely comedy, and it contains a genuinely comic character. It is Phil Hogan, Josie's father, a sly, hard-drinking and cantankerous old Irishman who is much more sober, sensible, intelligent and well-meaning than his bouts with alcohol make him appear. I admit I hadn't realized how amusing and interesting he was until I saw him portrayed by Ed Flanders, who is quite wonderful in this splendid revival. . . .

"The two central figures are among O'Neill's most brilliant creations. Josie, the bulky girl who thought she was so unattractive to men that she pretended to have many affairs, but confessed to James Tyrone that she was still a virgin, is not only a sad, lost woman but an indomitable one, who won't give in to the cruelty of fate. The ending of what is really a tragedy even becomes exultant, because Josie, who won't surrender to defeat, is determined to go on with her blighted existence bravely. . . .

"Miss Dewhurst is not only right for the role and looks very beautiful, but gives a truly magnificent performance. Jason Robards who was the best Hickey in *The Iceman Cometh* I ever saw, is perfect in all the phases of Tyrone's complex character, and I've already said how fine Mr. Flanders is. Since I didn't have to rush off to my typewriter Saturday, I could stay in the theater and watch the tremendous ovation the standing audience gave. It was a proper tribute to not only a great play but to the marvelous performances in it."

The piece on *Sweet Charity* is less a review than a wish. It is a benign and clear statement of personal preference.

His review of *A Moon for the Misbegotten* is intensely personal. It abounds in adjectival enthusiasm, probably appropriate but he makes no attempt at qualification or argument. Certainly Watts is open-hearted and unpretentious. O'Neill's play, its actors, the director, and production are his only concern—not himself. His reaction is visceral, and it is the reaction of a theaterlover of taste.

Random examples of Watts' opinion of other plays follow:

1973: "Jean Anouilh is the drama's foremost apostle of disillusioned romanticism. *The Waltz of the Toreadors* is his best, funniest and, in a curious way, most beautiful play. It is certainly one of the masterpieces of the modern stage, not only of the French. It is a delight to see, and it is being given a satisfying production at the Circle in the Square-Joseph E. Levine Theater, where it opened last night, with Eli Wallach and Anne Jackson in the central roles. . . .

"The mood and action are farcical, and hilariously so. Indeed, in view of the play's comic spirit, it may be hard to convince anyone who has not seen *The Waltz of the Toreadors* that it is basically a little sad, but that is the case. Gen. St. Pé is a figure of fun, and he is quite an absurd fellow, but he is considerably more than that. For his romanticism, though it makes him behave idiotically, is real and touching, and he can talk about it eloquently. And he won't give up, even if the odds grow steadily against him."

1973: "What kind of play is *The Merchant* [*of Venice*]? Everyone has his own interpretation, but I haven't any original one of my own. All I can say is that, in addition to being a fascinating combination of drama and comedy, it can be very exasperating. There isn't a completely sympathetic character in it. Even Portia has an irritating touch of sadism and practical joking. Since she was going to save Antonio's life, why did she have to make him go through the last minute's fear of death before doing so? And wasn't it a dirty trick she played on her husband about that ring?

"As for Shylock, it can only be said for him that he is the best of a bad lot. I think it is likely that Shakespeare originally intended him to be an anti-Semitic villain to please the Elizabethan masses. Then the creative process took over in the Bard and he became the play's one living figure. I have always· suspected that, if Shylock had boldly gone through with his vengeance and cut off that pound of flesh from Antonio, he would have been perfectly safe because they would have found no ounce of blood in the stuffy merchant.

"What a strange play it is! Much of it is based on the fact that the characters aren't very bright. When the Prince of Morocco and the Prince of Arragon go courting Portia and have to pick the right casket that will entitle one of them to her hand, you would think they would have had the sense at least to suspect that it was unlikely to be either the gold or the silver one with their pompous inscriptions but the modestly inscribed one of lead. Yet the poor idiots go immediately to the bait for their self-esteem. They are good scenes, though.

"After the famous scene of Shylock's discomfiture, the play really has no place to go, but the craftsmanlike Bard knew how to pad. As annoying as it is, Portia's trick about the ring is also entertaining, and the scene toward the end in which the characters have brief speeches beginning with 'On such a night' contains some of the loveliest lines in all of Shakespeare. It should be noted, by the way, that there is cynicisim in a few of them. For all his romanticism, the Swan of Avon was a realistic writer."

1973: "One hates to think what any playwright but [Tennessee] Williams would have done with this material, and I rather wish he had come up with some other idea. But the skill that has made him the foremost living American dramatist hasn't deserted him, and *Out Cry* has been written so expertly that it not only retains an astonishing share of theatrical interest but creates two characters who may be lunatics but are both believable and touching. The relationship between the brother and sister is genuinely and decidedly moving in their affection."

These excerpts speak well for Watts. The Anouilh play—a comedy—he finds touching. His view of *The Merchant of Venice* is a thoughtful and interesting effort to explain a play that invites argument. The brief segment about Tennessee Williams' play demonstrates the reviewer's ability to recognize special qualities in an unsuccessful play. Watts, unlike many other reviewers who did not comprehend the play, was not cruel to it or its talented author.

In closing, I would like to quote a part of Watts' review of Edward Albee's latest play which received anything but a generally enthusiastic press. It is interesting that Watts—the elder statesman—found it "fascinating."

1975: "*Seascape* is one of Edward Albee's most brilliant and fascinating plays and marks a fresh departure for him. It is a kind of allegorical comedy and has a warmth of heart not always to be found in his distinguished work. Dealing with mankind's rise from the primordial slime, it offers us a philosophical glimpse of evolution in addition to being characteristically witty and richly entertaining. . . .

"Albee always begins with a great advantage. He invariably writes such beautiful prose. No contemporary dramatist can use the English language so gracefully, and *Seascape* is wonderfully eloquent as well as witty. I don't see how even those who don't care for the play itself can fail to recognize that the writing is downright superb. It has been noted that, on the whole, the lizards have the best lines and the evening doesn't reach its peak until they arrive. But the husband and wife aren't neglected, and indeed they have some valuable ideas for their—and our—undersea ancestors. At times, the discussion seems almost Shavian, but it remains Edward Albee at the top of his form."

GEORGE OPPENHEIMER

I should next like to quote excerpts at random from Mr. Oppenheimer's reviews. First, from a Sunday reconsideration of Pinter's *The Homecoming*, February 11, 1967:

"My complaint with Mr. Pinter is that he prepares us too sparsely for this kind of world. The events preceding its revelation are more realistic and less opaque than in most of his plays. We need to be prepared for this sort of startling metamorphosis. However, this is the habit (I almost called it the arrogance) of Mr. Pinter. Being a thoroughly unconventional playwright, he ignores the ordinary conventions of exposition, of establishing situations, of sustaining moods or characterizations. Our mad world changes madly as does Mr. Pinter's. You'll find no more rhyme or reason in a Pinter play than in the violence and virulence that surrounds us daily. The life he portrays is the life he sees and for us to see it clearly and understandingly, we must do so through his eyes.

"What we see are scenes of violence and sex, not for their shock effect but because violence and sex are indigenous to the members of this ruttish household. And what we hear are dark hints and earthy humor and the rhythms of common speech made into uncommon poetry. Our vision is apt to become blurred and our hearing defective when Mr. Pinter abruptly darkens a meaning or befogs a motivation. What we hear also is the rich humor that flows naturally and effortlessly from the characters who, odd though they are, never become caricatures. They are real people who inhabit Mr. Pinter's world and it is only the world itself that becomes something of a caricature to our conventional eyes. . . .

"Whatever its shortcomings, *The Homecoming* should be seen, not as a duty but as a stimulus, an entertainment and one more step in the development of the unique mind of the amazing Mr. Pinter."

This is a simple, honest, and personal view of the Pinter play. It is direct, substantiated, and readable. Without liking it wholeheartedly, Mr. Oppenheimer tells his readers that it "should be seen" but tries to prepare them for the kind of surprise that he himself experienced.

The following excerpts about *Darling of the Day* and *The Happy Time* have comments about music as an integral part of musical-show architecture. These are constructive observations about two shows that were not successes, but Mr. Oppenheimer's discussion in no way denigrates the estimable authors and composers. His view is astute and without animus. This piece appeared February 10, 1968:

"In my review of the new musical *Darling of the Day*, I said, 'It has one or two showstoppers but practically no show-advancers.' I did not then have space to enlarge on this idea which seems to me one of the basic faults in too many of our current musicals. Numbers are injected almost arbitrarily in the hopes that they will stop the show. More often than not they do. . . .

"A case in point is the number 'Not on Your Nellie,' which serves as a perfect song and dance for the enchanting Patricia Routledge in *Darling of the Day*. Sad and disheartened over the imposture of her husband, she goes to her local pub and proceeds to get slopped. She then sings the song, joined by the singing chorus, then by the dancers until it builds into a fast, rousing and entertaining production number. The hands go out and produce generous applause.

"What has been accomplished is twofold. Miss Routledge has shown one more facet of her many skills without revealing any new facet to her character and we in the audience have been provided with a lively number that was mentioned enthusiastically in the reviews, as it was intended to be. However, what has it done for the plot? How has it advanced the action or the characterization? The answer is not one bit. It comes toward the end of the evening, an excellent place for a show-stopper since it sends us out into the street in better humor than a quieter song might do. But what if the number really made us feel for Miss Routledge in her disillusionment and worry?

"Also in *Darling of the Day*, there is a song called 'Let's See What Happens.' It is, for me, Jule Styne's best number in the show with its charming lyrics by E. Y. Harburg and its infectious melody. More than that, however, it accomplishes more adroitly than most dialogue scenes could do the growing attraction between Miss Routledge and Vincent Price, who plays a famous artist disguised as his valet. Here is a splendid show-advancer, moving the plot forward, helping the characterizations, progressing the romance.

"One of the best examples of this kind is 'Adelaide's Lament' by Frank Loesser in his *Guys and Dolls*. In Stanley Green's *The World of Musical Comedy*, the best book on that subject that I know, he says of this song, 'Loesser changed the lyric to make her suffer from psychosomatic ailments ("A person could develop a cold") because her marriage to Nathan has been postponed so often. 'Adelaide's Lament,' one of the most brilliant of all comic love songs, is a perfect example of Loesser's dictum: "I try to examine characters, not events." '

"Think back to the four classic musicals of Rodgers and Ham-

merstein—*Oklahoma! Carousel, South Pacific* and *The King and I.*
These were integrated shows in which the music and dances fitted
into and advanced the stories. They were show-stoppers, plenty of
them, but they did not stop the flow. . . .

"I believe that if we could get back to the integration of story,
character and numbers, our musicals would profit vastly. This
season they have been particularly lifeless except for the lively off-
Broadway duo, *Hair* and *Your Own Thing*, the former closer to
revue than musical comedy and the latter an irreverent and hilarious spoof of Shakespeare's *Twelfth Night*, whose numbers fit the
mood and help tell the story."

George Oppenheimer wrote of the revival of Odets' *Awake and
Sing* (1970). He was seeing the play for the first time and related it
to the angry young writers of 1970. His conclusion about the "disciples of formlessness and obscurity" is especially relevant.

"In 1935, when Clifford Odets' play, *Awake and Sing*, was produced by the Group Theatre, I was out of New York. I read it with
great admiration but it was not until last night, when it was revived
at the new Bijou Theater on West 48th St., that I finally saw it
performed. It is good to report that it lives up to everything I had
heard about the original production.

"Under the sensitive and perceptive direction of Arthur A. Seidelman, every one of the actors is outstanding. As a result, Mr. Odets'
portrait of a Jewish family struggling to survive the Depression and
the hostilities engendered from living together in such close quarters, still remains rousing, absorbing and passionately honest. While
it evokes the feel of its day, it is in no way dated but, on the contrary, is relevant to our own times. . . .

"Here is a play of protest of the Thirties. Unlike too many of our
current crop of ungrammatic protests, it is well made, well written
and without the constant presence of despair. Odets had great
humor. He had anger, too, but it was tempered with compassion
and an understanding of his expertly drawn characters. . . .

"I wish that the disciples of formlessness and obscurity would
every one of them see this play and learn how effective protest can
be with a form and a clarity that contains character, meaning and
entertainment. *Awake and Sing* deserves to be as great a success as
it was in 1935."

It is interesting to observe that although Mr. Oppenheimer is a
senior citizen, he nevertheless displays considerable understanding
of new talents. Excerpts from three reviews follow: *The Me Nobody
Knows, Operation Sidewinder*, and *The Basic Training of Pavlo
Hummel*.

"Based on a book entitled *The Me Nobody Knows,* which consists
of texts spoken and written by public school children between the
ages of 7 to 18 from Harlem and the Bronx, a musical by the same
name opened last night at the Orpheum Theater. It has been edited
by Stephen M. Joseph, with the original idea credited to Herb Schapiro, music by Gary William Friedman and lyrics by Will Holt.
And before we go any further, let me urge you to see it.

"The 12 youngsters, eight black, four white, in this simple but
highly imaginative production, directed by Robert H. Livingston
with musical numbers staged by Patricia Birch, vary from children
to teenagers and they are all of them naturally talented. . . .

"The show is at its best when it is singing and dancing, although
I was greatly moved by a series of letters to a benefactor by a
touchingly grateful young slum boy. 'These are children's voices
from the ghetto,' says a quotation in the program, 'in their struggle
lies their hope, and ours. They are the voices of change.'

"Do not let me give you the impression that this is a preachment.
Especially in its first act, the propaganda is muted and when it becomes louder, angrier and more forceful, it contains righteous but
not, as so many protest plays do, militantly offensive indignation.
Time and again I felt a catch in my throat as these youthful performers talked and sang. One song, in particular, touched me. It is
called "Let Me Come In" and it is an honest and compassionate
plea by all 12 of these appealing young people to be allowed to
share in some of the good things of a world that has too long
deprived them. . . .

"There are moments in the second act, a very few of them, when
the mood breaks and the action becomes repetitious. Almost immediately Mr. Friedman comes to the rescue with a song, while Mr.
Livingston restores the mood and the cast rouses you, moves you or
entertains you.

"To conclude, *The Me Nobody Knows* is one of the happy sur-
prises of the season."

The simple and often overwhelming emotional pull of *The Me
Nobody Knows* made it considerably easier to relate to than the
other two more abrasive plays. George Oppenheimer comprehended
their virtues as well as some faults and he has spelled them out
simply.

"There is a great deal of everything, some good, some bad, in
Operation Sidewinder, which opened last night at the Vivian Beaumont Theater.

"Its author, Sam Shepard, who has been produced mainly off off-
Broadway, is possessed of an incredible amount of fantastic imagination, so much so that it affects his play to an almost schizophrenic

degree. And yet, here is total theater, beautifully directed by Michael A. Schultz and well produced by the Lincoln Center Repertory Theater.

"There is melodrama, protest, comedy (its weakest point), fantasy, pageant, ballet (an exciting snake dance performed by an Indian tribe), music (plenty of rock, again some good, some bad, all loud, played well and composed by a weird-looking hippie combo, known as The Holy Modal Rounders that performs between all of the many scenes). It is psychedelic and, quite often, psychopathic. It has one foot in science-fiction and another in the Theater of the Absurd, but whatever it has or is, it is never for a moment dull.

"Don't expect me to tell you the plot. I have a strong conviction that not even Mr. Shepard could do that for you. He is a completely undisciplined writer, who shows flashes of brilliance in isolated scenes and speeches, only to retreat into pedestrian prose, thwarted attempts at humor and situations that, at one moment, boggle the mind and, at the next, delight it. . . .

"With all its faults, and they are manifold, *Operation Sidewinder* captures the sound of today in its confusion and its cacophony. But it also reflects our times in a driving aliveness and excitement. Whatever may be said for or against Mr. Shepard, he is unmistakably a product of the age which he attacks so angrily, so bewilderingly, so imaginatively, so badly and so well. Like the wonder and the windiness of his age, he cannot be ignored."

The deliberate refutational elements within this piece somehow manage to give a very positive picture of the play, the meaning of which the reviewer was struggling to unravel. It is clear that he admires the talent of the writer, considers him important, and wishes he were a better craftsman.

George Oppenheimer's review of David Rabe's *Sticks and Bones* (1971) follows in excerpt. By now, four years after its production, this play is discussed as a kind of classic. So Mr. Oppenheimer proclaimed it.

"With this play a lagging season comes alive.

"Once again Rabe has written an anti-war play with a fury that mounts to an almost unbearable conclusion. It is a story of the return of a blind soldier to an 'American Dream' home, consisting of his father, mother and kid brother. Their names are Ozzie, Harriet and Rick, his is David.

"Here is a trio that is even blinder than David, refusing to see what is going on in the shattered world of today. Ozzie has, at least, a dim perception, a restlessness and a distaste for his domestic life, but he has subordinated it to the comfort of home cooking and the anesthesia of television. Harriet is a clod, made up of cliches and phony optimism. And Rick, their banjo-playing, folk-singing son is a physically attractive and mentally retarded dolt.

"Then David the blind soldier comes home, embittered, suspicious, hostile, antisocial. With him is the ghost of a Vietnamese girl whom he has loved and left behind to become a whore. His sense of guilt adds to his disorientation, to his inability to fit, as he once did, into the almost criminally smug family circle. With his arrival, things are no longer cozy. David rejects brutally their clumsy efforts to temper his affliction with copious food and idle talk and empty cliches. He scares them and means to and suddenly their world begins to fall apart as they face themselves and a grim reality.

"As he did in *Pavlo Hummel*, Rabe blends reality with fantasy. The figure of the Vietnamese girl, never speaking, gliding about unseen by everyone but the blind man, is an intrusion into the mood of the play. And when the father is finally forced to see her, there is for me, too abrupt a transition into symbolism. However, this is a small flaw in a drama that clutches at your throat, that makes you laugh and cry, think and mourn at the waste and the despair that have occupied our lives with this evil war.

"There is a scene when an unctuous priest comes to see David and, filled with arrogant confidence, tries to talk him into passiveness. Suddenly David has had enough and lashes out at him with his white-tipped cane, while the priest is both terrified and exalted by his martyrdom. It is a fearful and yet strangely comical scene. . . .

"Here, at long last, is a magnificent play by a man who may well become our most important new American playwright."

If, as Clive Barnes has said, the critic's function is the expression of his own taste, both Watts and Oppenheimer have always discharged this obligation. They have done it simply and honestly, and have served their readers and the theater. Their unpretentiousness has probably lost for them a cocktail-conversation audience, but for those who cared honestly for their judgments, they have provided it clearly and consistently for about half a century.

5

Peripheral Newspapers

EDWIN WILSON

The Wall Street Journal, a daily with a circulation of 1,367,430, deals principally, as its name implies, with commerce and the economy. It is a splendid newspaper, and it considers theater among many other special subjects. Edwin Wilson*, who is employed as reviewer, writes fairly, intelligently, readably, and without animus about the things he sees.

The following extracts from several of Mr. Wilson's notices are amply reasoned. He is a distinct plus among the ranks of opinion-dealers.

To begin with, there is the 1974 *London Assurance* imported from England. In addition to a detailed description of the star's performance, there is an interesting consideration of nostalgia.

"In the part of Sir Harcourt, actor Donald Sinden has played the role off and on for four years and he appears to have lost none of his zest for the part. Sir Harcourt is a fop: a man who wears a wig of

---

*Born in Nashville in 1927, Wilson is a graduate of Vanderbilt University, University of Edinburgh, and Yale University Drama School. He has taught drama at Hofstra University, at the Yale Drama School, and at Hunter College. He has served as production assistant for Broadway and off-Broadway plays as well as for several films. In addition to teaching and being theater critic for *The Wall Street Journal,* he is author of several books on theater.

spit curls and sees himself as the height of fashion. To everyone else, of course, he is a fool. But what a grandiloquent fool. As played by Mr. Sinden, Sir Harcourt strikes an operatic pose, one hand held aloft behind his head like a fencer at the ready, the other hand carving arabesques in the air, and we are transported to the early 19th Century.

"Mr. Sinden and his colleagues from the Royal Shakespeare Company give us a good replica of the exaggerated style of the past, when women fell faint across couches and men ceremoniously lit their cigars after dinner. But Mr. Sinden goes further; he does not simply reproduce the style; he embellishes it. Sir Harcourt has trouble with his teeth—they are false, one assumes—and to keep them properly aligned Mr. Sinden must occasionally rearrange his face: He drops one eye, twists his cheek, quivers his chin, and eventually manages to restore them to their rightful place. He can carry on these contortions for thirty seconds or more, and they are outrageously funny. So, too, are those moments when Polly Adams, in the role of Grace Harkaway, faces the audience to deliver a sententious set speech on humor or the pleasures of early morning. ('When I with joy behold the first tear that glistens in the opening eyes of morning' is the first line.)

"[Boucicault's] talents were just right for the demands of the commercial theater and *London Assurance* is a good example. . . .

"As adapted and directed by Ronald Eyre and performed by Mr. Sinden and his colleagues, it retains the original satire, but another layer has been added. It becomes a satire of a satire, for we are laughing at a form of theater once taken at face value.

"This has been a little-noticed element of the nostalgia and revival boom. Frequently our pleasure comes from making fun of our forbears—of the things they took seriously or the styles they found admirable—whether in the '20s, at the turn of the century, or, as in the case of *London Assurance,* in the 19th Century. This kind of amusement will always be with us, and doubtless there are things we hold sacred today which generations hence will find the subject of great mirth. The preponderance of laughs today at the expense of the past, however, leads one to ask why we lean so heavily on this form of amusement. Is it that we have so little in our own day to laugh at, or that we secretly admire and yearn for that which we satirize and use our laughter to mask those yearnings, or, perhaps, that we feel less badly about our own inadequacies when we can point to shortcomings of those who lived before us? The questions come easier than the answers."

This is an interesting and literate view which seems to have appeared nowhere else.

Next, some of Wilson's thoughts on *The Contractor* (1973) and its author, David Storey, his "methods," and the general plight of playwrights.

"In the present state of the theater, finding his own voice is perhaps the single most difficult task facing a playwright. The winds of the past and future whirl round his head so furiously that he has trouble locating his own center. The theater of the past sometimes seems contrived and artificial. As for the present and the future, a cursory glance suggests chaos; theater is performed in streets, garages and warehouse lofts, frequently with the playwright conspicuous by his absence.

"Amid this turmoil one writer who has found a solution is British playwright David Storey, who seems successfully to have planted one foot in the past and another in the future. . . .

"In all his work Mr. Storey writes realistically but eschews artificiality: There appear to be no plot coincidences—no timely phone calls or unexpected letters—and no big show-down scenes between the main characters. As with his other plays, *The Contractor* does not follow a plot so much as present an event:

"On the surface it looks simple, but Mr. Storey's method is deceptive. Like Chekhov before him, he employs artifice to hide his artifice. The men seem to be an ordinary bunch of workmen, most of them unemployable elsewhere because they drink and are lazy, and their conversation has the ring of authenticity—greatly aided by Storey's extraordinary ear for dialogue—but actually there are a number of crises in the play. . . .

"Perhaps Mr. Storey's single most successful device, however, is the notion of the tent itself. Both in *The Changing Room* and *The Contractor* Storey has found a physical activity which becomes a ritual. *The Changing Room* showed us a group of rugby players in a locker room before, during, and after a game; the counterpart here is the raising and lowering of the tent.

"Young people today are intrigued with ritual—those group activities which, through repetition, take on special meaning (perhaps to replace those time-honored religious and family rituals which have been eroded in our day). Mr. Storey has rediscovered ritual in a group of men undertaking a sports event or a joint task of physical labor.

"He reminds us how much texture and resonance is to be found in these seemingly simple tasks when they are performed regularly by a team, providing sustenance to those who take part, and even a kind of joy."

In this review, as in most of Wilson's, the writer relates the play under discussion—new or old—to today's audiences and conditions, an important function of all criticism.

The following excerpts deal with two plays (1974) which Wilson discusses concurrently and relates to each other. Liking some aspects of each and disliking others, he nevertheless is respectful of the two writers who, in spite of anyone's feeling about their current progress, have earned our gratitude.

"Two strong craftsmen came back to Broadway on successive nights this week, both showing evidence of their customary skill, but neither quite on target; one fell a bit short of the mark while the other has overshot it.

"The one this side of the mark [*In Praise of Love*] is [by] Terence Rattigan. . . . Lydia Cruttwell, knows she is dying of a rare disease, but she does not want her husband to know. Her husband, an absent-minded literary critic for the London *Sunday Times,* knows of his wife's illness but does not want her to know he knows. Under the pressure of the situation, the husband comes to realize how much he loves his wife, and she, in turn, comes to recognize his love —something she was not certain of before. Neither says anything outright to the other of their secret feelings but they pervade the entire final portion of the play and are quite touching. The way Mr. Rattigan has made their love so understated on the one hand and so unmistakable on the other is a tribute to his superb technique.

"He is greatly abetted by his actors. . . . Where, then, has Mr. Rattigan gone wrong? The answer is in taking so long to get to the denouement. He always builds his plays carefully, but here he builds too carefully, with endless rounds of medical reports, confessions to confidantes, and hints of what the future might bring. We care about the characters at the end, but we have had too little to care about along the way.

"If Rattigan has the ability occasionally to make us cry, Neil Simon has the ability all too easily to make us laugh. His new play, *God's Favorite* at the Eugene O'Neill Theater, is a retelling of the Job story from the Bible. . . .

"Mr. Simon hasn't done much for the Job story, but the story has done a lot for him, providing a clothesline on which he strings a never-ending assortment of gags.

"The point is, if you are inclined to laugh at anything—a building in ruins, a man writhing on the floor with an impossible itch, or gag lines like "your mother can't see you, she has her ear plugs in"— you will have a high old time at *God's Favorite*. If, however, like this reviewer, you are one of those who will forgo a barrage of belly laughs for moments of genuine humor, you will wish that Simon had used his facility for making jokes less and his insight more. Then his hero, instead of being the butt of a joke, might have been a true comic character with a heart and a head. In speaking of creating a poem, Dylan Thomas said, 'The best craftsmanship always leaves holes and gaps in the works of the poem so that something that is *not* in the poem can creep, crawl, flash, or thunder in.' There are no holes or gaps in *God's Favorite*: they are all filled with yocks, gags, and laughs. In warfare it is called overkill, in economics, the law of diminishing returns.''

Next, Wilson tilts with a difficult and perhaps inconclusive play, *When You Comin' Back, Red Ryder?* (1973). Most reviewers found it confused but could not dismiss it readily. Here, the writer treats it with tacit importance because it has piqued his interest and he dares to raise pertinent questions for which he has no ready answers. It is conceivable that these questions might have been of some help to the author.

"*When You Comin' Back, Red Ryder?* which opened recently at the Eastside Playhouse, is a disturbing play in more ways than one. On one level it is a well-crafted suspense play. . . .

"But Mark Medoff, author of this play, is writing more than a chiller; he is trying to tell us something, and it is here that the play becomes disturbing in another way, because it is not clear what he is trying to say, and where it seems clear, his message is not entirely satisfying. Teddy, the chief character, is reminiscent of the main character in the film *A Clockwork Orange,* and in their mixture of sentimentality and sadism there is some resemblance between the film and Medoff's play.

"These young men seem to be reacting against something and this raises two questions: Against what are they reacting? And assuming there is a definite provocation, does it adequately explain, let alone justify, such gratuitous violence? These are important questions because the growing incidence of gratuitous violence and impromptu malevolence in our society is cause for genuine concern.

"Why, then, does Teddy of the play act as he does? Someone asks him whatever became of 'peace and love' among the young, and he replies that he has nothing to do with that, he is one of the 'disaffected.' But disaffected with what? With society, of course, and hypocrisy, but these are too general, and besides, they are nothing new. In Teddy's case his chief lament is the loss of the hero in American society. The Red Ryder of the title is the name of the frightened young man who works in the diner, but also of the comic book Western hero, and no one could stand more in contrast to a legendary hero than this scrawny kid. The answer to the question in the title, when is Red Ryder coming back, is 'never.'

"What does all this mean? Does the loss of past heroes explain his present behavior? Does he have insight on this question that others do not? Is his distress genuine? Is he the new American hero? It is impossible to tell.

"These people all have inhibitions and hang-ups—who doesn't?—and Teddy probes them with the skill of a satanic surgeon, exposing the raw nerve ends. The question here is whether Teddy, in his ability to expose flaws, is superior to the others or simply a sadistic punk? A second question is whether his presence is therapeutic or a form of malignancy? When he leaves he seems to have worked wonders: the scrawny kid talks back to his boss for the first time and leaves town and the violinist has discovered a new independence from her husband.

"There are other ambivalences as well—whether Teddy is a real character or more of a catalyst, for instance—but the aforementioned are enough to indicate that Medoff has raised more questions than he has even begun to answer. Still, they are important questions, and we should welcome him as a playwright who is willing to grapple with them, demonstrating considerable technical skill as well. His play is provocative if inchoate, leading us to ask, in the vernacular of the title: 'What you gettin' at, Mark Medoff?' "

Lorelei and *Gigi* gave rise to the following critical thoughts:

"One gets the impression with these recent revivals like *Gigi* and *Lorelei* that someone thought they had a bright idea: 'The movie *Gigi* had all those wonderful songs, and it's never been on the stage. Why not try it?' Or, 'Carol Channing is still in great form, why don't we cull the best songs from *Gentlemen Prefer Blondes* and wrap them in a new package?'

"This might be all right for a night club revue, but not for a Broadway musical. The stakes are too high. Not only does it cost half a million dollars or more to produce, it is an occasion for those who attend. They expect and deserve the real thing. Of course it's fun to hear Carol Channing sing 'I'm Just a Little Girl from Little Rock' and 'Diamonds Are a Girl's Best Friend' as only she can sing them. On a cross-country tour for the past year she has pleased thousands singing them, but you could hear the same thing in *An Evening with Carol Channing*. How much more delighted and entertained those same thousands would have been if they had seen her in numbers fully integrated into an exciting piece of work.

"Nostalgia has its role in theater. Who would have thought that works based in the late 1950s and the early 1960s could evoke nostalgia, but in the musical *Grease* and the film *American Graffiti* they are doing just that. Those two pieces work because they are original, and were among the first to treat these periods. With the 1920s, however, as well as with *Lorelei* and *Gigi*, we have been around the track a few times.

"A revival can be given new life but it requires a point of view.

As with an original interpretation, it also needs a fierce passion to bring the past alive. Broadway can give us revivals and nostalgia by all means, but it should give them to us with freshness, creativity and a new vision."

These thoughts are sober and relevant. They can be taken seriously because they are not arrogant, and they don't take advantage of less than ideal situations to be ironic. They are adverse without being caustic or angry. They are coolly analytical and specific.

In his review of *Irene* (1973), Wilson is a dissenter, with reason. He also makes it clear that this is not a "revival"—an important fact since it seems to have gone unnoticed by too many reviewers.

" 'Something old, something new, something borrowed, something blue'; this is one way to describe *Irene*.

"The something old is the show itself. The something blue is 'Sweet Little Alice Blue Gown,' a song from the original production which in this version is sung not once or twice, but three times.

"The something new is a revised book and a series of new songs written to fill out the story.

"Although the humor runs to the banal, up to this point everything is fine. But when we get to the something borrowed we get the feeling *Irene* went a bit overboard.

"Signs of it are everywhere. Patsy Kelly, who plays Irene's mother, does a buck and wing very much as she did in *No, No, Nanette*. And Debbie Reynolds, who is making her Broadway debut playing the part of Irene, even resorts to twirling a broomstick—a feat borrowed from the days when she was a baton twirling champion in Burbank, California.

"In a number where chorus girls carry parasols, one girl cannot open hers. The audience notices her plight and begins to worry. Here it is opening night and she cannot make her parasol work. Poor girl! Then at the last minute she pops it open; we realize she could have done it all along. It is one of the oldest tricks in the business, borrowed from no telling how many shows.

"*Irene* resembles one of those galas—usually given in tribute to an esteemed performer or for some worthwhile charity—in which great routines from the past are strung together with a bit of well-intentioned horseplay.

"Ordinarily you expect borrowing in a nostalgic musical. You want to see the old dance numbers and admire the period costumes, to hear the banjo and recognize familiar songs. We get all of that in *Irene*. . . .

"But for borrowing to work to best advantage it must be integrated into a new whole; the high spots must be all of one piece;

they cannot remain fragments from another world. With *Irene*, no one could decide whether it was an authentic period piece, a revival, a parody, a potpourri, or just what.

"When that happens a production has no life of its own, no anchor or center of gravity. Every theater piece, from the most serious drama to a frivolous farce, needs something at its center which the performers can hold on to. When they do not find it, they run for cover—and so do directors—usually to something that has worked before, whether it fits or not.

"One result is that no one trusts the material: the big number, yes, but not the stuff in between, even when it is good. An example is the opening of the second act. It is a quiet musical number; a real sleeper from the original production called 'The Last Part of Every Party.' The men are in tails, and the ladies in evening dresses; they stand in a line singing in harmony like a glee club chorus. The song is surprisingly lovely and the effect quite disarming. But rather than let it stand on its own, the director—or someone—breaks into it to give us a slapstick drunk scene."

The current *Equus* (1974) has been admired, discussed, and occasionally angrily dismissed. The majority of playgoers have agreed that it is an "experience." Edwin Wilson has found it so but he has varied the reasons. The following is an excerpt from his review:

"Theater is the art of bringing different worlds together: The audience comes together with the actors, the words of the playwright merge with the voices of the performers, characters on stage confront one another, and the vision of a director joins forces with the ideas of a playwright. When these elements strike one another with the proper force they set off sparks which light up the sky and illuminate the soul.

"Playwright Peter Shaffer understands this well, for in his new play *Equus,* which has just opened at the Plymouth Theater, he has brilliantly brought together several elemental forces of the theater. Though rare, there are plays which move us to tears and affect us deeply; they appeal to our emotions. There are other plays, equally rare, which provoke thought and appeal to our intellect. Rarer than either, however, are plays which combine the two: which strike a body blow to the gut at the same time that they set the wheels of thought spinning in our brain. Mr. Shaffer's *Equus* is just such a play.

"On one level the play is a psychiatric detective story. . . . On another level, the play is symbolic. . . .

"There are other levels to the play. Grand designs are set beside small human touches. . . .

"The play has many levels, therefore, but Mr. Shaffer has not set his ideas spinning on separate reels which never strike a common note. He has joined the heart to the mind and the symbolic to the real. The levels of his play bounce off one another; they collide, combine, and coalesce to form a texture of immense complexity. That alone is a significant achievement.

"With the collaboration of Mr. Dexter and his actors, Mr. Shaffer's words do become flesh. We do not merely hear about passion and worship; we are shown passion and worship as it unfolds before us on stage, and we take part in it ourselves. Mr. Shaffer's play is about many things—the Nietzschean conflict between the Dionysian and Apollonian impulses, the problems of normalcy and the attributes of insanity, the need we have to worship a god—and these ideas will be analyzed and criticized for some time to come. But like any exciting work in the theater, initially it should not be dissected; it should be seen and experienced. By combining so skillfully the primal elements of theater, by saying so much on the one hand and leaving so much to our imaginations on the other, *Equus* becomes one of the most powerful and provocative theatrical experiences of our time."

Finally, some opinions about Tennessee Williams' dark and enigmatic play *Out Cry* (1973), which was unsuccessful. Extracts from several critics are presented concluding with Edwin Wilson.

First, a respectful if dissident voice from T. E. Kalem (*Time*):

"It is because Tennessee Williams once was just such an artist that the appearance of *Out Cry* is immensely saddening. Here, the man who suffers and the mind which creates are no more separate than a drunk and his crying jag. In the plays that earned Williams his reputation as America's finest dramatist, he showed that he could impose the order of art on his darkling terrors and forge passion and compassion out of pain. *Out Cry* is devoid of those gifts. . . .

"A Williams groping for words, parched for images, fumbling in dramatic craft—all this seems incredible, but alas, it is true."

Richard Watts (*New York Post*) had this to say:

"The most remarkable thing about it is, that for all its continuous befuddlement, it is almost steadily interesting."

Both respectful, one "saddened," the other found it "interesting." Now comes Martin Gottfried, who saw only Act One:

"Merrick's [the producer's] presumed intentions are appreciable but, I think, misguided, for they are tantamount to humoring and pampering, when what Williams needs is tougher judgment than ever before. . . .

"The relationship between the brother and sister is never developed beyond the basic fact of its being incestuous.

"Even that is suspect since the sister is plainly a homosexual-substitute, Williams evidently feeling that incest is more palatable to general audiences than homosexuality. In these days of gay liberation, such theatrical subterfuge is even more absurd than it always was.

"Given the shapeless, aimless, self-indulgent script, with its embarassing use of the theater as a confessional, autobiographical medium and therapy, the actors could only pretend to play. . . .

"I spent the whole first act fearing abusive shouts from the audience to the play, its author and the actors, and left at the intermission, relieved that if such a possible and awful thing was to happen, at least I had not witnessed it."

Once again, Gottfried would deal roughly with a playwright whose work he disliked, saw only part of the play and failed to comprehend what he did see. Once again he alone finds a character "plainly a homosexual-substitute" (Williams was indeed writing about himself and his sister). Gottfried, like Wozzeck, sees blood everywhere, even in the sunset.

In contrast and strongly apropos, Karyl Roosevelt wrote an adverse review of Williams' recent novel, *Moise and the World of Reason,* in *The New York Times Book Review* of July 13, 1973. However, in the final paragraph, the writer said with appropriate respect: "Yet Tennessee Williams cannot be permanently fuddled. He's too good for this scrappy book and there will be more to come."

Doesn't the author of *The Glass Menagerie, A Streetcar Named Desire* and other distinguished works deserve this much faith?

In conclusion, here are some sections of Edwin Wilson's review which explains that the play was "difficult to grasp."

"Tennessee Williams' new play *Out Cry* is a difficult piece—difficult to grasp and, in the concluding section, difficult to endure. For this reason it is doubtful that it will have a long run at the Lyceum Theater, where it opened last week. But whether we realize it or not, we have a stake in it, and it would be a mistake not to look at what it tried to do and where it might have failed. . . .

"From the outset it is clear that the play is on several levels and that Williams is dealing in symbols, many of them an outgrowth of his own experience. It is a matter of public record that Williams has been battling a number of private and public ghosts in recent years. He has undergone serious doubts about his work, and in his personal life he has encountered problems which led to a breakdown. He has since recovered to the point where he is once more functioning well—completing this play and a full length autobiography to be published soon.

"Quite often artists transform such struggles as Williams has had into works of art. This, one suspects, is what he was attempting to do here. For much of the first act he succeeds. Everywhere there are reminders of his past. Even the set contains odd fragments from former plays: an old phonograph from *The Glass Menagerie* and a spiral staircase and louvered door from *A Streetcar Named Desire*. But they are not insisted on, and it is even doubtful if many in the audience are aware of the connection.

"As with the scenery, many personal references transcend Williams' life. The brother and sister stand on their own, but they could be Williams himself, or they could be autobiographical in another way: Williams has a sister who has been institutionalized for many years and of whom he has taken great care. Such echoes are searing in their honesty, but they are handled with subtlety and discretion.

"In dealing with the sense of failure; with charges of insanity (the other actors send a telegram to the brother and sister telling them they are insane); and with the need to go on 'Sometimes the impossible is necessary') Williams translates his own anguish into a broader vision which has meaning for us all. There are sections in the play more powerful than anything he has written since his halcyon days.

"But he cannot maintain it. Time and again, at the point where we have accepted his theatrical metaphor and entered his world, he loses his objectivity and crosses the line from artistic statement to personal disclosure. Having set up an atmosphere of madness or hysteria he comments on it once too often, or he introduces self-conscious lines.

"In some cases these are small transgressions but their sum total is that for all the play's incandescence and poetic excitement it does not fulfill its promise. If that is the case, one might wonder, why bother? In the Broadway ledger a miss is as good as a mile. We bother partly because it is Tennessee Williams and he is a writer of proven talent. He seems to have recovered some of his former powers and it would be good for him to recover them all.

"In a broader sense, however, we bother because his loss is our loss and this due to the plight of the serious play on Broadway. The situation is dire indeed. . . .

"And so, when a playwright—and particularly one of our best—does not altogether succeed, we are the poorer for it. The out cry in Williams title is a cry for help. In this case, it takes on a special meaning for theater-goers."

This last excerpt reveals Wilson's best qualities. He is respectful of a leading playwright, even in that playwright's failure. He bothers to analyze the play without excoriating it or its author. He relates the play to its sensitive talented author and its failure to the Broadway theater. Wilson is a critic, a humanist, and a credit to his *Journal.*

JOHN BEAUFORT

The Christian Science Monitor's (daily circulation 200,000) John Beaufort* writes for readers in a wide area in a publication that somewhat resembles Washington's *National Observer* in that both contain besides news coverage, many feature articles pertaining to fine arts and letters as well as cultural critiques. These are in particular contrast to the New York *Daily News'* many feature columns that deal with more popular subjects.

In Beaufort's reviews of New York theater openings, his gentle tone is consistent with the paper's mood. He is a lover of the theater and his attitude most often is one of encouragement. As an example, here is an excerpt from a 1973 coverage of the City Center Acting Company's production of Chekhov's *The Three Sisters.*

"The City Center Acting Company has launched a three-and-a-half-week repertory season with a limpid and moving production of *The Three Sisters*. It confirms the earlier displayed promise of the young troupe. The virtues of the performance staged by Boris Tumarin begin with the clarity of each characterization. Mr. Tumarin has guided his youthful players in a way that takes advantage of their most evident capacities at this point: forthrightness, ardor, and a sensitive idealism that dedicates itself to the text.

"Inevitably, some of the company's players fill roles beyond their age, and this is a problem. There is also the fact that plumbing the full depths of a dramatist like Chekhov requires experience and maturity.

"Yet there are riches and rewards aplenty in the beautifully composed production at the Billy Rose Theater. No essential element is

*Born in Canada in 1912, Beaufort attended public and private schools there and in the United States, and Rollins College in Florida. He began his career as a copy boy at the *Christian Science Monitor,* and after filling various news and feature assignments, became a member of the paper's theater and film department. In 1939 he became New York resident dramatic critic. After service as the paper's war correspondent overseas, he became chief of the *Monitor's* New York News Bureau, then editor of the Arts and Magazine section, and finally resumed his position in 1951 as New York dramatic and film critic. He subsequently served in other departments in London, Boston, and New York and has contributed Broadway reviews to *The Times* (London). He has lectured extensively to college and community audiences.

slighted. All the tenderness, gallantry, foolishness, and pathos of these turn-of-the-century Russians as Chekhov perceived them come vividly to life. . . .

"The company at the Billy Rose achieves a performance transparency which enables us to perceive once more the humor and humanity, the hope and despair, the devotion and the sometimes heartbreaking happiness of this lovely play."

Here there are neither extravagant claims of superiority, perfection, nor cries of delinquency, but acknowledgment of "forthrightness, ardor, and a sensitive idealism." Beaufort, while recognizing a lack of "experience and maturity," accentuates the company's virtues. This is a fair statement in behalf of a young, serious group that is obviously trying hard to sustain itself while it strives to grow. This attitude is exemplified by Thierry Maulinier's comment on Colette as critic: "There is no true criticism without charity."

In line with the preceding review and its intent is a 1959 piece about a talented playwright's first Broadway offering—Lorraine Hansberry's *A Raisin in the Sun,* a "black" play seen at a time when black plays were nearly unique.

"Quite apart from its appeal as a lively, poignant, stimulating comedy about believable human beings and their problems, *A Raisin in the Sun* embodies several remarkable achievements. Lorraine Hansberry, its 28-year-old author, makes her debut at the Ethel Barrymore Theater as the first Negro woman to achieve a Broadway production. It is also reportedly the first Broadway offering staged by a Negro (Lloyd Richards). It elevates Sidney Poitier to New York stardom. And incidentally, Philip Rose and David J. Cogan, the producers, are theatrical neophytes.

"Miss Hansberry borrows her title from a poetic question posed by Langston Hughes—

> What happens to a dream deferred
> Does it dry up
> Like a raisin in the sun?

"Miss Hansberry wisely refrains from attempting to impose an answer. With an intuitive talent for the establishment and development of character, she allows the Younger family to grow and mature as they begin to distinguish between false dreams and true. . . .

"*A Raisin in the Sun* surmounts such shortcomings as a fairly obvious plot by the authenticity of its dialogue, its candor, honesty of character delineation, and lack of special pleading. The attitude is preserved in Mr. Richards' direction."

This review does not patronize but accentuates the play's virtues while not ignoring what Beaufort considers to be its shortcomings.

The year 1956 marked the American debut of Samuel Beckett's *Waiting for Godot,* a play so new as to have been predictably controversial especially at that time. While offering no specific interpretation, Beaufort trusted the experience he *felt* plus his intuitions and he wrote impressions that now, nearly two decades later, seem to have struck pay dirt.

"*Waiting for Godot* is an extravagant illustration of the theory, shared by this reviewer, that a stage play may take any dramatic form that can be put on a stage. Mr. Myerberg, whose affinity for the unconventional has previously exhibited itself in such ventures as *The Skin of Our Teeth* and *Lute Song,* has outdone himself with the present venture. Or perhaps it would be more accurate to say that he has been outdone by Mr. Beckett. For here is a drama without plot, action, or other conventional means of support which meanders with studied aimlessness from nowhere to Erewhon, and yet which casts an unmistakable spell.

"Out of the mundane inanities of small talk, Mr. Beckett produces a flow of language which, though scarcely ever self-consciously poetic, in the end produces the effect of poetry. Described as a 'tragicomedy,' its dire view of the human condition is expressed in dialogue which ranges from the hilariously sublime to the pathetically ridiculous. Almost invariably, the strange tale of Gogo and Didi comes to pause on a note of compassionate tenderness.

"Amid its ambiguity and volubility, its playing with and upon words, its obscurity, recurrent crudities and vulgarities, its pessimism and high-flying nonsense, *Waiting for Godot* creates an impressionistic montage of humanity's hopes, fears, superstitions, sleeping and waking nightmares, rationalizations, and religious yearnings. Such a report as this can offer only a sampling of Mr. Beckett's observations—on man ('There's man all over for you, blaming on his boots the faults of his feet'); on hope ('Tomorrow everything will be better'); on the play itself ('Let us try and converse calmly, since we are incapable of keeping silent' and 'Yesterday we spent blathering about nothing in particular. That's been going on now for half a century.'); on human companionship ('We don't manage too badly, eh Didi, between the two of us?').

"Near the end of the play, Didi remarks: 'What are we doing here, *that* is the question. And we are blessed in this, that we happen to know the answer. Yes, in this immense confusion, one thing alone is clear. We are waiting for Godot to come—. . . Or for night to fall. We have kept our appointment and that's an end to that. We are not saints, but we have kept our appointment. How many people can boast as much?'

"*Waiting for Godot* is absolute rather than program playwrighting. Some hearers consider this insupportable in a stage piece. Others, who accept Christopher Fry's definition that poetry in the theater is 'the action of listening,' find the Beckett play a strange, mystifying, sometimes absurdly comic, experience in the living theater, a work whose loquacity is often obscure and even impenetrable, but never boresome as acted at the Golden."

The following excerpted review deals with John Osborne's *The Entertainer* (1958), starring Laurence Olivier. Here is a vivid account of the play and the chief actor. Although Beaufort found serious faults with the play, his review piqued readers' interest.

"*The Entertainer*, which has come for a limited engagement to the Royale Theater, is valid theatrically because it is literate and trenchant; because it evokes an emotionally charged atmosphere in masterfully employed stage terms, and because it is subject to vivid interpretation by the brilliant cast assembled for Tony Richardson to direct.

"The spectacle of one of England's most renowned classic actors strutting and crooning and telling deliberately bad jokes accounts for much of the interest in Sir Laurence's portrait of a ne'er-do-well. But this is notable play acting. It gets under the layers of Archie's makeup as the entertainer moves between a seamy resort theater and the squalid lodgings where the Rices measure out their private lives in gin glasses and domestic strife. . . .

"As a study of character, *The Entertainer* is almost documentary in its observation. As a dramatic work, it suffers from Mr. Osborne's perfunctory plotting, particularly in the final scenes. As a statement about man and the nature of human feelings, against the background of England today, it succumbs in the end to its preoccupation with a character and a situation which are at core sordid, repugnant, and devoid of any genuinely appealing quality.

"The notes are sour because the emotional strings are false."

Archibald MacLeish's verse-play *J.B.* (1968), based on the biblical *Job*, found little favor with critics and ran for a limited time. In the following excerpts, John Beaufort describes the production graphically. He also points out what he considers to be the play's virtues. He is sympathetic with the author's endeavors without crediting them with total achievement.

"The production of Archibald MacLeish's *J.B.*, at the ANTA Theater, distinguishes with the work of a major American poet a theatrical season of prevailing triviality. Whether Mr. MacLeish's humanistic version of the Job drama ultimately achieves the place of a literary landmark, its immediate eminence is unmistakable.

"Boris Aronson's visual framework for the performance is brilliantly integrated into the bold totality of Elia Kazan's staging. A curtainless, varileveled platform—extended, and with steps leading down to the auditorium—represents the interior of a universal circus tent which has seen more than its share of time, travel, and weather. Mr. Aronson, a devotee of the big top, has caught the forlornly deserted atmosphere of a show stand between performances.

"The main tent pole supports a circular stairway leading to a kind of costume loft and, above it, a platform which also suggests a pulpit. At one point early in the action, a great spread of canvas rises against the cyclorama, like a film of atmosphere separating earth from cosmos. The global image of the ring is repeated in what I take to be an astronomer's armillary sphere suspended from above; the double circle incorporates several of Tharon Musser's ingeniously arrayed lights. . . .

"On first encounter, the writing seemed over-explicit, too self-conscious in its casualness. A certain rhetorical element is never quite surmounted except in the occasional passages taken from Scripture: they stand out monumentally. . . .

"If the poet's conclusion is touching rather than deeply moving, he is at any rate compassionate, aroused, humane. In the murk of crowding negatives, few western writers are willing to risk even the approach to a positive statement. Those who speak up at all on the big themes too often assume the prevailing Existentialist tone of a Sartre or a Beckett. The author of *J.B.* settles for a modestly hopeful vision. He leaves his hero with something more promising to do than await a chimerical Godot. Mr. MacLeish concludes his exploration of a transcendent theme not with a bang but with a whisper, not with a sunburst of affirmation but with a hopeful ember of love to shed promissory light in a dark circle."

In no way has Beaufort muted his adverse feelings about a less-than-satisfying play, but he has bothered to accentuate the good qualities in the work of a major American poet.

The following final excerpts are taken from reviews of two revivals. First, the 1974 production of O'Neill's *A Moon for the Misbegotten* evokes enthusiasm. However, in this review, Beaufort has not been careless with adjectives but has built and supported eloquent arguments for play and actors. A segment from the start of the notice follows:

"Among the pleasures of constant playgoing are those rare moments when the delivery of a speech or line elevates, intensifies, and deepens the emotion it is expressing. For want of a better phrase, this sort of consciousness raising is the fourth dimension of performance: something to which all the customary elements contribute but which cannot be measured on any precise critical scale.

"Such a moment occurs in the fourth act of Eugene O'Neill's *A Moon for the Misbegotten*, at the Morosco Theater, when hulking Josie Hogan cries out her love for the man she knows is lost to her and to himself. As Josie, Colleen Dewhurst fills the declaration with a passion, tenderness, and heartbreak that are deeply revealing as well as moving.

"With characteristic detail and deliberation, O'Neill has brought the situation through its long night's journey into day. The moon and the spectator have watched as Josie awaits Jim's promised but belated visit; hears out his agonized confession of degraded behavior at the time of his mother's death; discovers her father's shabby plot to compromise Jim; and finally cradles him in the sleep that assuages some of his tormenting remorse.

"But James Tyrone Jr. is doomed, haunted by all the unforgotten ghosts of the past, and Josie realizes it. When, after his final departure, she tells her father, 'I love him,' the declaration exposes not only her sense of loss but a depth of feeling to which nothing in her squalid life has ever moved her before. Miss Dewhurst conveys with a special poignancy the ardor of the normally rough-spoken country amazon. The moment punctuates a fine performance and proves, as it should, memorable.

"Yet Miss Dewhurst's achievement could not and does not stand alone. Its lengthy preparation includes Jim's lurid confession—erupting in Jason Robards' brilliant portrayal as if from some pit of remorse and self-loathing. Mr. Robards plays the part unsparingly. The context is completed by the indecorous Yankee-Irish comedy of the early scenes. Here as elsewhere, Ed Flanders exposes all the irrepressible meanness and mischievous humor of Josie's rapscallion of a pa."

In closing, I would like to quote passages from John Beaufort's review of Boucicault's *London Assurance* (1974). Here the "altered version" of the play that Martin Gottfried took foolish exception to, is found "to heighten its acceptance by a latter-day audience." The descriptive aspects of this piece provide a welcome guide to the reader.

"Mr. Sinden's outrageously affected Sir Harcourt Courtly is (as that Francophile himself would opine) the *pièce de résistance* and *raison d'être* of this stylishly extravagant re-creation of Boucicault's durable script. The program describes it as 'Ronald Eyre's adaptation and production,' which presumably means that it has been altered to heighten its acceptance by a latter-day audience.

"Altered but not diminished. 'Am I too florid?' inquires Sir Harcourt of Maximilian Harkaway, his plainspoken friend from rural

Gloucestershire. Sir Harcourt is referring specifically to his cheeks, whose cosmetic rosiness is about as natural as the jet black of his curly wig. The query might also concern the performance itself. But while the play-acting is sometimes florid to the point of hyperbole, the company at the Palace stays within the permissible bounds of tongue-in-cheek foolery.

"For *London Assurance* belongs in the honorable tradition of the complicatedly farfetched plots, the impossibly mistaken identities, and the assorted machinations by which playwrights like Boucicault achieved their comic effects and obligingly pat denouements. . . .

"Mr. Sinden's Sir Harcourt is a comic portrait of masterly detail which requires no retouching. His poses in the pseudo-Japanese manner, his pouter pigeon posturing, his disdainful stares, his ceaseless pretensions and creaky gallantry (once down on his knees, the knight can scarcely rise)—all these and more comprise the consummate caricature of a pompous ass. . . .

"*London Assurance* is premium fun."

Beaufort's reviews are simple and consistent, and they communicate his own experiences clearly to his readers. His judgments are gentle but by no means evasive. He is a lover of the theater and his critical approach is loving.

VARIETY AND *DAILY VARIETY*

The show biz bible, *Variety*, and its West Coast *Daily Variety* (latest ed., Vol. 277, No. 9) deal with the biz of show biz. They report on films, video, TV, radio, music, night clubs, recordings, personal appearances, concerts, books, and stage. They publish opinions (usually box-office oriented) addressed to the trade, statistics related to tours, grosses, trends. *Variety* contains massive pages of advertisements intended to influence bookings of all sorts. Commerce in entertainment is its stock in trade. Its jargon is its own and is based on abbreviations and slang.

It is not addressed to the public but to the entertainment business fraternity. It tries to predict what will sell—on the road, on the West Coast, and in New York. It also publishes weekly dollar reports. These figures are of great commercial interest and three sets of grosses appear side by side: potential gross at capacity, last week's, and the current one. It is obvious that this practice, translated, contrasts possibilities with trends.

An example of a pre-Broadway review has a Cleveland by-line

and concerns the then on-coming musical *Odyssey*. (Later, as *Home Sweet Homer*, it ran for one performance on Broadway.)

"Odysseus, the cunning king of Ithaka whose victorious return from Troy was frustrated by the enmity of Poseidon, has a few more frustrations to overcome with this prospective Broadway musical by Erich Segal and Mitch Leigh, staged by Albert Marre.

"Whether *Odyssey* can be brought in is a challenge to the best editing and rewriting of an overworked second half after the sparkle and imaginative first act. It is reported that at least 20 minutes have already been excised from the three-hour production.

"The ingredients are there. Yul Brynner, in a welcome return to the stage, portrays the lusty, flamboyant adventurer with a deft technique with the women as he is cast about from island to island on the way home. His vibrant stage command more than offsets a not-too-strong singing voice.

"Particularly promising is his meeting with his son, Telemachus, played by Russ Thacker. The youth's devotion to his mother, along with his own escapades, adds a credit to the show.

"Joan Diener plays the queen, Penelope, but the sound system was faulty on the opening night, and her rich voice did not come through. There was no mistaking, though, her portrayal of the queen who is sought by eight muscle-bending pleasure-seeking suitors headed effectively by Martin Vidnovic and Bill Mackey.

"Segal's book, based on the Homer legend, has the proper Greek flavor, subject to substantial cutting. The costuming, staging and choreography are the strongest points in the production.

"There are good scenes of Kalypso's Isle and on Phaikia, the former with Catherine Lee Smith doing a creditable job and the latter with Shev Rodgers and Diana Davila adding pluses to the show. Of the nine songs, 'Tomorrow' may click.

"Cleveland audiences reacted favorably to the show. The opening, scheduled Dec. 9, became a dress rehearsal and the actual premiere was held Dec. 11. Despite the Newspaper Guild strike which has closed both dailies, the *Plain Dealer* and the *Press*, there was strong business for the show, which is continuing its tryout tour this week in Washington."

In this and similar pre-Broadway reviews there is small attempt at making artistic judgments. The thrust is toward a kind of crystal-ball prognosis of box-office expectation.

Although the end product on Broadway is treated similarly, in New York there is greater attention paid artistic evaluation. In New York, the critic, whose signature is "Hobe," is Hobe Morrison. Morrison's notice reaches the general public *only* if the producer chooses to quote from it in a newspaper advertisement.

The following is "Hobe's" reaction to Neil Simon's (December 1974) *God's Favorite*.

"The story of Job with jokes. That's what Neil Simon has attempted to dramatize in *God's Favorite*, last Wednesday night's arrival at the Eugene O'Neill Theater. This time, the author of such hilarious comedies as *Barefoot in the Park, The Odd Couple* and *Plaza Suite* has written a parable for the doubting modern world.

"*God's Favorite* is a provocative and interesting play that doesn't quite work, but seems to be saying that in the face of perplexity and possible catastrophe man's salvation lies in faith. It is a show that may not satisfy either the serious-minded or diversion-seekers.

"The story involves a devoutly religious man who credits his business success to divine will. As predicted by a kooky messenger claiming to represent the Almighty, he is afflicted with material disaster and agonizing illness to test his faith, but refuses to renounce God.

"This is the most serious play Simon has written, but still contains many of the kind of laugh lines and funny situations that are his trademark. A few literal-minded may be offended by elements they regard as frivolous or even sacrilegious. Others may be amused, but see the comedy as a deeply felt religious expression.

"Under the fluid direction of Michael Bennett there is a strong performance by Vincent Gardenia as the sorely plagued but resolutely trusting title character. Charles Nelson Reilly mops up in the showy part of a witty, effeminate holy messenger. Maria Karnilova, Terry Kiser, Lawrence John Moss, Laura Esterman, Rosetta LaNoire and Nick LaTour are plausible in ill-defined supporting roles.

"William Ritman has designed two settings representing an Oyster Bay mansion before and after the holocaust. There are acceptable costumes by Joseph G. Aulisi and lighting by Tharon Musser.

"Neil Simon is not content with smash hit comedies, but has been trying to write more profound plays, and *God's Favorite* is his most ambitious thus far. It is not a fully realized work, but should have moderate popular acceptance. Even so, the author may prefer that to the funnier works that have made him one of the most successful playwrights in theatrical history.

"Incidentally, this is at least the second Broadway play about Job. Another was *J.B.*, the Archibald MacLeish drama and Pulitzer Prize winner of 1958–59. According to some authorities, the Old Testament story of Job was taken from an ancient Greek tragedy."

Morrison's paragraph beginning "Neil Simon is not content" recognizes clearly the author's aspiration which is the play's *raison d'être*.

The first paragraph of "Hobe's" account of the recent *Where's*

Charley? revival tells the whole production story succinctly: "As a Christmas holiday show for the family, *Where's Charley?*, last Thursday night's arrival at the uptown Circle in the Square Theater, should serve the purpose. It's a relaxed song-and-dance romp that will convulse unsophisticates but demands tolerance from Broadway audiences."

The first paragraph of a review of *Good News:* "If nostalgia and desire to see former Hollywood stars are enough, there could conceivably be sufficient public interest to make a success of *Good News*, which opened Monday night at the St. James Theater. On the basis of entertainment quotient alone, however, the revival of the 1927–28 musical is inadequate."

The first and last paragraphs of a review of *All Over Town:* "If the basic premise and characters were believable, there might be a hilarious farce in *All Over Town*, last Sunday night's opening at the Edwin Booth Theater. In the matter of dizzy plot twists and goofy bits of business, Murray Schisgal's play rivals some of the Georges Feydeau concoctions, but it seems forced and sporadically amusing rather than consistently funny.

"There are 17 people in the cast. That's more than enough for most operating budgets, but perhaps not excessive for a producer not unduly concerned about break-even—as Adela Holzer was with last season's *Bad Habits*."

Peter Ustinov's *Who's Who in Hell* opened and closed quickly. "Hobe" 's notice contained the following: "It's a lost cause, however. *Who's Who in Hell* isn't strong enough for Broadway."

These direct, unpretentious reviews are clear, commercially oriented, and without hocus-pocus.

In *Daily Variety*, published in Los Angeles, "legit" reviews are signed "Edwa" (Bill Edwards). The point of view is similar to weekly *Variety's*. The problems are only slightly different and are geographically conditioned.

"Edwa" covers shows before and after Broadway. He is also sincerely concerned with budding Los Angeles projects, and since the West Coast paper is published daily, Edwards' reviews affect the lives of local shows.

Edwards' abbreviated notices, while commercially oriented, are also artistically concerned.

First, I would like to quote from some West Coast reviews of shows previously seen in New York. The second paragraph and the next to last of *Sugar* follow:

"All of Wilder and Diamond's story is there, show being a literal transference to the stage. Peter Stone's book is like an edited carbon copy of the filmscript with tunes by Jule Styne and lyrics by Bob Merrill. . . .

"Overall show is a lot of fun. Full of laughs, but empty in substance. Morse's antics are the real trip. . . ."

The first and last paragraphs of a review of *Two for the Seesaw:* "*Seesaw* is the singing-and-dancingest musical to come along in a coon's age and its zest and zing are due mainly to director-choreographer Michael Bennett and a Tony Award-winning dancer with the unlikely name of Tommy Tune. . . .

"The Ahmanson stopover, for just three weeks, should bring a bundle of cash if word-of-mouth can go out fast enough. Just on the strength of the dancing, show could possibly go into a long run if a local theater was available to house it. (Move over to Huntington Hartford would be ideal—if it were possible.)"

The beginning of the *Applause* notice: "There doesn't seem to be a bitchy bone in Nanette Fabray's body and one would think that in the role of the supreme bitch of all time, Margo Channing, Fabray might do less than what is needed for the role. But Long Beach Civic Light Opera's presentation of *Applause,* the tuner based on *All About Eve,* allows Fabray to mould the role to her own limitations and result is superb. Overall, production is doubtless the best piece of musical theatre currently appearing in the Greater Los Angeles area. LBCLO's box office is going to be a beehive of activity for next three weeks and all that busy-ness will mean money."

The opening two paragraphs of *The Sunshine Boys:* "As has been true in the past 15 years, Neil Simon's name is magic at any box office. And it's no different with *The Sunshine Boys,* a current offering at the Shubert Theater, where tills are bound to tingle madly for the next several weeks.

"Also as is true with Simon, show is a collection of one-liners strung together with very little story, but because of Simon's special touch, to quote the musical Benjamin Franklin, 'the damned thing works.' "

The first four paragraphs of the West Coast production of *A Little Night Music:* "The Harold Prince–Ruth Mitchell production of Hugh Wheeler's and Stephen Sondheim's tune-up of Ingmar Bergman's film *Smiles of a Summer Night* is a delicate pastiche of valentine romantics and sophisticated bedroom farce. *A Little Night Music* is in for an 11-week run at Shubert Theater in Century City and will need a lot of hardsell word-of-mouth to fill the run at the advanced ticket prices.

"Directed by Prince with a certain kind of magic touch that only he seems to be able to bring about, *Music* is simultaneously a comic operetta, a new form of high musical comedy and frosted Rabelaisian romp amongst turn-of-the-century 'beautiful people.'

"Greatest asset is Sondheim's lyrics which capture the mood of the piece and round out each of the characters with fresh clarity and clever rhetoric."

Whispers on the Wind was a beguiling but unsuccessful off-Broadway show (twice) in New York. The first paragraph of Edwards' notice follows: "After a number of not-so-good efforts at its new home, Theatre Rapport has come up with a winner that might possibly play all summer if group's schedule permits it. It's *Whispers on the Wind*, a charming little musical in the light vein of *The Fantasticks* that starts out sort of like *Spoonriver Anthology* and ends up in a manner similar to Gordon Jenkins' *Manhattan Tower*."

The Center Theater Group played a revival of *Saint Joan*; Edwards' last paragraph about it follows:
"This offering is a strike-out for CTG Ahmanson which would be okay if it were just a show that doesn't make it and producers could take their lumps and go on to the next one. But it's locked in to the subscription season with an assured run. Subscription buyers might even see it as just a bad apple in the barrel and feel the rest of the season has been and will be better. But the students who will be going are the ones who are likely to be hurt. If this is representational 'professional' theater, then they are getting the wrong kind of education in setting standards for what to expect in 'good' theater."

The first paragraph of the review of *The River Niger:* "Life amongst the brownstown dwellers in Harlem can't be all as tidy as Joseph A. Walker makes it for Johnny Williams' family in *The River Niger*, else there would be no reason for the militant uprisings that have developed over the last 100 years."

Variety and *Daily Variety* fulfil their unusual assignments in a simple unadorned manner which is the prerequisite of these periodicals' public. The writers say what they have to say directly. They are concerned with the *business* of theater, although both Morrison and Edwards do consider other aspects. One admirable view of their work must be pointed out: neither writer is snide. Both report what they see, feel, and believe, and both are succinct. These are not inconsiderable accomplishments for reviewers.

ALLAN WALLACH

Long Island's leading newspaper, *Newsday*, grows in influence in direct proportion to the exodus from New York City. It has a daily circulation of 452,586, and sells almost as many copies on Sunday.

Recently with the retirement of George Oppenheimer as daily theater reviewer, Allan Wallach* became his successor.

Allan Wallach is a fair judge of quality in the theater, and what he has to say is clear, consistent, and communicative.

I should like to commence with Wallach's entire review of Roy Dotrice in John Aubrey's *Brief Lives* because this piece describes plainly what the production was like as a script, what it looked like, the style of the presentation and the actor's quality in the solo role. There is plenty of contagious enthusiasm in this review and no bias.

"In the seven years since Roy Dotrice first performed *Brief Lives* in London and New York, it has become the standard against which all other one-man shows are measured. Last night, he returned to Broadway to show why.

"Dotrice's performance as John Aubrey, the 17th-Century biographer, antiquary and man of letters, is an extraordinary amalgam of the actor's skills. At the Booth Theater, he is creating a portrait of a solitary old man with a lifetime of memories for company that is colored by humanity, warmth, humor, wit and—despite the great age of his subject—the savor of life. It is truly a one-man show for all seasons.

"He emerges from sleep, his face waxen and his beard dingy-white, to shuffle through lodgings of incredible clutter (Julia Trevelyan Oman's canny setting), a labyrinth of tables, dressers, piles of dusty papers, stuffed animals, carvings, game hanging beside an oven, a suit of armor, a glowing fireplace. He turns the act of getting dressed into an acrobat's trick, and the task of boiling milk over a burning log into a clown's routine. He speaks in a high-pitched voice encrusted with age, cackling with delight over a treasured memory, pausing to direct a glare of mock reproof at someone in the audience who happened to laugh too quickly.

"There is never a sense that this is a young man playing a 72-year-

---

*Born in New York in 1927, Wallach attended the College of the City of New York and Syracuse University, majoring in journalism and political science, and was graduated Magna Cum Laude. He worked two years as a technical writer on radar, then as a reporter and copy editor on two newspapers before moving in 1957, to *Newsday*, where he served in many different capacities. He was named daily drama critic in 1972.

old—Aubrey's age at his death in 1697—but rather that it is Aubrey himself sharing his reminiscences with us.

"Patrick Garland, who adapted and directed Brief Lives, has culled the selections shrewdly from Aubrey's *Lives of Eminent Men* (better known as *Brief Lives*) and other writings. The selections, seamlessly joined, range from stories about the great men Aubrey had known or known about—Shakespeare, Sir Walter Raleigh, William Harvey and others—to funny, sometimes ribald anecdotes about lesser folk, ideas on medicine and education and recollections of his own boyhood.

"Aubrey had a wonderful way with a story, and Dotrice burnishes every detail to a high gloss. When the biographer wrote of Sir Walter Raleigh's execution, he noted that "he took a pipe of tobacco a little before he went to the scaffold . . . to settle his spirits," and somehow the tiny detail makes the scene come alive. Dotrice recounts gleefully how Raleigh once angrily struck his son at the dinner table and how the younger man, not wishing to strike his father, instead hit the man seated on the other side of him, saying, 'Box about: 'twill come to my father anon.'

"Frequently, Dotrice/Aubrey will begin by saying, 'When I was a boy . . .' or 'In Queen Elizabeth's time . . . ,' contrasting that time with the raucous age in which he finds himself, and the effect is as though some ancient veteran of our own Civil War had survived into the Age of Watergate to remind us of Lincoln and Sherman.

"The reminiscences of Aubrey's boyhood are among the most entertaining moments in *Brief Lives*. Dotrice's eyes gleam and the solitary tooth in his blackened mouth glistens at the recollection of the way a headmaster repeated a nonsense phrase like 'Crinkumcrankum,' or agonized over the long hair of his students. Later, as he observes how much learning dies with the death of a learned man, his expression darkens at the intimation of Aubrey's own hovering death.

"Aubrey likens the biographer's skill to the art of a conjurer summoning up the dead from their graves. In summoning up Aubrey himself so vividly, Dotrice is displaying a conjurer's art to rival Aubrey's."

Wallach's review of the late revival of *Good News* makes a unique point. This review is precise and keen, and though it is decidedly adverse, it is not abrasive.

"By now, the nostalgia musical has become so machine-processed a genre it probably should be discussed in terms of merchandising instead of theater. In *Good News,* at the St. James, the warranty covers all the parts so dear to the hearts of trivia lovers: A movie star of the past plucked out of retirement (Alice Faye); an assortment of songs familiar enough to be applauded during the overture (the justly admired 1927 score by Buddy De Sylva, Lew Brown and Ray Henderson), with dances to match; fashions recalling an era as it existed mostly on stage or film (pleated skirty, yellow slickers, pork-pie hats with upturned brims, all cannily designed by Donald Brooks); most important of all, a foolishly innocent book that lets us cluck over the good old days like indulgent parents."

I have not read a better appraisal of this kind of production.

Similarly in his review of the recent (1975) revival of *Private Lives*, Wallach is astute about the play, in particular about its "sadness." He is also perceptive about the character and its relationship to Maggie Smith's performance.

"Maggie Smith takes the role of Amanda Prynne and flings it around herself as flamboyantly as if it were a gaudy feather boa. In the process she runs the considerable risk that her performance will be described as 'mannered.' Well, yes, it is, but she plays the part as though to the mannerisms born.

"*Private Lives* is a comedy that almost cries out for artifice, and Miss Smith's Amanda is a contrivance that seems to be made out of sequins and eye shadow and odd bits of illusion. She underscores her sharper sallies with a quirky nasal twang, and she occasionally breaks a word apart as though she were applying a coat of acid to each syllable before reassembling it. When she casually dismisses a rival as 'fundamentally stupid' or gently admonishes her brand-new husband to try not to be pompous, clouds of malice swirl around the stage. . . .

"Beneath all the casually elegant chatter of *Private Lives*, Coward was toying with an idea of some substance: the relationship between two people who are unable to live together, yet unable to live apart. . . .

"Because Amanda's and Elyot's situation is as sad as it is combustible, Miss Smith and Standing play their scenes with just an echo of a sigh behind the banter. There is tenderness in this entertaining revival, even though it has to fight hard to survive in the comedy of bad manners and outrageous mannerisms."

A review of the Yale Repertory Theatre's production of a dramatization of Joseph Conrad's novel *Victory* is pithy and precise. Although few of us saw this play, Wallach gives us an excellent idea of what it was like. The following are excerpts:

"In Joseph Conrad's 1915 novel, *Victory*, men and women isolated both by their own imperfections and the remoteness of tropical islands are maneuvered by fate into tragic confrontations. The story is imbued with a theatrical sense of inevitability that makes it ideal for transfer from printed page to stage.

"The Yale Repertory Theatre in New Haven has done this as directly as possible in its current production, employing the Story Theater technique that was pioneered there. Characters step out of the action to address the audience as narrators, using chunks of Conrad's novel. This double sensibility that makes them both observers and participants keeps the production true to Conrad's novelistic vision without becoming false to the requirements of theater. . . .

"Conrad has cast his story as a conflict between the 'tame' members of society and the untamed ones who prey on them. Much of the success of the Yale Rep production results from the way it captures the ambiguities that keep his characters from belonging completely to either category."

The controversial *Flowers* opened late in 1974 and ran for only three weeks. The press ranged from hostile to tolerant, but the majority opinion was stinging. Some writers expressed their dissatisfaction in jokes, which, under the circumstances, was the easiest and cheapest way of disposing of what had set out to be an honest artistic essay. Some reviewers found the play too far removed from Genet who allegedly was its spiritual father. Others made sport of its quite open homosexual ambience. Many found it revolting.

The remarkable part of Wallach's review is that it presents a clear view of what he saw and leaves judgment to the reader, or, more probably, to the spectator. In this case, the writer is not avoiding judgment, nor is he behaving in a cowardly fashion. He seems to feel that the subject matter and style are so strange and personal that he does not wish to hand down a decision that would probably not satisfy anyone. He has not felt strongly one way or another, and so he has left the fate of the show to its interested audience.

"Jean Genet, that poet of perversity, creates in his words a subterranean world peopled by murderers, pimps and glittering drag queens.

"In *Flowers*, which arrived at Broadway's Biltmore Theater last night after an acclaimed run in London, Lindsay Kemp attempts a visual collage suggested by one of Genet's most important novels, *Our Lady of the Flowers*. Largely through mime and dance, Kemp offers a succession of images in which androgynous figures in whiteface move with a kind of frozen horror, like bizarre sea creatures drifting in the deepest recesses of the ocean.

"At their best, these images are stunning, at once beautiful and grotesque, as if Hieronymus Bosch had painted a homosexual vision of hell. But repeatedly, Kemp undercuts his effects with cheap camp humor that suggests he is not at all confident of his creative powers.

"*Flowers* has been devised, designed and directed by Kemp, a British mime, dancer and all-around man of the theater who also plays a starring role. In addition, he collaborated on the lighting, which plays a major part in creating the show's ambience of decadence and mystery.

"The show doesn't attempt a literal re-creation of Genet's novel, although some of its scenes resemble episodes in the book. Instead, it takes figures akin to those described by the French author—transvestites with painted lips contorted in anguish; a young murderer aware of his beauty; gay sailors dancing a ludicrous waltz—and sets them prowling through a grotesque mime show in which male nudity and homosexual practices are important elements.

"The measured pace of *Flowers* is somewhat reminiscent of the disorienting, slow-motion theater of Robert Wilson. *Flowers* begins with a striking scene in a prison filled with writhing, onanistic men, suggesting the prison in which Genet wrote *Our Lady of Flowers*. Wordlessly (there is virtually no dialogue), it moves on to a black, rain-drenched funeral that turns into a homosexual orgy.

"Later, in a Montmartre cafe where sullen drag queens and their customers saunter languidly, a transvestite in shimmering silver (Kemp) enters, her chalk-white face a ravaged mask. That figure, suggesting the character called Divine in Genet's novel, dominates the remaining scenes: She goes through a mock marriage to a grinning man in evening clothes; flutteringly takes him to her garret; loses him to a rival drag queen; becomes involved with the beautiful young murderer and suffers at his execution.

"Much of that is unfaithful to the spirit of Genet, whose underworld people achieve a triumphant sanctity through their crimes. Far from triumphing, Kemp's whitefaced figures are pitiable creatures whose characteristic expression is anguish. And Kemp's stabs at comedy—transvestites in ragged mesh stockings singing old Judy Garland songs and tap dancing listlessly—are from a world far removed from Genet's. This humor is reflected in the music stitched together by Andrew Wilson, which jumps from a requiem to the bleeps of an electronic synthesizer to snippets of Al Jolson and Billie Holiday.

"Much of this humor of incongruity is funny, as camp humor often is, but it reflects an uneasiness at the heart of *Flowers* that makes it partly a remarkable visual experience and partly a sister-under-the-skin to Charles Ludlum's Ridiculous Theatrical Company."

Finally, I should like to reproduce Wallach's review of *London*

Assurance, the 1974 importation from London. This is a "yea" notice. I particularly like the writer's saying, "the kidding succeeds because of the genuine affection that sustains it," and his evaluation of Boucicault: "[his] dialogue and plotting were more stageworthy than inspired." There is honest criticism in this piece, but the total effect—so important to the reader and potential theatergoer—makes *London Assurance* as attractive as I myself found it to be.

"London, which is fast turning into the most successful tryout town Broadway ever had, has now sent over for American enjoyment one of the lightest and brightest of its comedies.

"The latest arrival is the Royal Shakespeare Company's production of *London Assurance* which opened last night at the Palace. Like *Sherlock Holmes*, the other Royal Shakespeare attraction currently on Broadway, *London Assurance* gently kids the stage conventions of an earlier time. The results in *London Assurance* are still more felicitous; the company revives Dion Boucicault's 1841 success with such assurance that the production manages to be both permeated by charm and saturated with fun.

"Much of the reason is the approach taken by Ronald Eyre, who adapted the play and directed it for the company's 1970–71 season. (The present production has been directed by Euan Smith.) Although *London Assurance* pauses on occasion to let us savor the extravagantly romantic effusions of its young heroine or the posturing of an aging dandy, it is never condescending toward the inanities of Boucicault's plot or characters. The kidding succeeds because of the genuine affection that sustains it.

"The other reason this far-from-brilliant comedy is so entertaining is the deft comic playing of its British cast. As Sir Harcourt Courtly, an elderly rake who refuses to yield to the ravages of time, Donald Sinden is great fun. He mugs more than a stateroom full of Marx Brothers; under a wig of tight black curls, his rouged cheeks quiver, his lips puff, his eyes bulge as a look of astonishment passes across his face. To demonstrate that he still cuts a dashing figure— even if the figure requires the aid of a corset—he strikes a balletic pose guaranteed to strike a libidinous spark in the heart of any maiden not overcome by mirth.

"The production abounds in skillful performances. Polly Adams sparkles as Sir Harcourt's intended bride, Grace, who is determined to be governed by reason. There is fine work too by Elizabeth Spriggs as a horsey outdoor woman; Roger Rees as Charles Courtly, Sir Harcourt's amorous son; Bernard Lloyd as a quick-witted idler named Dazzler and John Cater as a meddlesome lawyer named Meddle.

"Their work brightens a play that Boucicault, the Dublin-born actor-playwright, dashed off in four weeks when he was not yet 20. *London Assurance* became an immediate London hit in 1841 and, like the current production, was later transplanted to New York.

"The comedy is in the style of an earlier era; Boucicault evidently chose as his models the dazzling comedies of Sheridan and Gold-smith, although he was hardly in their league as a playwright. He utilized the sure-fire contrast between the preening of a city-bred sophisticate and the simplicity of rustics, and tossed in such crowd-pleasers as scenes of mistaken identity, eavesdropping, and duels and elopements that don't quite come off.

"In Boucicault's handling of these elements, the plot is little more than a device to frame some sturdy theatrical stereotypes. Sir Har-court, his son Charles and the lovely Grace form a romantic triangle that is more comic than romantic. Charles is compelled by circum-stances to pose as someone else—a pose that leads to most of the complications—while Dazzle and Meddle do their best to muddle the plot.

"Although Boucicault's dialogue and plotting were more stage-worthy than inspired, his audiences evidently found the comedy a work of verve and charm—qualities that are retained not only in the playing of the current cast but the flavorsome settings of Alan Tagg and the costumes of David Walker and Michael Stennett.

"Only toward the end, when the playwright's invention flagged, do things begin to run down somewhat. By then, however, it scarcely matters; *London Assurance* is captivating not because of Boucicault's inventiveness but the skill of the company that is restoring it to the stage."

THE VILLAGE VOICE

The *Village Voice*, published in New York, speaks in behalf of whatever it considers to be new. Like all journals, its level of ex-cellence wavers. Although its leading drama criticism is written by John Lahr, many other writers contribute.

I should like to quote, without comment, the first part of a re-view by one Michael Feingold. Since the *Voice* published it (June 1974), I must assume that it was read by someone beforehand.

"Shakespeare, for some reason, has become largely a summer sport in this country. I'm not sure why. You would think, in a sea-son of trifling and lazy-minded relaxation, the last sort of theatre people would want to attend would be a great thick pile of blank verse and complex counterplotting, full of words and customs long fallen into disuse. Even granting that many of the Shakespeare theatres are outdoors, how can people bear to sit, sweltering and fighting off mosquitoes, just to soak up the flood of verbiage, meanwhile racking their brains to dredge up from long-forgotten footnotes exegeses of the tithe-pig and the buttery-bar, King Cophetua and the lady of the Strachy, for the purpose of hearing two actors pretend to argue about whether one of them lives by his tabor (because he earns his living by it) or by the church (because his house is next door to it)?

"Probably, it's because Shakespeare, as befits his intellectual bankruptcy, has gone into public receivership, and received ideas are just what is wanted for summer amusement. If we ever started performing Shakespeare more consistently in the winter, he would have to be taken seriously as adult entertainment, and approached at his own highest level. Which would make it considerably more difficult to perform and direct Shakespeare, and would leave the critical tooth nothing to mumble over, of a summer, except stock packages of Neil Simon, a fate distinctly worse than death.

"At Stratford, Connecticut, where the indoor theater is air-conditioned and the textual obscurities are minimized along with the sweltering, Shakespeare is not taken so seriously. Instead of being deeply explored as an artistic challenge for the audience, he is fidgeted with, for the purpose of making him tolerable to those who don't know him well, and newly 'interesting' to those who think they know him all too well. Shakespeare wrote a play, and therefore we must put the play across, with a few little explanations for the philistines, and a few little kinks and gewgaws for those of you who know the texts by heart and are bored stiff with them."

6

Magazines

THERE ARE MANY more weekly and monthly magazines carrying theater reviews than are included here. Some, like *Mademoiselle* with its Leo Lerman, have a national reading public but the reviews are not extensive and they appear too late to be of much help to a show in trouble.

The general level of scholarship among those represented here is high. The reviewers, faced with space limitations, have cultivated —perhaps *invented*—a style that, while it is somewhat telegraphic, nevertheless manages to communicate clear ideas to a wide audience.

These reviews help to raise the level of taste among the millions who read them and succeed in enlarging audiences when the three New York daily writers permit a show to survive long enough for belated magazine encouragement to be of service.

The Nation is read by the serious-minded few and employs perhaps the best of all American critics to assess theatrical values— Harold Clurman. *Time* and *Newsweek* interest an enormous audience whose first concern is news. T. E. Kalem and Jack Kroll are both excellent theatrical barometers. The witty and well-informed Brendan Gill (with his associate, Edith Oliver) inform readers of the widely read *New Yorker* about matters theatrical. This indestructible magazine maintains a high standard of adult humor that reaches not only inhabitants of New York but discriminating people everywhere. The *Saturday Review* has undergone recent and frequent alterations in editorial policy and perspective and now appeals to the scientific-minded as well as to those concerned with literature and the arts. *New York* goes in for sensationalism, places more emphasis on hawkish irony than on matters of human concern, and attempts to arm its small, mainly local public, with as much icy incivility as possible. Its critics are well informed but they put riposte above communication. *Cue* guides its readers to entertainment.

The following samples of weekly reviewing are liberally representative.

HAROLD CLURMAN

It is not surprising but shameful that some directors know little about their own craft and even less about acting. Similarly, many playwrights know little about acting. Many actors simply "act" without having learned any technique. Many critics know little or nothing about any of these elements technically and their reviews are mere impressions of what they saw with insubstantial judgments of what pleased or irked them.

Harold Clurman is a notable exception to these deficiencies. Educated extensively in theater, in Paris and New York, he worked as actor, stage-manager and as director of such distinguished plays as *Golden Boy, Awake and Sing, A Member of the Wedding, The Autumn Garden, The Time of the Cuckoo, Bus Stop, Tiger at the Gates, The Waltz of the Toreadors, A Touch of the Poet,* and many others.

Clurman was a founder of the Group Theatre, has taught acting for professional actors, lectured, is theater critic for *The Nation,* has been guest critic for the *London Observer* and *The New Republic,* and has written a number of books on theater and criticism.

Harold Clurman is one of the most knowledgeable, capable and fair-minded critics in the world. Many of his views on critics and criticism are combined in the introduction to his book *The Divine Pastime,** and I should like Clurman to speak for himself from this introduction.

For the reader of the daily newspaper (the critic) is one who issues bulletins in the manner of a consumer's report. . . . He is to tell his readers in no

*New York: Macmillan, 1949, 1974.

uncertain terms, "I like it or I don't like it. . . ." All these words are vague.

First: who is the "I" that speaks? Why should his assertion carry any particular weight? . . .

Second: what does the critic mean by the word "like"? I like pretty girls and I do not particularly "like" Samuel Beckett's work, yet I do not rush to a show which boasts a cast of pretty girls (I can meet them elsewhere) and I hope never to miss a Beckett play.

Above all: what is the "it" that the critic likes or dislikes? . . . The primary obligation of the critic is *to define* the character of the object he is called upon to judge . . . the definition should precede the judgment. . . .

. . . the reviewer whose reaction to a play is contained in such ejaculations as "electrifying," "inspired," "a thunderbolt," "a mighty work," "a dismal bore," may be in each instance right, but his being right does not by itself make him a critic. For those epithets indicate only effects: pleasure or displeasure. The true critic is concerned with causes, with the composition of human, social, formal substances which have produced the effect. . . .

For mv own part, I do not often know what I really think about a play as I leave the performance. Momentary satisfaction and immediate irritations frequently warp my judgment. My thoughts and feelings become clear to me only when I read what I have written. . . .

I would encourage playgoing . . . not by rave reviews of mediocre plays, not by discussing "genius" in every promising talent, but by being wholly committed to saying, with due regard to all the complexity of the elements involved, what I feel at each theatrical occasion I am called on to attend. . . .

. . . it is not at all necessary or desirable to judge every new play on the basis of that ideal (some absolute standard). There is even something inimical to art in such a practice. . . .

"Entertainment," "good theatre," "beauty" are not enough. We must know what these virtues actually do, how they work. The critic's main job, I repeat, is not to speak of his likes or dislikes as pleasure or distaste alone, but to define as exactly as possible the nature of what he examines. . . .

Merit in acting is weighed chiefly by the degree of personal appeal it exercises. The actor is rarely judged for his relevance to the play as a whole since the play's meaning to begin with is frequently unspecified. . . .

In a review of *A Streetcar Named Desire*, Clurman wrote about actors:

"The actor becomes creative only when he reveals the life from which the play's lines may have emerged, a life richer perhaps than the lines' literal significance. The creative actor is the author of the new meaning that a play acquires on stage, the author of a personal sub-text into which the play's lines are absorbed so that a special aesthetic body with an identity of its own is born . . . an actor who does not create a life beyond what was there before he assumed his role—belies the art of the theatre."

Later in the same essay, Clurman has something to say that relates strongly to criticism:

"It is substance—not the conclusion—of an argument that gives it validity."

In 1946, Clurman wrote a tribute to one of our finest actresses, Laurette Taylor. I should like to quote a sentence which transcends this one actress and applies significantly to emotion itself as it is received from the stage.

"Without being especially identified with 'mother roles' or the generally disagreeable type of 'good woman,' she becomes a symbol of the enduring woman, the very modesty of whose suffering is more personally touching than the martyred mother of heroic myth."

At the very end of Clurman's review of *My Fair Lady* (1956) he wrote:

"What makes me enjoy all these players most of all is a quality of *bravery*, a certain professional sturdiness and reliability which are characteristic of the English actor at his best. They are disarmingly impudent, self-confident and modest at the same time. They are entirely immersed in the fine task of being entertaining. They are our humble servants and have a grand time at the job which they have taken pains to learn thoroughly. What they bring to the stage is not their private selves, but a craft which has somehow ennobled them for our pleasure and admiration. The total effect is in the honest sense wholesome. It is strange—but that is how I would finally describe the show."

A section of Clurman's essay on *The Merchant of Venice* is not only arresting in itself but it uncovers another aspect of this controversial play. (In another part of this book, Walter Kerr is quoted relative to still *another* aspect.)

"I have always thought of *The Merchant of Venice* as an ironic comedy about 'capitalist' hypocrisy. Antonio and his companions —their whole society in fact—live on unearned income. Most of them are wastrels parading as gentlemanly gay blades. They hate the Jew for being a money-lender which was virtually the only profession open to one of his religion in the sixteenth century. But they require his money when they have been profligate in the use of their funds. After they escape the consequences of their improvidence and bankrupt the Jew, they turn once more to their thoughtless fun and games. This explains the last act, which is superfluous, even fatuous, unless the play is so understood. . . . He [Shakespeare] planned to write a play with lots of laughs and pretty diversions, a melodramatic comedy which would also contain the menace of a fantastic creature, a *Jew*, who in the England of his day was an unknown phenomenon, since the Jews had been banished many years before."

The following is taken from Clurman's review of Giraudoux's *The Madwoman of Chaillot* (1949):

A painful example of the inadequacy of our producers' and directors' approach to plays of quality is the current production of Jean Giraudoux's last play, *The Madwoman of Chaillot.*

Here is a play that may well deserve being called a masterpiece. It is a socially keen comic fantasy. It is a model, in one special vein, of what I believe the contemporary theatre should aim for: the discovery of concrete symbols whereby a vision of modern life can be conveyed through poetic and picturesque imagery. . . .

The Madwoman of Chaillot is a play that might be done in any number of unforgettable productions by a variety of talented directors. But in New York it has fallen prey to that commercial destiny whereby one of the production units least equipped to present it adequately has been bequeathed its treasures. . . .

The disgrace of this vandalism is that it is not deliberate. The producer-director undoubtedly loves the play and appreciates its beauties as much as anyone else. He simply hasn't the slightest understanding of how such a script should be translated to the stage. Indeed, he could not have realized that a production of such a play must be a *translation,* that is, a transference of material from one medium (the written word) to another (the theatre).

One of the reasons for this ignorance is that, aside from a few consciously trained theatre craftsmen, most of the audience—including a majority of the reviewers—is equally in the dark on the subject of what constitutes stage direction. Most comments on *The Madwoman* indicate that its present production is either regarded as an acceptable one or that the play itself is considered tedious! It is as if the manuscripts of the Mozart symphonies still existed but no one was left to play them except the musically semiliterate.

For example: the play opens with one of the most scintillating speeches in any modern play since the early Shaw, a speech in which the president gives a commandingly epigrammatic summation of his career and his philosophy as a financial wizard who has learned to turn unreal values into gold. The speech is read with ponderous complacency as if the author intended to portray a smug fool instead of a creature of electric intelligence and drive. The gendarme who sits down to drink beer at the café terrace and bets the gold button from his uniform against the madwoman is a type that must be played by a character actor like one of the men who surround Raimu in the *Marius* series. Instead he is played by an actor who is embarrassed at his own curious behavior, as well as by his proximity to the play's star! The life of the café is not created; the café gives the impression of being empty and one that is not much frequented, whereas it is supposed to represent a teeming center of prosperity around which the suppressed people, like inhabitants of a marvelous underworld, flit about to trouble the conscience of the evil ones on their sidewalk thrones. This calls for a series of Daumier-like impressions; what we get at the Belasco is a collection of small-part actors who have been made to feel that they are hardly anything more, because they have been given no specific image or outline to fulfill.

Finally, the madwoman herself is conceived as a kind of trim but musty elegant with a greenish tint, like a mask, around her eyes, as if she were a character out of some English Gothic romance. Giraudoux's madwoman is romantic in the sense that she is old and as real as Paris itself, with its dirt, its decay, its accumulation of ancient memories, traditions, defeats, wisdom. The madwoman shouldn't be played with that movie glamour which reveals a once-famous beauty upon whom an eerie shadow is thrown; she is glamorous because above the misfortune of her abject neglect rises the pride of age-long human experience—complex, majestic, triumphant. It is the essence of Giraudoux's conception that the spirit of the old Paris buried beneath the surface of the smart city must win out for a human order to be restored. In his sets—the first with its series of empty window frames rising and spreading in endless monotony like a throng of featureless faces; the second with its moldy riches thrown haphazardly in all directions like exploded and unheeded treasure—the designer has attempted to suggest some of this meaning. But our producers no longer know even how to read a play in terms of the theatre. In its transformation into show business, the theatre has become a dead language.

From a review of Beckett's *Waiting for Godot* (1956), Clurman again wrote of the conveying of emotion to an audience as he had earlier in his Laurette Taylor tribute. There he referred to the actress, here to the playwright's method.

"The form is exactly right for what Beckett wishes to convey. Complete disenchantment is at the heart of the play, but Beckett refuses to honor this disenchantment by a serious demeanor. Since life is an incomprehensible nullity enveloped by colorful patterns of fundamentally absurd and futile activities (like a clown's habit clothing a corpse), it is proper that we pass our time laughing at the spectacle."

In a discussion of acting (1949) Clurman makes the following comment:

How Chaliapin made his Boris what it was is part of the technique of acting, part of the mystery of "personality" which is at the core of all art. My point here is that an appreciation of the opera's music or words would be insufficient to explain or even to recognize the quality of Chaliapin's Boris. Something was made of these elements through the body and soul of the actor that was new and not to be truly grasped by a separate analysis of each element.

This last phrase, "not to be truly grasped by a separate analysis of each element," is pure gold. Perhaps many people have known it all along. I have. But too often, especially in the cases of some reviewers, a hasty scorekeeping tally is made, and at once this is supposed to account for all the faults as well as the virtues of a theater-piece as though, in such a complex experience, this type of analysis were desirable or even possible.

Clurman makes other points about acting (1949):

> To act on the stage means to behave under "unreal" or imaginary circumstances as though these circumstances were real.

This point is rarely understood by actors, directors or playwrights. Writers also need to translate what they write, when it is for the stage, so that it *appears* real on the stage. In actuality, even what is written is not real.

> "Interpretation" is a word often loosely used to indicate almost anything the actor happens to do with his part. More strictly, it should apply to what the actor chooses his part to mean. We call a writer "good" not simply to compliment his skill in the use of language but to approve his content. One may agree that an actor shows interesting skill and yet find in him a lack, or a falsity, of interpretation. Boyer's Hoederer in *Red Gloves* seemed to me to have very little interpretation, just as the Morley of *Edward, My Son*— part social wit and part actor—strikes me as an amusing and fortunate "misinterpretation."

> I have seen actors give remarkable acting performances in plays which they virtually wrecked. Years ago Jacob Ben-Ami played the name part in Giraudoux's *Siegfried*, a play about a Frenchman who, having lost his memory in the war, gains a high post in German diplomacy. Ben-Ami gave an unforgettable portrayal of the tragedy of living one's life without memory of one's past, but the play happened to be a comedy about the delightful difference between the French and German mentalities.

". . . remarkable acting performances in plays which they virtually wrecked" is a serious matter too infrequently comprehended. While this is often the fault of the actors themselves, it is sometimes due to grave casting errors.

One (there are unfortunately many) example of the actors' misjudgment can be illustrated by the London versus New York production of Jean Cocteau's play *The Eagle Has Two Heads.** An unknown actress, Eileen Herlie, achieved stardom in the part in London where it enjoyed a run of two years. At the time of its London

---

*Clurman in Eric Bentley, *In Search of Theater* (New York: Knopf, Inc. and Random House Inc., 1947–1953). "I saw *The Eagle* in a pre-Broadway showing at New Haven, and it didn't come off. Miss Tallulah Bankhead was unsuccessfully trying to turn a delicate fantasy into a beefy melodrama: Bankhead and Cocteau canceled each other out. Cocteau protested, I believe, that Miss Bankhead is doing a play for which she is not suited."

opening, great pains and haste were exerted to secure the principal role for Tallulah Bankhead for Broadway. The play was accordingly produced in 1947 in New York, where it received—the play, that is—a bad press, although Miss Bankhead was given glowing tributes. The American production was terminated after twenty-nine performances; Miss Bankhead destroyed the play.

Similarly—but not her fault—the Arthur Schwartz–Dorothy Fields musical, *A Tree Grows in Brooklyn,* based on the popular novel, *starred* Shirley Booth in what should have been a secondary role. Miss Booth was at the top of her best form. The result was a disproportionate stage-piece in which the two struggling lovers—the true principals—were put in shadow behind a great divertissement —Miss Booth—and the show itself was faulted. Ironically, it was probably due to the presence of Miss Booth that the show ran 267 performances. Nevertheless, the real values were unwittingly destroyed.

Clurman has the following to say about criticism (1952):

Criticism bespeaks awareness, sensitivity, discrimination as to the nature of one's feelings, above all and to begin with, an openness of the senses and the heart. Our critical severity is a commercial reflex: we don't want to be fooled—we must like or praise only what is accredited. That is why we have so much "criticism" in superlatives of praise or blame—both equally distorted. And the tendency of our official criticism is to imitate our practice rather than to correct it. Our practice consists in treating the theatre as a business rather than as free expression and play—even though the playgoer is not in the theatre for business.

In this way we are not only killing our pleasures in the theatre but ultimately the institution itself. When we measure the theatre mainly in terms of snobbish opinion or box-office profits (the two slowly coalesce) the need for theatre ultimately disappears: there are more rarefied pursuits to be snobbish about and entertainments that are more profitably popular. We often say that this state of affairs is due to the economics of the theatrical situation: I am sometimes inclined to believe that our approach to the theatre encourages, indeed necessitates, its ruinous economics.*

Here are, at random, a number of points from Harold Clurman's criticism which I feel are of great significance and too seldom voiced.

I do not see life as Pinter does. But it is imperative that he reveal his view of it: it is part of the truth. He is an artist, one of the most astute to have entered on the world stage in the past ten years. Those who do not respect and appreciate his talent understand little of our time or its theatre.

*From *The Divine Pastime.*

The decentralization of the theatre is not the result of any special "idealism" but the response to a need for using all our unused gifts.

There is little point in speaking of the theatre as a social art and ignoring in practice the actual society in which the theatre finds itself.

Yet in collapse [of the theatre] may lie our only hope.

There is no use in a critic's pretending that he is never influenced. He would be less than human—therefore a poor critic—if this were so.

Harold Clurman, through talent, experience, much thinking, and clear investigation, is one of our best contemporary theater critics. He is impassioned because he loves the theater that he has worked in and now writes about, but he is not essentially angry, even though—with ample reason—he is impatient with many things that ought to be better. Not the least of these deficiencies, in his opinion, is criticism and critical standards.

I find it deeply regrettable that Clurman, writing for *The Nation*, can exert only minor influence on the public and the theater due to the fact that his periodical is a weekly and its circulation is limited.

The theater and its audiences are in need of him.

JACK KROLL AND T. E. KALEM

Newsweek and *Time* are competitive weekly news magazines. *Newsweek* has a circulation of 2,933,158 copies and *Time*, one and one-half times that many. Both appeal to readers of better-than-average intelligence, are succinct, informative, and while the accent is on news—domestic and worldwide—both periodicals include up-to-the-minute coverage of business matters, science, sports, entertainment (film, theater, TV, music), books, education, law, medicine, religion, and art.

The number of their subscribers does not nearly represent the extent of their reading public since both magazines are familiar to airplane riders, visitors to doctors' and dentists' offices, barber and beauty salons, or almost anywhere people are apt to spend time waiting.

Inasmuch as both are weekly magazines, their theater influence has a delayed effect on any Broadway show. However, if the New York dailies have not killed the show at once, and provided, of course, the critics of *Newsweek* and *Time* have issued sufficiently favorable opinions, business at the box office will pick up. The out-of-town visitor—an important if delayed customer—will be strongly influenced by these reviews.

Jack Kroll and T. E. Kalem are sober critics whose opinions are well stated and clear. Both obviously have strong backgrounds in theater and evidence enthusiasm for it when they are stimulated to do so. These reviewers are firstly concerned with evaluating the vehicle—play or musical—and secondly with acting and production values. This, I feel, is the correct order of business since, if the vehicle does not work, there is, especially today, little opportunity of providing a satisfying evening in the theater. Once when there were stage superstars like Barrymore (John or Ethel), Nazimova, the Lunts, Muni, Mrs. Fiske and a few others, these provided ample excitement. Without having seen them myself, I am certain (Shaw and others have spelled it out) that Duse, Bernhardt, Rejane, Rachel, Booth, and others whose names still reverberate in our ears often turned evenings spent with such writers as Sardou, Belasco, and even their inferiors into hours of magic.

Today, in the absence of superstars and with more sophisticated audiences, the vehicle must engage us, and during this period of experimentation and transition especially, the interpretive voices of astute reviewers are needed more than ever to provide average readers with some positive point of view.

Kroll and Kalem are able, thoughtful and independent thinkers. As a rule, they neither oversell nor annihilate. They are inclined to raise the sights of the average reader and still interest the better informed.

Jack Kroll of *Newsweek* most recently has helped to parlay two shows—both meritorious in differing degrees and both crucified by the three New York dailies into hit and run categories: *The Wiz* and *Shenandoah*. (Details about these are to be found elsewhere in this book.)

Kroll is an independent. He writes analytically without being didactic or cluttered in the limited space allotted him. He is eminently readable and interesting.

The following excerpted from his review of Joe Papp's production of David Rabe's (1973) *Boom Boom Room* represents a loner view. Kroll is strongly in favor of the production without giving total approval. The show was not a success.

"Criticism starts with a spontaneous personal response, and I cannot remember when I was so involved in what was happening on the stage of the Vivian Beaumont Theater.

"*Boom Boom Room* is by 33-year-old David Rabe, the author of the acclaimed *Sticks and Bones*. The new play confirms something central in the sensibility of this developing young writer; his driving force is an intense, even anguished compassion for anguished people—the human race—leavened by a black wit and a powerful sense of the surreal nature of modern life which more and more is breaking through its mundane façade.

"*Boom Boom Room* is a courageous, indeed foolhardy play for Rabe to have attempted these days. From beginning to end the play is headed by Rabe's feeling for his heroine Chrissy, a feeling complicated, even confused, but affectingly powerful and of unmistakable moral authenticity.

"These are important and rare credentials for an artist these days —a heartless, repellently wised-up time if there ever was one. The go-go girl is a vivid image of this time—gyrating alone in her cage suspended in the pinball din of rock music, the eternal feminine lobotomized to an apoplectic travesty of its femininity. Chrissy is a victim; the men in her life are either studs like Al, who brutalizes her out of his own enraged spiritual impotence, or boys like Eric, panting in a wet dream of melted-down idealism, a no longer practical lust for the woman as goddess, mother and whore.

"There is a strong, O'Neill-like Catholic streak in Rabe. Eric's feeling for Chrissy is like a parody of the Jesuit thinker Teilhard de Chardin for whom woman was 'the lure and symbol of the world,' and Chrissy is haunted by the thought that her mother didn't want her—'My mother,' she says, 'made me nearly an abortion.' Chrissy's father is a former small-time crook, now sick with prostate trouble and his own rough nausea at the emptiness of life, who gave her vodka when she was a baby, voluptuously whipped her as a young girl and who sees her now as one of those 'hippie-groupie people' who both frighten and excite him.

"Rabe's play is so strong, so affecting, so truly felt that one is angry at him because he has let it get in its own way—it is too long, repetitious, overindulges in verbal shock, and moves uncertainly between the real and the surreal. Papp probably made a mistake with his first director, Julie Bovasso, whom he dismissed a short time before opening, taking over himself. Nevertheless, *Boom Boom Room* is an extraordinarily moving play, full of moral courage, remarkable insight into women as the 'other,' and a grimly hilarious humor. . . .

"Tighter direction would have helped Miss Kahn, but she is extraordinary in the quality of her emotion, her evocation of a fighting vulnerability, her struggle to seize the sweetness of her humanity."

Tom Stoppard is surely one of the most evocative playwrights of our time, often one of the most difficult to comprehend, requiring considerable concentration and imagination. Even with concentration, Stoppard's intentions can be maddeningly elusive.

The following (incomplete) review by Jack Kroll presents the reviewer's interpretation of *Jumpers*, which was not long-lived. While Kroll's view is not the only possible one, it is nevertheless lucid and goes a long way in a reasonable direction toward clarifying a special and controversial theatrical experience. This is a first-class example of the writer's fulfillment of a basic critical obligation. *Jumpers* was a 1974 production.

"We owe a debt of gratitude to the Kennedy Center for the Performing Arts in Washington, D.C., for bringing over from London Tom Stoppard's dazzling play, *Jumpers*. Stoppard is, to coin a phrase, a playwright of our time. To earn that merit badge his basic weapon is a luminous sense of the dreamlike absurdity of modern life. In *Rosencrantz and Guildenstern Are Dead* Stoppard stood tragedy on its head by focusing on Hamlet's two finky friends and showing that they, and not the tragic hero, were our contemporaries.

"A lover of logic but a luster after paradox, Stoppard in *Jumpers* attacks the biggest, fattest paradox we have—the breakdown of certainty through the proliferation of knowledge. He does this by creating an astonishing and immensely appealing theatrical form in which he both uses and parodies such genres as bedroom farce, detective story, science fiction, comedy of manners, surrealist dream play and more. It all adds up to a metaphysical farce that seems to have been written by an airmail collaboration between Wittgenstein and Groucho.

"Stoppard's play becomes a mad microcosm of England (and the Western world) in a lunatic state. His hero is George Moore, a seedy middle-aged professor of moral philosophy whose name (the same as that of the great English philosopher) ironically underscores his all-round status as a loser. George's career has ground to a halt, and so has his marriage to the much younger Dotty, a retired singing star who has long barred him from sexual privileges. Dotty (as *her* name implies) has troubles of her own, which are attended to by Archie, or Sir Archibald Jumper, vice chancellor of the university, philosopher, psychiatrist, lawyer and amateur gymnast. Dotty retired from show biz right in the middle of a song, stricken by the knowledge that men had gone to the moon, thus wiping out the entire realm of spirit and romance.

As *Jumpers* unfolds, the first two British astronauts have in fact landed on the moon. Their contribution to the space age is a brawl on the lunar crust when a power failure allows only one man to take off. At the same time the Radical Liberals have just won a general election, and at a gala celebration in the Moores' Mayfair house entertainment is provided by the Jumpers—members of the philosophy department who tumble on the side—by George's secretary who strips while swinging on a chandelier, and by the glamor-

ous Dotty who makes a mini-comeback only to sink back into
despair when she sings a medley of 'moonie-Junie' songs. The main
action is triggered when one of the jumpers is shot to death right
out of a human pyramid.

"There is a headlong, nonstop, delirious invention of insane action, including Dotty's attempt to hide the corpse, which has
mysteriously been placed in her custody, in her lavish bedroom.
Holding everything together is the shabby but lovable figure of
George, shuffling distractedly between his study, where he is composing a lecture, and Dotty's bedroom, where he manages not to see
the dead body and not to connect, as usual, with Dotty's live one.

"George's lecture, which is both a parody of technical philosophy
and a good example of it, is the heart of the play. In it the moral
philosopher tries with desperate bravado to justify his clinging to
absolute values—beauty, goodness, God. 'I don't claim to know
that God exists,' he says at one point. 'I only claim that he does
without my knowing it.' But he is the odd man out in a world
where professors of logic outrank professors of moral philosophy—
indeed, the murder victim was the professor of logic and that makes
George a prime suspect in the eyes of the intrepid Inspector Bones.

"George's chief philosophic rival is his wife, who sees the moon-
mad, logic-bound Radical Liberal world heading for apocalypse.
George crosses verbal swords with her, but even he admits that
philosophy has run into a dead end. 'Language is a finite instrument
crudely applied to an infinity of ideas,' he says, 'and one consequence of this is that modern philosophy has made itself ridiculous
by analyzing such statements as 'This is a good bacon sandwich.'
The beauty of George as a character is that he is a kind of metaphysical clown and yet he is the last humanist, clinging with mad
gallantry to his values. Stoppard creates a genuine humor of heartbreak, rising to a fine climax in a dream sequence in which all the
play's elements come together in an explosion of irresolute revelation—including the question of whodunit.

"The play is fiendishly difficult. . . .

"It is a brilliantly humane comedy about the only animal in the
universe trapped in the toils of its own over-developed consciousness."

To continue with Kroll's view of the new and the difficult, here
is how he handled Peter Handke's *Kaspar* (1973) which was "caviar
to the general." In the ensuing excerpts, Kroll succeeds in conveying
his own experience to his readers. He is at pains to interpret, to
translate; Kroll is not lazy nor is he a dullard. He has the patience
and the ability to elucidate and he obviously feels it important to
pass on to his geographically scattered readers his analysis of a
play they will probably never be able to see for themselves.

"Handke's plays are about the most explosive and disturbing action human beings are capable of: the effort to grasp one's own nature and the nature of the real world. His *Kaspar* was suggested by Kaspar Hauser, a 16-year-old boy who turned up mysteriously in Germany in 1828, arrested in a state of early childhood, unable even to walk or speak.

"Handke's Kaspar is a twentieth-century homunculus who represents the confounded, bollixed-up condition of modern man. As the play opens we see him garbed in a clownlike checked suit and hat, his features covered with a kind of postnatal film. Over and over he repeats the sentence: 'I want to be someone like somebody else was once.' At the same time he struggles like a comic version of Frankenstein's monster to coordinate his movements; he is unable to do the simplest things—walking, standing, sitting—without going into a scary split, a cross-legged collapse, a crashing fall.

"From that first sentence, with its anguished desire to shed his sense of primal isolation and join both his species and its history, Kaspar gradually shapes up into a reasonably coordinated humanoid, moving on to more complicated language sometimes under the prodding of four 'Prompters' on catwalks who call out to him through megaphones. As his 'education' proceeds it is accompanied by television monitors which play back, either in real time or in replay at various speeds, both his activities and those of the prompters. Presently he is joined by four other 'Kaspars,' dressed exactly like him, who perform contrapuntal or antiphonal versions of his activism.

"The strong intellectual and dramatic excitement of the play is in watching how the very process of .mastering reality leads to Kaspar's alienation from reality. Basic axioms like 'Become aware that you are moving' inexorably develop into the tautologies of self-consciousness ('I exist too much . . I am lost among the objects') and then into the fatuous maxims of modern man's bad faith—'The criminal is scum, but a human being nevertheless.' At the end Kaspar is drowning in superfluous, contradictory overawareness—the true tragic fate of modern, non-tragic man.

"The tensions, releases and climaxes of Handke's play are mirrored precisely in a superb production. . . ."

The following (excerpted) deals with another new play (1973) which Kroll appreciates and interprets. In spite of the flaws that he points out as well as his own disappointment he is neither belligerent nor abusive—a difficult and objective style that not all drama reviewers are able to achieve.

"The family may be washed up, according to the hip new thought, but young American playwrights seem to be having an awful time combing it out of their hair. In *Sticks and Bones* David Rabe showed the family as a TV-comedy gang that couldn't handle the moral horror of the Vietnam war. Michael Weller's *Moonchildren* were college kids forlornly euphoric in their false freedom from the folks back home. In *Baba Goya*, his third play to be produced at the American Place Theatre, Steve Tesich sees the family as a vocational school for the absurdities of American life. . . .

"Like other expatriated East European writers such as Jerzy Kosinski, Tesich's vision of American madness seems colored and accented by his experience of European madness.

"The result is something very strong but still unresolved. Where the families in Ionesco or Rabe are solidly conceived and believable as families, no matter how hilariously or bitterly insane their conduct may be, the family in *Baba Goya* seems too often to be a vehicle for Tesich's ferocious comic impulse. . . .

"Tesich wants that last word to resonate as the triggering atom for a new world of new relationships, replacing the old worn-out ones. OK, but his funny, genuinely alive play, sharply staged by Edwin Sherin, is a little too pleased with its own wit and energy; it lacks the shock that comes with the real moral force of *Sticks and Bones*. But Tesich remains one of the most promising young American playwrights, and American Place's commitment to him is a rare and exemplary thing in U.S. theater."

Still writing about new plays, Kroll tackles the successful and now much-discussed *Equus*. Along with most other reviewers and with a majority of the theatergoing public, Kroll admires, is excited by and recommends the play and production. He also points out what he believes to be limitations—elements which do not coincide with others more usually to be found. In spite of some basic carps, Kroll's review is a model of thoroughness, succinctness, and encouragement to a potential audience. This review is presented in its entirety (1974).

"As theater, Peter Shaffer's *Equus* as staged by John Dexter is dynamite, reminiscent of such other English imports as Peter Brook's production of *Marat/Sade* and Peter Hall's staging of Pinter's *The Homecoming*. But the greatest theatrical dynamite is implosive as well as explosive; it's a kind of instant integration of your faculties as well as a blowing of your mind and viscera. *Equus* provides one of the biggest blows in many years, but it takes a long time to pick up the pieces.

"Like most of Shaffer's plays (*Royal Hunt of the Sun, Black Comedy*), *Equus* stems from an 'idea,' in this case Shaffer's hearing about the case of a teen-age boy who blinded some horses with a metal spike. From that horrifying mystery he has spun out his play, which becomes a confrontation between the boy, Alan Strang, and a psychiatrist, Martin Dysart.

"Using hypnosis, a false 'truth drug' and his own persuasive sincerity, Dysart breaks through Alan's shell to find a boy torn between his mother's rote Christian piety and his father's rote Socialist atheism. Ever since Alan was picked up on the beach as a child by a stranger riding a horse, that animal has been lodged deeply within his psyche as a symbol of wholeness, ecstasy and transcendence. But the horse also represents Alan's dissociated state, as we —and Dysart—learn in a revelatory scene involving the boy, his beloved horses, and a girl in the stables where he worked.

"Having 'solved' the mystery, Dysart is racked with despair because all he can do for Alan is make him fit for a sterile life in a sterile society. And he excoriates himself for his own sterility—his sterile marriage to a 'Scottish lady dentist,' his sterile poring over pictures of centaurs while 'Alan is trying to *become* one in a Hampshire field!'

"This is a familiar theme of the modern mind, finding a psychological expression in Freud's *Civilization and Its Discontents* and a powerful literary expression in much of D. H. Lawrence's work. And Shaffer's use of the horse to represent the power and danger of the unsublimated instincts also resembles Lawrence, who went so far as to use a hobbyhorse to that effect in one of his stories. But if Lawrence is still under attack today for muddleheadedness in his attempt to body forth the struggle between Natural Man and Civilized Man, certainly Peter Shaffer cannot expect to get off scot-free.

"Dysart's attitude toward his patient echoes that of British psychiatrist R. D. Laing, who blamed disturbed behavior on a sick society. But Laing decided that he would have to include radical social action in his therapeutic armory; this is a serious missing element in Dysart's view, which stops at self-pity.

"It is, however, the most explosively eloquent self-pity you've ever witnessed on a stage. In fact, Anthony Hopkins's performance is such a brilliant flight of virtuosity that he almost overwhelms sympathy for his proclaimed impotence with the potency of the proclamation. As Alan, Peter Firth is equally astonishing; he and Roberta Maxwell as the stable girl play the most blazingly effective nude scene in our age of Total Hangout.

"Equity's rule against all-English casts always precludes perfection in ensemble acting, but especially fine are Frances Sternhagen as Alan's mother and Everett McGill as Nugget, the most important of the six horses. These are superbly mimed by actors wearing beautiful equine masks of silver wire designed by John Napier, who also did the stark and suggestive semi-abstract setting. I thought Shaffer's

play too pat in its intellectual substance, but it is a devilishly masterful work of craftsmanship. And John Dexter's staging has the detail, shading and shattering rhythm of the creative mind itself. As
pure theater *Equus* is not to be missed."

Short Eyes (1974), a remarkable and shocking play by a non-
playwright, is the subject of the following excerpt. Here again, Kroll
is precise in his reasoning as well as his feeling—the latter responsible for setting the former into motion.

"*Short Eyes* is unexpected even from that master of the unexpected, producer Joseph Papp. Written and mostly acted by young
ex-convicts, former inmates of the Bedford Hills Correctional Facility in Westchester County, N.Y., *Short Eyes* is an astonishing
work, full of electrifying exuberance and instinctive theatricality.
While it won't vie with Somerset Maugham or Terence Rattigan
in an anthology of 'well-made' plays, *Short Eyes* needs absolutely
no apology—it isn't occupational therapy and it isn't a freak show;
it's an authentic, powerful theatrical piece that tells you more about
the anti-universe of prison life than any play outside the work of
Jean Genet.

"Written bitingly by Miguel Piñero and directed like a choreographed whirlwind by Marvin Felix Camillo, *Short Eyes* portrays
the tragicomedy of people festering in prison like bread being baked
in a malfunctioning oven. The young convicts—heisters, muggers,
druggies, whatever—act out a violent and ironic parody of straight
society, complete with its racism, its conflicting codes, its moralities
that are hard to tell from corruptions. For the cons the supreme
sin is to be a 'short eyes'—a sexual molester of children. On this
one point everyone—black, white, Puerto Rican, Muslim fanatic
and tough Irish Catholic—all come together, and the short eyes gets
the book thrown at him, from ostracism to the indignity of being
dunked in the toilet to a final act of terrible 'justice.'

"The brilliance of the play is to show these violent young men in-
stinctively reaching for a balance of personal expression and communal structure. It isn't easy to show the paradox of destructive
impulses that want to be creative ones, but *Short Eyes* does this
better than most 'straight' works, especially in a number of powerful and hilarious set pieces, stunningly performed. . . ."

Here is a short section from Kroll's review of David Storey's *The
Changing Room* (1973). The writer has made out a clear case for a
remarkable play and is able to encompass in a single paragraph
what it took other writers several columns to tell.

"On one level, the play seems to be a documentary eavesdropping
on the changing room (locker room) of a semi-pro Rugby team in

the industrial north of England on the day of a game. It is transformed by Storey's humanity and beautiful craftsmanship into something subtly larger than life, a brilliantly clear magnifying lens placed over the vulnerable flesh of these worker athletes, for whom violent sport is an uneasy recompense for lives of subservence and quiet desperation. And Storey's inescapable use of total nudity becomes a moving ritualization of mortality—the scene in which the trainer dresses an injured, semiconscious player is theater as noble and moving as any you are likely to see. . . ."

The following section of Kroll's criticism is taken from a kind of United Nations series of revivals: plays by a Russian, an Irishman, a Frenchman, and an American.

I quote from Kroll's *Uncle Vanya* notice because, as is usual with this writer, more is said than pertains to this one play.

"Anton Chekhov was the first great dramatist of the modern malady, the first to dramatize the tragicomic fact that modern consciousness was so refined, so overcooked, that it had boiled off all its qualities, like coffee left on a burner over a weekend. In *Uncle Vanya*, as in *The Three Sisters* and *The Cherry Orchard*, Chekhov's characters are like neurons in a giant brain whose prolonged, self-generated thinking has resulted in a stupor of subtlety. Chekhov was a doctor, and in these plays he is showing us how the cells behave in a pathological organism.

"Because Chekhov is a great dramatist this organism is not only Russian society just before it was flushed away by revolution but the over-all society of modern Western man. The paralysis of will he diagnosed remains one of the most profound perceptions of our own condition any artist has had. He knew, and knew how to show, exactly in what mixture we are sad and funny, impossible and yet somehow possible. . . .

"How does an artist help us to live? By telling the absolute truth, no matter how dispiriting, and at the same time somehow insinuating that the shape and energy of truth breeds the appetite not only to live but to change life. This is what Sophocles and Shakespeare do, and it is what Chekhov and the grimly chuckling Beckett do. . . .

"Through an astonishing synthesis of pathos and absurdity Chekhov brings his microcosm to a kind of grand stalemate, forcing our own vision deeper into the meaning of these bollixed-up, ridiculous, exasperating lives that move, veer, subside and smell so much like our own. It is not 'identification,' but rather a detonation of insight triggered by an artist as original and shockingly effective as Cézanne in his ability to make us see."

The following account of Joyce's *Ulysses in Nighttown* illustrates

Kroll's acute perceptivity as well as his behavior in the face of dissatisfaction; it is cool, critical, appreciative, objective, and even
grateful. Contained in this notice also is a history, an evolution of a
performance and a careful interpretation of Joyce's basic intentions.

"In 1958, the production of *Ulysses in Nighttown* at the tiny,
rickety Rooftop Theatre in Greenwich Village epitomized every
thing that was meant by 'off-Broadway.' Going up in the shaky
elevator, you knew you were on a voyage to the impossible—trying
to put *Ulysses* onstage was a Quixotic fantasy. But as it turned out,
Marjorie Barkentin, working closely with that splendid poet and
friend of James Joyce, Padraic Colum, had turned out a brave and
intelligent piece of work that captured at least a cadence from the
heartbeat of Joyce's gigantic masterpiece. Thanks also to director
Burgess Meredith, choreographer Valerie Bettis, and most of all
Zero Mostel, the result was one of the most memorable landmarks
of the entire off-Broadway movement.

"Now *Ulysses* has been revived at one of the biggest Broadway
houses, the Winter Garden, complete with a fight over the direction
of Burgess Meredith, the purported intervention of Mostel and
other such blessings of the big time. The result is an ambiguous
and uneasy atmosphere that only the prepotent ghost of Joyce
can dispel.

"And prepotent it is. Joyce's Dublin of 1904 is the seed-city of the
modern world, a spawning ground for every soiled exaltation and
transcendently base seduction of modern man. And, in his parallel
with Homer, Joyce makes the climactic Nighttown section the
'Circe' episode of his modern epic. Homer's Circe changed men into
swine; Joyce's Circe is the madam, Bella Cohen, who changes men
back into their lustful animal natures. Bella and her whores turn
the guilt-tormented Stephen Dedalus into a drunken travesty of a
poet and thinker. And it is Bella who triggers the masochistic fantasies of Leopold Bloom. In the process Bella herself turns into a
man, and this scene, with Swen Swenson in whip-wielding drag,
shows perhaps too much relish in the scatological subjugation of
Bloom.

"Such pitfalls of emphasis bedevil this production. In one of
several additions to the text, Stephen speaks to the British soldier
who beats him up: 'You die for your country . . . But I say, let my
country die for me.' But in the novel Stephen adds: 'Up to the
present it has done so. I don't want to die.' Here Joyce's complexity
has been reduced to a banality.

"Still, it's intermittently exciting to see this lovable masterwork
fleshed out. And there is plenty of flesh, including that of Fionnuala
Flanagan, who does Molly Bloom's great soliloquy (or part of it) in

the nude. Not only does Miss Flanagan create one of the most beautiful images you'll ever see, but her authenticity of feeling and style turns Molly's four-letter words into musical monosyllables that shock you, not by their 'dirtiness,' but by their fierce and primal pathos.

"I remember Zero Mostel's original Bloom as one of the most thrilling performances I've even seen. Some of that thrill is gone, along with the relative innocence of a great actor at the beginning of his fame. But the amazing thing is how good Mostel still is. With a mixture of grave dignity and clownish self-abasement he goes through a miniature Odyssey, seeking in cold fact and hot fantasy to put together his fractured roles: cuckolded husband, hapless lover, sonless father, Everyman. For all the faults of this production, Mostel's sad and funny, tragic and triumphant incarnation of Joyce's immortal character is something that should not be missed."

From Kroll's review of Anouilh's *Waltz of the Toreadors*, revived in 1973, here is a brief but perspicacious section about the play, and an incisive appreciation of Eli Wallach's performance.

"In the preface to one of his plays, Jean Anouilh wrote: 'I suppose I am not very serious; after all, I work in the theater.' A civilized attitude, that, a bit sub-Shavian, with a not unattractive whiff of ennui, even of corruption—the pleasant corruption that upholsters the moral furniture of the Western middle class. Like a superb couturier of the theater, Anouilh divides his plays into styles, cuts and colors: the 'rose' plays, the 'black' plays, the 'brilliant' plays, the 'irritating' plays, the 'costume' plays. His 1952 *The Waltz of the Toreadors* is one of the irritating plays—that is, one of the plays in which Anouilh smiles, laughs, weeps and grimaces at 'human' folly.

"In this play you see before your very eyes the theater of the West at a pitch of civilized polish—the heir to every virtue of genius. Fair enough; in such plays, well produced, an intelligent audience is literally entertained—that is, held up, supported, maintained in a firm and friendly admonitory grip, like a child being held by a sage and cynical uncle who talks seductively of the bittersweet pleasure-pains of life. It is great fun, this eloquent caressive scolding, the almost lecherous scolding of a seducer who thrillingly tells us: 'What darling fools you mortals be!'

"Wallach is not one of your godlike thespians; he's a little guy who probably has to watch his diet and he has a squeaky voice with New York adenoids. But in everything he does, from Mexican bandits in dopey Western movies to a performance I shall never forget in Ionesco's *The Chairs*, he positively vibrates with a libidinous love of acting. As the general, he does a thousand little things and enough big things to add up to a funny and touching performance that makes you like, quite properly, both actor and character."

As the final review-excerpt dealing with revivals, I quote from Kroll's notice in appreciation of *A Moon for the Misbegotten* (1974) which includes an analysis of Jason Robards' performance. Kroll's view of the play differs from that of other admiring writers, but is without any strain for originality.

"*A Moon for the Misbegotten* is the most Irish of Eugene O'Neill's plays. The ineradicable incense of Irish Catholicism in which he ambivalently struggled and wallowed as a young man, the puritanism and profanity, the love and lust, the nameless, nagging sense of self-corruption and the proud protocol of a self-aware artist—all of these polar opposites appear here in their most 'ethnic,' one might say anthropological, form. And, although they are focused in the character of James Tyrone, who in real life was O'Neill's older brother, Jamie, they are of course the stuff of which O'Neill himself was made and unmade. . . .

"Robards gives one of the best O'Neill performances I've ever seen. His Jamie is a frayed gentleman, a spoiled poet and polluted idealist. In the climactic scene Robards gives an amazingly clear, detailed, subtle and powerful portrayal of a man in the fourth dimension of alcoholic fog, lurching between past and present, being wrenched about by his agonized memories of the train ride with his dead mother, his desire for Josie and his counter-desire that he shall not 'poison' her with the bad faith that has poisoned the others he has loved and lusted after. These wrenching transitions between time zones and psychic states are superbly played by Robards; his hands move in a piercing emotional calligraphy, finally coming to rest within one another, picking at wisps of straw in the aftermath of a gestural passion."

In conclusion, I offer a trio of musical review segments: one revival and two new ones.

Irene (1973) having been largely "created" for this production should not be called a "revival," although if history remembers it, it will doubtless be so designated. Kroll finds his own pigeonhole.

"*Irene* represents in conception and intent a barbarism older than Attila: the barbarism of naked, impudent commercialism. Nevertheless, just as there was something admirable even about the old Scourge of God, one must stand at least semi-aghast at the sheer, blazingly stubborn energy that this farrago of theatrical misfeasance has generated in its undaunted struggle to survive. This struggle has given the show a kind of perverse state of grace, a

weird humanness that—almost—transcends its original impulse to
cash in on the lotus-land nostalgia that has seeped into the be-
calmed spirit of the country.

"From the show's very first sound—a banjo—it is shamelessly
selling us everything from our father's mustache to the Sweet Little
Alice-Blue Gown that is the most famous of its museum of musical
keepsakes. (These also include the title song and 'You Made Me
Love You.') And Debbie Reynold's entrance—a pratfall—seems almost to deliberately dedicate this show to all losers who keep getting up. You watch Debbie twirling a broom, leaping off a piano,
showing her knickers, uncorking her tomboy straight right to the
jaw when the rich boy dares to kiss her, and you think: yeah, take
that, Liz Taylor.

"Nothing is too outrageous for *Irene's* wild-eyed determination
to sell you: Patsy Kelly as Irene's mother mugs like three Jackie
Gleasons, George S. Irving as Madame Lucy the couturier, passionately grabs Patsy's veteran breast, a chorus boy crosses himself before taking off in a flip. Peter Gennaro's choreography features as
much yelping as it does dancing, but it has a crazy lumpen-Dionysiac
ecstasy that gets to you. In a way *Irene* is beyond criticism; you
sense it *belongs* to somebody—yes, to those out-of-towners, those
affable Attilas whose moment this is. *Irene,* you made them love
you."

Kroll defines nostalgia in the first paragraph of his piece about
Over Here!

"Nostalgia has become a semi-permanent part of the American
psyche, and why not? Nostalgia is nature's way of telling you the
road to Utopia is blocked straight ahead, so swing around and try
the back road through the past. Revivals like *Irene* and *No, No,
Nanette* have tried to fan our flagging passions by turning us into
necrophiliacs—with some success. But *Over Here!* is the first show
to use nostalgia with good faith and sophisticated self-awareness.
In the process, the smart, talented people who made it have come
up with a show that hugely entertains you by hitting you where
you live—and where you used to live."

Finally, here are segments of Kroll's review of *A Little Night
Music* (1973):

"For several seasons, producer-director Harold Prince, composer-
lyricist Stephen Sondheim and their collaborators have been keeping the idea of 'Broadway' barely alive pretty much by themselves
with their attempts to update the musical form. Their new show,
A Little Night Music, like *Company* and *Follies,* deals with the
illusions and disillusions of love—and so it's of more than passing

significance that the new show is based on one of Ingmar Bergman's best films, *Smiles of a Summer Night*.

"Bergman's 1955 film was a subtle, funny, touching and even profound exploration of love among the not-so-naked apes of high Western civilization. But in turning from their brilliantly sardonic exploration of the great lost tribe of the mid-twentieth century, the megalopolitan middle class, to the turn-of-the-century Europeans of Bergman, Prince's team has given up something in the dubious pursuit of a 'higher' art. The two earlier shows made my skin bristle (A.E. Housman said that's how you recognize real poetry); *Night Music* inspired a cool, distanced admiration for fine work by superb professionals. . . .

"It must be added that Prince and Sondheim have earned the necessity to be measured against the highest standard—their own. By any other standards *A Little Night Music* is an emerald in a box of gooseberries. Technically Prince's integrity, taste and concern for detail are as strong as ever, and Sondheim continues on one of the most brilliant creative streaks in the history of American musical theater. His songs here, all in some form of waltz time, completely transcend the book (even more than they did in *Follies*) and set up their own universe of wit, rhythm and melody that does indeed have a bristle-producing power."

Whether or not you agree with Kroll, he invariably puts most things in perspective. He writes clearly, interestingly, and supportively. He is never angry, a fact that adds to his credibility as a critic.

T. E. Kalem,* reviewing for *Time*, provides an interesting contrast to Jack Kroll. Often the two agree in principle but their reasoning is very different. Supportive reasoning is one of their excellent qualities. Whether due to space limitation or preference, Kalem's writing is usually less fulsome than Kroll's.

The following excerpts—with a single exception—deal with shows that have been considered in the earlier part of this chapter. My own comments will be brief. Only the first quote concerning *Sgt. Pepper* (1974)—which was not included in the Kroll segment—is

*Born in 1919, T. E. Kalem was book reviewer for *Time* from January 1951 to September 1961 when he became drama critic. Kalem majored in sociology at Harvard where he graduated *cum laude* in 1942. His plans to attend law school were interrupted by World War II in which he served three and a half years mostly as infantryman in the Pacific. Afterward he turned to another of his interests—finance, and for two years wrote weekly stockmarket letters, then book reviews for the *Christian Science Monitor*. During his early years at *Time* and while serving as book reviewer, he wrote many cover stories on playwrights. He has twice been president of the New York Drama Critics' Circle.

given in its entirety. This is as explosively antithetic as Kalem ever becomes. Given my own "druthers," it would have been more violent, contributing as the show did, to the proliferation of juvenile delinquents.

"If a medical dictionary of the theater should ever appear, one entry would be a grotesque disease known as O'Horganitis. Its chief aspect is the metastasis of spectacle over substance. Its subsymptoms are bloat, inanity, hallucination, sexual kinkiness and contagious vulgarity. The disease reached plague proportions in the late '60s, but sporadic outbreaks still occur; and if one wishes to be mortally infected, the place to go is Manhattan's Beacon Theater where *Sgt. Pepper's Lonely Hearts Club Band on the Road* is on germy display.

"Exploitation is at the core of this show. The idea was to cash in on the popularity of the Beatles. Their songs are probably as original and innocently evocative of the flower-child world of the '60s as they ever were, but here they are trampled under the dreck of Tom O'Horgan's grimagination. Just to offer one example, his notion of enhancing a song like 'When I'm Sixty-Four' is to have two doddering floor-to-ceiling puppets paw lewdly at each other. As for plot, he tells a fragmentary tale of a Candide-like rock singer, Billy Shears (Ted Neeley), who meets and marries Strawberry Fields (Kay Cole) —the characters are christened from Beatles' songs. But Billy loses her to death and his own integrity to Maxwell's Silver Hammermen, Jack (Allan Nicholls), Sledge (William Parry) and Claw (B.G. Gibson). They are dressed in something resembling chain mail and apparently represent the Hell's Angels of the commercial music business. Billy's true bête noire is an extremely comely black temptress named Lucy. She is played by Alaina Reed, who is a richly dramatic alto and could qualify for a leading role in some other musical after *Sgt. Pepper* stops malingering on the road across the country.

"For the rest, O'Horgan simply grubs around in his museum of Halloweens Past and bemuses the audience with such papier-mâché wonders as a huge walking dental plate. The faggy odor of the show may be sniffed at its gamiest in a Beef Trust chorus-girl number featuring women padded out with lardy stomachs and grossly enlarged behinds. . . .

"Sociologically, *Sgt. Pepper* proves that the infantile youth cult of the '60s, the drug scene and all the militant minirevolutions are now a series of receding bad dreams. It takes a decadent nightmare of a show like this even to conjure up their ghosts."

Following are reviews of two plays by David Storey: *The Changing Room* (December 1972) and *The Contractor* (November 1973). In the first of these, Kalem assigns a "central concern" to all Storey's plays—an interesting and original point of view.

"Life is war on the installment plan. With deceptive quietude, that is what David Storey, the most remarkable playwright to come out of England since Osborne and Pinter, has been telling us. The theme comes clear in *The Changing Room*, which is having its U.S. première at New Haven's Long Wharf Theater.

"Playgoers and critics alike may be excused for having missed Storey's central concern. In his earlier plays, his spare, meticulous and almost detached naturalism tempted us into thinking that Storey was dealing in slivers of life, when he was actually showing us life being shot away. Almost nothing happens in his plays. Ah, but on any given day, nothing much happens in life or war. In these enterprises, tedium is as certain as death is sure.

"What are these segments of mortality as explored by Storey? In *Home*, Storey told us of the war against old age, quavering forays into the land mines of memory, desperate territorial imperatives like holding on to a chair in the sun at a home for the insane. In *The Contractor*, which also had its U.S. première at the Long Wharf, Storey told of the daily war of work, the campaign that liquidates itself with the setting sun and must be fought again the very next day. Man and his toil—Sisyphus *agonistes*. Men put up a tent for a wedding party and then take it down. That is all that happens, and it is like watching an entire life unfold and then fold.

"If *The Changing Room* is Storey's most powerful and moving drama, it is because he has found in sport his purest metaphor for the war of existence. The characters are a semi-pro English north country rugby team. Six days of the week, they are peaceable, nondescript employees somewhere. On the seventh day, they gird up their loins for gory combat. The changing room is where they come and go from their catchpenny Armageddon. In Act I, the men perform their initiation rites, strip down, loosen muscles, get into their uniforms. In Act II, they come off the field of combat, boy-toy soldiers, some broken (George Lithgow), all muddy and bloody. In Act III, after a late-minute victory, they are roaring, towel-flipping conventioneers with a communal shower for champagne.

"That is all there is, but it is enough to make this the finest new play seen on the North American continent this season, barring a miracle. . . ."

Kalem's view of Storey's emotion-conveying mechanism is explained in his article on *The Contractor*, excerpted here.

"One of British Playwright David Storey's avocations is painting, and as a dramatist he depicts still lifes. His detractors emphasize the 'still'—nothing happens in a Storey play. His admirers emphasize the 'life'—everything that constitutes the experience of a lifetime has been distilled into two hours of stage time. When playgoers choose up sides, their vehemence, all by itself, testifies to one thing: we are in the presence of a playwright of consequence.

"Though it was written prior to *Home* and *The Changing Room*, *The Contractor* may be the best play of the three. Few dramas exemplify with greater purity the classic concept of a beginning, a middle and an end, while adhering as well to the unities of time, place and action. To be sure, nothing much happens. In Act I, some workmen put up a spacious lawn tent for the wedding of their boss's daughter. In Act II, they decorate it for the bridal-reception party. In Act III, they clear away the debris of empty champagne bottles and strike the tent.

"The metaphor is not the meaning. What emerges subliminally from *The Contractor* is that life runs the inevitable course of the rising and setting of the sun, that it moves with deceptive torpor yet is shatteringly brief, and that the sum of all its tediously accumulated fractions is a melancholy zero.

"Rather depressing stuff, some may argue. In reality, it is not. This is partly because Storey peppers the play with a fusillade of humor, much of it of the caustic one-upmanship variety at which the British have few equals and no superiors. In *The Contractor*, as in *The Changing Room*, Storey reveals himself as a celebrator of communal male effort. The task of playing a rugby game knits the men of *The Changing Room* together in pleasure and in pain. The task of putting up and taking down the tent in *The Contractor* is not a stage charade. It is real and intricate work, a team effort that requires the subordination of individual and abrasive personalities to the communal effort. That is why Storey's casts always look like veteran ensemble companies. They have to be to get the work of the play done.

"This also reveals why Storey is a stage animal down to his bones and marrow. In any satisfactory theatrical experience, any single member of an audience feels a communion of spirit with those around him. That is how audience emotion builds so that the entire theater seems to erupt with laughter or stills to a rapt, absolute hush. . . ."

Kalem's view of Chekhov's method of dramatic composition is explained in the following passages from his article on *Uncle Vanya* (1973).

"Chekhov's drama moves almost in reverse. Instead of a conflict of wills, there is a frustration of desires. None of his characters do much of anything or expect to get anywhere, but all of them are aware of a nagging, infuriating immobility. Climaxes are anticli-

maxes. Precisely because life has passed Chekhov's people by, aged
them, defeated them, they bear eloquent witness to how avidly men
and women hunger for life. The laughter and tears in Chekhov arise
from the recognized or unrecognized disparity between the life one
wants and the life one gets.

"All of these elements are present in *Uncle Vanya*. . . .

"Chekhov's compassion for his characters' bruised hearts never
blurred the amused clinical eye he focuses on their petty, self-deluding
foibles. Chekhov frowned on directors who made his plays too
glum and autumnal, and Nichols, with his agile comic flair, has
certainly avoided doing that. He gets marvelous assistance from
Nicol Williamson, whose Vanya is compacted with a mischievous,
sardonic, self-mocking wit that not only defines his own character,
but also makes a comment on the situation of everyone in the
play. . . ."

Here, excerpted, are Kalem's interesting views of *The Waltz of
the Toreadors*. His opinion of Wallach's performance is in contrast
to Kroll's.

"In this play, first seen in New York in 1957, Jean Anouilh caricatures
the romantic attitudes that get men betrayed. It is a black
farce with a bitter personal tang, an overprotesting cynicism, a disillusionment
so dark as to suggest illusions once far too rosy. . . .

"Thanks to Anouilh's vividly ironic vision, much of the evening
is howlingly funny. Wallach has always possessed perfect comic
pitch and he displays it again here. However, he lacks that certain
panache which makes St. Pé a dualist with destiny rather than a
Good Soldier Schweik taking fate's pratfalls. Jackson is an awesome
virago who delivers her lines like bayonet thrusts. . . .

"The brisk playfulness of Brian Murray's direction somewhat
masks the vein of melancholy that runs through Anouilh's best
characters. Their gaiety is inverted mourning. They suffer with a
quip on their lips while stretched on a rack that is the distance between
the way things are and the way they want them to be. . . ."

From a review of *A Little Night Music*: ". . . the mood of the
evening is impeccably sustained and, rather surprisingly, it is not
so much jolly and summery as *triste* and autumnal. It is as if these
world-weary beings had sated their artistic tastes on almost every
experience except the simplest of joys. Designer Boris Aronson's
nobly brooding setting of towering white birch trees seems almost
like a comment on the frivolity and emptiness of the characters'
lives.

"Nothing lends the show quite so much strength as Stephen
Sondheim's score. It is a beauty, his best yet in an exceedingly dis-

tinguished career. The prevailing waltz meter is more suggestive of *fin de siècle* Vienna than the Scandinavian north, but why carp? In a show almost without choreography, Sondheim's lyrics are nimble-witted dances. Literate, ironic, playful, enviably clever, altogether professional, Stephen Sondheim is a quick-silver wordsmith in the grand tradition of Cole Porter, Noël Coward and Lorenz Hart. There are three standout numbers. One is 'Liaisons' (Gingold), a lament that courtesans are not the elegantly larcenous creatures they used to be. Equally arresting are 'Send In the Clowns' (Johns), a rueful gaze into the cracked mirror of the middle years, and 'The Miller's Son' (Jamin-Bartlett), a gather-ye-rosebuds-while-ye-may paean to the flesh.

"Producer-Director Hal Prince, who demands mere perfection from a cast, gets very nearly that here. He has curbed Gingold's hammy excesses, lit up the sexy enchantress in Johns, and released in Cariou a presence, as well as a voice, that marks him for the top of the U.S. musical stage. Ardent admirers of Prince's *Company* and *Follies* may be startled and a trifle dismayed that he has devoted his formidable skill and inventive energy to what is basically a bittersweet operetta. But then, the only predictable thing about Hal Prince is that whatever he does is the best of its kind."

Whether one agrees in toto with this point of view, Kalem earns our respect for his sober thinking and for what he recognizes as exceptional.

The fact that Kroll and Kalem contribute so tastefully, interestingly, and knowledgeably to their respective publications—widely read by the general public across the United States—is fortunate for the theater of Broadway. Both writers are thoughtful. Considering the geographical range of their reading public, both could do their jobs decently enough and yet forgo consideration of newer, less popular and predictably more fleeting plays than many that they are at pains to introduce and interpret. This is certainly to their great credit. They labor intelligently and well for our theater world.

BRENDAN GILL

New York has two weekly magazines which, in some respects, are similar. *The New Yorker*, with a circulation of 487,206 and by far the older, and *New York* address themselves to somewhat similar readers. The older is perhaps understandably the gentler. *New York* is somewhat like the adolescent "Frankie" in *A Member of the Wedding:* she tries hard, and sometimes with dirty words, to prove that she is grown up, when it is apparent that she is struggling to attract attention and to escape from her cocoon.

Brendan Gill, drama critic of *The New Yorker*, is grown up, while John Simon, in the other, goes through the motions. Like all weekly reviewers, judgments have little effect on the new Broadway show, which has often succumbed before the weekly arguments appear.

Reading Brendan Gill's reviews makes it clear that he is knowledgeable and that he is a member of the human race, first class: He is a gentleman.

Being a gentleman seems to generate beneficial side effects. First, Gill's reviews are seldom impatient. This suggests that his writing is considered. Then, too, critical destruction of an actor, a playwright or anyone else is not a help to the object of the demolition and it is distinctly unfair to the reader who is subjected to an irrational personal tantrum. The *bon mot* of itself is the *raison d'être* and is unconnected with any serious consideration. Anger or ridicule cannot be accredited to considered criticism.

What Gill writes is forthright, is based on considerable background; his judgment is never ambiguous. When he dislikes something or finds it imperfect, he is nevertheless able to recognize whatever good qualities it may contain and he frames his review in such a way that the reader may feel impelled to attend the show in spite of the objections clearly presented but not featured in Gill's piece.

Gill dislikes Rattigan's *In Praise of Love*, but is "grateful" to the playwright for providing a vehicle for Rex Harrison.

"Mr. Harrison is one of the most accomplished actors alive, and he has reached a point in his career at which, in part by the perfection of his timing and the unction of his utterance and in part by our gleeful anticipation of that perfection and that unction, he can make the merest scrap of a three-word throwaway seem charged with meaning; a flicker of an eyelid, an infinitesimal clearing of the throat, and—presto!—a pinch of wit becomes an epigram. The skimpier the play, the more resourceful Mr. Harrison, with the result that we find ourselves perversely grateful to Mr. Rattigan for giving us so little substance and thus requiring of his star that he give us so great a display of his magicianship."

A third play in the same article is Neil Simon's *God's Favorite*. For me, this was the fairest and most accurate of all reviews of this play.

"*Who's Who in Hell* was paved with good intentions, and so is *In Praise of Love*, but Neil Simon's new play, *God's Favorite* (at the Eugene O'Neill), consists entirely of bad intentions, in the form not of pavings but of pitfalls. Mr. Simon has dug these pitfalls laboriously, one gross shovelful after another, without seeming to notice how deep they are and how often he has tumbled into them. To my surprise, my response to *God's Favorite* is one of indignation. I would have expected to content myself with reporting that, despite its having been written as a comedy, it amounts to a grim and often distressing medley of trumped-up, unfunny jokes, ill told and thoroughly unsuited to the action they purport to embody; instead, I find that I feel more strongly about the play than that. I find that it looms before me as a colossal impertinence—a jeer not at religion, though Mr. Simon in his ignorance manages to affront both Judaism and Christianity, but at literature.

"The Book of Job is one of the most exquisite poems ever written; its words are always in our ears:

Where wast thou when I laid the foundations of the earth? declare, if thou hast understanding.
Who hath laid the measures thereof, if thou knowest? or who hath stretched the line upon it?
Whereupon are the foundations thereof fastened? or who laid the corner stone thereof;
When the morning stars sang together, and all the sons of God shouted for joy?

It is also superbly dramatic. The description of Job's many afflictions requires only a few verses; the rest of the poem is a series of debates between Job and three old friends, Job and young Elihu, and Job and God. If our ears (in Hopkins' phrase) are rinsed by the music of the language, our minds are ravished by the give-and-take of the dialogue. And it is this masterpiece that Mr. Simon has decided to retell, in the colloquial New Yorkese that one hears on the stage and on television but that is a parody of true New York street speech. . . .

"The Book of Job begins, 'There was a man in the land of Uz, whose name was Job; and that man was perfect and upright, and one that feared God, and eschewed evil.' Mr. Simon's Job is a repellent humanoid, who suffers and survives; good and evil and the fear of God are far beyond him. . . ."

What Gill specifies here is the playwright's dereliction in creating a play on as lofty a theme as the Book of Job, of necessity by-passing one of its chief attributes—its poetry, which was replaced with pale jokes—and with failing to create as its central character a man of sizeable inner dimensions.

Flying in the face of all of the daily critics, Gill—necessarily belatedly—dared to admire the National Theatre of Great Britain's production of *As You Like It*. Barnes panned it—if one can decipher his review—mainly because he had seen a star cast in this production seven years before. This means that Barnes did *not* review the performance that we pitifully few witnessed and many of us loved on opening night. Is Barnes' reason valid? Gottfried disliked it for his own muddled reasons. Watt didn't like it. The New York daily press was solidly opposed, and the show simply ceased to exist. I quote most of Gill's review which contains some learned reasoning and certainly no prejudice.

"I would have expected the National Theatre of Great Britain's production of *As You Like It* to prove a welcome addition to our current London season, but few of my colleagues appear to have found it as delightful as I did, and so it has departed from the Mark Hellinger with a regrettable precipitance. A pity, because the experiment that distinguished the production—having all the roles in the play, whether male or female, be taken by men—was an interesting one and deserved to have judgment passed on it by a large audience. In Shakespeare's day, women's roles were played by boys, and I have always been curious to know how readily I would be able to respond to this convention. Given that I couldn't possibly work my way back into the sexual attitudes of the last decade of the sixteenth century and therefore never imagine precisely how an Elizabethan twin of mine would feel about an adolescent boy playing Cleopatra or Lady Macbeth, nevertheless the nature of my response this late in the twentieth century would be bound to be of value to me; it would heighten my apprehension of Shakespeare the dramatist in something like the same fashion that a knowledge of the pronunciation of Elizabethan English heightens one's apprehension of Shakespeare the poet. (It is amusing as well as instructive to realize that the first Hamlet would have spoken his soliloquy with an accent and lilt not unlike that of any bartender in contemporary Dublin.)

"If how I might respond to boy actors playing Shakespeare's women remains moot, the National Theatre's production of *As You Like It* revealed that with no difficulty whatever I was able to accept men actors playing at least four of Shakespeare's women. The risk that the play might be thought to have been turned into a vehicle for mere voguish transvestite parody was easily avoided by the director, Clifford Williams; moreover, he made plain how much better the play works in terms of its plotting when all the actors are male than when they are not. For reasons that remain obscure to me—and that I hope are not deeply, darkly sexist—actresses who play Rosalind, Celia, and other prankish types are tiresomely implausible when the plot calls for them to dress up as young men, while actors who play young women manage to do so most convincingly. Shakespeare was obviously aware of this and of the comic advantage to be taken of it by contriving to have boys-playing-women suddenly turn into boys-playing-women-playing-boys. A

Pirandello-like ambiguity of gender appealed very much to the Elizabethan mind in general and to Shakespeare's mind in particular (his sonnets bristle with it); it appeals to our minds as well, both off the stage and on. The uniformity of dress and vocabulary manifested by the young of both sexes in 1974 would seem at first glance wholly at odds with the marked differences in dress and vocabulary manifested by the young of both sexes in, say 1599 (the probable date of *As You Like It*), but by a paradox they pursue the same goal: Shakespeare made witty art out of an assumed disparity between the sexes and we make wit, if not art, out of an assumed identity between them."

Gill's discussion of the male-female aspects of this production and its relationship to such productions in Shakespeare's day is laudable and he makes it clear that in his opinion "mere voguish transvestite parody was easily avoided." His reasoning that Shakespeare was obviously aware of . . . the comic advantage "of boys playing girls' roles seems logical and suggests to me that much of the fairly general critical disagreement with what this production accomplished so well was due to static generated by today's local theatrical climate—the drag syndrome—and not what this company intended, or what it was actually successful in doing—or what Shakespeare had in mind.

This thinking of Gill's leads to his conclusion that this production "deserved to have judgment passed on it by a large audience." Alas, general critical misjudgment closed it prematurely.

Later, in the same review, Gill urges audiences to see *London Assurance*. The following is the last paragraph in the review, which probably is a reply to Martin Gottfried's usual high dudgeon set in motion by just anything he can attach his caboose to, and without regard to reason. (In this case, Gottfried attacked the "version" of the play.)

"Go to *London Assurance* with a light heart and don't worry too much about what the author would think of so wanton a travesty of his work. Boucicault, an Irish bastard of notably elastic morals, did much the same thing to many another author's plays. In any event, he is buried here in town; if he is spinning in his grave, we ought to be able to bend our ears earthward and by good hap hear him hum."

The reader will find in the lengthy opening paragraph of the review of the recent *Cat on a Hot Tin Roof* revival, a kind of small masterpiece in Gill's statement of enjoyment, which nevertheless contains a good deal of criticism. Here the enjoyment far outweighs his querulousness, and what emerges is a happy endorsement.

". . . what a rousing melodrama it is and how the present company enjoys immersing itself in all those luscious roles! Williams is a playwright in the nineteenth-century tradition, and one observes in him the qualities that our ancestors admired in Dion Boucicault; nothing is here for tears and scarcely anything is here even for credulity, but the evening roars past in a glory of gorgeous Southern fustian, and one leaves the theater like a happy sleepwalker, reluctant to be waked. One has had such a good time that to question the means by which the prestidigitator-playwright has achieved his effects would seem a dour Yankee incivility. Let the Technicolored dream go on and on, let the bright birds flutter up and out of the black cape perpetually."

In the same article, Gill writes of the *Gypsy* revival, which he found wanting. Although I disagree with his findings, I respect his reasoning and admire his saying at the outset that "everyone else who has seen it likes it better than I do."

". . . the character of Rose, Gypsy's mother, is so unremittingly self-centered, self-aggrandizing, and, at last, self-destructive, that not a shred of humanity adheres to it. Rose's inhumanity didn't matter very much when, fifteen years ago, she was being acted by Ethel Merman; listening to that matchless voice, we had no reason to take the role seriously. Miss Lansbury is far from having a matchless voice; she has great warmth, charm, and energy, and she has brought these qualities to bear on a part that can make no use of them. Gallantly, she has sought to give us a Rose capable of having children, of loving them, and of failing them; it is a Rose that Mr. Laurents omitted to invent."

In reviewing another revival, Gill not only thinks clearly and writes well, but he is also unostentatiously and interestingly erudite.

"A close neighbor of *Scapino* on Broadway is *Candide;* the two shows have it in common not only that they are among the most joyous events of the season but that they achieved their first success at the Academy of Music, in Brooklyn, and have hopped from a big island to a little one with undiminished zest and grace.

"*Candide* and *Scapino* have something else in common: a point of view. *Candide* is a musical adapted from an eighteenth-century novel in a twentieth-century *commedia-dell'arte* style, obviously with tongue in cheek. *Scapino* is adapted from a farce written in a seventeenth-century *commedia-dell'arte* style, no less obviously with tongue in cheek. For Molière was concocting a prankish potboiler, and he knew it. Some of his more fastidious admirers were distressed to observe him descending to such a level—he was simultaneously preparing a ballet-tragedy with Corneille and Lulli—but Molière had heard that sort of highfalutin talk before; he was a manager as well as an actor and an author, and he needed not only a full house but a vehicle to keep himself and his company employed. As it turned out, *Les Fourberies de Scapin* was a failure. It opened in May, 1671, with Molière starring as Scapin, and ran but a short while; Molière never played in it again, and it wasn't until after his death, two years later, that the farce gradually earned a place for itself in the canon of playable Molière.

"*Scapino* is so rude and lively and English-music-hall-like in its action, and so free and easy in its language, that one is startled upon going back to the original to discover that most of *Scapino* is taken word for word from *Les Fourberies*. A line that becomes increasingly hilarious as it is repeated throughout a scene and that sounds so intensely English that one would swear it had been written by Sir Noël—'What the *devil* was he doing in that boat?'—is, of course, a precise translation of Molière's '*Que diable allait-il faire dans cette galère?*' (One of the most famous tag lines in literature, it was borrowed from Cyrano de Bergerac's *Le Pédant Joué*. Molière said of such borrowings, 'I lift my good things from wherever I please,' and in *Les Fourberies* there are a few good things that he was brazen enough to lift from himself.)"

The following relate unfavorably to new plays. However, when Gill is dissatisfied, he tries hard to discover the reasons. He makes his points without resorting to ridicule. The reader must feel that the writer is making an honest effort to explain an intelligent negative point of view. When he is able to be, Gill is constructive—as in this review:

"John Hopkins' *Find Your Way Home,* at the Brooks Atkinson, is a good play—indeed, for the first two of its three acts it is a very good play, and only in the last half hour or so does it begin to falter and break up, not because the playwright lacks invention or stagecraft but because he cannot bear to stultify himself in order to provide a tidy ending. He is an artist and not an actuary, and the lulling serenities of double-entry bookkeeping are not to be applied to the messy hodgepodge of heartbreak. Having pitched his characters headlong into an entanglement from which there can be no quick and orderly withdrawal, Mr. Hopkins must bring his curtain down upon an ambiguity; it is an ambiguity 'just like real life,' as some kindly soul is bound to say in these circumstances, but real life and a work of art have very little to do with each other, and we are right to feel that the playwright has failed us, however honorably. Impertinent and schoolmasterly though it may sound, I wish Mr. Hopkins to continue working on his play."

Review of the next play was unique since—unlike at least two of the daily writers—Gill refrained from making obvious jokes.

"*Saturday Sunday Monday*, at the Martin Beck, is the sort of play that one feels sorry for, simply and without anger. It is a domestic comedy by the celebrated Italian playwright Eduardo de Filippo, who is also prominent as an actor and a producer. Mr. de Filippo has written no fewer than forty-six plays, many of them big successes, so it is plain that he knows how to please his countrymen. I suspect that Americans will find his handiwork old-fashioned and self-indulgent; at any rate, this American does."

The following review is one of a kind. Some writers were "respectful," but most were outraged and impatient. There was a general attitude that equated *Flowers* with X-rated porno films. It is easy to expect such a point of view since many homosexual acts were simulated. However, *Flowers* had a more serious artistic intention which most reviewers preferred to ignore. Gill's perceptive review follows in its entirety:

"*Flowers* is an admirable embodiment of the homosexual transvestite's ideal of parody, which seeks less to ridicule the original work than to achieve a connection with it. One is reminded that, all questions of sexual orientation aside, mime is more successful at conveying pathos than it is at conveying wit. There is something infinitely touching about the silent gesture; that is the reason Chaplin in his early pictures could break our hearts at the very moment that we were laughing at him, though once he began to speak, using words precisely as we did, our hearts stopped breaking. I found a little to laugh at and a good deal to be moved by in the damply glowing flowers of evil that Mr. Kemp has gathered up and scattered before us. He has the help of a company of six men and a woman, whose young bodies, often entirely naked, are lithe and well disciplined and a great pleasure to watch."

Gill's impatience with *Molly* is direct and amusing. But *Molly* had nothing to recommend it and most writers took advantage of that fact by making sport of it. (Isn't there some ancient admonition about not kicking a man when he's down?) Here, there is no kick, but Gill invents a harmless and witty device. His entire notice follows:

"*Molly*, at the Alvin, is an atrocious musical. Perhaps it will help to temper my irritation if I think about the theater instead of about what I saw there. *Molly* is one of the ugliest shows ever to reach Broadway, and, wonderful to relate, its ugliness appears to be intentional, but the Alvin is very pretty. It is in the Adam style, with charming Wedgwood medallions let into the walls; the lounge in the basement is a hundred feet long and contains a fireplace and a bar. *Molly* is listed as having six producers, some of them in the branch of show business called personal management. It would be natural to suppose that what we have here is a case of too many cooks' having spoiled the broth; not so—the broth was no good to begin with. The show is based on a footling piece of hackwork called *The Goldbergs,* which was both a popular radio show and a play. Written over a quarter of a century ago, its clumsy caricature of lower-middle-class Jewish life in the Bronx has not improved with time. The heroine, Molly Goldberg, is the usual huffing and puffing stage-Jewish mama, bent upon suffocating everyone within reach in the name of unselfish devotion. Molly is played by Kay Ballard, who is totally unconvincing; her Yiddish phrases are uttered with as little felicity as if they were in Basque. She has a big voice, whose size calls attention to the skimpiness of the songs (music by Jerry Livingston, lyrics by Leonard Adelson and Mack David) she has been given to sing. The time is the thirties, and I little expected, watching that period of our history reel under the blows of its misuse in *Children of the Wind* and *Veronica's Room,* that it was so soon to receive another pummeling. The thirties were indeed grim, but they are far from deserving these deeds of retroactive betrayal and rebuke. Marsha L. Eck designed the repellent thirties costumes, which may well be accurate. The Alvin was designed by the distinguished theater architect Herbert J. Krapp. The two men who built the theater and made up its name out of the beginnings of their own—Alex Aarons and Vinton Freedley—can scarcely have supposed when the theater opened in 1927 that it would someday house a musical in which fat middle-aged women would parade around the stage in grotesque bathing suits and tennis frocks in order that fat middle-aged women in the audience should laugh at them: The opening show at the Alvin was the Gershwins' *Funny Face,* starring Adele and Fred Astaire."

Gill's view of *Lorelei* is filled with generosity for its star. He manages to recall the original, *Gentlemen Prefer Blondes,* relates the problems of a tour to the present production and genuflects before the image of Carol Channing in two paragraphs.

"Back in 1949, a musical called *Gentlemen Prefer Blondes* opened here and was turned into a dazzling success by the presence in the starring role of what was then a comparatively novel apparition among us, Miss Carol Channing. She played the dumb-seeming but ever-calculating young gold-digger Lorelei Lee with an energy that might well have served to scoop out the Grand Canyon, and her most popular song, 'Diamonds Are a Girl's Best Friend,' has long since passed into the language, along with 'Hey, There' and the Gettysburg Address. Miss Channing opened last Sunday evening at the Palace in a show called *Lorelei,* which turned out to be a shameless plundering of whatever the producers thought was still

usable from the original work, twisted askew and placed in a new
and repellent context. The result is a botch of a particularly unpleasant sort, in which poor Miss Channing first appears as a middle-
aged widow in deep mourning and then plunges back into the remembered happy days when she and the century were still in their
twenties. It was heartless of whoever stands behind this production
to have urged Miss Channing to play in what amounts to a ghost
story; twenty-five years is a very long time indeed, not only in
terms of changing styles of musical comedy but also in terms of
human life. Miss Channing continues to be an impressive national
resource, all the more precious to us when so many other sources
of energy are running low, but how unwelcome a compliment we
pay her in saying that her imitation of herself in youth is a remarkable one!

"Miss Channing is what is known as a superstar, and superstars
are in constant jeopardy of being unwisely exploited. *Lorelei* has
been on the road for almost a year; the reasoning behind that long
period of travel appears to have been that the show could be
hammered and patched together as it moved from city to city,
taking in enough money along the way, thanks to Miss Channing,
to retrieve much of its capital outlay before it had to face the supreme gamble of Broadway. Given the current cost of transportation
and other business factors, that premise has probably proved faulty;
as far as the quality of the show is concerned, I find it hard to believe that it has not lost along the way whatever little freshness it
may once have possessed."

And finally, there is Gill's version of the much-discussed *Equus*.
This excerpt demonstrates original thinking, an original conclusion
regarding the author's intention, and he outlines the action briefly
but fairly completely.

"On its most readily accessible level, Peter Shaffer's *Equus*, is a
mystery story: somewhere in England a quiet and well-behaved
stableboy takes a long steel spike and plunges it into the eyes of
six horses, blinding them. What has been the occasion for this
monstrous event? It is obviously an act of madness, but madness
explains nothing—it is only a device for not explaining things and
thus for avoiding instead of resolving problems that prove intoler-
ably difficult for a community to face. The woman magistrate before whom the boy is brought is shocked by the deed but is honorably determined to get to the bottom of it. She appeals to a friend,
a doctor in a local psychiatric hospital, to take on the case. The
doctor demurs; he is already overworked, and the last burden that
he wishes to accept at such a moment is still another specimen of
adolescent derangement. Nevertheless, the magistrate prevails; the

psychiatrist consents to see the boy. When he attempts to question him, the boy responds with a litany of singsong TV commercials. So the struggle between them is joined, and what a struggle it is! The ignorant stableboy and the learned doctor prove to be admirably matched adversaries, for what the boy lacks in knowledge and experience he makes up for in cunning; he has been desperately mutilated in his upbringing, and this mutilation has served to make him a master of self-concealment. For his part, the psychiatrist, also much mutilated, is a master at luring his patients into revelations of their darkest secrets. The plot of *Equus* is all simply and artfully, in a series of questions and answers, the working out of the mystery: How did an innocent boy come to reach the point where he felt obliged to blind the horses he loved?

"Mr. Shaffer is an ingenious playwright. . . . He is also a superb writer of dialogue, and in *Equus,* which he might once have been content to turn into an exercise (this time for ten fingers, and perhaps for ten toes as well), he has taken far greater chances than before. His psychiatrist poses questions that go beyond the sufficiently puzzling matter of the boy's conduct to the infinitely puzzling matter of why, in a world charged with insanity, we should seek to 'cure' anyone in the name of sanity. The doctor faces in his personal life a misgiving likely to paralyze him in his practice; he discovers that the boy, sick as he seemingly is, has had the joy of passion greater than any that the doctor himself has ever felt. If he cures the boy, it will be at the expense of that passion, which the doctor envies and would like to share.

"Mr. Shaffer offers his big, bowwow speculations about the nature of contemporary life in the midst of a melodrama continuously thrilling on its own terms. The confessions of the boy evoke onstage the presence of his parents, of the keeper of the stable, of the pretty girl who seduces him, and even of the horses he has blinded —men wearing simulacra of horses' heads and horses' hooves, who lend an eerie, pre-Christian, totemistic air to the judgment being passed on the boy who has made them his victims. Mr. Shaffer convinces us that there is a pagan 'horseness' separate from the life and death of individual horses and well worth our reverence; we violate it at our peril. The word 'equus' stands for more than a single horse, as the word 'man' stands for more than a single man. It appears to be Mr. Shaffer's conviction that if only we could be who we are without having to bear the crushing weight of an identity, we would have no need for violence."

The New Yorker's drama critic has a responsibility to its above-average reader to report and comment intelligently about the theater. Brendan Gill might have made jokes in the manner of some of his

colleagues. Instead, and very much to his credit, he has chosen to
be serious without being somber, informative without assuming
the role of pedant, and, above all, comprehensive and fair. His
readers do not have to agree with him, but it is difficult to quarrel
with his reasonable and intelligent point of view. His able assistant,
Edith Oliver, deserves more praise than this paltry acknowledgement allows.

JOHN SIMON

We are aware that there is a class of connoisseurs . . . who shudder at every
temptation *to admire,* as an unpardonable crime, and shrink from whatever
gives delight to others, with more than monkish self-denial. These kind
of critics are well described by Molière, as displaying, on all occasions, an
invariable hatred for what the rest of the world admires, and an incon-
ceivable partiality for those perfections which none but themselves can discover. The secret both of their affection and their enmity is the same—their
pride is mortified with whatever can give pleasure, and soothed with what
excites only pity or indifference. They search out with scrupulous malice,
the smallest defect or excess of every kind: it is only when it becomes painfully oppressive to everyone else, that they are reconciled to it. A critic of
this order is dissatisfied with the *embonpoint* of Miss Stephens; while his
eye reposes with perfect self-complacency on the little round graces of Mrs.
Liston's person!

This passage from William Hazlitt's essay on *The Beggar's Opera*
(1813) describes John Simon with amazing accuracy.

What any critic has to say about himself is less related to the
truth than what he has to say about the subjects he criticizes; both
leave wide-open spaces for inference and the real truth about the
critic is to be found lurking somewhere in the vicinity of his own
statements.

John Simon, critic of *New York* Magazine, is knowledgeable
about many things, he writes superbly, is entertaining and has the
rare ability to communicate his experiences as a theatergoer interestingly, usually without boring his readers by synopsizing plots.

The fact that he can be brutal and brusque, that he can indulge
himself wantonly because by doing so he can also be amusing,
is not only inhuman, but serves no critical purpose. Since he is
innately brilliant, it is a pity that he should find it necessary to
resort to making harsh personal quips to someone else's indefensible
embarrassment. Simon's caprices have often been attributed to an
attempt at attracting attention to himself. He is not a force in the
theater but a smart after-dinner or cocktail party conceit.

In a recent issue of the *Drama Review*, John Simon responded
to questions regarding criticism. I should like to quote some of his
replies.

. . . If [the critic's] a serious critic, [he] is an artist . . . like any other
talent, his responsibility is first and last to himself. . . . That's first and last,
but in between there is an audience and an audience that matters. . . . They
are to be provided a piece of reading that will be pleasurable enough for
them to enjoy. . . . They are to be taught something by it . . . educated by
way of elucidation . . . explication . . . teaching. . . . The writer should
use the work of art as a springboard for philosophical speculation about life,
about existence, about what it means to be a human being . . .

I must cite some extracts from Mr. Simon's reviews that seem to
contradict his benign "what it means to be a human being. . . ."

In this review of *Minnie's Boys*, one of the most dishonest and
untalented musicals of recent years, Simon railed often and at
length against its star, Shelley Winters.

"Miss Winters is a disaster or, considering her vast expanse, a
disaster area. She looks like a tea cozy surmounting a sack of flour,
perhaps to remind us that man does not live by bread alone, but
also tea and simpering. Yet 'simpering' does not begin to convey
what issues or, rather, does not issue, from Miss Winters' mouth.
Sitting very close, so as to get the full benefit of the ample amplification that nowadays is the tinny sine qua non of a Broadway musical, I was nevertheless able to miss many of her utterances. This did
not, however, perturb me; a miss was as good as a mile of script,
indeed better. And I am not even talking about her singing, or
speaking of the song; I am talking about her speaking of her lines.

"Miss Winters has a talent for letting her words dribble into her
beard—mind you, she does not actually have a visible beard, only
an audible one. Into that sound-deadener drops line after line, as
into a coffin, the whole process accompanied by a facial paroxysm
from which it is hard to deduce whether, at this particular funeral,
Miss Winters is fighting back tears or laughter. Her face constantly
looks like an embarrassed body railroaded into a nudie show and
trying desperately to cave in and crawl inside itself for conceal-
ment. While this shows fine esthetic judgment, it does very little
for putting across a line. Furthermore, Miss Winters has extremely
uncertain emphases and rock-bottom comic timing. Along with
Groucho, Chico, Harpo and Zeppo, we now have a Zero Marx."

Then there is Simon's famous review about Zoë Caldwell in
Colette:

"Miss Caldwell is an actress of glibly spectacular competence,
who once, working at the Tyrone Guthrie Theatre, exhibited something more than that. In New York, she merely exhibits herself,

whether in *The Prime of Miss Jean Brodie* or the crime against Mme
Colette, a performance that is all shoddy histrionic trickery.

"Listen to her as the adolescent Colette asking her mother, Sido,
permission to touch a butterfly 'only just light-ly.' That breathless
pause between 'light' and 'ly'—held for enough of a silent beat to
explode on your inner ear—is hamminess itself. Listen to her saying 'I did have the habit, and still have, of maaaaaarveling . . .' with
enough a's in 'marveling' for three bowls of alphabet soup. Or catch
her switching on her poet-nostalgia voice in 'Always, always my
thoughts take me back to Sido,' like a double bass vibrating away
close to bursting. And when she intones the arietta, 'Mother, I
luuuuvvv him!', that melismatic monosyllable is clearly aimed at
echoing down the corridors of time. On top of which, Miss Caldwell is fat and unattractive in every part of the face, body and
limbs, though I must admit that I have not examined her teeth.
When she climactically bares her sprawlingly uberous left breast,
the sight is almost enough to drive the heterosexual third of the
audience screaming into the camp of the majority. Colette had sex
appeal; Miss Caldwell has sex repeal."

In still another review which is a kind of interpretation of these
and other similar criticisms of women, Simon tries to explain:
"There is something particularly horrible about any out-and-out
plain woman carrying on onstage as if she were a raving beauty:
it is so utterly unconvincing, presumptuous and dishonest that, in
a sensitive spectator, it produces not only esthetic revulsion but
also moral indignation."

Two by Two: ". . . but Madeline Kahn, who has at least two 40-inch
busts, is an outrageously vulgar caricature of a Mrs. Ham."

Now when did any person living or dead ever *see* Mrs. Ham
(Noah's daughter-in-law) or even a portrait of her?
Score: ". . . Miss Wilbur has the most beautiful breasts I have seen
in a long time, on or offstage. I recommend them unqualifiedly."

The Gingerbread Lady (Maureen Stapleton): ". . . but she sorely
lacks any sort of grace, charm, poise, sexiness that would suggest
either music or glamor in her past."

Abélard and Héloïse: "Diana Rigg, the Héloïse, is built, alas, like a
brick basilica with inadequate flying buttresses. . . ."

Come Back, Little Sheba (Trish Hawkins as Marie): "On top of her
uncommunicative acting, she sports a face of insurpassable banality,
and legs like a pair of wounds."

The chief questions arising from these excerpts are 1) What has
any of it to do with dramatic criticism? 2) Aren't these opinions

purely personal and even psychopathic? 3) What imaginable purpose could these invectives and paeans serve?

And are these illustrations of "what it means to be a human
being"?

G. B. Shaw, *au contraire,* wrote in *The Saturday Review* (June 15,
1895) a piece *contrasting* Sarah Bernhardt and Eleanora Duse. This
is an essay on two female faces. Both ladies were then internationally
famous and adored. Bernhardt was fifty-one, Duse thirty-six. Both
were playing *La Dame aux Camellias* and Sudermann's *Heimat*
simultaneously in London.

Shaw's essay is filled with gibes at Bernhardt—mostly because of
elaborate (French) makeup and partly her extravagant style of acting.
Duse apparently employed little (visible) makeup and her acting
style was obviously the simpler of the two. What is truly remarkable about Shaw's writing is the graphic picture he presents of what
each of the ladies was like. The criticism, harsh as it was for the
French lady, presented an interesting contrast of acting styles. An
excerpt follows:

This week began with the relapse of Sarah Bernhardt into her old profession
of serious actress. She played Magda in Sudermann's *Heimat*, and was
promptly challenged by Duse in the same part at Drury Lane on Wednesday. The contrast between the two Magdas is as extreme as any contrast
could possibly be between artists who have finished their twenty years'
apprenticeship to the same profession under closely similar conditions.
Madame Bernhardt has the charm of a jolly maturity, rather spoilt and
petulant, perhaps, but always ready with a sunshine-through-the-clouds
smile if only she is made much of. Her dresses and diamonds, if not exactly
splendid, are at least splendacious; her figure, far too scantily upholstered
in the old days, is at its best; and her complexion shews that she has not
studied modern art in vain. Those charming roseate effects which French
painters produce by giving flesh the pretty color of strawberries and cream,
and painting the shadows pink and crimson, are cunningly reproduced by
Madame Bernhardt in the living picture. She paints her ears crimson and
allows them to peep enchantingly through a few loose braids of her auburn
hair. Every dimple has its dab of pink; and her finger-tips are so delicately
incarnadined that you fancy they are transparent like her ears, and that
the light is shining through their delicate blood-vessels. Her lips are like
a newly painted pillar box; her cheeks, right up to the languid lashes, have
the bloom and surface of a peach; she is beautiful with the beauty of her
school, and entirely inhuman and incredible. But the incredibility is pardon-
able, because, though it is all the greatest nonsense, nobody believing in
it, the actress herself least of all, it is so artful, so clever, so well recognized
a part of the business, and carried off with such a genial air, that it is impossible not to accept it with good-humor. One feels, when the heroine
bursts on the scene, a dazzling vision of beauty, that instead of imposing
on you, she adds to her own piquancy by looking you straight in the face,

188 of The Critics

and saying, in effect: "Now who would ever suppose that I am a grandmother?" That, of course, is irrestistible; and one is not sorry that one has
been coaxed to relax one's notions of the dignity of art when she gets to
serious business and shews how ably she does her work. The coaxing suits
well with the childishly egotistical character of her acting, which is not the
art of making you think more highly or feel more deeply, but the art of
making you admire her, pity her, champion her, weep with her, laugh at
her jokes, follow her fortunes breathlessly, and applaud her wildly when the
curtain falls. It is the art of finding out all your weaknesses and practising
on them—cajoling you, harrowing you, exciting you—on the whole, fooling you. And it is always Sarah Bernhardt in her own capacity who does
this to you. The dress, the title of the play, the order of the words may
vary; but the woman is always the same. She does not enter into the leading character; she substitutes herself for it.

All this is precisely what does not happen in the case of Duse, whose
every part is a separate creation. When she comes on the stage, you are
quite welcome to take your opera-glass and count whatever lines time and
care have so far traced on her. They are the credentials of her humanity;
and she knows better than to obliterate that significant handwriting beneath a layer of peach-bloom from the chemist's. The shadows on her face
are grey, not crimson; her lips are sometimes nearly grey also; there are
neither dabs nor dimples; her charm could never be imitated by a barmaid
with unlimited pin money and a row of footlights before her instead of
the handles of a beer-engine. The result is not so discouraging as the patrons
of the bar might suppose. Wilkes, who squinted atrociously, boasted that
he was only a quarter of an hour behind the handsomest man in Europe:
Duse is not in action five minutes before she is a quarter of a century ahead
of the handsomest woman in the world. I grant that Sarah's elaborate Mona
Lisa smile, with the conscious droop of the eyelashes and the long carmined
lips coyly disclosing the brilliant row of teeth, is effective of its kind—that
it not only appeals to your susceptibilities, but positively jogs them. And it
lasts quite a minute, sometimes longer. But Duse, with a tremor of the
lip which you feel rather than see, and which lasts half an instant, touches
you straight on the very heart; and there is not a line in the face, or a cold
tone in the grey shadow that does not give poignancy to that tremor. As to
youth and age, who can associate purity and delicacy of emotion, and simplicity of expression, with the sordid craft that repels us in age; or voluptu-
ous appeal and egotistical self-insistence with the candor and generosity
that attracts us in youth? Who ever thinks of Potiphar's wife as a young
woman, or St. Elizabeth of Hungary as an old one? These associations are
horribly unjust to age, and undeserved by youth: they belong of right to
differences of character, not of years; but they rule our imaginations; and
the great artist profits by them to appear eternally young. However, it
would be a critical blunder as well as a personal folly on my part to suggest
that Duse, any more than Sarah Bernhardt, neglects any art that could
heighten the effect of her acting when she is impersonating young and
pretty women. The truth is that in the art of being beautiful, Madame
Bernhardt is a child beside her. The French artist's stock of attitudes and

facial effects could be catalogued as easily as her stock of dramatic ideas; the counting would hardly go beyond the fingers of both hands. Duse produces the illusion of being infinite in variety of beautiful pose and motion. Every idea, every shade of thought and mood, expresses itself delicately but vividly to the eye; and yet, in an apparent million of changes and inflexions, it is impossible to catch any line at an awkward angle, or any strain interfering with the perfect abandonment of all the limbs to what appears to be their natural gravitation towards the finest grace.

Although concerned with female pulchritude, the review is really about acting: vivid, precise, and meaningful, with nothing demeaning or inhumanly personal.

In answer to the critic's responsibility to art and artists, Simon doubts "if a critic really influences the practitioners of the art."

While I would doubt Simon's power to curtail the run of a show or his ability to cause an actor's dismissal, his jibes can certainly not be calculated as helpful. On the other hand, with his considerable knowledge and background, if he were to allow himself to be taken seriously as a critic, a natural endowment which he abuses disgracefully, he could indeed "influence practitioners of the art." This influence would be helpful if only he had the innate desire to use it meaningfully. Too bad that he does not.

(A perfect example of a critic's "influence" on "the practitioners of the art" can be observed in the writings of John Martin, dance critic of *The New York Times* [its first] from 1927 until his retirement nearly forty years later. Under his aegis and due largely to his support, analysis, encouragement and occasional adverse but studied reasoning, the dance in America grew enormously both as a native art and in quantity of activity. [The opposite is happening today in the Broadway theater. The major newspapers are fairly choked with announcements of dance companies that attract enormous attention.] But more importantly perhaps was the fact that Martin was an aisle-sitter at the start of the careers of Graham, Humphrey, Weidman, Limon, and a great many others. He, in a big sense, "promoted" them, for he interpreted and praised them to what was at first a small audience that grew in time to sell-out proportions.

But Martin also criticized their lesser achievements, and although this criticism was often resented, it resulted in rethinking, editing and remodeling that often led to a fuller realization.

Martin helped importantly to usher the maturity of great serious talents onto the stage and he transformed an often hostile audience into an understanding, worshipful one.

So much for John Simon's "doubts."

Further on in the *Drama Review* interview Simon says that "the reviews are for the public, for the readers, and for the record, you know, for ages to come, of what it felt like to this particular mind and this particular sensibility to look at the theater of that period."

"The public" is, in Mr. Simon's case, very small. *The New York Times* has nearly three times as many readers every *day* as *New York Magazine* has each week. *Time* Magazine (also a weekly) has about eleven times as many; *Newsweek* nearly ten times as many. Mr. Simon's "public" is circumscribed. But when Mr. Simon even *considers* that he is writing for posterity, he is in trouble. No major artist in any period created for any time or place other than his own. The very *idea* of creating for posterity which is, in fact a result—not a cause—is most inhibiting.

> . . . that is a step
> On which I must fall down, or else o'erleap,
> For in my way it lies.
>
> *(Macbeth)*

Simon surprisingly expressed an oft-confused concept in answer to a question of a "different critical standard or approach to the Broadway theater than to off-off Broadway or non-Broadway theatre" when he replied ". . . whether it is a serious art form, like a comedy or a tragedy, or whether it's a less serious art form, like farce or musical revue. . . ."

I cannot comprehend how, in the mind of someone as bright as Simon, there can be any confusion between subject matter and seriousness of art. Surely no one supposes that Mozart's *Marriage of Figaro,* Shakespeare's *A Midsummer Night's Dream,* Feydeau's *Hotel Paradiso,* Verdi's *Falstaff,* Molière's *Doctor in Spite of Himself,* and many others are less "serious" as art works than pieces built on darker subjects such as Wagner's *Götterdämmerung,* Shakespeare's *Macbeth,* Ibsen's *Ghosts,* or Sartre's *No Exit.*

Further on, Simon said ". . . you don't expect as much from an impoverished little regional group as you do from a big, Broadway, heavily-financed production."

Here, again, there is a measure of confusion. On the one hand, certainly no one can argue an "expected" difference between what *may* be encountered in a regional theater and a Broadway production. On the other hand, the regional (New Haven) Long Wharf Theater's productions of David Storey's *The Changing Room* and Peter Nichols' *The National Health,* Washington Arena Stage's *Raisin,* earlier importations from Tyrone Guthrie's Minnesota Theatre Company, San Francisco's American Conservatory Theatre, and Margo Jones' theater in Dallas need no apologies: They were simply not inferior, and the best of what they did succeeded later on Broadway, often without cast changes.

However there is a deeper confusion in contrasting "impoverished little regional groups" and "big, Broadway, heavily-financed presentations." While it is incontestable that the regional group does (is able to) and must operate on a budget smaller than Broadway's (largely due to union price-tags and New York real estate) I must object to this contrast and its implications.

Of course, any Broadway production has to, of necessity, be "heavily-financed." However, money raised for a Broadway production (and with increasing difficulty) is used for a single show. If the show receives a poor press, it usually closes at once or in one, two or three weeks, and at a total loss. No matter how "heavily-financed" it is, if the show fails to get its audience, there is no money left in the till and no show.

I fail therefore to see why the hypothetical regional production should be treated with more tender loving kindness. In fact, the Broadway fiasco undoubtedly required more time to get on the boards, expended more professional expertise, cost, lost more money and put more people who were dependent on its success for their livelihood out of work than any show presented by any regional theater. Also, the money raised for a regional theater pays for a series of productions.

Besides, John Simon is among the first to call attention to attempted Broadway money-saving, unquestionably essential. The play and players are never enough; the production must appear to have been costly. Examples:

Following the Phoenix Theatre's production of *The Visit* (the Phoenix tries hard to be a quality theater and is always in need of money), Simon wrote: ". . . decor—consisting mostly of a few black abstract cutouts looking like Rothkos painted over by Ad Reinhardt, and some metallic screens looking like nothing at all."

For *Hedda Gabler* (starring Claire Bloom): "John Bury's set is at best rudimentary."

For *A Doll's House* (again Claire Bloom): "That master craftsman, John Bury, has come up with his least suggestive set and lighting."

For Albee's *All Over:* "Rouben Ter-Arutunian's set is the essence of anonymity, and, being considerably smaller than the stage, appears to be merely camping out on it."

For *Gypsy:* "The sets by Robert Randolph and costumes by Raoul Pène du Bois have a perfunctory proficiency. . . ."

For *Naomi Court* (off-Broadway): "The setting for both plays is Naomi Court, a condemned apartment building whose insufficiently developed atmosphere contributes precious little by way of local color or symbolism."

Let's just assume that Simon's opinions—these and many others —dealt fairly with the scenery. Isn't this the sort of criticism that, under today's producing conditions, is so unimportant and so injurious that it were better ignored? Certainly the choice between *no* theater and theater with inadequate scenery (for whatever reason) is not open to discussion.

In response to "Has your concept of your role and responsibility changed since you began writing criticism?", Simon replied: "I don't think so. I think the role of the reviewer may change, according to what newspaper he writes for, according to what the particular crisis in the theater may be. . . ."

This is a fair point of view, but does Mr. Simon act as he speaks?

The theater of Broadway has been in a steadily worsening crisis for many seasons. The entire world is in the grip of a forbidding inflation, perhaps unmatched by any other in history.

I selected a volume of Burns Mantle's *Best Plays* at random. The season was 1927–1928, forty-seven years ago. At that time, 174 plays, 39 musicals, and 19 revivals were produced.* In the last currently available volume, 1972–1973, there were 15 plays on Broadway (four successes), 14 musicals (two successes), 18 revivals (three successes), 5 imports (two successes), 4 one-, two-, or three-person shows. On off-Broadway, there were 37 plays (four successes), 24 musicals (seven successes), 17 revivals, 6 imports, and 1 one-person show.

Is this then not a time of crisis? Is not this a time for critical assistance?

In the same interview Simon said that "power is always in the dailies." There can be no disagreement about this. Out of the total of fifty-one shows produced on Broadway in the 1972–1973 season, 6 played fewer than five performances, 15 played fewer than ten, 9 fewer than twenty, 5 fewer than thirty, 2 under forty. Five of these gave only one performance and another, two. The daily press sponsored these closings.

*In Poggi's invaluable *Theater in America* (Cornell), he claims a total of 264 productions that season.

I should like next to quote examples of Simon's ridicule which too often seems to constitute his sole *raison d'être.*

The Andrews Sisters in *Over Here!:* ". . . seldom have so few had so much to be modest about: their quota of talent, charm, personality, and looks is not just meager but positively miserly."

Richard II: "Richardson's King is a distasteful, flaming queen (no wonder Barton cut out the character of Bagot, for fear of slangy rhymesters). . . ."

City Center Repertory Company: "This is the sort of group that gives repertory, which we so desperately need, the kind of name that should be reserved for massage parlors."

The Iceman Cometh: "Two policemen, walk-ons. They can walk. Less good when they talk."

Boom Boom Room: ". . . as for that colorful gallery of supporting characters, most of them could be sued for non-support."

Lorelei: ". . . and the dances by Ernest O. Flatt are earnest and flat."

The Tempest: "As Ferdinand, Mark Metcalfe . . . is a gangly, spastic puppet aspiring to be the first animated totem pole. . . . *The Tempest* functions on many levels. . . . Berkeley and his myrmidons have leveled it down to one: the dregs."

Othello: "Of John Tillinger's Rodrigo I felt that his interest in Desdemona was just a cover for his true craving to be mounted by Othello."

In the same review: "Mail address to an actor c/o 'Crashing Bore Theatre' should just as surely reach him at the American Shakespeare Festival."

An American Millionaire: "The wispy phantasms flitting around the stage under Theodore Mann's condignly non-existent direction, are at best seven ectoplasms in search of a spiritualist."

These proclivities of John Simon are sadly wasteful. Given the wealth of knowledge he possesses in so many areas, his ability to write vividly and, when he wishes, meaningfully, his articles could be truly significant and importantly beneficial to the current straitened theater world. It would appear from the preceeding examples (and there are books full of similar ones) that Simon too often fails to care, that he too seldom allows himself to worry about the theater as it exists rather than as he might wish to be,—and that he too frequently sells his soul for a quip. I wish that as a critic he felt a greater responsibility to others and a bit less (as he has said) to himself.

I should like to list and then substantiate some of his extraordinarily good qualities. These are presented in no particular order.

When Simon admires a play or performance, he is able to express himself not only directly, but with considerable clarity and logic. Of George Rose's performance in *My Fat Friend*: ". . . witty, silly, ingenious, occasionally dense, toying flamboyantly with both his happiness and grievances, a well-adjusted homosexual not without fleeting regrets, bitchy yet also kind—and all this in an unbalanced, asymmetrical, unpredictable mixture. As George Rose embodies him—and this is another definitive performance in an indefinite play—he is childish and adult, sensible and absurd, but not in any measurable, definable, chartable proportion or sequence. It is the old, sound business of a character taking over, of an author letting his creation dictate to him rather than the other way round, of a lot of loose ends somehow, mysteriously, coalescing into a knotty ball of truth."

". . . And as for George Rose, no one has ever portrayed the sheer joy of living with greater sophistication, and greater innocence.

In contrast to this in-depth analysis, Martin Gottfried did a wrap-up based on his predictable phobia: "I'm sorry that George Rose is beginning to be type-cast as prissy fags—he is much too fine an actor for that. . . ."

Regarding *Good Evening* (Peter Cook and Dudley Moore): "The two work together like clapper and bell, and what rings out is to laughter what Big Ben is to clocks. Why, you may ask, is the best British humor so clearly superior to ours? Partly because it is more satirical, which is to say it is about something, not just sealed off in a vacuum; and partly because of its unconcern about who might not understand it, and about whom, and how many, it might offend."

This brief discussion of British humor, is clear and meaningful. From the review of *Short Eyes*—a play about prison life written by a former prisoner: "There are plays, not the greatest, but not the least, either—that move us not so much through their art as through their authenticity and humanity, by laying bare less known and grubby aspects of life with an emotional insight that no merely documentary account can equal. *Short Eyes* is such a play. . . ."

Chekhov's early play *The Wood Demon*: "It is good to see *The Wood Demon* once and then to forget it; just as an occasional visit to the monkey house is good for a look at the chimpanzees, the better to appreciate Homo sapiens, who came from there. But David Giles's staging is a must: an example of how to get the maximum of movement, psychological detail, and pictorial composition into a slice of life without letting it become a piece of Martian fruitcake à la Peter Brook. See it and marvel."

I admire these closing lines because Simon has not really liked the play—something he has made abundantly clear. He has also been able to separate the director's contribution from the author's and to tell precisely why he applauds the former.

Of *Liza Minnelli:* "What can one say about *Liza?* Miss Minnelli's one-woman show should not be reviewed by drama or music critics, though it certainly abounds in sound and fury, but by reporters who cover landslides, avalanches, derailments, and other second-rate disasters. She is a phenomenon as sad as it is garish: a tiny, overeager talent given enormous electronic amplification from under which emerges a shrilly desperate call for fame, for love, for help. . . ."

I believe these are representative examples of Simon's clear, serious, critical logic.

"At Georges Feydeau's *Chemin de Fer* laughter becomes chronic. Wild, absurd conceit rubs shoulders with ridiculous lumps of mortal logic, sans-culotte farce and periwigged high comedy miscegenate brazenly in full view, lies and truths intertwine in a sinuous dance, jokes are built up with the relentless precision of complicated performing automata. We howl with merriment as the predictable catches us by surprise, lapse into paroxysms of laughter as the flimsiest contrivances hit us over the head with their incontestableness. Human destinies bounce up and down, as if Feydeau had written not with a pen but with a seismograph needle, and great gusts of our guffawing accompany each rise and fall. Only supreme mathematics, architecture, and musicianship could calculate, build, and orchestrate as surely as Feydeau plotted, erected, and detonated his laughs in farces where all the world's a bedroom, and all of us the constantly reshuffled players in it."

A brilliant account of an almost indescribable style of play without any attempt at unfolding the labyrinthine plot. A superb delineation of an extraordinary experience.

David Storey's painful and poetic *Home* is certainly one of the most difficult plays to describe and I should like to quote from Simon's perceptive account.

". . . I suppose, in reaction against the British Empire style—Storey writes a gray, chilly, discomfitingly damp prose, occasionally clearing into wistful little patches of sunny amiability, the exact linguistic equivalent of English weather. The atmosphere is one of postwar English equity's cheerless triumph over pomp and circumstance, as a classy society gallantly sinks into raucous class-lessness. In *Home*, five variously affected victims of train sickness in a society in transition and amid values in transit to oblivion, discover madness as the only outlet for uprooted mediocrity.

"There is something extremely exquisite about the diverse ways in which these people juggle their despair; whether it is colored balls of delusion, knives of nastiness, or just common garden chairs balanced in one hand, whatever sails, hurtles, or hesitates in this air (and these airs) is the identical desperation. There is humor here as well as touching awkwardness, there are the fuzzy edges of quotidian trivia in gruesomely sharp focus as well as discreetly un-insistent, self-effacing bits of symbolism."

I am puzzled by Simon's spending nearly two columns discussing the production of a play (in this case, Bertolt Brecht's *The Good Woman of Setzuan*), then after detailed recounting of the plot, criti-cism of acting, direction, scenery and translation—mostly thought to be inferior—he closes with:

"Do see *The Good Woman of Setzuan;* the play's virtues can absorb the deficiencies of any production, and you may find this the rare kind of dramatic event that prevents the gods from destroy-ing the theater altogether."

Even if Simon's adverse criticisms were appropriate, I am puzzled by his leaving his strong plea, to *see* the play for the very last sen-tence. If he is indeed sincere, why would it not have been more efficacious of him to have *begun* with it?

Simon paid tribute to the late William Inge's *Come Back, Little Sheba*, and his brief summary of the central character's role is es-pecially exemplary. The star in this production was Jan Sterling.

". . . the portrayal of the terrible battle between waning good looks and time with its scorched-earth policy, and of the heartbreak-ing fragility that only women whose one defense was allure can display when they must finally shiver in a nakedness of soul for which the nakedness of the flesh is no longer adequate covering.

"The actress brings out all of it: the fundamental, doomed flirta-tiousness that cannot quite comprehend why it can no longer walk through walls, the puzzled sweetness that so moves us by refusing to turn hostile, self-flagellating, or sour, but persists in sending out waves of great, kindly ineptitude. And when this gallant helpless-ness is finally at witlessness's end, it is to Miss Sterling's immense credit that universal catastrophe becomes visible beneath the dimin-utive drama—that, like an inspired cook, she manages to make humble, almost skimpy, fare become profoundly sustaining."

Too little has been written about the behavior of audiences. However, within the past five or six years, in keeping with the "freedom of expression," nondiscipline (lack of regard for everyone else) and similar movements which have flared up under the guise of "liberation," extraordinary, uncomfortable and worrying behavior have been too often apparent. Such carryings-on affect the performers, break the audience's concentration and are, in the end, supreme examples of gaucherie and selfishness. John Simon called attention to some of these "happenings" in several articles. The first of these reported incidents that occurred at the opening of *Short Eyes*, the brutal, noisy, imperfect but effective play (the author's first) about prison life.

Simon wrote: ". . . On two separate occasions, downtown and uptown, I watched an audience largely composed of blacks and Puerto Ricans, but containing also a goodly number of more or less hippified whites, behave with abominable inhumanity. The fact that they talked or shouted back at the stage (a barbarous habit, admired, oddly, by such different critics as Brustein and Barnes) is merely uncivilized. It does express involvement that makes it impossible for others to hear, and for its exhibitor to stop and think, is imbecile, antisocial, and worthless. What truly appalled me, though, was the unbridled ecstasy with which these audiences savored— pealingly laughed, deafeningly cheered and applauded—the victim's being hung head down in a filthy toilet bowl, threatened with sexual assault, brutally hounded and mauled, and finally slaughtered. Similar ovations greeted other homosexual acts, fist fights, and even the least show of violence.

"There is no excusing this on grounds of unsophisticated spontaneity, childlike identification, unconventionalized forthrightness. It is, I am afraid, bestiality, and though it may function also as catharsis, there remains the hideous underlying fact that any society that needs that much catharsis, of so gross a kind, can never get enough of it from the theater or other harmless sources, and is in grave trouble indeed."

Commenting on Sammy Cahn's successful evening, *Words and Music*, Simon reports an audience reaction which has grown steadily more annoying.

"A great evening for the kind of audience that lives to display its savvy by applauding a song it recognizes and so drowning out one third of it. . . ."

Recalling the applause-just-anywhere syndrome, I wish Simon had carried the ball a step further. For, in recent times, audiences applaud scenery at the opera. They applaud jokes in the theater thereby rendering ensuing dialogue incomprehensible. (There was

a time when laughter—the reaction writers and actors pray for—
was sufficient.) In line with general and new audience misconduct
should also go the fairly new practice of providing just any and
every show with a standing ovation—once-upon-a-time meaningful
since it was more spontaneous, less habitual, and reserved for truly
extraordinary experiences and artists.

Simon's review of *Equus* is filled with distortions. It is obvious
that Simon, far from having given himself to that theatrical experience, remained outside it, to score-keep. Most of what he pointed
out as faulty was probably incorrect.

Perhaps one reason for his noninvolvement from what happened
in the theater is hinted at in his first-paragraph mention of the audience's "lapping and clapping it up." On occasion, this *can* alienate.
I experienced it at the opening of *My Fair Lady* when I heard the
explosive laughter at Shaw's jokes: I was irked by the fact that now,
nearly three quarters of a century later, so many people were obviously hearing the lines for the first time.

(In a review of *The Norman Conquests*, Clive Barnes wrote: "Let
me admit that had the audience enjoyed itself a little less, I might
have enjoyed myself a little more."

Simon was put off by *Equus* and he never recovered. Most of his
objections are expressed by the following: "We are told that insanity is more desirable, admirable, or just saner than sanity."

Where? He must have reference to the doctor's final soliloquy.
What the doctor actually says is: "My desire might be to make this
boy an ardent husband—a caring citizen—a worshipper of abstract
and unifying God. My achievement, however, is more likely to
make a ghost! . . . Passion, you see, can be destroyed by a doctor. It
cannot be created."

At no point does the doctor indicate that "insanity is more desirable." He is, however, envious of the boy's passion—a quality
which the doctor lacks—and even the boy's distorted sense of joy
with its feeling of freedom, as when he gallops at night. The doctor
concedes the boy's "pain" which he promises to remove. What
bothers him is his inability to replace it with anything more than
"normalcy" which *may* lack passion for anything. "With any luck,
his private parts will come to feel as plastic to him as the products
of the factory to which he will almost certainly be sent."

Simon describes the boy's "crazed passion [which] . . . drives him
viciously to blind half a dozen harmless equines. . . ."

This act was incontrovertibly horrifying, but "vicious" it was not.
The boy had been driven wild by the imagined notion that his
horse-gods had *seen* him kissing and trying to have intercourse with

the girl, being unfaithful to them. He blinds them—of course, un-reasonably—as a result of his very real feelings of guilt.

Simon says that *Equus* "at its campiest [is] a farce like *Bad Habits*." Has anyone but Simon thought that *Equus* was, at any point, campy? Or farcical?

And why should not a doctor be a "spokesman for normality" al-though he is "an unhappily married man"? Is there something ab-normal or the least bit unique about an "unhappily married man"? Is such a state unusual and does it disqualify such a person from being a "spokesman for normality"? If it did, then there would be no writers, artists, philosophers, or anything else.

"What has this common stableboy to lose if . . . he makes love to a nice girl?" I think I have already pointed out Shaffer's answer to *that* one: *This* boy might—if altered by the doctor—lose his passion for anything. Mr. Simon surely has observed any number of human shells who have survived hopelessly after this sort of exorcism. They *do* exist and unfortunately they are not unique. And what about the Victorian "common stableboy"?

". . . note the almost reverential ardor with which the psychiatrist treats and gazes at his ephebic patient's mind and body."

Isn't it true that when any teacher finds himself on the verge of discovering the answer to a particular student's problems, he feels "almost reverential ardor"? It is not an uncommon feeling. As for "reverential ardor with which [he] gazes at his . . . body," I think Simon is deliberately trying (as did Martin Gottfried in a since-retracted first review of this play) to read into it meanings that exist nowhere either in the text or on the stage.

". . . the girl is, of course, the aggressor" is literally true, but the inclusion of "of course" seems to indicate that in *this* play, girls are viewed as objectionable. (Another oblique reading of homosex-uality into the play.)

Clearly, the girl from start to finish is depicted by author and director as a sympathetic, sunny, normal, fun-loving, attractive character. She has sympathy for the boy and *believes* she under-stands his failure to have intercourse with her. (It is certainly not her fault that he does not.) Because the boy's proclivities are far from normal, she must be the aggressor (too harsh a word, perhaps "leader"). But she attempts gently and affectionately to lead him to do what he actually *might* have consummated had the two of them not *had* to have been in the stable, within the sound of the horses.

Farther on, Simon objects to the "semihappy ending . . . the boy at least, will be cured—as if psychotherapy were such a simple matter. . . ."

That, again, is Simon's reading. The doctor does not claim that it is "simple." To the contrary, he recognizes at most only superficial good in its eventual outcome. He says: ". . . I do ultimate things. Irreversible, terminal things. . . ." Does this sound as though the doctor believed "psychotherapy were such a simple thing"?

Finally: "Then comes the grand nude blinding scene, showing off the boy's organ to best advantage, and all that, combined with the far-fetchedness of this whole notion of hippophilia, makes me agree with Martin Gottfried's view that what is really meant here is pederasty."

I fail to comprehend Simon's meaning in "showing off the boy's organ to best advantage." At that point in the play I was embarrassed. I felt that we were looking with a sense of shock and horror at a fetus—a baby about to be born. I felt deep compassion; I was witness to a very private revelation.

Simon's statement is as obtuse as "Two times two equals chocolate." It simply does not add up to the scene as actually presented.

In the play it is psychiatry which is "a shriveler of souls," but by this review it is John Simon.

T. S. Eliot's comment is appropriate here:

The critic, one would suppose, if he is to justify his existence, should endeavour to discipline his personal prejudices and cranks—tares to which we are all subject—and compose his differences with as many of his fellows as possible, in the common pursuit of true judgment. When we find that quite the contrary prevails, we begin to suspect that the critic owes his livelihood to the violence and extremity of his opposition to other critics, or else to some trifling oddities of his own with which he contrives to season the opinions which men already hold, and which out of vanity or sloth they prefer to maintain.*

Finally, and perhaps a bit unfair to Simon, I should like to reproduce four sections of an important article on words, "Must The Rest Be Silence?" Unfair only because I am unable to reproduce Simon's entire argument.

. . . but I do think that what the theater is most afflicted with is the agony of the word. The word, which was in the beginning, threatens to drop out at mid-point, or wherever it is that we are. . . .

Though non-verbalness first affects the general public, its indirect effect on the theater is still a mighty blow to the windpipe. . . .

But truly, young people astonish me with their inability to speak even in sentences, never mind paragraphs. . . .

Let our youthful rebels beware: social and political commitment without commitment to articulateness and poetry will do little for the world beyond

*T. S. Eliot, "The Possibility of Relevance" in *Selected Essays* (New York: Harcourt, Brace & Co., 1950).

transforming it into a monstrous discothèque, free and equally brutalizing
to all. The necessary revivification of the word might well start in the
theater. Just by ceasing to shout, by talking softly to people, it might oblige
them to listen. . . .

In this Simon has taken an almost unique position, and he has
certainly made a strong stand with regard to black theater, which
suffers from misleading acclaim.

In his review of *My Sister, My Sister,* Simon takes vigorous exception to this fairly general practice of patronage.

"Clearly the playwright is treading the dangerous ground of plati-
tudes, melodrama, and soap opera; equally clearly, he tries to tran-
substantiate his ingredient by continuous, dizzying shifts in time.
From one moment to the next, Sue Belle switches from six to
eighteen, or any number of intermediate ages, and we are never
sure whether we are watching a precocious child or a retarded
young woman. Often we don't even know what is happening. Actually, Sue Belle is a conglomeration of commonplaces—sociologically tragic data never coalescing into dramatic solidity and originality. The bewildering fragmentation and jumbling are only one
problem; another is the poverty of language ('I should have screamed
out through my thick black darkness of despair'; 'Your face scratch-
ing me like black sin . . .'); and still another is the insufficient development of such key figures as the mother and father—to say nothing
of a dramatically gratuitous appearance of Jesus Christ. The parents
are recognizable, but you can get recognition from a newspaper account; from art, you expect very much more. Lastly, there's a ghost
here appreciably more real than the others—that of Tennessee Williams. Mr. Aranha's play looks like bad Williams in blackface.
. . . But it is, ultimately, the play that so far from being 'strong
and demanding theater,'* merely demands a strong stomach and
backside."

In refutation of the idea that Simon is selfish, careless about the
world and the people who inhabit it, I must point out two examples
of his overwhelming concern with justice, and his indignation at its
deflection.

The first of these outcries is heard in his review of *Inquest.*

"*Inquest* has been too lightly dismissed by those who rightly object to its jerky structuring, boggling lacunae, palpable special pleading, less than smooth production. But to go from this to pronouncing
Donald Fried's documentary play about the Rosenberg case not
worth seeing, or declaring the 'theater of fact' bankrupt, seems to

*From a review by Clive Barnes.

me as unwarranted as the trial of Ethel and Julius Rosenberg was unjust. For the conclusions we reach in *Inquest*, despite the excessively good intentions that have paved the way with cobblestones, are acutely important: *this* is what it was like to live in a frenzied country under a hysterical government and an intellectually and morally inadequate President; *this* is how faulty trial by jury really is. These are fearfully relevant matters, regardless of whether the Rosenbergs were guilty or not. Even if they were, however, their trial was a monstrous farce, and to that point the play speaks with ample eloquence. . . . To be sure, the dramatis personae in the Rosenberg case were nowhere near so articulate and complex as those in the Oppenheimer case; yet their poignancy and the urgency of their terrible needs are no more dead than the theater of fact. The Rosenbergs, alas, are; their case, however, should be reopened."

Simon's concern with moral values again emerges in his review of *The Trial of the Catonsville Nine*, Father Daniel Berrigan's play about the trial of his brother Father Philip, seven other Catholics, and himself. The following excerpt constitutes nearly one third of the review.

". . . *The Catonsville Nine*, whose nineness was as inspiring as that of the Muses, as righteous as that of the Supreme Court, were —are—ahead of their times. And the times are always legalistic, which is to say cautious and benighted and no more able to recognize true greatness than to practice it. Think of what would have happened had these women and men been pronounced innocent and set free—instead of having heavy sentences meted out to them for burning papers to prevent the burning of lives. It would have meant the millennium—that, whether or not God was dead, man was alive, and that, through him, even the Divine might become a living truth. But the defendants at Catonsville were not Philip and Daniel Berrigan, Thomas and Marjorie Melville, Mary Moylan, George Mische, Thomas Lewis, John Hogan and the late David Darst; the defendants were the policies of the United States, human obtuseness and stubbornness, and the powerful archfiend Stupidity. These defendants, alas, were set free, released to plague us and make our mortality almost the lesser of evils we have to contend with.

"About the production, I shall say only that it is good: the grandeur of the matter rubs off even on the less able actors, and a few of them really are flawless. Gordon Davidson has directed with a rapid yet lucid flow, out of which jut, rocklike, great jagged moments of sublimity. The technical aspects are well managed, and the final use of film footage of the actual event is most apposite and overwhelming. Daniel Berrigan has condensed it all beautifully:

there is even a great deal of fine, ironic humor in this tragedy. If I had a fraction of these people's heroism, I would, at the very least, post myself outside the *No, No, Nanette* box office and beseech prospective customers to buy tickets to this show instead. It may not redeem our suicidal society, but it does, coincidentally, stay the doom of our theater."

It should be clear that John Simon is many things. What is legend about him is his caustic wit, his frequent disagreement with the opinions of his colleagues and his destructive jibes at just anyone, too often lacking relationship to dramatic criticism.

On the other hand, Simon has many excellent qualities as a writer; a superb, enviable intellectual background; and enough courage to take the calculated risk of being indiscreet.

He is generally mistrusted by producers, directors, writers, actors, and his colleagues. A great part of this is attributable to fear of what Simon will write. Even this is largely unjustifiable since his power is limited by the necessary tardiness of his review and the comparatively small circulation which his periodical claims.

However, John Simon has succeeded in attracting considerable attention from a kind of local cultist clique, which, having no stake in the theater, laughs the pavements wet because of his journalese.

It is my feeling that John Simon is split somewhere down the middle and I wish profoundly that he could become a serious critic who would perhaps force himself to care consistently about the theater and its inhabitants—the same theater that on his few good days he obviously loves.

HENRY HEWES

Saturday Review's Henry Hewes (b. 1917) has had the advantage of considerable education and training. Early in his life, he worked on *The New York Times* in various lowly positions. In 1952, he became drama editor of the *Saturday Review*, and since 1954 he has been drama critic. He has adapted and directed a number of plays, has lectured extensively, and is the author of numerous articles.

Since Hewes has been a contributor to the *Saturday Review*, his influence on the comings and goings of Broadway theater is limited by both the circulation of his magazine (500,000 copies every other week, much of it outside New York City) and the time-lapse between a show's opening and the appearance of Hewes' opinion. Besides, the primary interest of many readers of the *Saturday Review* is in books, and only secondarily in science and the other arts.

However Hewes' knowledge and taste are apparent in his articles. In the 1954 Blitzstein adaptation of the Weill-Brecht *Threepenny Opera*, his was at the start almost a solo voice raised in praise of a distinguished work given a marvelous production in an appropriately small off-Broadway house. In the end, it ran for nearly 2,700 performances. Excerpts from Hewes' review follow:

"What a wonderful surprise it is for a reviewer to return from London and Paris and find right in his own backyard such a genuinely exciting piece of theater as *The Threepenny Opera*. This musical comedy written by Kurt Weill and Bertolt Brecht in 1928, and now adapted lovingly into English by Marc Blitzstein, completely captures its audience from the instant the curtain of Greenwich Village's Theatre de Lys rises and a tattered, but elegant streetsinger moves slowly and deliberately along a London street to sing with malicious hoarseness:

> O the shark has pretty teeth, dear,
> And he shows them pearly white;
> Just a jackknife has Macheath, dear,
> And he keeps it out of sight.

This "Ballad of Mack the Knife" is sung to music as flamingly contagious as any tune ever written for the non-operatic stage, and most of the audience would have been satisfied to listen to it for two hours. But dramatically the ballad's great value is that it tells us that we are to be offered both a romantic and a harshly realistic view of life simultaneously.

"Since we live in a rich country at a prosperous time, the romantic view will tend to predominate. We will enjoy the gaiety of a dashing Macheath, the broad humor of the operation of an organized beggars' racket, the quaintness of a wedding supper conducted with awkward elegance by a band of uncouth cutthroats, a picaresque chase which leads through the London underworld to Newgate prison, and a merry ending which kids the old-fashioned operetta.

"But spiking and adding character to these events is the author's awareness of the tragic contradictions that attend the struggle for power and survival in this life. J. J. Peachum, who has found that the secret of his beggars' syndicate is that 'the powerful of the earth can create poverty, but they can't bear to look at it'; Jenny, who can daydream of nothing better than having a pirate ship come and blow up the whole business and carry her off fully revenged for the indignity and misery that has been heaped upon her; Mrs. Peachum, who understands the contrast between delicate sentiments of love and the cruder demands of sex; her daughter Polly, who can love Macheath in that 'anywhere-you-go-I-will-go-with-you' way and at the same time reconcile herself to becoming his widow and inheriting his estate; the police commissioner, Tiger Brown, who cannot bear violence or cruelty when it is put on a *personal* level; his daughter Lucy, who turned down the good men who made her feel a lady only to be ruined by a rogue who didn't; and finally Macheath himself, with his slavishness to social habit and to the amenities of life which finally interferes with his business ruthlessness.

"The songs employed to make these comments are distinguished beyond their individual pleasantness by an economy that keeps their romantic quality dry of mush. In addition, Mr. Blitzstein has most appropriately inserted a song from 'Happy End,' another Weill-Brecht show. This is 'The Bide-a-Wee in Soho,' a number telling of Lucy's ability to find the acme of pleasure in a tavern whose principal virtues are a smelly alley, nasty words scrawled on the door, and beer puddles on the floor.

"While there are some who will quarrel with such materialistic philosophy as 'even honest folk may act like sinners unless they have had their customary dinners,' it will be hard for anyone to refute the final bitter stanza that so truly describes a society that tends to divide the world into villains and heroes, and insists on happy endings:

> So divide up those in darkness
> From the ones who walk in light.
> Light 'em up, boys, there's your picture,
> Drop the shadows out of sight.

"*The Threepenny Opera* is a theater masterpiece, and Mr. Blitzstein and the production's sponsors are to be thanked for making it available to New York theatergoers who may find a trip to Christopher Street the most rewarding of the season. I did."

The 1965 review of John Osborne's *Inadmissible Evidence* is equally perceptive and goes to the core of the play. This is an excellent example of the reviewer's "offering insights to the reader."

"If I could see only one of all the attractions currently playing on Broadway, I would pick *Inadmissible Evidence*. Not that John Osborne's extended personal statement is a play with a beginning, middle, and an end, or even with an orderly progression of crises and denouements. But it is all-out theatrical statement, naked and shattering yet ultimately soaring above the desperation it so relentlessly presents.

"For what Mr. Osborne has done is to reflect in one stubborn

individual's irrational resistance to his times a fierce portrait of our
backwardness and our forwardness, both of which strike him as
unsatisfactory. He is not making a plea for tolerance or corrective
action, but, as Shakespeare did in *Lear*, simply and superbly expressing a horrifying nightmare. Osborne's latest protagonist, like
his Neo-Luther, Archie Rice, George Dillon, and Jimmy Porter, is a
visceral and crude-speaking man who needlessly and purposelessly
offends and alienates everyone, as he tries to remain loyal to his
own anger and insolence. . . .

"What *is* he driving at? He is, driving at everything in modern
society that demeans the individual, wastes his talent, and punishes
his emotional expression. There is complaint that the play, which
is shorter here than in London, is still too long. But this comes
from those not yet able to perceive that *Inadmissible Evidence*
is one of the great works of the modern theater."

In 1959, Jack Gelber's *The Connection* created a sizable stir. Produced by the Living Theatre (off-Broadway) it gave rise to much
discussion. Henry Hewes' review (reproduced here in its entirety)
is vivid and sensitive. It also re-creates for the reader Hewes' initial
experience. Although I, for one, never saw *The Connection*, I am
nevertheless able to comprehend a good deal of what it must have
been like.

"In *The Connection*, now playing at the Living Theatre (Four-
teenth Street and Sixth Avenue), twenty-seven-year-old playwright
Jack Gelber has attempted a remarkable thing. He has tried to lo-
cate modern man's position in the universe not cleverly but well,
with a method inspired by the one jazz musicians use, where the
individual soloists take turns improvising on a more or less agreed-
upon theme.

"Mr. Gelber has selected as his soloists a group of dope addicts
who perform for us in two phases of their normal existence. The
first phase, the waiting at low ebb for the man with the heroin to
show up, emanates irritability and anxiety relieved only by bitter
jokes and some interludes of cool jazz supplied by a quartet of
junkie musicians. In order to give his hipsters something to punch
against, Mr. Gelber has invaded their privacy with a few squares.
There is a producer who fancies himself as being hip, and who
tells us that what we are about to see has no basis in naturalism
and that it is neither 'a sociologist's report on the packing order of
Bowery bums' nor is it similar to the recent plays and films that
treat dope addicts as exotics or as society's problem children. There
is a playwright who dislikes the producer's introduction because
it is a little too phony, and yet resents it when the actors shy away

from 'carrying out their dramatic assignments.' He also bemoans his own inability to take a strong and conclusive attitude toward his subject matter without becoming artistically dishonest. And there are a couple of cameramen who glare photofloods into the faces of the already miserable junkies. These intruders are constant reminders that hard truth and audiences are apt to be inimical. As someone in the play says, 'You can't find out anything about anything by flirting with people.' And when we move into the play, we are conscious of a degree of non-wish-fulfilling truthfulness seldom found in the theater. Its characters turn out to be no more 'freaks' than the rest of us. They happen to be hooked with heroin. We are hooked with more legal but nonetheless compulsive and habit-forming things: 'the next dollar, the next new coat, the next vitamin . . . aspirin . . .'

"The action takes place in the apartment, or pad of a man named Leach, who is suffering from a boil. As described by one of his tenants, 'Leach is a queer without being queer. He thinks like a chick . . . Sometimes I wish he would stop fighting it and make the homosexual scene. It would be easier on all of us. Besides, he would swing more himself.' Leach is surrounded by a variety of cats: Sam, a Negro whose morality consists of not stealing from people he likes; Solly, a Jew of great wisdom and knowledge; Ernie, a psychopath with a persecution complex; and four musicians.

"These are all waiting for a benevolent Negro known as the Cowboy to show up with some heroin. He is their connection, through whom they will be turned on. When one of the photographers asks if 'the big connection' might also show up, Sam's simple answer is that there is no such man. He says, 'I am your man if you come to me. You are my man if I go to you.' While this narcotics-anonymous arrangement may not be strictly true in its literal denial of an international dope-peddling organization, it suggests an interesting idea. Perhaps the universe has not, as so many religions would have us believe it has, a big Almighty God who directs its activities every instant. Perhaps instead it is a self-winding eternity of mutual interaction that requires no big boss. Perhaps the divine spirit is manifested in these fundamental human connections.

"When the Cowboy does show up, his gentle Christ-like humility towards his fellow men encourages us to think even more in these terms. He says, 'What's wrong with day jobs? Or being square? Man, I haven't anything against them. There are lousy hipsters and lousy squares. Personally I couldn't make the daily work scene. I like my work hours as they are. But it doesn't make me any better.'

"And yet he is refreshingly selfish when he admits that he'd be sorry to see legalization of the free administration of narcotics put into the hands of the doctors because he would be out of a job, and they (like organized religion) would become the big connection.

"The Cowboy himself was saved from a run-in with the police through the help of an elderly Salvation Army woman who returns to the pad with him and whose unshatterable innocence is comic and blessed. She seems right out of Saroyan as she asks everyone if they know a Harry McNulty (presumably her connection). Indeed, there is a mysterious character known simply as Harry who drifts in a couple of times during the play to make the simplest connection of them all. He quietly plugs in a portable phonograph, listens to one jazz record, and departs without saying a word. Could this Harry be *the* Harry McNulty Sister Salvation spoke of?"

It is curious to note Hewes' inimical feeling toward Beckett's *Waiting for Godot* and *Endgame* as alluded to in his praise for *Krapp's Last Tape*. This review is luminous and perceptive.

"As a man who found *Waiting for Godot* exasperating and *Endgame* stifling, it is a joy to report that Samuel Beckett's newest effort lets loose a passion for life and a robust poetry that were deplorably manacled in the aforementioned plays. Titled *Krapp's Last Tape*, this short character study begins unpromisingly as we watch a filthy old man rummaging about his disordered, dimly lit room. Too much time is taken for us to see the suggestion that man is an animal torn between primitive satisfactions (represented by a drawer in which Krapp keeps a supply of bananas) and intellectual ones (represented by a second drawer in which Krapp keeps his last spool of unrecorded tape). But from the moment Krapp puts away a banana he has started to eat and decides to listen to a particular tape in his vast collection of reminiscences recorded over a forty-year period (here we willingly allow Mr. Beckett the poetic license of pretending that tape recorders were in use many years before 1946, when they actually were put on the market), the play acquires energy and dramatic tension.

"It is not a man revisiting his real past as Emily did in *Our Town*, but a man revisiting his past as he recalled it in shorter retrospect. Moreover this man is not the depressed, half-alive specimen that squirmed on the microscope slide in Mr. Beckett's other plays. He is a man of extraordinary acuity, sensitivity, and vigor. And finally Krapp has an honesty that permits him to share his human weaknesses with the audience. At one point in the tape he is playing he hears his younger self launch into some romantic overstatement of life's meaning which makes him furious with himself, and he rushes to push the button that will allow him to skip that painful portion.

On another occasion, as he is listening with more ease to the old tape, he belatedly hears himself use the word *viduity*. In disbelief he replays the sentence again, angrily stops the machine, rushes to get a dictionary and looks the word up. In this sequence, Mr. Beckett has not only been eminently theatrical, but he has also demonstrated for us the wonder and greatness of language, which most of us must use too pedestrianly.

"A little later he skips too far along the tape and comes in at the end of what appears to be a juicy description of a love affair. As the tape moves on into a calmer philosophical post-mortem, Krapp jumps with comic, understandable fervor to the rewind button. The description, when we do hear it, is richly poetic, and puts us all to shame for the relative poverty of our own experiences. We feel this poverty both in our depth of feeling and in our unwillingness to treat it with the importance and beauty it has to offer.

"At the end of the play Krapp is left with his arms about the tape recorder, an old man clutching the heat of life with an appreciation that has grown proportionately with his diminished power to live it."

The second half of the same bill celebrated Edward Albee's debut in the New York theater. Due to space limitations, Hewes' review of *The Zoo Story* was delayed an extra week. Although it is overwhelmingly favorable, it is interesting, in the light of fifteen subsequent years in Albee's career, to read Hewes' reservations. This analysis of the play is interwoven with an account of the plot.

"Mr. Albee's play is quite simple in form. A dull, respectable man with that upper-middle-middle expression on his face is reading on a park bench when an obnoxious stranger approaches him with irritating personal questions and remarks. The stranger has a desperate need to make contact with someone, and as a last resort pushes his listener to violence.

"The details of these events are made fascinating by the actors George Maharis and William Daniels. To the role of Jerry, the beatnik, Mr. Maharis brings a quietly hypnotic rhythm that comes across as theatrically colorful yet integrated with his own personality. And as Peter, the square, Mr. Daniels provided a genuine humor. He is at his best in the early part of the play where the tone *is* humorous, as Jerry ridicules the clichés he is able to smoke out of Peter's Madison Avenue existence. Of course, this ridicule has itself become a cliché, and if unimaginatively played would seem merely tired and predictable satire. But director Milton Katselas has permitted each actor an awareness of the situation and of what the dialogue means to the one who speaks it. Jerry tends to have this awareness at the precise moment he speaks. And Peter has it a second or two after he has said his line. Even an ordinary interchange (JERRY: 'Well, *Time* magazine isn't for blockheads.' PETER: 'No, I suppose not.') becomes subtly hilarious when given this particular treatment. And it is not just funny, for as he considers each random question, Peter becomes more and more aware of inadequacies not really faced before.

"Jerry, on the other hand, seems compelled by an inner, not quite understood drive, an unwillingness to stop short of scraping out the last layer of truth. And even when he is using such colorful language as 'But that was the jazz of a very special hotel,' it is not done for effect, but rather because that is the best way he knows to express his nostalgia without oversentimentalization. The high point of his performance is reached when he tells 'The Story of Jerry and the Dog.' In the parable Jerry attempts first kindness and then cruelty to a dog that tries to bite him every time he comes into his boarding house. The result is an eventual compromise in which both Jerry and the dog arrive at a state in which they neither love nor hurt because they no longer try to reach each other. This state—the basis of so many relationships in modern adult society—is what has driven Jerry into his present pilgrimage up Fifth Avenue to the zoo, where he had hoped to find out more about the way people exist with animals, animals with each other, and animals with people. As he tells Peter the story of what he saw at the zoo, Jerry attempts, through cruelty, to provoke some animal feeling in Peter, and though the ending is melodramatic and violent, Jerry—like Christ—succeeds at the cost of his life in arousing the human soul out of its deep modern lethargy to an awareness of its animal self.

"*The Zoo Story* is done so well that we can afford to point out that Mr. Katselas might have made this production even more effective if he had been able to highlight some of the author's points more distinctly and had found a more interesting way of expressing the animal stirring within Peter at the play's melodramatic end. We can also afford to wonder if Mr. Albee's suggestion that Jerry's boarding house is a West Side purgatory in which God is a queen who plucks his eyebrows and goes to the john is not one that needs the fuller development he might give it in a longer play. And doesn't his description of Jerry's deceased mother ('She embarked on an adulterous turn of our Southern states . . . and her most constant companion among others, among many others, was a Mr. Barleycorn') owe something to Tennessee Williams? No matter, Mr. Albee has written an extraordinary first play, which, next to Jack Gelber's *The Connection,* constitutes the finest new achievement in the theater this season. Thank God for off-Broadway, and, I guess, thank God for beatniks."

An off-Broadway event of no small importance occurred in 1960 with the opening of the Jones–Schmidt *The Fantasticks* which, in 1976, is still running! Hewes' account of it is clear and knowing. As in all of Hewes' notices, the style is simple and straightforward.

"One of the happiest off-Broadway events in a season that has been happier off of Broadway than on is the new lighter-than-air musical *The Fantasticks.* Using a plot suggested by Rostand's *Les Romantiques,* author-lyricist Tom Jones and composer Harvey Schmidt have worked with a professional expertness equaling the best Broadway has to offer and with a degree of artistic taste that Broadway seldom attains any more.

"*The Fantasticks* is a sophisticated story about innocence. It tells a childishly simple romance with an air of knowing at the same time its value and its absurdity. . . .

"The songs are distinguished and delightful. There is a clever patter song of parental wisdom which advises that to manipulate children you must merely say 'No,' and which points out along the way, 'Your daughter brings a young man home, says, "Do you like him paw?" Just tell her he's a fool and you've got a son-in-law!' Another catalogues the varieties of rape to be enjoyed, of which my personal favorite is 'the military rape done with drummers and a big brass band.' And a third gets fun out of comparing the mixed pleasures of raising children with the surer ones of raising vegetables.

"The show also contains three lovely ballads. The first, 'Try to Remember a Day in September,' provides a nostalgic frame for the entire proceedings. 'Soon It's Gonna Rain' creates a delicate and breathless mood. But the best of all is 'They Were You,' which has a compelling insistence similar to that of 'Mack the Knife.'

"Under Word Baker's direction the performances manage the difficult but crucial task of being whimsically charming and at the same time steering clear of conscious cuteness. The actors seem rooted in the earth even though they are proliferating in high thin air. . . ."

Peter Brook's *A Midsummer Night's Dream* has been beautifully described in Hewes' review. For those not fortunate enough to have seen it, it is a clear delineation of the production. Hewes' evaluation is likewise to the point.

"Peter Brook's new Royal Shakespeare Company production of *A Midsummer Night's Dream* manages to be immensely popular entertainment while practicing the highest standards of theatrical

art. It sets out with the dedicated austerity one associates with productions at La Mama, announcing immediately that its approach
will be non-literal and that Shakespeare's text will be used rather
than illustrated.

"Even before the players appear, this commitment is established
by Sally Jacob's setting. A large white box and two plain doors in
the rear wall form the basic background. Above this, reachable
by ladders, is a black balcony, a sort of elevated offstage area where
actors and musicians can watch the onstage action. Clearly this is an
artistic gymnasium, a three-dimensional blank canvas on which
the performers will paint and erase.

"With a roll of the drums, the players pour onstage, greet us, and
assume their places for the opening scene. Theseus and his bride-
to-be, Hippolyta, are dressed in bright-colored but simple robes as
they discuss Theseus's anxiety about the four-day wait until his
love can be consummated. To this concern is added the problem of
Hermia, in love with Lysander, but commanded by her father to
marry Demetrius, who is loved unrequitedly by Helena. And there
is a group of workmen in modern work clothes, who are rehearsing
a love tragedy for presentation at Theseus's nuptials.

"Now the tale moves to the Athenian woods, which are created
by actors on the balcony dangling coils of wire from fishing poles.
The lovers remain themselves, but, as if in a dream, Theseus and
Hippolyta have become Oberon and Titania, King and Queen of
the Fairies, and Theseus's major-domo, Philostrate, has turned into
Puck, a mischievous courier in pantaloons. They also are served by
four fairies drably accoutered in gray.

"Fairyland magic is imaginatively represented. Puck swings in on
a trapeze. Titania is suspended on a red feather-upholstered stretcher.
And Bottom is turned into an ass merely by the addition of donkey
ears and a nose bulb. The saving grace of these stunts is that they
are never illusionistic, but are always done in the 'let's pretend'
spirit of children's games. Furthermore, they are delightfully playful.
For instance, when Puck passes the magic love potion to Oberon
he does so by spinning a silver saucer on a stick and handing it to
Oberon, who takes another stick and precariously juggles the still-
revolving saucer on it.

"Brook's direction is similarly playful, with the actors speaking
lines while climbing ladders, running down the aisles, or hanging
from trapezes. Occasionally, they even sing some of the dialogue
to musical accompaniment. A splash of 'oh, hell' sponetaneity is
added when Bottom calls for a calendar and someone throws it
onstage. And most outrageous of all is the moment when the dimin-
utive Hermia blocks Lysander's exit by hurling herself horizontally

across the open doorway and remaining comically transfixed there by the force of Lysander's rush.

"Since *A Midsummer Night's Dream* is about the frustrations of people who want to make love, Brook has not neglected the play's opportunities for physical lustiness. Helena begs Demetrius to love her while she lies on top of him. Oberon tempts Titania by caressing her belly. And most audacious is the scene in which Bottom becomes excited, and an erection is indicated by an actor's thrusting his bare arm through Bottom's legs. Indeed, it is made funnier still by having the actor bend his arm and snap it back straight every time Bottom roars 'Hee-haw.'

"But beyond the fun and the artistic innovation of this production, there is a subtler virtue. Because every effort has been made to avoid prettiness and the artificial decorums the nineteenth-century theater enameled over the play, the characters now seem more vulnerable and genuine. As a result, a fresh beauty emerges naturally from Shakespeare's words, and we find ourselves moved gently by the compassionate way these flawed people deal with the disorder of love."

I particularly like Hewes' view that this production avoids "prettiness and the artificial decorums the nineteenth-century enameled over the play . . . a fresh beauty emerges naturally from Shakespeare's words."

Hewes' review of Edward Albee's *All Over* (1971) is an example of a critic's honest attempt to come to grips with an estimable playwright's work, his failure to agree with it altogether, and his respectful regret. Too many reviewers lack the ability to be negative after a sincere but fruitless search for meaning in an artist's work without a cruel, facetious or even angry kiss-off. Hewes, unlike these writers, is interested in the play and the future of the playwright and not in attracting attention to his own desire to amuse.

"The relative joylessness of modern life appears to be driving some of our foremost playwrights to abstraction. The latest instance is Edward Albee's *All Over*, in which an American Everywife awaits the death of her affluent and famous husband. Awaiting with her are "the other woman"; his middleaged son and daughter; his best friend; an eighty-six-year-old doctor; and an elderly nurse. We never see the dying man, who is lying in a coma behind a hospital screen at the rear of the stage. Nor do we learn anything specific about him, for the playwright wants our attention on the other characters. The dying man is there to give them a reason to gather and to converse with more candor and emotion than usual, and to suggest that, with his passing, his satellites are moving into a fallow finality.

"Because of the play's characters, its literary dialogue, and its subject matter, one is immediately reminded of the late T. S. Eliot. But the differences between Eliot and Albee soon become apparent. It is not just that Eliot wrote verse that sounded like prose and that Albee writes prose that sounds like verse. It is the almost complete lack in *All Over* of the sense of nemesis that in Eliot's plays acted as a driving force against which the characters could struggle. Eliot believed in God and fate, and Albee, in this play at least, chooses not to. This choice is certainly appropriate to our times, and it makes *All Over* a realistic and honest effort to reflect contemporaneity. Yet, it leaves Albee with the difficult task of finding some other conflict that will be equally dramatic.

"The obvious way to create such drama would be to find deeply revealing points of dispute between the characters. This would have been easy to do for none of them like one another very much, and the wife is firmly opposed to complying with her husband's wish that he be cremated. Yet, again Albee has resisted. Why? One can only guess that he prefers to show us the overriding despair that reduces these people's lives to dispassion and makes their decisions unimportant.

"Thus, *All Over* becomes a play of carefully orchestrated conversations in which recalled random thoughts and petty unresolved bickerings fill in a mosaic of waste. The husband presumably had a vital career, but those around him who used his wealth and supplied him with conventional satisfactions have diminished into stagnant, decaying people. Even his mistress seems unable to express the joy of her long relationship with him and instead recalls the ecstasy of a former love affair, which because of its brevity remains more perfect in memory.

"The wife, on the other hand, can't remember falling in love with her husband. She repeats several times throughout the play, 'Oh, God, the little girl I was when he came to me,' and ultimately confesses that his appeal had been the serene security of being attached to an older man. Nevertheless, even though she briefly tried a sexual liaison with her husband's best friend, she knows she is incapable of loving anyone else. Both she and her husband's mistress foresee an unhappy old age without the man who has given their lives some meaning. That this meaning was made shabby for both of them is sad, but is implied to be the legacy of a generation driven to indecisiveness by the breakdown of old traditions.

"Would their lives have been less shabby if the husband had divorced his wife and married his mistress? Perhaps. But divorce is seen by the playwright as a kind of killing. Indeed, it is suggested that the threat of divorce was responsible for driving the best friend's wife to insanity. The subject is enlarged upon by the doctor's deliberations about the shift from Old Testament-inspired severity to New Testament-inspired mercy. The latter is more humane, but the older tradition may have produced a more vital Western civilization. Without advocating that all men with mistresses be cruel enough to divorce their wives, Albee has pointed out that indecisive living is an important factor in what many see as the decline of the West.

"It is not just indecisiveness that is being criticized. *All Over* goes beyond that to examine the myth upon which the meaningfulness of marriage and love is based. In one of those characteristic Albee dissections of word distinctions, the mistress tells how she first became aware of 'a faint shift from total engagement' in her affair with the husband, which led to a knowledge that all her sharing had been not 'arbitrary' but 'willful,' and that nothing had been 'inevitable or even necessary.' Existentialist philosophers may find glory in our ability to continue with such awareness, but in *All Over* the wife and mistress do little more than resign themselves to an insoluble unhappiness. In this respect, the play disappoints. Two hours of deathwatching would be more dramatic if they led to a release or a revitalization.

"Also disappointing is the flatness of the other characters, about whom we never learn very much. The best friend is mousy. The son is a washout, whose response to his father's fame has been to become an uncompetitive time-server. And the daughter, who has become involved with an opportunistic and unscrupulous married man, is cynical without being witty.

"Director John Gielgud has apparently given the playwright the kind of production he wanted. There is a minimum of movement and color as the various characters speak more to the audience than to each other. Furthermore, although Rouben Ter-Arutunian's neutral setting of black velour and aluminum never distracts us from what the people are saying, it fails to supply a feeling of warmth and of being in a house where old tradition is passing.

"Jessica Tandy brings a gracefulness of speech and manner to the role of the wife that noticeably exceeds the comparative tonelessness of most American performers. Colleen Dewhurst exhibits an understated inner strength as the mistress. And Betty Field is lively and forceful in two or three brief forays as the nurse.

"However, it requires great effort on the audience's part to follow the quick shifts of dialogue and to appreciate some of Albee's set pieces of conversation that seem to lead the action nowhere. Because the emotional and intellectual rewards of doing this work are elusive, *All Over* commands our respect more as Albee's obstinately drawn abstraction of the state of things than it does as a dramatic work."

Henry Hewes is observant, concerned about theater, and precise in conveying to his readers what he sees and how this affects him. The many elements of theater are so thoroughly integrated in his reviews that cutting them becomes next to impossible. His gentleness and tolerance are seriously in his favor, but as the world of "Have you read what so-and-so wrote about *Up Yours!*" goes, Hewes has been underexposed. Pity.

MARILYN STASIO

Cue is a weekly magazine that has served New Yorkers for forty years. Beginning as a kind of grand timetable of entertainment (movies, plays, TV, radio, concerts, etc.), it expanded its format to include reviews of these happenings plus related feature articles.

Marilyn Stasio from Boston is a graduate of Regis College and Columbia. She edited a weekly newspaper in Bensonhurst, then became feature editor of *Cue*, "second-stringed" Emory Lewis in the late sixties as drama reviewer, then succeeded him. She teaches at N.Y.U. and is the author of a book on the theater, *Broadway's Beautiful Losers.**

Ms. Stasio writes regular theater reviews—three, four, or more in each issue—and occasionally contributes related essays. Her views are clearly her own. She exhibits a love for the theater, is not influenced by other critical voices, is tersely analytical, not abrasive. She gives attention to Broadway and off-Broadway as schedules permit, and has only one standard applicable to both.

I would like to quote passages from some of Marilyn Stasio's thoughts on off-Broadway.

The following is from a review of a 1975 Negro Ensemble Company presentation. This excerpt (first and last paragraphs) tells of talent, interest, and limitations.

The First Breeze of Summer: "At the Negro Ensemble Company. Leslie Lee is a talented, sensitive playwright with a lot of heart. His first professionally produced play is a family drama, low-keyed in mood and episodic in plot structure, about people who love each other. There is nothing remarkable about them, and nothing extraordinary about their problems, but they are such rich characters, such nice people, that it is a pleasure to meet them. . . .

*New York: Delacorte, 1972.

"The play's overlength and diffuseness are rescued by Lee's admirably clean and direct language. More crucial a flaw is the insufficiency of strong, pivotal scenes, those sustained moments of clash and confrontation which would give the play its missing focus and would allow these likable characters the full and dramatic realization they deserve."

As brief as these excerpts are, they are precise, they communicate a feeling of the reviewer's experience, enumerate the new playwright's good qualities, and pinpoint what, in the reviewer's opinion, are his weaker ones.

In the following excerpt, Ms. Stasio details her delight with Liv Ullmann's performance in *A Doll's House,* and her dissatisfactions with most of the rest of the production.

"At the outset, she is radiantly beautiful, the perfect woman-child creation of her society. Her character is a fascinating composite of innocence, instinctive good sense, silliness, gullibility, shrewdness, and ignorance. Liv Ullmann's strongest contribution to the role is her acknowledgement of Nora's own acquiescence in the shaping of her artificial role as woman-as-toy. This Nora hasn't the benefit of a modern sensibility; she is a nineteenth-century woman, a responsible part, as well as a passive product, of her society. The interpretation gives poignancy to the slow drawing of her self-understanding, and Ms. Ullmann is intensely moving in her final scenes.

"This lovely Nora is not so dazzling, however, that she can hide the uninspired banality of the supporting performances. Barbara Colby's Mrs. Linde is excepted; hers is an intriguing and well-thought-out piece of work, although her obvious modernity is out of step with the production's strong sense of period. Michael Granger and Barton Heyman bring little substance to Dr. Rank and Krokstad, who have as little life as the unused pieces of furniture in Santo Loquasto's dull, ungainly set. Sam Waterston's pompous-ass approach to Torvald confirms the chichéd notion that the man is simply a blustering boor. Someday, some actor might have the nerve to interpret him as a strong, fiercely ambitious, sexually attractive, intellectually dominating, slightly sadistic human being. Someday. Obviously not today. Not in this upright but limited production."

The next review—in its entirety—briefly covers Robert Wilson's extremely lengthy *The Life and Times of Joseph Stalin,* which not many people saw. Wilson is progressing along a unique and difficult path and Ms. Stasio is respectful of his efforts. She also manages, within a brief space, to convey some notion of what the unusual production was like.

The Life and Times of Joseph Stalin: At the Brooklyn Academy of Music. "Although physical exhaustion claimed me after seven hours of Robert Wilson's marathon twelve-hour theater epic, you may number me among the hooked. Not numbered among its fascinations are such conventions as plot or conflict, character development, intelligible dialogue, or motivated action. Yet it is magical, a hypnotic experience with moments of transporting beauty. The beauty is almost wholly visual. Using 18,000 pounds of elaborate scenery, a veritable parade of gorgeous costumes, and the lushest lighting effects, Wilson creates panoramic spectacles of color and design that are as trippy as anything Coleridge ever fantasized in an opium haze. If there is a central scheme, it seems to be based in surrealist principles; Wilson establishes a specific painterish landscape, strongly redolent of Magritte, let us say, or Boudin or Rousseau, and then introduces eccentric variables—from dancing ostriches to giant turtles —whose pure incongruity forces you to expand your perception of the scene. The attractions of Wilson's highly original and distinctly bizarre notions of theater are not closed to analysis; but his is an aesthetic vision that demands first-hand experience."

As a final sampling from off the mainstream, Ms. Stasio writes of a spoof that Martin Gottfried said "couldn't be more fun." While not antithetical to the production, the reviewer was not carried away by any unalloyed brilliance.

Bullshot Crummond: At Theater Four. "The Low Moan Spectacular, the company that wrote and presented *El Grande de Coca Cola*, calls its new opus a 'satiric reminder.' More precisely, it is a send-up of the detective mysteries written in the '20s and '30s by the British novelist Sapper. Sapper's macho detective hero was Bulldog Drummond, one of a line of square-jawed, aggressively virile heroes in the obnoxious guns-and-groin tradition of James Bond and Mike Hammer. It is a distinct pleasure to see him reduced to Crummond and satirically skewered by this irreverent crew.

"The problem with the show is the same problem in the original material—they are both so trivial and esoteric that they are scarcely worth the technical craftsmanship lavished on their creation. 'B. S. Crummond' has been staged with real ingenuity and moves along at a nice clip. But the production works best when the actors relax their grip on their idiotic subject and concentrate on characterization. When Diz White satirizes an upper-class lady of quality and teeth, and John Neville-Andrews plays a downtrodden waiter from the lower orders, we are treated to a taste of what this clever company might accomplish with more demanding material. (Closed.)"

Finally, and still off-Broadway, some gleanings from a piece covering a new play (1975) by Thomas Babe. While admiration is expressed for what the reviewer feels are the author's good qualities, these are not overshadowed by the limitations she also observes.

Kid Champion: At the Public Theater. "It is an uncommon and exciting event when a writer of talent, substance, and passion makes his debut. Thomas Babe deserves notice; he has written a problematical, unrealized, but remarkable first play. . . .

"Babe clearly means his rock star to represent an entire generation and a very specific period of American life and culture. Played to dazzling effect by Christopher Walken, the charismatic Kid is beautiful, vulgar, intelligent, narcissistic, cruel, messianic, sensitive, vital, decadent, and doomed. He embodies all the beauty and ugliness of the '60s—not merely its strange new music and bizarre folk heroes, but all its ambivalent values and dreams. Although he strains against his savior role, at the end of the play the recycled young god has begun his transformation into a new 1970s model.

"It's too much, all that Babe wants to say; the play can't handle it, and the breakdowns are tragic. What does come through is Babe's dynamic stage voice, a highly individualistic idiom that blends lyric beauty with hard-edged realism. One of the Kid's followers pleads, 'We still need somebody like you.' We should say the same to Babe."

The new author is clearly appreciated and warmly hailed, and although found somewhat flawed, not discouraged.

Now, Broadway. First, extracts from a review about a difficult and not altogether satisfying play by the notable Tom Stoppard (1974). Stasio presents her interpretation of a complex experience.

Jumpers: At the Billy Rose Theater. "Tom Stoppard's new play is a philosophical farce that is brilliantly funny but ill-developed and dramatically unresolved. Its diabolical puzzler of a plot starts with a bang—the shooting of an acrobat in the middle of a dazzling performance—and weaves down some ·pretty bizarre byways that include the retirement of a singing idol, the murder of a Professor of Logic, the defilement of the moon, and the death of a rabbit. But when these plot elements are put together, a shocking world emerges, no less horrific for being comic. Stoppard creates a civilization that is a macabre, surrealist version of our own modern world. In this society, all traditional values are either reversed, perverted, bypassed, or crushed altogether: the Archbishop of Canterbury is an agnostic; athleticism is as important as scholarship; government is now dictatorship; God, the moon, and popular music are all dead. In the midst of this comic and disturbing nightmare stands a Professor of Moral Philosophy, the only man who won't jump (literally) to the new tunes. In Brian Bedford's marvelous performance, as insightful as it is delightful, the man is the Don Quixote of the space age. Hilariously and yet poignantly out of touch with his times, he doggedly pursues the question 'Is God?' (or, as he sometimes states it, 'Are God?'). Affirming God, he also affirms the validity of good and evil and the existence of moral values, thus confirming his own position of isolation in an amoral society. He is a superb stage creation, and the play turns tedious when he leaves the stage to his wife and her lover. . . .

"For all the scope of his stunning wit and flashing verbal humor, Stoppard seems to have forgotten the special formalistic demands of the stage."

There is no doubt as to what the reviewer saw, what she admired, thought, and found wanting. Her presentation is clear and vivid.

The next review finds brilliant performances in a not-altogether satisfying play. In Ms. Stasio's opinions, the one more than compensates for the other.

In Praise of Love: At the Morosco Theater. "Once in a blue moon we get a chance to see a stage performance so special that it remains with us for years afterwards. Thanks to Donald Sinden, John Wood, Peter Firth, and Jim Dale, that rare blue moon has appeared with astonishing regularity this year. Now it's out again, to shine on Rex Harrison.

"In Terence Rattigan's latest play, and Broadway's latest import from London, Harrison plays an irascible, acerbic, abominably selfish literary critic. With sublime disinterest in anybody's nervous system but his own, he is impartially insensitive to wife, son, friend, and all authors living or dead, not excepting Shakespeare. He is an irresistible, madly charming s.o.b., and Harrison plays him brilliantly. His vocal equipment is gorgeous and he remains in constant and consummate command of it; his phrasing is immaculate, his timing sublime, his gestures exquisite.

"He has a wife, poor thing, played beautifully by Julie Harris in another superb example of acting craftsmanship. The lilting voice and sensitive face are delicate instruments, which she keeps flawlessly tuned. Actually, she is altogether too lovely to convince anyone that she was once a death-camp survivor in Germany, or that she is now suffering from a terminal disease—but what the hell.

"Rattigan's gracefully crafted love story—which persistently echoes that 1950 two-hanky movie, *No Sad Songs for Me,* starring Margaret Sullavan—constantly hovers between bittersweet sentiment and flat-out sentimentality. Its steady flashes of wit serve as ballast. Much of the time, wit wins, and when it doesn't, Harrison and Harris charm it back on its feet—superbly."

Like nearly all the other reviewers, Ms. Stasio was not delighted with Neil Simon's treatment of the Job tale. It did not, however, provoke her to anger, nor was she blind to some of the play's virtues. She was also not swept away by performances. Her judgments are briefly suggested. The following is excerpted:

God's Favorite: At the Eugene O'Neill Theater. "As the audience's favorite for the last decade or so, Neil Simon would naturally be intrigued by the biblical figure of Job, God's favorite. What is surprising and disappointing about his new comedy is how little Simon has explored the comic and spiritual possibilities of his subject. . . .

"There is humor here, but the cleverness is mere contrivance. The play's laughter does not grow out of a full-fleshed character, but is dragged out of schematic situations in which Job is little more than a passive receptacle. Unless the target is running, fighting back, or giving a lot of backtalk, it's no fun watching him get stomped. The biblical Job had a lot more fight in him.

"Vincent Gardenia's saintly schnook is a sweet and baffled patsy, matching his wonderfully mobile face with the delightful deadpan of Maria Karnilova, as his luxury-loving wife. But Charles Nelson Reilly, who has Simon's best laugh lines as God's weirdo messenger, keeps getting hilarity confused with hysteria, a situation director Michael Bennett might have controlled."

Now for a Broadway musical. *The Wiz,* considered elsewhere, was largely panned by the New York daily press, rescued by the magazines and additional financing, and is now a secure hit. Ms. Stasio explains her own reasons for enjoying it.

The Wiz: At the Majestic Theater. "When L. Frank Baum dreamed up his children's classic, *The Wonderful World of Oz,* he surely never had visions like the ones you'll see in this fantastic new musical. But Oz is whatever your imagination wants it to be, and a lot of talented, creative minds want it to be a trip to remember.

"All the essentials of the beloved story of Dorothy and her friends are retained, but in William F. Brown's witty book, every familiar character and situation has been given a sly, hip, and very funny contemporary twist. The wicked witch is a big mean mama, and the Cowardly Lion gets himself distracted by some very unusual poppies. Baddest of all is the Wiz hisself, a dude who really got his act and his wardrobe together.

"There's a lot of magic in Geoffrey Holder's production, and the most potent of it all is Charlie Smalls' dynamite music. The overall mood of it is joyous rock, with sweet excursions into gospel, blues, and even an old-fashioned ballad or two. Finely orchestrated by Harold Wheeler, the songs have the force of the tornado that blew Dorothy to Oz.

"An extraordinary all-black cast makes each lavish musical number an event. At the top of this veritable heap of talent—let's hear it for Mabel King, Dee Dee Bridgewater, Hinton Battle, Andre De Shields (what a Wiz he is!), and veterans Ted Ross, Tiger Haynes, and Clarice Taylor—stands phenomenal Stephanie Mills, a fifteen-

year-old wonder who plays Dorothy with sassy charm and a gigantic voice.

"This is one musical where no creative element is played cheap.
The costumes and sets are as dazzling as the show's conception demands, and George Faison's non-stop choreographic inventions are
the most exciting Broadway has seen in years. If you're wondering
how a tornado can be choreographed, Faison's solution will knock
you out. This new musical has breakneck energy, glorious spectacle,
and all the good humor of a circus. Maybe this isn't exactly the Wiz
that wuz but it's the Wiz that is, and it's a wow."

In closing, I would like to quote liberally from one of Ms. Stasio's
essays, this one written in January 1974 about the theater's "vital
resources" as of that time. This optimistic piece from a reviewer is
in sharp contrast to the pointlessly discouraging *New York Times*
lead article of the preceding September by Robert Berkvist.

The theater still has a great wealth of energy, and miraculously a large portion of that submerged vitality has surfaced this season, just when we need
it most. This energy bank rests not in the quiescent professional commercial
theater, but in the non- and semi-commercial theater companies which,
after quietly growing in strength in recent years, have emerged as the back-
bone of our theater today.

The signs have been evident, of course, for some time. The New York
Shakespeare Festival alone has supplied Broadway with two consecutive
seasons of top-quality, award-winning theater; Broadway's best dramatic
offering nowadays is *That Championship Season*, a NYSF production. As
slim as the current off-Broadway season has been, it would be slimmer still
were it not for *The Hot L Baltimore* and *When You Comin' Back, Red
Ryder?*, both plays courtesy of the off-off-Broadway Circle Theatre Company,
and *Moonchildren*, which originated at the Washington Arena Stage. These
theater companies have been injecting new life into the commercial theater
arena for several past seasons, but this year they have emerged full-force
with vivid and strongly individualized identities.

The Chelsea Theatre Center is already solidly into an impressive season.
Not only did the Brooklyn company open an attractive Manhattan branch
theater this year, but it christened its new home with appropriate ceremony
—a fine production of David Storey's important work, *The Contractor*, at
last given its American premiere. Their second production is a dilly, an
ebullient resurrection of Leonard Bernstein's musical *Candide*, inventively
re-interpreted in the vivacious Chelsea manner. And Chelsea does have
an identifiable manner, characterized mainly by its love of experimentation,
its quicksilver energy, and its very large sense of delight. More than anything else, Chelsea means fun. The company thrives on challenge, whether
in the form of a complex new play by a young writer like Heathcote Williams, or a formidable classic like Gay's *Beggar's Opera*, which demands a
contemporary approach that must be both merry and meaningful.

The American Place Theatre traffics in challenges of another order, dealing most successfully in intellectually posed puzzlers. Although all APT work is characterized by an exceptionally high level of professional craftsmanship—direction and design are minor forms of poetry with this company—its primary imprimatur is its bold approach to the more complex contemporary dramatists. If anybody is going to have a successful go at Robert Coover, Jack Gelber, or Joyce Carol Oates, you can count on its being this venturesome company. An interesting facet of APT is its ongoing obsession with the theme of the American family in dissolution. Comically treated last season in Steven Tesich's *Nourish the Beast* (later transferred to off-Broadway), the theme reappears in *Bread*, the company's second show this season. It's comforting to know that somebody's minding the hearth.

Now that so many of our developing theater companies have come to some degree of common maturity, it has become possible to look at their aims and accomplishments in just this broader perspective. It is now possible to appreciate how each group is striving to arrive at its own distinctive identity through the recurring statement of pet themes. For one example, the Performance Group, as is dramatically evidenced by its current productions, Sam Shepard's *The Tooth of Crime* and Michael McClure's *The Beard*, has long been fascinated by works exploring the shifting identity of the American mythic hero. The Circle Theatre Company is on the same wavelength, but with a different emphasis. More naturalistically oriented in style, this company shows a continuing concern for the moral confusion of a country whose traditional idols and ideals have proved inadequate to modern-age challenges.

The ecletic New York Shakespeare Festival, which this year wrote a new chapter in theater history by moving into Lincoln Center while maintaining its Public Theatre activities, resists all analytical labels. Still, there is an observable pattern to Joseph Papp's checkered record of follies and triumphs. More now than ever before, the NYSF has come to represent a platform for unconventional and often unpopular positions, a theatrical home for dramatic characters and philosophical points of view not easily acceptable to the conventional theater. Both onstage and on the offstage creative level, the company has proved consistently hospitable to women, blacks, and young people; to the avant-garde and the experimental in style; and to politically and socially controversial dramatic themes and issues. One must admire Papp's choice of *Boom Boom Room*, a tough play about an ex-prostitute, to open the season at the Vivian Beaumont. It is both an affirmation of the company's principles and fair notice that its new location in the bosom of the establishment will not compromise the company's concern with the assaulting of established ideas.

On the other hand, two key companies dedicated to upholding the theater's classical tradition are making an admirable showing. Both the revitalized New Phoenix Repertory Company and the Circle in the Square have come through impressively, with sparkling productions of *Holiday*, *Chemin de Fer*, and *The Visit* by the Phoenix, and from the Circle, a splendid production of *The Iceman Cometh*. As if this were not heartening enough, yet another classical company, the young City Center Acting Company, has returned for a second public season to reaffirm its bright promise for the future.

An energy crisis in the theater? Just plug in, and prepare to be pleasantly shocked.

> Sweet are the uses of adversity which . . .
> Find good in everything.

Refreshing.

7

Some Critics Outside New York

"Critics are parts of communities, each with
its own particular history and need."
—Harold Clurman

The American theater has always been centered in New York,
although, from time to time, there have been stock companies in
many other cities and theaters across the country that served as important way stations for touring groups.

In every part of the country, residents looked to local newspapers
to announce and enlighten them as to what to expect in entertainment at home as well as in New York.

From the beginning, star names were the magnets for audiences.
If a show had itself earned a reputation in New York, theatergoers
around the country looked forward to seeing it on their own stages.
Some of these productions played one-night stands, others perhaps
a week when business warranted. There were 339 touring companies in 1900!

It was inevitable in time that the cost of touring, advertising and
salaries would rise, and that productions would become increasingly
shabby.

Motion picture and television productions were never shabby (at
least physically), stars were plentiful, and tickets for movies were to
be bought at a fraction of the cost of theater tickets, while television
required no dressing, no traveling, and was free. The theater could
not hope to win out over such odds.

But all cities were by no means alike in their relationship to theater, and local reviewers found themselves struggling with a variety of different and special problems.

Chicago was a center for touring companies and remained so into our own time. Broadway hits came there *after* Broadway, or with a "second" company, while the New York company continued at its original stand. There was always the hope that the "Chicago company," as it was called, would do well enough in the Windy City to warrant a stay of six to eight months, or even a year, after which it would then travel on to other points west.

While Boston and Philadelphia often saw Broadway hits after completion of their New York runs, more frequently these cities were used as testing grounds for new shows in need of practice and improvement *prior* to Broadway. Sometimes these companies went on to Detroit or Toronto.

Within the last decade, with the decline of movie-making in Hollywood and increased television production, Los Angeles has spawned more theater work, since a large number of actors who have gathered there in the hope of finding television or occasional movie work are eager to perform in even tiny theaters (similar to off-Broadway and off-off-Broadway houses) just to be able to work at their craft.

There are special and different kinds of theater in many key cities; Chicago, Boston, Philadelphia, and Los Angeles especially. And there are resident theaters of prominence in Minneapolis, San Francisco, Washington, D.C., New Haven, Boston, Dallas, Houston, Princeton, and more than a dozen other cities.

Critics have served a variety of functions in each of these places and are faced with a variety of situations which cast them in vastly different roles.

In the main, those who deal with the road companies from New York are at pains to accept on behalf of their citizens only what they consider to be worthy and they can and do drive out anything they consider second-rate.

Those who deal in pre-Broadway tryouts attempt honestly to evaluate—often for the first time anywhere—the intrinsic worth and the defects of the offering, endeavoring to help set it right. They also attempt to tell their readers whether or not the production is interesting.

Local newspaper writers dealing with resident theaters are faced with still another problem. On the one hand they want sincerely to encourage the local company and to help it acquire as large an audience as possible. But they also have a responsibility in criticizing what they think could be better.

In these outlying cities the reviewers carry an even greater weight than those in New York. They know the importance of getting the audience in immediately, or they try—in the case of an inferior touring company—to rid their city of the production at once. To a large extent, they possess the power to do either.

Space in newspapers outside New York is more liberally alloted for theatrical stories. A scheduled road company may provide the subject for many columns weeks in advance of its arrival: there are pieces about the play, the author, the star and often about smaller-part players. The day after opening the review is usually given great space along with additional "social" columns associated with local opening night luminaries, parties, etc. On the Sunday following, there are more articles and more photographs.

With these special conditions in mind, I should like to quote in some cases, too briefly, some reviewers who have played important roles in the theater outside New York.

CLAUDIA CASSIDY

Claudia Cassidy was the artistic arbiter on the *Chicago Tribune* from 1942 until her retirement in 1965. She helped to build Chicago's Lyric Opera, one of America's most highly rated organizations. She watched over the Chicago Symphony Orchestra, helping to secure the services of the distinguished Fritz Reiner, and then she fought for the tenure of conductor Rafael Kubelik when he succeeded Reiner.

Claudia Cassidy has always nurtured a dream for Chicago. She envisioned her city as a center for the arts and never could accept a lesser role for it. Her sights were raised high and she has spent her life (she continues at the present with a radio program and occasional Sunday essays) trying to encourage all Chicago artistic institutions to be nothing less than the best.

In the process, especially outside the city, she has incurred a reputation for viciousness that has been based almost entirely on her refusal to accept anything that she considered second-best.

Before quoting from some of her theater reviews, I should like to reproduce several passages from a 1951 article about Miss Cassidy by Richard B. Lehman which appeared in *Theatre Arts* Magazine.

The fear which some producers, directors and actors hold for Miss Cassidy may in part be motivated by a realization of their own inadequacy and unwillingness to recognize the truth; it may actually have something to do with the lack of vitality, confidence and imagination that prevails in the present-day theater. The great majority of critics, bombarded as they are continually by mediocrity which would have been unbelievable to reviewers of fifty or even twenty years ago, have suffered a gradual decline in taste and have allowed their standards to relax. Miss Cassidy has somehow managed to keep her sights as high as they were in the beginning of her career; she has never become indulgent or coddling toward the second-rate. . . .

If there is a single reason for her acidity, it must be connected with her unhappiness at the thought of what has happened to theater and music in Chicago, and indeed in this country, during the past quarter-century. When she first arrived in the city, it was still in its golden age. There was a first-rate opera company, she recalls, and the plays that originated there or came in from out of town were put together with the same professional care and attention ordinarily accorded Broadway productions. Chicago was an exciting place to live in the twenties; it was the fountainhead of a vigorous school of writers, painters, and other creative people. And then, gradually, they all began drifting eastward to New York and to Europe. . . .

Miss Cassidy writes a daily piece on drama, music, and the dance. She is not only an excellent writer; she is honest, outspoken, fearless and highly intelligent—which must make some of her colleagues on the *Tribune* wonder uneasily what she is doing in their midst.

The question is not hard to answer. Miss Cassidy is one of the five most perceptive, informed and scholarly critics in American journalism. A brilliant phrase-maker, she has the ability to make people continue to read her no matter what they think of her notions and opinions. She can incite violent controversy with a passing remark, and few modern reporters are as deft as she at acquiring enemies, or, for that matter, friends. On more than one occasion her column has pulled over 2,000 letters in a single day.

Another *Theatre Arts* article, "America's Dramatic Critics" (November 1956) says, in part:

"She's tough as hell, her standards are high, and she generally scares hell out of actors and producers. But she's a wonderful person to have on your side when she likes a play, and she's been known to like a few. Playgoers who read the *Chicago Tribune* follow her verdicts and depend upon them. She gets people into a theatre. Her enthusiasms have the effect of those of the late Alexander Woollcott; she has frequently turned a seeming flop into a smash hit." Such is the comment of a Chicago showman in speaking of Claudia Cassidy, who holds the post of dramatic critic for the powerful *Chicago Tribune*. . . .

Miss Cassidy writes with skill and fluency; her wit is sharp, her phrasings are apt, and she is as important to the theatre of Cook County, Illinois (and as much of a force in it), as, say, Brooks Atkinson is to the drama of the port of New York.

Chicago's indomitable Miss Cassidy has actually cheered for many of the worth-while plays that have come before her knowing eyes and ears, but it is never a great surprise to find her denouncing a play that has been a success in New York. And she is always unwilling to accept a cast that is by any means below the Broadway standards. Producers can't slight Chicago and get away with it—not with Miss Cassidy on duty in the *Tribune* tower.

One of Claudia Cassidy's critical triumphs became historic. Tennessee Williams, whose *Battle of the Angels* was such a flop that it never reached Broadway, wrote *The Glass Menagerie* which played Chicago (1944) en route to New York—an infrequent happening. Cassidy's morning-after review began this way (and the reviewer returned to see the play at its second performance):

"Too many theatrical bubbles burst in the blowing, but *The Glass Menagerie* holds in its shadowed fragility the stamina of success. This brand-new play, which turned the Civic Theater into a place of steadily increasing enchantment last night, is still fluid with change, but it is vividly written and, in the main, superbly acted. Paradoxically, it is a dream in the dusk and a tough little play that knows people and how they tick. Etched in the shadows of a man's memory, it comes alive in theater terms of words, motion, lighting, and music. If this is your play, as it is mine, it reaches out tentacles, first tentative, then gripping, and you are caught in its spell."

In November of 1961, Williams' *The Night of the Iguana* opened in Chicago. Three sections of Miss Cassidy's notice follow:

"Two things arrested attention almost as soon as the Blackstone curtain rose on *The Night of the Iguana*—that Oliver Smith had created one of the finest settings in the bleached ruin of the Mexican hotel perched high in a tropical seaside forest near Acapulco, and that Tennessee Williams, who has enriched the theater for twenty years, had written a bankrupt play. I read somewhere that in it Mr. Williams shows more 'compassion' for his characters. There was more compassion in one radiant scene of *The Glass Menagerie* than you will find in the whole of this barren play. . . .

"My quarrel is not with the people Mr. Williams has chosen to write about. Many a time in earlier plays he has taken worse and made them fascinating. The problem with *Iguana* is that the people, the situations and the writing are bleakly dull. . . .

"Well, bankruptcy is fairly final. You stop that and do something better. You may also pause to note that in a bad play the perpetual sex life can be not just dull, but unimaginative."

The following Sunday Miss Cassidy wrote a piece about the earlier opening of *The Glass Menagerie* and concluded with remarks about *The Night of the Iguana*.

"To me, the valid violence in Williams' play comes from within, and that is why some of the best scenes in *Iguana* are played by Margaret Leighton, an actress of inner resources. *Iguana* is not a good play—for him it is a baffingly bad one—but the loud clatter of bad direction and some hopelessly incompetent performances is a scandal.

"An ambitious play is always important—no one wants to see it fail. But the really important thing about *Iguana* is the man who wrote it. He is one of the theater's greatly gifted men, as some of us have known since that blizzardy night nearly seventeen years ago, and that he should find his way again is a matter of the deepest concern. Without Tennessee Williams the theater and all who value it would be irretrievably bereft."

For those people—mostly from the theater—who dreaded Miss Cassidy, I would like to point to her review of *The Night of the Iguana* in which the role of Maxine Faulk was played by Bette Davis. Miss Davis is mentioned as the performer, her costume is described, but there is no comment on Miss Davis's performance. Nor is this treatment made to appear snide.

For the Cassidy detractors whose inaccurate memories seem to recall that all Chicago companies that changed stars were murdered, a part of La Cassidy's notice about *La Plume de ma Tante* refutes this.

"Something special moved into the vastly improved McVickers last night—a really funny show. *La Plume de ma Tante*, which has been roaming the world for years and years, came to our town as fresh and gay as something just out of a Parisian hatbox, with Robert Clary and Liliane Montevecchi heading an altogether engaging cast. This swift and zany revue has often been called a French *Hellzapoppin*, and up to a point that makes sense. Anything can and does happen. But to one who found Olsen and Johnson wonderful offstage, and their show a noisy bore, the point of demarcation is the whole point. *La Plume* is in its absurd way an endearing show, with the cachet of charm and style.

"The first thing you see is a bewitching circus curtain by Marcel Vertes. It sets the mood, being crisp, sunny, amusing and a touch farouche, the last in honor of a quality found most pungently in the extraordinary Montevecchi, who is among other things wild, fierce, sullen, and behind those black silk bangs, shy. What Mr. Clary is I am not entirely equipped to tell you, except that he has what it takes to come on constantly and yet never enough. He is small and droll and versatile and confiding, and few shows robbed of Robert Dhery could hope for such replacement luck."

Another example of Miss Cassidy's reaction to a new cast is to be found in her review of Lillian Hellman's *Toys in the Attic*.

"When it comes to plays, Kermit Bloomgarden takes care of his own. Howard Bay's setting is as imaginative as it is resourceful. The new cast is a good one, the variations in types probably shift the performance considerably. Anne Revere's elder sister is what she must have been from the start, strong enough to stand alone, wistful enough to remember a fragment of Schumann in a bad moment. Patricia Jessel is a demon driven wisp as the incestuous one, Penny Fuller a half mad child as the terrified one. Scott McKay's Julian is a traveling salesman without customers. Constance Bennett does not mar the sketch of the rich one, nor does she develop it. Clayton Corbin's Henry makes you wonder, which is half the actor's battle."

No account of Claudia Cassidy's reviewing would be complete without inclusion of some of her famous barbs:

On *Edward, My Son:* "Its writing, though often pungent and stagewise, is otherwise undistinguished, its settings are a calamity, and if the direction is more than routine, its quality escapes me."

On Margaret Phillips in *Summer and Smoke:* "My own conviction is that she seriously weakens an already unstable play . . . an actress of singularly limited range and almost no perceptible depth. . . ."

On *The Respectful Prostitute* and *Hope Is the Thing with Feathers:* "Both productions seem to have been thrown together on the train."

On *Funzapoppin':* "Olsen and Johnson dispensed refrigerators, sun lamps, heating pads—in fact, almost everything but entertainment."

On Olivia de Havilland in *Candida:* "A pallid, one-dimensional heroine in a kind of comic-strip Shaw. When she enters, she is an interruption, nothing more."

I first had the pleasure of knowing Claudia Cassidy and her husband, Bill Crawford, when I fought at the battle of the Great Lakes Naval Training Station (1942–1944). I think of her as warm, sincere, beautiful, and honest. She has always had courage largely in behalf of her charge: Chicago. Like all idealists—and Claudia Cassidy is a bona fide idealist—she dreams.

Once during a hospital stay, she wrote:

. . . part of my stay was a busman's holiday. Toward the end I began to write stories in my head—strange how special they seem then, only to vanish like mist when you try to put them on paper. Still with me, tho, are familiar imaginings of what Chicago would be like on my beat if I could wave a wand.

The Chicago Symphony Orchestra and Fritz Reiner—what better when they are at their best? I gave them a new hall, a magnificent one with an intimate theater lurking in its depths. I merged all the best chamber music in one glorious season in a perfect setting. Stretched the Lyric season to three months—November thru January, with budget to bring the best singers, conductors, directors, and designers, to build a resident company in the finest style, and to house it in a modern theater with superlative production facilities. Opened a repertory theater with a classical base and an adventurous head in the clouds. Cleared the concert decks of the dull stuff managers peddle and managers buy. Opened a resident ballet troupe, a good one, built several new theaters as decorative as stimulating, and brought all the best shows from New York, London, Paris, etc., while they were fresh and exciting.

Pipe dreams? Maybe. But the dream comes before the reality. And hospitals, for recuperators, are fine places for dreaming.

ELLIOT NORTON

Theatergoers in Boston as in many other cities outside of New York have been increasingly chary about patronizing shows prior to Broadway unless they could boast performers of some special magnitude or star writers such as Rodgers and Hammerstein, Lerner and Loewe, or others of similar status.

During at least two and a half decades (the forties, fifties and part of the sixties) Boston was one of the chief pre-Broadway stops for New York-bound shows. It was customary for such productions to remain in the city from two to four weeks, all the while rehearsing, cutting, rewriting, and sometimes recasting.

As of 1956, there were seven daily newspapers in Boston that published the comments of seven reviewers. (At this writing, there are only two.) The local critics were responsible for many of the changes. Chief among these in this 1940–1960 period was Elliot Norton, who wrote for the *Boston Post* from 1934 until it closed in 1956, then the *Record American* that became the *Herald American* and the *Sunday Herald Advertiser*. Norton has reviewed more than five-thousand shows in forty years, published books, and given many courses on theater at Boston College, Boston University, and at Harvard. He has also been the recipient of many awards in recognition of his critical contribution.

Norton's reviews bore considerable weight, not only with the public but especially with writers and producers who respected his opinions and conclusions. Often, Norton's opinions have been helpful and have seldom (in relation to pre-Broadway exercises) been abrasive. He has a nearly unique penchant for moral matters that include language as well as subject matter and stage deportment. While he is not a prude, this proclivity runs throughout much of his writing.

Here are some of Elliot Norton's reviews of new shows Broadway-bound.

The first is from *Subways Are for Sleeping* (1961). This article—

a second—was written near the end of its Boston run after considerable revision of the show. It imparts more than a hint of the sort of trouble new shows can encounter. The atmosphere of perpetual change and uncertainty are made frighteningly clear.

"One scene was eliminated from *Subways Are for Sleeping* and another substituted during the Boston engagement. But when the show moved on for a Broadway opening it had not been changed substantially; it was pretty much what it had been, and by no means the best of all musical comedies.

"Betty Comden and Adolph Green had written a few new snatches of dialogue to make the character of Tom Bailey, their hero, a little more substantial. What they achieved was hardly enough. What Sydney Chaplin, as Tom Bailey, did with their lines was uninspiring. On a second visit, the performance of Mr. Chaplin seemed even more puzzling than on the first night.

"Sydney Chaplin crashed into the theater five years ago in *The Bells Are Ringing* as a natural leading man: big, handsome quintessentially male, with a good light comic touch, natural authority and ease. In *Subways Are for Sleeping*, he is attractive, but languid and lackadaisical most of the time, as though he were not really interested.

"At the first Boston performance, his languor was annoying, but appeared to be due, in all probability, to changes made in the script since Philadelphia. You can't expect ease from an actor who isn't yet sure of his lines. Surely he must have learned all the words during three Boston weeks; yet he was still acting half-heartedly.

"Perhaps because she was reportedly suffering from laryngitis on Friday, Carol Lawrence seemed less effective than she had at the premiere.

"Carol is darkly handsome. She has a bright, strong singing voice of operatic range, as she demonstrated in *West Side Story*. She is nimble, swift and graceful as a prima-ballerina. But her performance in *Subways* was a little too eager, and at times—as, for instance, in a bright interlude in the French wing of the Metropolitan Museum —a little too coy.

"Blame for the faulty performances of both Mr. Chaplin and Miss Lawrence—the one too casual, the other too eager—lies with the director, Michael Kidd, whose business it should have been to give Chaplin a little boost—or even a swift kick—while persuading Carol to act with a little less animation.

"The truth about Michael Kidd is that his work in *Subways* is disappointing. He is primarily a choreographer, the man who designs the patterns which the dancers execute. This time, he had a double responsibility, as choreographer and as director of the entire show. He has not demonstrated his usual brilliance—and that's a word that reasonably applies to some of his earlier work—in *Sub-ways*. His dancers are the usual wonders, especially the girls. But the patterns he has invented for their movements are too often reminiscent and sometimes haphazard.

"There are moments of excitement in the dancing when he ingeniously works a fragment of the Russian style into a dance that involves a group of Santa Clauses which is otherwise uninspired. (On second thought, it may well be that the hearty maleness of the conventional pot-bellied, ho-ho-ho-ing Santa Claus is out of the range of his admittedly skillful, yet limited, male dancers.)

"The only Kidd dances which suggested his old inventiveness occur at the very end of the show in a finale that brings them on in small groups, moving at sonar speed, in slick contrapuntal patterns.

"If Michael Kidd had been able to devise rousing finales for both the first act and the second, *Subways Are for Sleeping* would seem a far finer show than it does now.

"The best of *Subways*, at the end as in the beginning of the Boston run, was in the wonderful scenes between Orson Bean and the new girl in town, Phyllis Newman. Their material is first-rate and they handle it magnificently, she with 'I Was a Shoo-In' and he in 'I Just Can't Wait to See You with Your Clothes On,' which is a masterpiece in a musical comedy that isn't."

In 1963 Norton reviewed *Stop the World—I Want to Get Off* after it had enjoyed a run of 556 performances in New York. Norton was not afraid of calling it "ugly," "tedious," "uninspired," "cheap," "coarse," and many other derogatory things. He also found the "stand in" (Kenneth Nelson) superior to the original, Anthony Newley. The following is excerpted.

"From England by way of Broadway, in a 'national' company which has been touring the United States, *Stop the World—I Want to Get Off* is an uncommonly ingenious and just as uncommonly harsh and ugly musical play, with its head in the clouds and its nose in the gutter. Anthony Newley, who wrote it and starred in the London and New York companies, is a highly imaginative man with a sordid sense of humor and a sorry kind of wit, given to pathetically juvenile jokes and expressions. In one scene he offers a limerick as coarse and witless as any of those that closed the Old Howard many years ago.

"At the Shubert, his show is very well played and sung by Kenneth Nelson, pleasantly supported by Miss Lesley Stewart and somewhat less effectively by a pair of pert twins and a rather notably unattractive chorus of eight or ten girls.

"An American in a distinctly British role, Mr. Nelson is presented to Bostonians as Littlechap, who is Newley's version of Everyman, a symbol of the little fellow who makes good though he is no good in any sense of the word. . . .

"The overall idea is imaginative, and in staging it with song and dance Director Newley has made it move some of the time with an agreeable rhythm of its own. Sometimes he lets it bog down in tedium or endless choruses of uninspired songs.

"When he moves from the large vision to the individual scenes, he has almost nothing to say and almost nothing to sing that isn't cheap and coarse in a boyish way.

"Lots of English writers are bitter about the world in which they have grown up and in which they struggle for recognition. Newley is not only angry about England, he is angry about everyone and everything and where you might expect him to admire and feel sorry for his Littlechap, you find, instead, that he despises him.

"In the end, Littlechap does begin to understand his own folly and the author has him put his newer feelings into eloquent words in the best song of the show, 'What Kind of Fool Am I?'

"But his regeneration is late, and before he arrives at it he has dragged about in the pettiest kind of disorder and duplicity as the most unpleasant heel the stage has yet offered in the guise of a hero.

"His affairs are puny and sordid, whether with his wife, by whom he is 'lumbered' into matrimony, or with a Russian party member in Moscow, a German maid at home or an American night club entertainer in New York.

"His liaisons with these women are presented as the silliest kind of smoking room stories. The wonder is that Newley didn't manage to get a farmer's daughter onto the stage.

"As he himself played Littlechap in New York, Author Newley emphasized the man's petty fraudulence by his own bitterness. Although his Boston standby, Kenneth Nelson, is not nearly so good a comedian, he gives the show a lift because his personality and manners are pleasant. He is, also, a good singer with a strong, resonant voice. He deserves a great deal of credit for carrying the entire show on his back from beginning to end."

I would like to call attention to the courageousness of this review. The show had exhibited strength on Broadway. Undoubtedly the Boston public, which has always patronized Broadway-proven successes, had looked forward to it and its tremendously successful paean to self-pity, "What Kind of Fool Am I?"

In December 1963, Ronald Alexander's play *Nobody Loves an Albatross*, starring Robert Preston, opened in Boston prior to Broadway. (For the record, the play rang up 212 performances in New York after a less-than-enthusiastic critical reception.)

In the view of this writer, Norton was precise in his feelings about the defects of both the play and the production. He was as potentially helpful as any "doctor" might have been. But either those involved in creating and producing the play failed to believe the critic, or chose to disregard his feelings, or simply were unable to effect appropriate improvements.

"Although it has Robert Preston as its principal player and he makes it move much of the time, *Nobody Loves an Albatross* is a comedy that doesn't work. In any case, it didn't work at the Wilbur on opening night, and unless somebody does something drastic about it right away it is unlikely to succeed in the foreseeable future.

"That it has some merit is certain: some of the lines and some of the scenes are sharply amusing. And for all its trickery, it is ultimately as honest as it is cynical and bitter. In satirizing the men and women who create the commercial television shows of the nation, it is cool and contemptuous from beginning to end, with no apologies, no punches pulled and not the slightest sop to the sentimentalists.

"If it can be made to work on playwright Ronald Alexander's terms, which are tough, it will blister the walls in all the halls of Hollywood where TV shows are written.

"It could conceivably do for the Great Wasteland what *Once in a Lifetime* did for the movie industry, though Moss Hart's play was a sweet and innocent charade compared with *Nobody Loves an Albatross,* which is brutally blunt.

"The trouble with the play is, first of all, the character of Nat Bentley, who despite all the charm of Robert Preston, is utterly repulsive.

"If you sympathized with this monster, if you felt he did what he did because he had no other way to earn a living, you might accept his pitiful bravado. Or, if he were consistently amusing and ingenious, you might embrace him as a comical rogue. But he is funny only part of the time; and some of the time he and his author are straining too hard for laughs.

"Monday's performance was the first on any stage, and that accounts for the fact that Robert Preston got the play off to a bad start. Presenting his man in scenes with his twelve-year-old daughter, his aggressive housemaid and a pretty new secretary, he was too loud, too rapid, too cocky and too obviously fraudulent.

"Later, he and some of the other actors—all of them first-rate, got closer to the proper tone and tempo of the piece and that made some difference. But by the time the star regained his balance something intangible but important had been lost forever.

"Probably the best moments in the play are the bitterest, in which Bentley and other writers, along with a cold-blooded feminine star and a couple of leeches from the agencies, wrangle and snarl at one another in a story conference that seethes with hatred, distrust, suspicion, and cruel humor.

"Gene Saks, as director, has yet to find a key to the play which would make it possible to fit all the performances into a single coherent pattern of farce and satire."

The following (excerpted) review of *Funny Girl* (January 1964) is particularly interesting for a number of reasons. There is the vivid picture of Barbra Streisand in her second show (*I Can Get It for You Wholesale* was her first) and the show's inadequacies, some of which are spelled out in Norton's review. Then there is the additional news item which appeared in the same paper a few days later.

It can be assumed that the show was vastly improved as it enjoyed a run of 885 performances on Broadway where it also had Streisand and several hit tunes by Jule Styne and Bob Merrill.

"At the Shubert, *Funny Girl* is one of those heartbreaking shows which run down and down and down as they run along, to end in tedium. This despite songs that are bright and jaunty, happy dancing spectacles that jeer grandly at the big production numbers of the twenties, and despite Barbra Streisand.

"Miss Streisand, who stars in it as funny Fanny Brice, is one of those rare young women born to dazzle and delight an audience; a plain girl who seems at times a stunning beauty, a capering clown with a flair for lunatic jokes, a singer with a strange belting style that makes modest lyrics sound like the pure romantic poetry of a great master.

"She has hits enough in *Funny Girl:* sad songs and mad ones, sentimental ballads and corny comical tunes. Not all of the music of Jule Styne is as good as his best and, occasionally, a lyric of Bob Merrill's is awkward or inept. But the good ones are there and Barbra lifts up her head time and again and lines them out into the topmost Shubert balcony.

"Nobody sings like Barbra Streisand, whose voice has its own strange timbre. Her tones are small, her pitch absolute, her range considerable, her delivery tense. She can sit or stand almost without moving, her eyes fixed on the back wall of the theater, and command every eye and every heart in the audience.

"But for all her spirit, her personality and her unique high style, she is only a performer. She needs a libretto to make some dramatic sense of *Funny Girl*. She needs, too, a good deal of help as an actress; there are some solemn scenes in which her acting is not persuasive. . . .

"The trouble begins in *Funny Girl* when the show gets away from Fanny Brice's onstage antics to Fanny's private life.

"That Fanny fell in love, married and ultimately divorced the swaggering gambler Nicky Arnstein is a fact. That their relations were as dreary as they are made to seem here is most unlikely. . . .

"*Funny Girl* is at this time, altogether too long, and surgery will help pull it together and lift it out of the doldrums. But a great deal more is required. Some of the writing is just plain labored. And the acting too."

Item: "The condition of *Funny Girl* is still so precarious that Jerome Robbins has been called in as play-doctor consultant during the musical's pre-Broadway run in Philadelphia. Director Garson Kanin, husband of Wollaston native Ruth Gordon, took it with good grace. It was apparently a question of S. O. S.—save our show. Its troubles were all too accurately forecast by our astute drama critic Elliot Norton at its try-out here. The growing but still unconfirmed rumor is that one of the prominent members of the cast may be replaced. Those who saw the show here may be able to guess who it is. And it sure ain't Barbra."

As a result of the foregoing notice, a most interesting interview took place between Jule Styne, the composer and Elliot Norton, the reviewer. In view of Norton's piece about *Funny Girl*, this interchange is particularly engaging.

"Jule Styne asked a good question. The composer of the songs in *Funny Girl* and other popular musical shows wondered if critics should expect from girls like Barbra Streisand anything more than great singing.

"Should such a star be required not only to sing magnificently but also to give a persuasive acting performance? Shouldn't a reviewer settle for good songs, greatly sung, and not worry about Barbra's failure, as an actress, to emulate Katharine Cornell, or Helen Hayes, or Duse, or Bernhardt in portraying Fanny Brice, in what is, after all, only a musical comedy?

"Styne believes that Barbra Streisand is, in her way, unique and extraordinary. She is, he says—and everyone agrees—a great 'performer,' an unusually brilliant singer who can hold any audience and fire them to enthusiasm.

"Now, such performers are no longer common in the theater,

though they have been replaced in most shows by actors and actresses who are rarely ever able to sing.

"When one like Barbra appears, Styne believes, she should not only be cherished but also protected, because she is needed by the theater more than she needs it.

" 'In cafés today,' he declared, 'in places like Las Vegas, this girl can now earn $15,000 a week.'

"What Barbra is getting now in *Funny Girl* is a secret between her and her producer, but it is much less than $15,000 a week.

"In other words, she could be prosperous, even triumphant, in the world of cafés and long playing records without ever bothering about stage rehearsals and tryouts, and the tensions of theatrical opening nights.

"All this being so, shouldn't critics be 'nice' to her, praising her brilliance and glossing over any lapses from perfection in her acting? From a girl of twenty-one, in any case, can a reviewer expect total perfection?

"One answer to these questions is that Miss Streisand's praises should, most certainly, be sung in loud and joyous canticles. She should be acclaimed, nay adulated, as far as the written word can be pushed. In this era of the superlative let her be wreathed in superlatives, all signifying greatness.

"For she is, in truth, a great entertainer, and when the band plays Jule Styne's songs and Barbra sings them she illuminates the Shubert Theater till it shines like a magic castle, as all theaters should at all times.

"Nevertheless, in *Funny Girl*, she doesn't act persuasively as Fanny Brice, and this must be recorded, in the first place, because it is a simple, elementary fact and readers are entitled to the facts, and in the second place because this young star is not a child to be flattered but a great performer whose work must be reasonably evaluated.

"If she were no more than a sweet child of seven, singing a pretty song pleasantly, it would be necessary to say no more than that about her performance. Or, if *Funny Girl* were no more than a conventional old-fashioned musical comedy, it wouldn't matter if she couldn't act, so long as she sang effectively, told her jokes, looked attractive and managed to keep from falling down while walking across the stage.

"But she is an adult artist in a musical play of some pretension, as a mere matter of respect, to analytical criticism: friendly, but honest. This she has received—and nothing more deadly than this.

"Yes, she could get along well without the theater in those areas of Show Business where there are no critics, only partisans and, occasionally, sycophants.

"If, however, flattery were necessary in order to keep her on the stage, she wouldn't be worth keeping.

"That she is worth keeping and cherishing must be obvious to everyone."

Since Norton's review of *Funny Girl* contained nothing but high praise for Barbra Streisand except "her acting is not persuasive," it is strange that Mr. Styne would have made so very much of this small, fairly harmless, gently expressed exception particularly since Norton's *real* objection concerned the show's libretto.

The following opening paragraph concerns Neil Simon's *The Odd Couple* (pre-Broadway) in February 1965. Norton voices his only quarrel with play and production, which he goes on to praise lavishly.

"For two happy acts, Neil Simon's *The Odd Couple* is a funny, foolish farce. In the third it runs down and out despite the prodding ingenuity of Director Mike Nichols and the stunning performances of Walter Matthau and Art Carney, both virtuosi in comedy and both at the top of their form. In the third, it loses momentum, runs out of steam, repeats or reworks once too often the jokes which had made the earlier episodes idiotically entertaining. There isn't enough substance to give it a final fillip."

Elliot Norton's stronger-than-ordinary views of morality are spelled out in the following Sunday piece that appeared in November 1963. What Norton is saying here to his Boston constituents is that the theater is unjustly accused of immorality—an idea that seems light-years and thousands of miles away from today. Not that the present writer opts in favor of immorality; it is just that by now *everything* seems to have been said and shown, including the very dull *Oh! Calcutta* which had nothing going for it, not even its nudity. However, if such things had been banned, there would have been explosions "not worth the powder it would have taken to . . ." Once permitted, they are usually dispensed with and seldom repeated for their own sakes when they are found not to be sufficiently engaging.

In 1963 Norton was telling his citizenry that the theater was a safe place for grazing.

"Although the U.S. theater has become highly sophisticated in the last forty years, its morals are still surprisingly good, reflecting the tastes, if not the habits, of the playgoing public.

"There is a segment of the audience, even in Boston, which leers or laughs at ugly innuendo and sometimes guffaws at the crudest kinds of single-minded coarseness. Yet most of the plays and musicals which most of the people patronize are seemly and innocent, though not quite so naive as were the operettas and the melodrama of an earlier period.

"Crime doesn't pay, but criminals always must in the really popular drama of today and although the good little heroine of the musical comedy romance is not always so good as she might be, she and her hero stand up for virtue.

"An occasional play like *Who's Afraid of Virginia Woolf?* does present characters who violate the commandments, the conventions and even the common code of polite behavior. But they are not glorified, they are represented as desperately unhappy, degraded and demoralized.

"There are occasional musical comedies which violate the proprieties to a greater or less extent. *A Funny Thing Happened on the Way to the Forum,* for example, adopts a pagan attitude of joyous immorality in telling an ancient Roman story of love and lust.

"It happens to be a very funny show, but it is not edifying.

"The English musical play *Stop the World—I Want to Get Off* is often sordid and in two or three places its use of gutter language is despicable.

"But these are exceptions. Almost every musical comedy success of the last few years has been moral in its tone and manner.

"*The Sound of Music* comes to mind as a prime example. This is the story of an Austrian girl who tried to become a nun but left the convent regretfully for marriage, who trained her children to sing, and who spends most of her time—and the audience's—in song.

"There has been no show more innocent than *The Sound of Music* in the history of the American theater, and few as popular on Broadway, or on the road.

"*The Music Man* is another innocent hit of huge proportions.

"*West Side Story* is sophisticated, yet its hero and heroine are good and its point of view moral.

"Consider the innocence of *Oklahoma!,* of *South Pacific,* or *The King and I* and *My Fair Lady.* These are the most successful, the most popular, the most acclaimed musical shows in the history of the American stage.

"At this moment, the musical comedy hits on Broadway—which is universally considered the epicenter of theatrical wickedness—are almost all entirely free of offensive attitudes, actions or language.

"This is true of *Here's Love,* the biggest of the new hits, which has Santa Claus as a central figure; of *110 in the Shade;* of *Oliver* which is based on Dickens' *Oliver Twist;* of *Jennie,* which stars Mary

Martin, of *She Loves Me* and of *How to Succeed in Business Without Really Trying.*

"The exceptions are the two shows previously mentioned, *Stop the World—I Want to Get Off* and *A Funny Thing Happened on the Way to the Forum.*

"Obviously, there is more to *Stop the World* than its coarseness, but this is the issue of the moment. . . .

"Of the plays without song and dance, the most popular are the small domestic comedies. These, when they please, become the real smash hits of the American stage.

"In the last three seasons, there have been three of these crowd-pleasers: *Mary, Mary; Never Too Late;* and the new '63 blockbuster, *Barefoot in the Park.*

"*Mary, Mary,* which has been running for nearly three years, and has been presented not only in New York but all over the United States, always with success.

"At one point, not long since, five companies were playing it here and abroad.

"*Mary, Mary* is innocent in word and deed, free of even the slightest hint of vulgarity, let alone immorality.

"*Never Too Late,* which opened in Boston a year ago with Paul Ford, Orson Bean and Maureen O'Sullivan starred, has been triumphant in New York ever since. In all the periods of bad weather, or during strikes, hazards, or catastrophes, it has flourished.

"*Never Too Late* is completely free of offense.

"*Barefoot in the Park* is so much admired you can buy seats only long in advance.

"It is sophisticated in tone, but it, too, is entirely inoffensive.

"All this is stressed at this time merely by way of setting the record straight. Occasionally, we do get ugliness, coarseness and immorality in the theater. On such occasions, some of those who dislike the theater anyway take up the ancient Boston chant that our stage is basically 'immoral.'

"They see—or, more likely, hear—about an ugly line or scene or situation in a given play, and conclude from that that all plays have ugly lines, or scenes or situations and that the theater is the chapel of Satan.

"That just doesn't happen to be the truth, or anything like the truth."

Norton, like the most illustrious critics of our past, has on occasion in one of his Sunday pieces given us portraits of some of our most cherished performers. Although he had found *High Spirits* (1964) less than desirable as a show, he gave a vivid, adoring description of its two female stars.

"Because life is not so very amusing and never has been, comedians are always in demand, and always, alas, in short supply. The good ones, that is, are in short supply; not every boob with big ears and two little heads is funny merely because he offers himself as the butt of a joke.

"Good comediennes are even scarcer, and this is not only lamentable but frightening; if women, who have always been wiser than men, lose their wit and humor, their ability to point out the difference between pompous fraud and simple truth, the end may be near. Let's not even consider the possibility.

"To get one funny girl in a show is a memorable achievement and that is surely the reason why *Funny Girl* goes back to Fanny Brice, who was one of the funniest, a rare one, an original.

"To find two who can work in tandem is a kind of wonder, possibly a miracle of some sort, a fracture of the theater's natural order. In *High Spirits*, at the Colonial Theater, there are two.

"Each of the two is unique, yet Beatrice Lillie and Tammy Grimes have certain admirable qualities in common.

"For example, they both have an exhilarating sense of nonsense and they share a common gaiety: they poke holes in the fabric of human folly not out of meanness or envy but from sheer experience.

"In or out of *High Spirits*, they are always high-spirited.

"Each has a bag of tricks, carefully utilized. Miss Lillie always speaks her deadliest and dizziest lines in a voice that is girlishly sweet, suggesting at times one of Louisa May Alcott's little women with Lizzie Borden's axe in her hand.

"For *High Spirits* she has cultivated a ridiculous walk. Strutting the stage as the addled Madame Arcati, she interrupts her march from left to right by skipping: this very gravely, of course, as though all reasonable people always walked that way.

"She is a mistress of the 'double take' which all comics use. Her Madame Arcati, at home with friends who have invited her to give a séance, is sweetly greedy and just as sweetly impervious to brandy till after the third swift jolt. Then suddenly her eyeballs seem to bulge as the alcohol hits the stomach and the stomach protests.

"In another high moment of *High Spirits*, she dances with hilarious gravity on little cat feet, then disappears behind a big fence, over which she tosses what would seem to be every stitch of her clothing. A moment later, still singing with idiotic sweetness, she reappears, fully dressed.

"What makes this funny is neither the striptease, nor her reappearance, but a sudden, seemingly casual glance she gives to the clothes on the floor.

"It is an instantaneous thing: grave, swift, and without elaboration.

She says nothing, does nothing, makes not the slightest gesture. But she conveys in total hilarity the mad idea that she is wondering how all those clothes, which look exactly like those she is wearing, could have got there.

"Tammy Grimes has her tricks, too. As Elvira, the high-spirited ghost who returns to coax her husband into eternity, she uses a small girl's precise voice and a clipped accent.

"When Elvira is wickedest, Tammy is sweetest, most charming, most mischievous and, so, nuttiest.

"Her Elvira is the most gleeful of spoofing spooks, delighted by almost everything including her own appalling tricks to get her husband across the great divide into eternity.

"Her skill in flying (on a wire, of course, like Peter Pan) is matched by her soaring joy. This aerial Ariel swoops up and down from her backstage heaven with a child's glee.

"That Elvira is not, however, a child, but a very womanly woman is part of the fun and part of Tammy's charm.

"On the stage or in the air, in *High Spirits,* she is the spirit of pure mischief."

Finally, I should like to quote from another Sunday piece by Elliot Norton, this one entitled "The Great American Musicals." What follows is the latter third of the article.

"What makes a musical great is a combination of qualities, appealing to sight and sound and sense. However fanciful, it must reflect something of the truth about life, and the joy in life, too.

"The philosophers, a gloomy lot, insist that 'life is a sadness.' The best librettists and composers agree with them privately and may hint at their thesis in shows like *Carousel,* whose hero kills himself. But they sing of man's humanity to man and to woman, too, exulting in conflicts that bring hope and sometimes peace.

"They suffer fools gladly, while mocking their follies. They liberate the emotions of their audiences by setting their people to dance and sing when words fail them, which is what all of us should do when words fail us and even, at times, when they come easily.

"The great American musicals, which are unmatched in the world, combine song and dance with story. If the stories tend to fall into conventional patterns, dealing most of the time with love in and out of bloom, they reflect with essential truth something of the American scene and the American dream. They are true to the American character after their fashion, or they are not great.

"The older musicals soothed and sometimes stupefied. The new ones, daring to come closer to life as it is, or as it might be under the smiles of a summer night, stimulate and exhilarate.

"In the ways they are put together, they are not only artful but artistic. *Oklahoma!* seems a trifle old-fashioned now, but when it was first played, sung and danced it fitted words, music and dance into a vibrant pattern that might have moved a Michelangelo. *My Fair Lady*, reproducing in the American way George Bernard Shaw's *Pygmalion*, reflected in new splendor all that Shaw had to say about a young woman who, like so many others, aspired to fulfillment, and did it in a setting of visual and musical splendor.

"There is something of the rowdily cheerful and optimistic American spirit in *Guys and Dolls* and in *Kiss Me, Kate,* and something of the rueful truth and beauty of romance in *A Little Night Music.*

"There is something gloriously optimistic in 'Oh, What A Beautiful Mornin','' the opening song in *Oklahoma!* and something buoyant and caressing in 'A Weekend in the Country,' the loveliest number in *A Little Night Music.* In between, all along the line, in the great ones, there are songs and sights and sounds and truths to recall and remember and to rejoice in."

This from a critic of seventy-two years of age is a remarkable affirmation of love and understanding of the American musical theater and indicates a continuing youthful spirit that takes no refuge in nostalgia, that has no need to resist the future.

However, even if Elliot Norton has not changed, conditions in Boston have. Mentioned earlier is the loss of five newspapers with their theater reviewers who twenty years ago made a stimulating hubbub the morning after a new show was first unveiled. Now with only two papers in Boston, the critical opinion is divided between Elliot Norton and Kevin Kelly, theatrical watchdog of the *Boston Globe.* Formerly the paper was sedate. Now as the *Boston Globe-Traveler* it has become far more outspoken and more powerful. Mr. Kelly, writing for the paper with the predominantly larger circulation, has become the dominant critic. Mr. Kelly is twenty-seven years younger than Mr. Norton and he is undoubtedly Boston's new force in the theater.

To Elliot Norton, *Ave atque vale.*

JOHN ROSENFIELD

The leading cultural voice in the Southwest for several decades was John Rosenfield, critic of the *Dallas Morning News.* Rosenfield was involved with theater, music, films, sometimes with books and pictures, and the dance. He was *au courant* with happenings in

all of these fields everywhere and had his own measuring sticks—
comparative scales—for use in his own sector of the world. He was
deeply conscious of the need for developing the arts at home and
was able to smell out promising talent, to nurture it, reprimand it
when he felt it softening or straying in the wrong direction, but
above all, to help it and help persuade local audiences to support
it.

While Rosenfield's influence was felt most directly at home in
Dallas, it nevertheless affected the public taste for good throughout vast areas of Texas, Oklahoma and Louisiana where his opinions were used as guideposts in all the arts.

Rosenfield was an evangelist in the best sense. While welcoming
touring companies, like Claudia Cassidy in Chicago he was apt to
be squeamish about second-rate ones. At home, he was decidedly a
significant factor in Margo Jones' growth from involvement in a
small theater, to a position of national prominence. He helped build
audiences for the summer Starlight Operetta, the Dallas Little
Theatre, for the Dallas Symphony, and later for Paul Baker's Dallas
Theatre Center.

It is most interesting to note in rereading John Rosenfield's reviews that while he most often praised productions, his admiration
was never expressed in the kind of adjectives he carefully reserved
for the best in theater. This he accomplished without condescension
and without *seeming* qualifications. For example, in Rosenfield's review of the Dallas Theatre Center's revival of *Can-Can* (1963), he
had this to say:
". . . pointing to the remarkable job by a couple of professionals,
neither affiliated with the Center. They were Tom Hughes, producer of the State Fair Musicals, one of the great summer operations in North America, and Toni Beck, his choreographer.

"When you consider a good musical's taxation on versatility, experience, assurance and natural endowment, Mr. Hughes and Miss
Beck had their nerve, and their gods were propitious. *Can-Can* is a
lively evening."

The Emperor Jones was done at Theater Three in 1964. After relating the play's history, Rosenfield "evaluates" the local production.
He supports it but does not give the same sort of praise he would
lavish on professional events.

"Theater Three, the local amateur stage, had the brilliant idea
Wednesday night to revive *The Emperor Jones*. It may awaken the
intense interest of youngsters curious about the art theater 'wows'
of forty-four years ago. It could make a point today of the imperish-
able validity of good theaters of any year. We found *The Emperor
Jones* not greatly dissimilar to the O'Neill play we saw on the night

of November 18, 1920, when, by golly, we 'covered' it in the capacity of a fledgling dramatic critic for a New York newspaper. Scenically, Theater Three, the arena stage on upper Main Street, is somewhat primitive but we doubt if it was surpassed to elaborate degree by the former stable in Macdougal Street off Washington Square.

"Theater Three has the right actor for Brutus Jones, William McGhee, Dallas businessman and laboratory worker who has specialized in Negro roles in local presentations of *Purlie Victorious, Mrs. McThing, The Bad Seed,* and *The Little Foxes.*

"Mr. McGhee has commanding presence, a rich musical voice and a vast range.

"We could have tolerated clearer articulation from him if only to occupy our mind with some of O'Neill's thoughts. *The Emperor Jones,* though, is largely an 'effects' melodrama and for voice and tonal color thereof, Mr. McGhee gave the full treatment. He broke the 'sound' barrier several times and whipped up matters to the tensile snapping point.

"While Mr. McGhee is not without stage and screen experience, he is no theatrical professional. . . ."

In his coverage of Ira Wallach's *Absence of Cello* (1966), Rosenfield dealt with a mediocre play and a company which he felt was only so-so. However, its presence in Dallas, an offering of the Community Course, was an "event" of sorts. The critic allowed his readers to feel that as an evening it had not been too disappointing but he gave the play far from a rave notice. Here the local critic is at pains to refrain from discouraging a continuing subscription series that could hopefully provide more stimulating theater fare to local audiences.

This same review following a Broadway opening would have spelled "curtains" for the show. In Dallas, the critic wanted to encourage his audience to resubscribe to next year's offerings: "Better luck next time" and "second-best is better than none" was the philosophy of the locale, almost a continent away from Broadway.

The following is excerpted:

"A rather good troupe struggled manfully with the acoustics at McFarlin Auditorium Thursday night to give a fair account of Ira Wallach's play of Broadway's previous season, *The Absence of a Cello.* And bless their little hearts, when the sound or lack of it got in the way of conscientious drama, acoustics didn't have a chance.

"The company headed by Hans Conried and Ruth McDevitt (she from the Broadway cast) may have obeyed that professional instinct to broaden the play in spots but this was inevitable, actors being as reflexive as they are. But the shape of the play was preserved for one of the Community Course's largest audiences. It may also be said, that Dallas saw a better *Absence of a Cello* than did New York. It did not seem quite as superficial here with Mr. Conried in the lead as Dr. Andrew Pilgrim, for such is the character's name. . . .

"Mr. Wallach has composed a talky play but one generally of good talk when not pushed to farcical gags. The one set, an inexpensive apartment in the worst possible taste, lives up to its function.

"The cello, symbolizing Dr. Pilgrim's Beethoven evenings with chamber music chums, darts into and out of view as the company man casts his all-seeing eye at everything including wife Celia's eleventh-century vase.

"Mr. Conried, who had lectured this same audience from the same stage last season with warm responsiveness, impressed them in a stellar acting role. He might have played with more subtlety at closer range.

"Florida Freibus, from Eva LeGallienne's Civic Repertory Theater, was both humane and decisive as the wife. Michaele Myers, with some Broadway and more road experience, was an attractive sister-in-law.

"Donald Buka, a graduate from the Lunt–Fontanne circle, did well enough as the absurd company man. There was always Miss McDevitt in an irrelevant part of a granny milking laughs where none was really written. Eldon Quick and Nancy Priddy were the juvenile interest.

"The Community Course, conducted by Southern Methodist University and Temple Emanu-El, and now twenty-seven years old, has been driven to a decision. R. C. Knickerbocker, executive director, reports that renewals for the 1966–1967 lecture-recital series now have reached 2,000 in a hall seating 2,400. Nothing like this popularity has ever before been registered before June or July. Shall the Course try for two audiences per attraction or not?"

In attempting to achieve a "delicate balance" in an inferior situation, Rosenfield has retracted his horns. He employed language that tells his audience it can feel free to like the current offering but he does not confer any superlatives upon it.

Now to present examples of Rosenfield at home—that is, the critic's recognition of and feeling for the distinguished talent that he found struggling for life in his own backyard. First he lauds Paul Baker, of Waco, Texas, who produced a new play by Gene McKinney, *A Different Drummer* (1955). (Subsequently, Baker established a new theater in Dallas where today, years after Rosenfield's death, it is prospering.)

"Waco, Texas: The Baylor University Theater, still famous for its schizogenetic *Othello* two years ago, has done it again.

"Friday night it began a run of Gene McKinney's *A Different Drummer*, which will challenge, enthrall, and divide playgoers at home and from afar. Everybody is likely to conclude that *A Different Drummer* is important theater and start the argument from there.

"Paul Baker, head of the Baylor drama department and base chemical of the directorial synthesis, is not smashing conventions to make cheap sensations. Students and faculty are experimenting with the theatrical vocabulary, hoping to find a phrase or a shape of enrichment. It is a tribute to the soundness of the aims and achievements that such laboratory work has turned out four times to be a whopping good show also.

"This time they did not throw Shakespeare into the test tube but their professor of playwriting instead, Gene McKinney, who came to Baylor from Tennessee and returned with faculty status by way of General Patton's Army and Columbia University. *A Different Drummer* (actually a trumpet player) proceeds from the late Prof. Koch's precepts of grass-roots inspiration.

"McKinney's locale is so regional as almost to be recognized as McLennan County. The virtue is that the Baylor student body, expressing itself impulsively, can be perfectly 'at home with the church-conscious small town and Main-and-Fourth street situations.'

"This is not to say that McKinney hasn't written the particular into something universal. . . .

"From the two-hour spectacle in Baylor's Studio One you can reach estimates that McKinney never wastes a speech, has a vein of gentle but inexorable satire, can limn a character of dimensions with a couple of thrifty speeches and can deploy a large cast easily through his staging resources. . . ."

The brightest jewel in Rosenfield's crown was his critical effort in behalf of Margo Jones and her tiny theater that opened in 1947 in the Gulf Oil Playhouse in Fair Park, a theater-in-the-round located on the grounds that for three weeks annually sprung into life as the State Fair of Texas.

Here are some excerpts from Rosenfield's review (July 10, 1947) of Tennessee Williams' *Summer and Smoke:*

"A playwright of recognized gifts intrusted a new manuscript to Dallas' Theater '47 Tuesday night and one hopes he gets here in time to see how well the resident repertory company does it and how much the local audience enjoys it.

"The reception by the 'world premiere' audience, which reached ovational volume, was not the ultimate test. This was a capacity audience of subscribers and backers to whom shy, informal Tennessee Williams is the glamour lad of the cause. They knew of his long collaboration with Margo Jones, managing director of Theater '47, and the romantic success story of *The Glass Menagerie* which brought both of them to Broadway in 1945.

"They knew, too, that rescuing such scripts as *Summer and Smoke* from the typewritten page and giving them life on a stage is the primary function of the theater they planned so long.

"So we can pardon them their ecstacy at finding *Summer and Smoke* meritorious. We think the less involved patronage at seventeen performances to come will find it skillful and absorbing. On the theory that no price is too great to pay for giving the world a valid esthetic expression, *Summer and Smoke* is worth all the waiting and all the money that Theater '47 has cost.

"It is a more rugged play than *The Glass Menagerie*. *Summer and Smoke* deals with elemental passions in the eternal conflict of the sacred and the profane. . . .

"We may as well face the fact that *Summer and Smoke* played with only partial effect in the four-sided stage of our theater-in-the-round. The area was altogether too small to set any one scene atmospherically. The night, the trees, the Gulf breeze and the fireworks of the fountain park rather eluded all suggestion. Miss Jones met her problem with extraordinary resourcefulness. We don't see how she could have managed better. But this play needs a stage and a big one. . . .

"The labor that went into the production of this play is no concern of the audience except in the finished result. However, it is reasonable to remember that there would have been no theater and no *Summer and Smoke* without community interest and driving leadership.

"*Summer and Smoke* should live in the repertory long enough to move from the floor to the stage, which may be many years."

Although the dominant theme of this review is not so much the Williams play as the deep pride in having it at Margo Jones' theater, Rosenfield nonetheless is able to see the unfortunate limitations of this adored playhouse, the inadequacy of its size for this play and the undesirability of presenting it in the round. This ability to sort out mingled emotions and recognize truth shows Rosenfield to have been a man able to search for and discover the heart of the matter, even when it must have somehow hurt him to admit it.

In January of 1955, Margo Jones staged Lawrence and Lee's *Inherit the Wind*, three months prior to Herman Shumlin's Broadway production. The following excerpts from Rosenfield's notice are interesting in themselves; however, in the very last line the critic reveals his honest feelings about new plays—a plaint which is not novel among members of the critical fraternity where obligatory attendance is frequent and too often unhappy.

"A new play of power, humanity and universal truth found its way into Margo Jones' Theater '55 repertoire Monday evening for what has to be an epochal three weeks of this anniversary season. *Inherit the Wind* is so worthwhile both in aspiration and writing skill that it is a game beyond the prize of even an active box-office.

"Judging by the reception there should be no trouble on that score either. The audience was engaged from beginning to end and escaped its engrossment only to applaud several spectacularly acted bits and to approve the rest. In tribute to Margo's inspired direction let it be said that her arena stage was crowded by her cast of twenty-one only when it was supposed to be.

"*Inherit the Wind* is the work of two Broadway-radio-television authors, Jerome Lawrence and Robert E. Lee, who were present to taste a triumph. It is a script of professional craft as well as sincerity. It is edited and burnished to an unusual degree for Theater '55's manuscript material.

"Messrs Lawrence and Lee have tossed off their share of potboilers and know how to be merely entertaining. This time, though, they have applied their gift to a subject that commanded their thoughts, their fervor and their hearts. . . .

"For an 'ideas' play, *Inherit the Wind* is argued in remarkably human terms. It would be absurd to push a comparison too far, but we feel like saying that Messrs Lawrence and Lee succeed where Messrs Shaw and Ibsen often faltered at the same thing. . . .

"The authors do not waste a line of dialogue. Every word goes somewhere. Clever is the opening, a colloquy between a lad collecting worms for fishing and a tiresome little girl who is afraid of worms. . . .

"*Inherit the Wind*, a title from the Scriptures, is one of the proudest, not to say exculpating productions of our unusual theater devoted sometimes painfully to new plays only."

The notice is proud, positive, and without palaver.

Finally, I would quote in its entirety an epitaph for Margo Jones (1965). It is sad and celebrative, and Rosenfield pointed ahead to the certain future of the Margo Jones theater, despite the death of its leader. This was of primary importance to him, as indeed it would have been to Margo Jones.

"A community theater located far from Broadway and running daily over a period of thirty to forty-two weeks a year.

"A theater employing only professional actors at Equity rates and professionals at all other posts.

"A theater devoted primarily to the presentation of 'hitherto unproduced' plays, varied by the revival of 'classic' or dramatic masterpieces at least fifty years old.

"Operation of a repertory company in which all actors rank alike and are paid alike; plus the 'repertory' repetition of the better plays for further seasoning of their values.

"This was the basis of Margo Jones' completely 'mad' idea, revealed to a few friends here in 1944. By 1945 the support had jelled among the supporters of the recently suspended Dallas Little Theater.

"There was encouragement in a donation by Eugene McDermott of $10,000. There was discouragement in the building situation, impossible costs of new construction, the lack of a single available playhouse.

"The Margo Jones idea became an actuality, however, in the summer of 1947 when it opened in the present quarters at Fair Park with *Farther Off from Heaven*, a new script by a chap named William Inge, who is not so obscure these days as the author of *Picnic* and *Bus Stop*.

"Theater '55, which changed its numeral by the year since Theater 47, was impossible to explain at first. As it operated with complete economic plausibility, it began to look simple and enviable. It became one of the best-known theaters in the world. It was imitated in hundreds of communities, if only for pointing the way to arena-type presentation.

"As an international force Theater '55 was treasured for its services to the playwright, which were two. It was the outlet for the new play and often a showcase for Broadway, movie, radio or television futures. But, better, it marshalled an audience for the play without reputation, gave it vogue and inspired many other theaters to entertain new scripts for the first time.

"Yet Margo saw to it that Theater '55 was a community theater. Technically it was and is owned by a civic non-profit group of which she was the paid managing director subject to orders. Actually, though, she was given a free hand and unquestioning support. She assembled staff and cast, arranged operations, selected plays without asking for anything but advice.

"In the shock, and, for many, the heartbreak of her death Sunday, can be found the nugget of her deep sincerity and love of the city she adopted and which adopted her. She left her dream and her organization intact as a civic institution, which can be carried on without so much as an amended by-law.

"The Margo Jones 'touch,' which she applied with the artist instinct, will be missing. Her longtime associate, Ramsey Burch, who has staged more productions of late than she, assumes her position.

"It was the ebullience of Margo's personality, her capacity to get things done in a jiffy, her hunches and inspirational leadership that made things hum for so long.

"This, we believe, has written a chapter in the whole world history of the theater. But Dallas gave Margo a testimonial luncheon last fall to celebrate her ten Dallas seasons. The point was that Theater '55 was a dream come not only to life but also to surprisingly long life.

"Those of us who were near her during those exciting years will never get over missing her.

"But she left in their custody a very solid and very precious factor in the culture of Western civilization. As never before Dallas must conserve it."

Although, as it happens, the quotations from John Rosenfield's voluminous writings were largely favorable, it must not be presumed that he was never a dissenter. For him, theater, then music, formed the core of his life. He devoted himself to interpreting them and educating audiences. He attempted to develop the tastes of local people who looked to him for guidance. He was often thought to be petulant and perhaps on occasion he was, but, if so, it was because of his ingrained love for the best in the arts, his undying hope that Texas—not only Dallas—would provide the proper climate for distinguished creativity. His dedication was always to the ideal of artistic excellence and growth.

RICHARD COE

*Richard Coe, of *The Washington Post*, is in a position somewhat similar to that of his colleagues in Boston and Philadelphia, since he also is sometimes faced with world-premieres of Broadway-bound theater pieces. In recent times Washington has housed more of these than the other two cities which formerly were considered inevitable stops before Broadway. This shift is due to the presence of the Kennedy Center with its several theaters (these are by no means the only ones in Washington), plus the enormous numbers of enter-

*Born 1916, Coe attended George Washington University, served in the USAAF (Middle East) and was editor of its *Stars and Stripes*. Coe was assistant drama and film critic on *The Washington Post* (1938–1942) and since 1946 has been its principal critic. He has lectured frequently, received the Newspaper Guild Award for Criticism (1949) and other related citations from the Washington (D.C.) Board of Trade, the General Federation of Women's Clubs, the District of Columbia Board of Commissioners, and was named Critic of the Year (1963) by the Directors' Guild of America.

tainment-hungry international displaced persons who inhabit the city and its environs.

Richard Coe has a keystone position. He is perceptive and knowledgeable, an excellent writer, and an impartial judge. While correct prognosis is not of true importance, it is nevertheless interesting to note that Coe's score is nearly infallible. Of more significance when considered purely as a critic, is Coe's comprehension of the many new works with which he is confronted. There he is discerning, wise, consistent, honest, and to the point.

Washington's admirable Arena Stage, which has become an increasing force in the American theater, produced John Whiting's *The Devils* (1963). The following is an excerpt from Coe's review:

"Alack, when our scientific age deals with devils and witchcraft it tends to confuse superstition with faith. At best an over-simplification, this quickly leads to that ignorance which contemptuously assumes faith to be passive muddle-headedness and denies the passionately activist quality which is the sine qua non of faith. So the 'scientific' view of the conveniently silent past is essentially supercilious and rapidly boring.

"Shaw, on the other hand, being a true humanist, was able to tackle superstition and witchcraft and the uses conniving statesmen and greedy capitalists made of them because he had a respect for faith and for people. Consider Joan, Bill Walker, Alfred Doolittle.

"This is why Shaw always insisted that *Saint Joan* be given with the epilogue. Without it, the play could not complete his statement. Without anyone of genuine faith involved, *The Devils* is only a paean of hate, not a play."

The same Arena Stage had a resounding success in May 1973 with a new musical, *Raisin*, that was as a result propelled onto the Broadway stage. The question of musicalizing Lorraine Hansberry's play *A Raisin in the Sun* is raised here (and answered), but without the offensive and baseless accusations attached to it by Martin Gottfried. Excerpts of Coe's review follow:

"At last! Something worth shouting about: *Raisin* at Arena Stage.

"Creatively inspired by the late Lorraine Hansberry's *A Raisin in the Sun*, this has a wonderfully varied score by Judd Woldin and Robert Brittan, a superlative cast of singing actors and an audience appeal that does your soul good. It is announced to run only through June 24; once the word gets around, Arena should just hold it for a couple of years.

"While I have a few reservations about spots here and there, the overall effect is so splendidly projected and the individual performances so right that those can wait.

"Like many others, I was fairly leery about the notion of musicalizing Miss Hansberry's basically serious drama about a black Chicago family of the early fifties that buys a house in a white neighborhood on Dad's life insurance policy. . . .

"The basic challenge rests on both book, to maintain the essentially serious story of this family ruled by a firm matriarch, and a score varied enough, true enough, to suit the action.

"Robert Nemiroff (widower of Miss Hansberry) and Charlotte Zaltzberg stick close enough to the play's development. . . .

"Nitpicking, I'd have liked Mama to have a quiet time of her own once Dad's insurance check arrives. And while I grant that an African dance which follows immediately is a wowser, it could have tighter incorporation into the whole. But the transition from the satiric 'Not Anymore' into the serious denouement is very well achieved, critical to the whole matter of accepting the play as faithful to its serious design.

"The score boasts the firmest melodic lines of any in recent memory, melodies that aren't afraid to take hold and sing. Anyone who follows musical theater surely is aware that composers' inability to sustain a melodic line accounts for the paucity of our recent musicals. Composer Woldin and his lyricist, Brittan, are reported to have spent five years developing their score and it's the best I've heard in years."

West Side Story opened in Washington in August 1957 prior to Broadway. Coe wrote a review the following day (excerpted here) and a Sunday piece ten days later (also excerpted). The reader should remember that these articles appeared nearly two decades ago. *West Side Story* represented the "newest" in Broadway musicals, and at that time Richard Coe was exploring what today we take for granted.

From the morning-after notice: "*West Side Story* is a work of art. Like all works of art, it is open to the conceptions of the creators and the observers. Watching the stage of the National we are moved, and tremendously moved, by a uniquely cohesive comment on life. It may not be our personal comment on life, but it is a vibrant memorable viewpoint.

"It is these things because *West Side Story* throbs with the comment of emotional thought. It is not quite throbbing with the reality of life because how can the teenagers of today find, in music, story, dance and philosophy, exactly what is on their minds? They don't quite know what is in their unrest, but they are indeed lucky to find commentators willing to try for explanations.

"The setting is not likely to have precise translators. We have a Puerto Rican gang of New York's West of Central Park and a group that's native born. There is romance here, but it is purposely not the romance of lyric theater; this is the romance of the lonely for the lonesome, not precisely the same wave lengths but close enough to be felt.

"The link, I think, is the music of Leonard Bernstein, sometimes soaringly melodic, sometimes cruelly sheer fighting rhythm and dissonance. There is conflict all the way, sheer, arresting, diametric, bitterly contrasting and searingly heartbreaking. In his music, eloquently projected in orchestra and voices, Bernstein is painting an emotional portrait. And the colors are always his, often ours but inevitably his.

"Fortunately, Arthur Laurents, nor Jerome Robbins who first got the feel for the idea, have not followed the pre-opening notion of giving us a strict Romeo and Juliet rewrite. They've a far more simple plan with the feel of warring factions without the textbook slavishness suggested.

"But it is Bernstein's flowing music that jells the vitality of these young people at their pitiably innocent warfare. It is senseless, but Bernstein's score makes us feel what we do not understand. Here we have the feel of today with no attempt to explain, with only the distrust that inhibits the young humans without background, intelligence or taste. It is a musical comment with only implied blame. . . .

"All told, *West Side Story* is a music drama to see and relish, to think about and remember and far too complex to be satisfactorily analyzed in a brief twenty-five minutes."

Now for a Sunday essay, ten days later: "Art, among other things, finds the beauty of truth in the ugliness of ignorance. This, to me, is the triumph of *West Side Story*.

"It is relatively trivial to compare the National's ambitious new musical play with others, though on the commercial level this is being spoken of as another *My Fair Lady*, a disservice to both.

"For here four men are taking a timeless view of one of our society's sorriest phenomena, the teen-age gangs of a great city. Without the book of Arthur Laurents, the lyrics of Stephen Sondheim and the nurturing of his original idea by Director Jerome Robbins, Leonard Bernstein would not have the framework for his music. But it must be admitted that without Bernstein's score, the framework would be only that. His music is the heart.

"Bernstein's challenge has been to strike an emotional chord, seeking to link this fortunately small segment of modern life to our whole society. Last year in *Candide* he was being intellectually brilliant: in its successor a deeper, emotional quality is involved.

"It is ridiculous to say that *West Side Story* glorifies young thugs; one might as well say that *Carmen* glorifies smuggling. What the music tells us is what, in our outrage, we easily forget: that within all of us beat the same emotions, primitive urges, lyrical dreams, cynical experiences, questioning fears.

"*West Side Story* is the sort of work that cries for definition because in our normal laziness we are far too tempted to pigeonhole anything as this or that. This fits into many categories, not just one.

"There are valid compromises in *West Side Story*, for in our democratic day art is becoming commerce. But when the boys of the Jet Gang sing 'Gee, Officer Krupke!' they also are telling us what they think of our concern about gangs. When the Puerto Rican Anita and the Shark girls sing of 'America' they state the conflicting views of young people in new surroundings. That these are wingding commercial numbers does not mean they have no place in the whole. Where they are, they fit.

"Bernstein's score also speaks to us more subtly: through rhythm —a number like 'Cool,' which has some of the hesitant beat of the young; through lyrical melody—'Tonight,' an infinitely moving modern comment on Shakespeare's balcony scene; through dissonance—in 'The Rumble,' a brilliantly staged fight scene; and with skilled musicianship the patterns of grand opera—'Tonight,' an astonishingly intricate quintet.

"There has been hemming and hawing over whether this is a modern telling of *Romeo and Juliet*. Of course it is and why not? Shakespeare frankly took his tale, names and all, from a poem of 1562, which stemmed from French and Italian sources. Love between rival clans is an ageless theme, including the Hatfields, and the 'Coys.

"Laurents and Sondheim have been amusing in their variations and one smiles about the friendly druggist (so expertly played by Art Smith), a descendant of the hapless apothecary of Mantua. And it is the representative of the state, now not a prince but a police officer, who tries to keep the peace and presides over the final scene of realization.

"This finale and indeed the whole second act is inevitable, just as are the long-recognized *Romeo and Juliet*. Yet to alter the inevitable is artistic fraud.

"Under Robbins' imaginative guidance the production is a model of exactness. . . ."

The next three excerpts concern new plays that failed to make it either in Washington or later on Broadway. Coe's views of them are clear and supportive. They were produced in successive years.

1956: "With *Night of the Auk* Arch Oboler is in the position of an architect who has designed a marvelous building and then can't decide where to put it. The peaks of idealism, the plains of realism, the vale of cynicism, the lake of philosophy, the shoals of despair, the cliffs of decision, the glen of poetry and the knoll of detachment lure the Shubert's playwright along a range of earnest search. . . .

"For earnestly as Oboler has meant to say something, there are too many things he's angry about for him to be positively positive about anything. He admirably hates wars; the irresponsibility of scientists toward their Pandora's Box; the Very Rich who are degenerate; the very opinionated who are so opinionated that they hate degenerates; the poor who might stoop to endorsing cigarettes; the advertising world which wants everyone to endorse anything and the general greed, ruthlessness and ambition of the human race.

"These are all laudable targets of attack and the audience was duly appreciative of the playwright's highminded anger as well as his marksmanship. The only drawback is that firing artillery at sitting ducks doesn't prove anything."

1957: "Great expectations are one curse of success. Last night at the Shubert, Tennessee Williams' newest play, *Orpheus Descending*, had its premiere and didn't get off the stage into that mesmerizing atmosphere that is Williams' own peculiar genius.

"As a playwright Williams has become his own prisoner. Shock values are expected along with his superb sense of dialogue, the shock values underlying the frank acceptance of sex in love. Usually his gift of poetic realism succeeds with his keen dramatic construction.

"This sound construction is fatefully missing in *Orpheus Descending*, which unquestionably has more to it than meets the ear. There is here, I suspect, thoughtful symbolism, but it comes out murkily in a story that moves by fits and starts, not through any fault of the excellent cast but through the shocks a Williams audience expects and is served and through the playwright's scattered shots at dramatic effect. . . .

"Williams' first dramatic weakness is evident in his first act, largely exposition of the sort one would condemn in any playwright not named Tennessee Williams. But, one argues with oneself, we shall see. His love of character—and how wonderfully well he can draw people in words—becomes Williams' next stumbling block, for he introduces several characters as a descant on his theme, but in the press of gathering events has no time to develop them. And so, ultimately, our attention is scattered and even a melodramatic last act comes off with a pop, not a bang. . . .

"The play is Williams' newest revision of *Battle of Angels*, his first produced play (at twenty-four) in 1940, when a chaotic Boston first-night signalled the windup of the tryout. In its new guise (85 percent rewritten), the play is not shocking, only murky, ineffective and sometimes tasteless."

1958 (first and last paragraphs): "Elia Kazan has transferred Archibald MacLeish's verse drama about Job, *J.B.*, from library to the stage with striking theatricality. That it is not a satisfying drama on the stage lies to an extent in the familiarity of the source, virtually a poetic drama. But the basic flaw is that Job is the same man at the end as he was in the beginning. This is noble but it is not dramatic.

"While I have found serious fault with *J.B.* I would like to welcome it as a long overdue essay in serious drama and production. What I suspect has happened is that being a man of warm erudition, MacLeish has sought to restate ancient glories and timeless triumphs. This he has done. He has given us an absorbing reminder but he has not employed the drama to its own limits."

These are thoughtful and reasonable "thumbs-down" notices; none is angry. Although Coe was deeply disappointed, he was deservedly respectful.

The following reviews (excerpted) concern two distinguished performances which Coe reacts to, analyzes and carefully re-creates for the reader. The first describes Ruth Gordon in Thornton Wilder's *The Matchmaker* (1956), long before its musical version *Hello, Dolly!* was dreamed of.

"At Miss Gordon's first entrance, lip rouge smeared carelessly around her jaw, red wig awry, you might get the notion that a very plastered star is about to disgrace her reputation. The creature, in full sail and bustle, lurches across the stage and your jaw drops in astonishment. She rolls her eyes shrewdly at her unknowing quarry and sputteringly repeats words from sentences she's just stammered over.

"Then it sinks in that you are watching one of the most brilliantly complex comic portraits of our time. You think of the people—nice ladies—you know who are like her. You recall how fond you are of them and their maddening, eccentric ways. And you settle down to adore the outrageous and utterly sensible Mrs. Levi. By the time Miss Gordon hits the middle of a loose-limbed, astute lecture on money, you are on the floor, vowing THIS you must see a dozen times."

The next review about Paul Scofield's *King Lear*, is even more graphic. The production, from England, played in Washington more than a year prior to its New York opening in May 1964. (Martin Gottfried refers to all long pre-Broadway tours as "cynical packages.") So much for "commercialism" and attempting to retrieve an investment. The play opened in Washington in April 1963. The following represents about one half of Coe's review:

"*King Lear* is less a play than an experience, something akin to one's first hearing of a Beethoven symphony, one's first sight of Durham Cathedral or the feeling when for the first time, one's flesh is swirled in an ocean wave, powerful, mysterious, haunting.

"The play depends almost entirely on its central player and there have been Lears, such as Donald Wolfit's, which suggest this. The melange of conflicting, unbelievable threads can scarcely be disguised but so towering are the thoughts which strike out from the play, so baleful are its thoughts on human cruelties and so glorious the poetry that when the entire company proves worthy, the result is a performance that will linger always with those who saw it.

"Last night's was one of those times and a ten-minute, standing ovation marked this as a memorable one in Washington theater history.

"The Scofield Lear is remarkable immediately for its quiet. Generally, in a voice of quite a higher pitch than he has used in other roles, he speaks with a quiet intensity, heightening the rage of the 'Blow winds' speech in the storm scene.

"He tackles the problem of giving his kingdom away and ignoring his tenderly sensible daughter head on. Scofield enters as a King, used to being obeyed, flattered and feared. He indicates he is weary, bone-tired, a subtle way of making foolish actions credible.

"He faces a line with brilliant use of his face, first listening, then thinking, finally speaking. This compelling concept, always brilliantly lighted, takes us into the old man who has so much to learn.

"And so each scene becomes a step in the progression of self-awareness. There are scores of memorable moments, brief pauses, the forming thought, then the hushed, weary voice: 'O, let me not be mad.' This is spoken flatly, tonelessly yet the effect will chill your spine.

"Old Gloucester, blinded now, seeks to kiss his hand and Scofield's Lear draws away, rubs it and mutters 'It smells—of mortality.' Cordelia, meeting her recovered father, asks 'Will it please you, Highness, walk?' and Lear looks at her, then nods, suggesting many things before he comes to his reply. . . .''

Edward Albee's latest play, *Seascape*, which this writer thoroughly enjoyed (along with "God and Clive Barnes," according to the acerbic John Simon), opened in Washington in December 1974. Parts of Coe's qualified notice follow:

"In *Seascape* Edward Albee has written a highly original, alternately funny and tender paean saluting the thinking creatures of land and sea.

"While I concede that for a less skilled production my enthusiasm might well be nil and also grant that some will find this far off their wave-lengths, the Eisenhower Theater's first-nighters were conspicuously alert and amused for the start of this four-week run last night.

"Less hearty fare than *The Skin of Our Teeth*, this does echo some of the affectionate wonder of Thornton Wilder's great human comedy and marks an aware turning from the theatrical acidity of Albee's *Who's Afraid of Virginia Woolf?* now in repertory at Arena Stage. A dozen years later Albee has found a perspective from the sand dunes.

"But he has not lost his verbal imagery; one listens, grasps and appreciates. . . .

"It is not an especially deep philosophy and there can be no ultimate conclusion to the play. Albee is only capturing a mood, one suspects a mere fleeting thought he might once have had at lovely, lonely Montauk. What remains is an insight: We of the universe are more alike than unlike. Distrust is our mutual enemy.

"That we accept the notion of the sea creatures communicating with the land creatures is one of Albee's technical achievements. Somehow we know that the spoken words are merely communicated thoughts. Some of the sport lies in the lizards' curiosity about hand shaking and human breasts. There's amusement in seeing the same qualities in males and females of whatever condition."

While this is far from a rave review, it exhibits an optimism for the play, respect for its author, and a desire on Coe's part to be helpful.

What follows is excerpted from Coe's review of *A Funny Thing Happened on the Way to the Forum* (1962). A discussion of musical shows in general is presented here. This was the year on Broadway that included *Little Me, Mr. President, Oliver, Sophie, Stop the World—I Want to Get Off*, and *Tovarich*.

"Blend is all in the exotic world of that popular, expensive hybrid, the Broadway musical.

"Of those which have had memorable Washington first performances, *West Side Story* and *Carnival*—to pick pertinent, divergent examples—were instantly recognizable as having that vital blend of material, staging and performance. They went on to triumph virtually as they were on their E street first nights.

"Last year brought another two, wholly lacking that sine-qua non, *Hail the Conquering Hero* and *Donneybrook*. Though a Broadway musical can be virtually about anything from King Arthur's court to the garment district, neither of these firmly established its intent and suffered accordingly, despite frantic tinkerings with material, staging and performance. . . . lack of blend has been all too evident in Broadway's big musicals this season.

"*All American* for instance, is essentially a satire on American life, adapted by Mel Brooks from Robert Lewis Taylor's book on Professor Fodorski. Every so often it is sharp, but through the casting of its particular, individualistic star, Ray Bolger, and the direction of Joshua Logan, *All American* avoids the blend. Ironically, Bolger and a fine cast, headed by Eileen Herlie, Ron Husmann, Anita Gillette and Fritz Weaver, seem better than their material, which surely must have been quite something else when practice started.

"*Milk and Honey*, a booming hit about some American widows touring Israel, has fairly heavy 'book' trouble. However, in performance this has the advantage of seeming better than it is because the production tone blends with the book which catches the exuberance in a new country. The dancing in this is first rate, the score matches the vigorous atmosphere and there is over-all cohesion.

"Triumphant blending of material with production is the cause of the *How to Succeed in Business Without Really Trying* uproar. Here, to start with, is the strong story line of Shepherd Mead's original book, detailing the rise of a window-washer to the company's presidency. As co-adapter and director, Abe Burrows never lets anything get in the way of that story line. Apart from 'staging' the musical numbers (which music and lyrics seem infinitely more clever than they do on Victor's original cast recording), Bob Fosse has contributed no strictly dance numbers. Sets and costumes, brilliantly detailed but always underplayed, never get in the way of the story's zestful drive.

"Because musicals have become our theater's most creative—and expensive—area of operations, the ultimate blend achieved by *A Funny Thing*, etc. will decide whether it ranks with *Carnival* or with *Donneybrook*. Which is what tryouts are all about, a matter of whether and whither."

Whether or not one agrees in toto with Coe's point of view, his opinion is thoughtful and relevant.

Coe is and always has been a valuable asset to his profession, to his city and to the theater. His opinions have almost invariably been a kind of Ambrose Lighthouse to Broadway. He knows. He allows himself to experience and he is not afraid of taking the initiative in saying what is on his mind.

JAY CARR

The Detroit News' drama and music critic, Jay Carr, is a discerning reviewer. He covers a wide range of performances and is obviously untouched by the opinions of others. Carr has problems similar to all out-of-New York writers. He covers theater of local origin, some pre-Broadway shows and touring companies, and he also journeys frequently to New York, London (Ontario and England), Ann Arbor, and other festival-type oases.

Carr writes well, communicates his own experiences to his readers, thinks and supports his judgments. After Broadway openings, his views are often at odds with those of the New York dailies. It is to his credit that he shows a lively interest in new, uncelebrated playwrights and wishes to acquaint his Detroit readers with their work.

I should like to begin with Carr's views of an amateur (local) production of Kafka's *The Trial* (1975). In his article, Carr dwells mainly on the author and his play, then deals with the director's resourcefulness. Following the quoted excerpt, the reviewer makes modest obeisances to the cast (John Rosenfield in Dallas did this). The review closes with dismissal of a local production of *Medea* which lacked a proper actress in the title role.

"One of the things that make contemporary life trying is the speed with which nightmares pass into the commonplace. No hell is private for very long, it seems. Not even the hells which were recently considered rather advanced, such as Franz Kafka's. Kafka may not yet be the darling of the TV networks. But he no longer speaks to us as a tormented outcast.

"He now seems one of us, partly, it is true, because we have had time to assimilate his vision. But no longer is he a terrifying opener of trap doors. The doors which in Kafka's day were barely clapped shut over guilt, dread, sexual and social anxiety, and the abnegation of human will have long been standing open. Today we all know only too well what a shaky thing a human identity is.

"This occasion for a fresh look at Kafka stems from an admirable staging of the Gide-Barrault version of *The Trial* at The Theatre on the Marygrove College campus. Rather than select one of the standard avenues of Kafka interpretation—the presaging of totalitarianism, the atomization of human will, the personification of feelings of helplessness and anxiety—director George Mallonee suggests them all in a lively and resourceful staging.

"Mallonee has deployed his large cast with insight, imagination

and purposefulness. At its center, of course, is Josef K, the bourgeois
bank manager whose world starts falling apart when two guards in
gray uniforms come to arrest him on the morning of his thirtieth
birthday. What is he accused of? Who is accusing him? He never
learns. He only knows that his shame and dislocation grow as the
knowledge of his impending trial spreads through the community.

"Mallonee has got the important thing right. Josef K seems, for
as long as possible, solid. The others swirl about him, brightly colored phantasmagoria. Sometimes they are benign. The advocate
rolled out on his canopied couch seems like a modern updating of
the caterpillar and his hookah from *Alice in Wonderland*. (Not that
Lewis Carroll is benign, but that's another piece.)"

This kind of notice educates without patronizing. It encourages
the striving local performers and producers to forge ahead, and
readers with intellectual curiosity are intrigued enough to attend a
performance. Its concern with the play rather than the young performers places the focus on the one truly interesting aspect of such
a presentation.

The Detroit Repertory Theatre revived Odets' *Rocket to the Moon*
(1975). Carr takes the opportunity to reevaluate and interpret the
play:

"Clifford Odets blazed across the American stage during the 1930s,
then got lost in his reputation as our Depression playwright. But
there is a lot more to his work than indignation at the way social
and economic systems diminish men. . . .

"It is not the current hard times that make Odets worth reviving.
Rather it is the fact that the pain in his plays is still fresh. . . .

"But deeper pain is caused by barrenness. Everybody is looking
for love. Some can't find it. The others can't accept it. Says a secondary character: 'Love and the grace to use it and expand it? Who's
got the time?'

"It may sound like soap opera in outline, but the emotions are
vivid, and Odets's compassion, his hatred of the nullification of life,
inflames them with unflagging tension. This isn't agitprop. Odets
seems to be working from the inside out, saying not that failed systems impose loveless lives on people, but rather that flawed so-
cieties arise from the difficulty of loving and accepting love.

"As is so often the case, the DRT production knows where the
values in the writing lie, but fails to get at them more than sketchily
and intermittently."

Again, the play's the thing. Carr does not support the performance but neither does he destroy it; and he makes the play something of an event.

It is apparent that Detroit—like many other cities in the United

States—abounds in local theatrical activity. The next excerpts are from a review of the Meadow Brook Theatre revival (1975) of *Death of a Salesman*. Here Carr treats Miller's play thoughtfully and with a fresh point of view.

"Has there ever been a more quintessential American on the contemporary stage than Willy Loman, that tragic personification of self-betrayal? 'You're too accommodating, dear,' his wife says at the beginning of the play. 'He had the wrong dreams,' says his son Biff at Willy's funeral. Both are only too right. Those lines frame a man who wasted his life trying to become what he didn't want to be. . . .

"His death is all the more poignant and all the more outrageous in its absurdity when the mercantile world he spent his life genuflecting to doesn't even permit him a dignified end. . . .

"*Death of a Salesman* makes us ask just as trenchantly in 1975 as in 1949 whether this isn't a land of the lost, overrun with Willy Lomans."

Detroit's Vest Pocket Theatre was the scene of a production of Lonnie Elder III's *Ceremonies in Dark Old Men* (1973).

"There are plays so strong and beautifully written that they ought always to be playing on a stage somewhere. Lonnie Elder III's *Ceremonies in Dark Old Men*, at the Vest Pocket Theatre, is such a play. Tender, rueful, loving, violent, bitterly ironic, and laced with explosive humor, *Ceremonies* is a radiant and deeply moving human experience. No stronger and more richly drawn cast of characters has inhabited any American play of the late sixties.

"Mr. Elder has created a world of stark, tragic beauty on a set representing a shabby one-chair Harlem barbershop. His play is about what people must do to remain alive and feel self-respect, but mostly it is about a dying old dancer's sad last fling, and its tragic consequences for his children. 'Dance any dance you can, but dance it,' the old man says. . . .

"But I didn't feel enough depth of character. Often the pace was rushed in a broad, muscular production which lacked the degree of nuance, tempo change, and sensitive phrasing necessary to fully realize the tragedy and plaintive poetry in the writing. The production is notable for energy rather than mellowness or poignancy. Recommended, then, with the above reservation."

Again, praise for a "strong and beautiful play" and reservations about inadequate performances.

Next, Carr's views of two traveling shows. The first is Mark Medoff's highly praised *When You Comin' Back, Red Ryder?* which made the Best Plays list, won an Obie and a Drama Desk Award in New York. Following a substantial run off-Broadway (201 performances),

the play came to Detroit (December 1974) with its author acting a
prominent role. The following extracts demonstrate the fact that
Carr is an independent thinker, although his was not the sole dis-
senting voice.

"Mark Medoff's overpraised play at the Music Hall, *When You
Comin' Back, Red Ryder?*, begins promisingly. A whining young
greaser named Steven Ryder (he likes to be called Red) has just
finished the night shift in a flyspecked roadside diner in New
Mexico. He's replaced behind the counter by a sweet, fat girl named
Angel, who pipes lovingly away at Red, ignoring his surliness.

"Then Medoff lets the play veer away from these two rich characters, leaving them stranded and undeveloped as he strides off
after Bigger Things. The evening thins out, seeming finally to decline into a stageful of borrowing—a little *Petrified Forest* nostalgia,
a little *Midnight Cowboy* transmogrification of myth, a little *Zoo
Story* showdown on the existential killing ground.

"The tipoff is that Medoff resorts to the mossy device of a loaded
gun menacing the innocents in the diner. Yes, there's suspense, but
it isn't dramatic suspense. It's suspense brought in by the prop
man. . . .

"I'm frankly tired of plays that mourn the loss of an innocence
we never had, and Medoff's play strikes me as slick and shallow."

The road company of *A Little Night Music* starring Jean Simmons reached Detroit in May 1974. Carr provides us with a "different" view of the show itself, which he admires.

"What *Der Rosenkavalier* is to opera, *A Little Night Music* is to
Broadway musicals. Worldly, benevolent, nostalgic, witty, and resigned, it waves wistfully to fin-de-siècle elegance and irretrievable
youth. It restores to the commercial theater a charm and sophistication for which it is starved. Here at last is nostalgia that doesn't
require you to disconnect your intelligence.

"Stephen Sondheim's haunting waltz themes make this treatment
seem deeper than the film that inspired it, Ingmar Bergman's *Smiles
of a Summer Night*. The film was an urbane comedy of manners.
Sondheim's washes of nocturnal sound have their inspiration in
Brahms, Ravel, and even Schubert. They are bittersweet, poignant,
intimate, and outdoorsy, and their colors match the show's autumnal emotions.

"The forest greens, golds, and russets that billow from the score
complement perfectly Florence Klotz's stunning mauve decade decor
and Boris Aronson's shadowy groves of birch trees that glide onstage
and off on plexiglass panels. There is a hint of Shakespeare's
Midsummer Night's Dream here. Nature smilingly imposes order

on the chaotic amours of supposedly civilized people. At the end all are resigned rather than resolved. They will act their ages. . . .

"There is a trimming of expectations rather than an expansion. Such qualities as resignation, irony and even self-mockery are a far cry from the traditional emotional surges and purges of musical theater. But here they are treated with exquisite urbanity and compassion. The unruly hearts of these sexual pilgrims are tamed with kindness.

"In no figure of the commercial theater do imagination and professionalism meet so satisfyingly as in Harold Prince, whose staging has exceptional style. This national company is patently a reproduction of the original, but it is a first-class production. Mr. Prince can always be trusted to lavish lots of care upon his work. . . .

"*A Little Night Music* handles the less than surefire theme of adjustment to one's years with exceptional grace, lyricism, and humanity."

We have seen Carr stimulating and encouraging Detroit-made productions. We have seen his treatment of travelers after the Broadway fact. Now I should like to present sections of two notices about shows en route to the lions' den (1974).

"It's a pity that words like romp have been cheapened by overuse. I mean what do you say when a real romp comes along? I'm thinking of the Royal Shakespeare Company's zestful revival of Dion Boucicault's 1841 comedy, *London Assurance*, which last night swooped into the Fisher Theater with arched brow and elegant drawl, the very sort of period entertainment that people flock to London in hope of seeing.

"Although the production has been around a few years, it is crisp, fresh and stunningly disciplined, actually a bit sharper and more nuanced than when I saw it at the Aldwych in 1970. Most important, it still has Donald Sinden's definitive portrayal of the overstuffed and overextended old fop, Sir Harcourt Courtly, who in a Gloucestershire country manor loses an heiress to his easygoing son.

"Sinden's Sir Harcourt remains the sublime comic creation. Mincing about like a decrepit dancing master, this rouged, preening ruin of a Regency rake comes on like Mussolini in drag. He has worked out every roll of his scornful eye, every curl of his gloved index finger, every disdainful ascent of his brow with bravura technique. He remembers to creak when he drops to one knee to propose, and is the most fun to have around when lines like 'Come, let us fly!' clear the air. *London Assurance* is a joy and Sinden's Sir Harcourt is stylized perfection."

This play and its star performer found the New York critics of two strongly opposite minds—Gottfried of course ranting against both. In New York, its run was brief. Carr reports a fun evening and a superb performance.

The Wiz (November 1974), despite a majority of New York daily paper put-downs, is a smash hit—a phenomenon dealt with elsewhere in this book. Jay Carr saw it in Detroit in the midst of its out-of-town troubles. Its eventual director—Geoffrey Holder—was at that time listed only as costume designer. Nevertheless, the Detroit reviewer recognized basic favorable qualities in *The Wiz*. I quote from his review.

"*The Wiz* is a dear little lollipop of a musical. It has charm, style, and flavorful characterizations. And it reminds us that there is more than one road to Oz. *The Wiz*, in case you haven't heard, is the black musical version of *The Wizard of Oz*, and I wouldn't want you to think it has dispensed with the Yellow Brick Road. It just has its own way of looking at it.

"*The Wiz* doesn't follow either the Frank Baum classic or the MGM movie with slavish literalness. While remaining true to the book, it has nevertheless taken it apart and rebuilt it in stage terms. . . .

"Charlie Smalls' music is smoothly accomplished, sitting easily in its soft-core rock, gospel and pop idioms. Many of the songs are a bit too facile, giving the feeling that you might soon hear one or two of them resurface as Chiclet or Chevrolet commercials. But the music was always rousing when it had to be, and it gives the principals and chorus enough to work with.

"The lyrics were more imaginative than the music and sat well against William Brown's book. But then one of the good signs about *The Wiz* is that there is no obvious division of labors, and that includes George Faison's choreography and Gilbert Moses's direction. The dancers were sensational, whether as blue mushroom-cap munchkins or funky monkeys. There are thin patches in *The Wiz*. But they frankly don't seem important. *The Wiz* brings a new confluence of talent to Broadway, which can use it. It is a warmly disarming show."

The following four excerpts are taken from reviews Carr wrote about productions he saw in New York.

First there is an evaluation of *Jesus Christ—Superstar* (1972).

"New York: I wasn't surprised to find the Broadway version of *Jesus Christ—Superstar* bristling with all the primitive Christian ferocity of a Nieman Marcus catalog. This was because of the directorial elephantiasis I had gloomily noted in the recent work of the man doing the staging, Tom O'Horgan. In *Lenny* it seemed to me that O'Horgan didn't trust his material and swamped it with overblown scenic effects.

"Too often he does the same thing in *Jesus Christ—Superstar.* The surprising thing about the Andrew Weber-Tim Rice score is that so much of it sounds as if it belongs in a Broadway musical. Yet O'Horgan and the producer, Robert Stigwood, seem to have thought they had something radically avant-garde, and that they had better conceal it under the trappings of what they thought was a typical Broadway musical.

"Much of the evening thus seems to be an unnecessary masquerade, a misguided exercise in lily-gilding proceeding from an effort to conform to a naively imagined Platonic essence of Broadway musical. The music is put in the position of having to work its way through the staging. Often it does. . . ."

The tone of this review, especially in references to O'Horgan, is as caustic as Carr ever gets. He is too resourceful an analyst to need rage in his tool kit.

The next is a brief selection out of a long piece about *Equus.* I quote these excerpts because they make several original points.

"Transatlantic crossings can be tricky, especially for drama of reach and depth, but *Equus* has arrived with its themes and its flavor intact. One of the things that make it so engrossing is its ability to be about several things at once and it brings its concerns to the stage with striking, personalized urgency. They are polarized in a squareoff between a teen-age boy and a hospital psychiatrist in southern England. . . .

"The probing that follows is more than a psychological detective story. It becomes a sort of spiritual love story too, as the boy and the doctor find their pained spirits intersecting in the spare, harshly lit arena that John Dexter's brilliant stagecraft has managed to turn into the black cave of the psyche. . . .

"The Doctor is an impotent romantic who must treat an impotent passionate man by purging him of his passion, and this is his dilemma. Either way, he kills something precious. . . ."

The following represents Carr's interpretation of David Storey's *The Changing Room.* It is unusual and sensitive.

"At first glance Storey seems to be at work meticulously inscribing a milieu and its inhabitants. But he is after more than just naturalism here. The changing room (it can't really be called a locker room because it doesn't contain any lockers) is not only the room where the players change their clothes. It is also the room where they change their lives for a few hours every Saturday. . . .

"In a program note we are told that this brand of rugby (Rugby

League) is a bruising working class game played for a dwindling working class audience. . . .

"The men pick up an extra $40 per game and they earn it by punishing their bodies on a frozen field. But for a few hours they change their lives. These mill hands, textile workers, civil servants and teachers yank a few hours of heightened existence and eventfulness out of their bleak, grinding lives.

"What we see is the gestalt of the team take shape slowly and fascinatingly as the men stumble in, dazed, out of the cold to slip first into their locker room identities defined by ritual jokes and digs and horseplay. Then, in evolutionary stages, the locker room identities are submerged in the gestalt that is the team.

"This is of course the story of all collective enterprises and it is built slowly and inexorably. The team takes shape from the specks of humanity that coalesce and encase themselves in blue and white striped jerseys, grows in strength until the tension in the changing room becomes unbearable, bursts out along the concrete ramp that leads to the field, and returns gasping and muddy and bloody and spent to catch its breath during the half.

"One of the superbeing's organs is lost. A large, dull fellow is kicked in the nose and is pinned to the rubdown table in pain as he is treated and sent off to the hospital, clutching a precious new electric drill that will be truer to him than his wife has been. The rich club owner and his flunky wait the game out in the changing room during the second half.

"And the team returns victorious, ignoring bruises, riding the jetstream of euphoria. Horseplay ensues in the shower. Water is sloshed around. The humor is exuberant rather than nervous this time and as the players sink, glowing into fatigue, the organism of the team that prowled and roared and tingled for a few hours, disintegrates until the following Saturday."

This is a perceptive summary of the play that describes its form as well as its content.

The last of these recent New York reviews concerns Edward Albee's *Seascape.* Carr is one of not too many reviewers who liked it. His interpretation is relevant, meaningful, and clear.

"New York: *Seascape,* Edward Albee's first play in more than three years, is a tender fantasia about an aging couple on a beach who encounter a pair of lizards ready to mutate from sea to land. The lizards don't come on until the first act curtain, and they are charmers, but long before their entrance the play has subtly begun to work on us.

"In several respects, *Seascape* is a high wire act, and Albee's skill as a craftsman enables him to gamble successfully. He gets away with some not very profound musings on the meaning of life, and he gets away with the anthropomorphic lizards. He even gets away with a dangerously low energy level in the first act. But *Seascape* is far more than the triumph of professionalism that Broadway successes usually, and merely, represent.

"The thing that distinguishes *Seascape* from Albee's previous plays is its straightforward expression of emotion. Emotion, when it has been expressed in Albee's previous plays, usually came out chilly, guarded, formal. But Albee and his characters have mellowed. The play begins with a suggestion of existential bleakness. But it ends in an affirmative gesture of outreach.

"Perhaps I should have made the point that *Seascape* recalls Shaw far more than Beckett, and in more ways.

"The lizards are of course embodiments of the life force, as is Nancy. Their personal destinies are of course inconsequential. What matters is that life presses forward on its own mission, recycling itself, changing itself, spawning countless generations of vessels to contain it during its cosmic voyage from primordial soup to string quartets and beyond.

"'Mutate or perish,' mutters exhausted Charlie, suggesting in his subtle jab, a tie to the academic world. The style of speech, incidentally, is another way in which Albee recalls Shaw. Like Shaw, Albee is often accused of being bloodless. Partly this is because again like Shaw, Albee doesn't write as people speak. He writes as he would like them to speak. There is a literariness, a wit, an exhilarating precision in his adroitly shaped language."

Finally, I should like to reproduce an entire review by Jay Carr, of Jean Genet's *The Screens* (1972). Produced by the enterprising Chelsea Theatre Center of Brooklyn, it had a run of only 28 performances but was included among the season's Best Plays. It was also voted a total of 18 points as "first choice" at the Drama Critics Circle by Harold Clurman, Henry Hewes, Jack Kroll, and William Raidy.

The review is a remarkable one in many respects. The mere fact that the Detroit drama critic would be at such pains to tell his readers, who would undoubtedly never see it, about such an unusual play is, in itself, commendable and demonstrates Carr's deep love of theater.

His graphic presentation of the play's theme and his successful efforts to reproduce his own experience are extraordinary. The story line of Genet's play is bound up with its philosophy and both are inseparable from the production. Carr's entire review follows:

"New York: When Jean Paul Sartre referred to Jean Genet as Saint Genet, he was being neither sardonic nor perverse, but simply descriptive. Sartre was calling attention to Genet's fierce determination to keep his poetry pure. Genet's plays belong to the theater of poetic event. They occur in a spiritual arena where religion and poetry have fused.

"Even those of Genet's supporters who have defended the decadent exteriors and particulars of his plays have tended to think of Genet as a perverse seeker of salvation and left it at that, missing the full scope and importance of the gesture he is making and the power of the poetic actuality he has forged. Genet is more than an anchorite out of Baudelaire.

"Precisely because he refuses to deviate from the business of the poet, conveying to us the experiences of his soul, he is a genuine and profound threat to society, since he necessarily must reject tradition. With tradition you save time because you do not begin at the beginning. But artists must begin at the beginning. Art respects no imperatives but its own, and is after adventure and newness, not a career as a brick in a wall.

"In addition to keeping his language fresh, Genet kept his spirit fresh by avoiding society's snares and artistic conventions as well. He felt drawn to subject matter that was anti-social and heavily laced with atrocity and perversity. Yet he wasn't being merely picturesque, as Toulouse-Lautrec was in portraying society's underside. Nor was he concerned with the drama of social conscience.

"Because his last play, *The Screens*, is outwardly a sardonic chronicle of the Algerian revolt against the French, its deeper significance is likely to be missed. Its nominal subject matter was enough to make the De Gaulle government lean hard on *The Screens*. It was written in 1959, but wasn't published until 1961, and wasn't performed in its entirety until 1966, when Jean-Louis Barrault's company staged it in Paris.

"Its recent production at Brooklyn's enormously enterprising Chelsea Theatre Group was only its second full production, and its first one in English. Because the Chelsea is a subscription house, and a new play was scheduled, *The Screens* had to close after a three-week run despite its being one of the hottest tickets in New York. The hope is that it will reopen off-Broadway.

"It would be a sad and particularly galling loss if, after waiting so long, New York were to so swiftly lose this sympathetic and inventive production of a play not likely to be staged in New York again soon. For all of its fascination, *The Screens* is unwieldy at times and is something of an endurance test, having about 80 speaking roles and taking about four and a half hours to perform.

"But despite the play's often irritating sprawl and deficiency of focus, it incontestably comes at you with the force of genius, albeit a somewhat softer kind of genius than that of Genet's previous plays. For one thing, there is more humor here. This time Genet is detached enough to allow irony to show, and he displays a ripely philosophical attitude toward death.

"There even is a picaresque quality about the string of travails involving the young Algerian named Said, his enduring old mother, and the unbearably ugly girl he marries. 'Evil is our only hope,' says this Algerian Mother Courage. 'It stays with us when everything else has gone to hell.' 'Said is like me,' she tells the scurrying little deformity of a wife. 'He likes things going wrong.'

Said and his mother embrace their down-and-outness. On the way to the wedding, Said cheers his old mother as she dances in her new shoes. And he laughs when his mother says to the cloth mask covering his wife's rotting face: 'We keep you covered because of the flies.' As the mother, Julie Bovasso is only makeup-deep, but she and Said are the play's connective tissue.

"The rest of the time director and translator Minos Volanakis makes exhilaratingly inventive use of the small stage space. A narcissistic homosexual killer of a French Foreign Legion sergeant swings smiling over his victims on a trapeze. A benchful of white colonials looking sugarfrosted in their white masks and costumes comes rolling out of the side wall.

"The richest whore in town uses her breasts as pincushions and sticks jeweled pins in them. A gendarme breaks into a dance in a municipal court. A white vamp glides across the stage on roller skates fanning herself with the butt of a .45 caliber pistol. A cadi with a heavy Yiddish accent makes a decision in court, shrugs, and says, 'If God is wrong, may He punish Himself.'

"An extravagant tumble of stage images then, and an anticolonial burlesque. A pith-helmeted colonial justifies white colonialism by citing Brecht's doctrine that things belong to those who make the best use of them. 'To save my son's patrimony, I'd sacrifice even my son,' he tells his companion. Then, as the orange groves are set on fire by the rebels, he observes sublimely: 'Smells like marmalade.'

"The plantation owner's son, coming upon Said and his wife, says to his lady: 'They look even worse off than we are. Maybe we can get some service around here.' But things have changed. 'Even their shade isn't what it used to be,' the son grumbles, as the French Foreign Legion is led on by a captain whose mind wanders. 'I want my men lyrical, earthy, and in heat,' he exclaims. 'War is a roaring gang bang.'

"By past standards, Genet is almost affectionate in his lampooning of the white colonials. He is hardly a great believer in the Algerian rebels either. In fact, the purity of the Algerian uprising is quickly corrupted. Every time the rebels win a battle, they seem more and more like the French in uniform. And the accounts of their victories are inflated by legends which are lies.

"Said and his mother drop pretty much out of sight during the play's second half, but she reappears just in time to be killed after herself strangling a French soldier who took his eye off her as he drank, permitting her to strangle him with the strap of his own knapsack. The scene called Among the Dead is the 15th of the 17 scenes in the play and it has a fey charm that might have been borrowed from Thornton Wilder.

"As the revolution's dead are gunned down, they reappear on a catwalk not far above the action, and they are bemused to find the transition so painless. 'Well, whaddya know? They make such a fuss about it,' is their entrance line. French and Algerians, soldiers and rebels join arms in instant rapport and cosmic wonder that they could have taken so seriously what went on below.

"The revolution is over down below, and it is clear that the rebels are enshrining a tissue of lies not vastly different from that of the colonials. The play is ready to come full circle, in a reconciling embrace full of awareness of our puniness and vulnerability, but suddenly the lightness is clouded over by the reappearance of Said, the incorrigible loner.

"With Said's reappearance Genet suddenly seems to throw off his attitude of beneficent reconciliation and snap back to his old wariness. Said's mother abruptly pulls herself out of the maternal coziness she had wafted into the boy she killed. 'Said, don't serve any cause,' she screams from the afterlife. 'They're going to make a folk song out of you.'

"Said refuses to publicly embrace the revolution. He goes further. He rejects it. He is shot. The conversational tone, the airy exits and entrances, the more easygoing quality of ritual seem to convey a more mellow Genet. But, Genet seems to open his eyes and lose his smile and sadly say, nothing has changed. Institutions demand loyalty or else.

"Said's chase after metaphysical absolutes is irreconcilable with service to an institution. In Said's case the fresh, indestructible actuality that the poet searches for turns out to be death. But for Genet's characters death can be a purification, a cleansing trip through the ashes, a purging of clichés, of lies, of cultural debris.

"In Genet's imagination lies the characters' renewal and their renewal echoes the poet's renewal of language and image. Like all poets, Genet is a soul brother to the early Christian ascetics, dead to the world so as to be more fully alive in spirit. That is why to think of *The Screens* as a gesture of solidarity with Algerian rebels or as a plunge into despair is to miss its point. *The Screens* is not about politics, but about poetry; not against death, but against corruption.

"*The Screens* is a ritual enactment of the poet's journey. It is a diffuse, cartoony, autumnal celebration of the kind of uncompromising spirit that makes poetry possible, and secondarily, it is a tenderly rueful acknowledgement of the inevitable difference between the political outlaw and the artistic outlaw. (The political outlaw runs toward power. The artistic outlaw runs away from it.)

"The artist clearly is the more dangerous outlaw because his rebellion is on a metaphysical level and he therefore is capable of generating a far more profound kind of upheaval. In their fever over Algeria, the French banned *The Screens* for the wrong reason. Its political content is negligible in comparison to its towering ability to transmit experience on an achetypal level."

Obviously the theater in Detroit—everywhere, for that matter— is served handsomely by Jay Carr. Any reader interested in theater would be indeed fortunate in having him as interpreter and critic.

DAN SULLIVAN

The Los Angeles drama critic is faced with problems similar to those peculiar to New York and Chicago. The film capital (semi-retired) finds itself today the capital of television production, which means that there is a plethora of actors, writers, composers, directors, and many others who are of necessity "between engagements." But performers, writers and directors crave action—on large or small scales, depending on whatever is possible.

As a result of up-and-down employment, Los Angeles has become a honeycomb of small off-Broadway– and off-off-Broadway– type theaters, most of them performing new shows to small audiences. There are at least five major theaters, four of them between large and colossal: the Dorothy Chandler Pavilion, which houses full-scale musicals as well as concerts, ballet and opera; the Ahmanson; the Shubert; the Huntington Hartford; and the smaller Mark Taper Forum, which seats more than seven hundred.

Some of these theaters produce shows and all of them book road companies that have left New York on tour or are practicing to go there at a later date.

Dan Sullivan, the critic of the *Los Angeles Times*, the most powerful of the critics, is a product of *The New York Times* where he served as an assistant drama critic. By most standards, he would be called "young." He is well backgrounded, writes well, and combines the New York situation (new works, off-Broadway, off-off-Broadway) with the Chicago situation (the road show, revivals, and pre-Broadway).

In addition, Sullivan and/or his associates cover ever-increasing activity in the universities, chiefly UCLA, USC, and UC, and they occasionally journey to San Diego, San Francisco, and other regional theaters when promising activities loom on the horizon.

Dan Sullivan, like Claudia Cassidy of yore in Chicago, battles inferior traveling companies. He frequently battles the Civic Light Opera for what he feels are old-fashioned, overlavish, "improved" revivals. He fights for what he considers to be higher artistic standards. He encourages new talents seen in modest surroundings, but he does not employ a double standard of criticism.

He has strong opinions about the roles of critic and producer. He feels that the critic has no obligation to theater business and that most producers run their businesses too haphazardly. He is in favor (Clive Barnes has expressed a similar idea) of producers being prepared financially to continue the run of productions for a period of time after opening, so that in the face of poor reviews they may through a hopefully good "word-of-mouth" increase attendance and eventually run indefinitely. He also believes that the subscription idea is the only sane method of operation for Broadway producers, especially at this time.

I would like to quote from a variety of Sullivan articles—most of them reviews. The first, however, states his position.

Sullivan has many sound things to say vis-à-vis producer and critic in an article entitled "An Open Letter to a Producer." In it, he states fairly his own position as critic and deals with the ill effects of "overselling" shows that the public subsequently finds disappointing.

Dear P (to use your corporate initial):

Thanks for your visit before your show opened and your thoughtful letter after my review appeared. It was good to see you again and to know that your allegiance to the kind of theater we both want for New York and Los Angeles is as firm as before. Of course, one look at your show was enough to prove that.

Your letter raises some perennial questions about the theater and the theater critic that are not going to be solved by return mail. But I do have some thoughts on a few of the matters you mention, which I offer not as a rebuttal but, let's say, as a definition of my job as in my view it relates to yours.

You have, you say, a problem. You would like to send more productions of the last one's high caliber (agreed) to Los Angeles and other American cities, both to increase the quality of theater across the country and to help pay off the cost of the New York production.

But unless enough people in the road cities turn out to see your shows, you will be worse off financially than before. (By "you," I mean, of course, your nonprofit producing group.) Were your shows to appear on a popular subscription series in each town, you would leave New York with at least X dollars in advance sales in the till. But road subscription lists are not what they were: nonexistent in many cities, preempted by resident producing groups (Center Theatre Group, Guthrie Theater, Arena Stage) in others.

"The result," you say, "is no substantial advance sale for a production that may have considerable merit but not be by Neil Simon or have a star who is a local folk hero." (Or, you might have added, not be a musical.)

Nevertheless in last month's instance, you took the chance, sent your production clear across the country—and were very disappointed at the review you got in the *Times,* which you read as respectful but not a rave. As a result of that review, you say, your play "will not find more than a small fraction of its potential audience in Los Angeles."

"I know you can only write what you see and feel," your letter continues, "and I cannot fault you. I am still puzzled whether I can in good conscience risk another production which in spite of my enthusiastic partiality [and that of the New York critics, as again you might have mentioned: really, P, you are too much of a gentleman] may not please you. You act as a watchdog for the L.A. audience and if you find yourself unimpressed they will take you at your word and stay away.

"It is an interesting problem—vital to us and I would guess vital to you in the long run. . . ."

Vital to me, indeed, P. As I am occasionally asked by some out-of-patience reader, where would theater critics be without a theater to criticize? (Writing about something else, I sometimes tell them, if it's been a bad day.) In the long run it is true that you and I are working for the same thing. But in the short run, which is the way life has to be lived, I can't work in quite the way you—and a part of me, too—would like. I cannot, that is, fake a reaction to a show.

Between the lines of your genuinely nice letter, that is what you are asking me to do. Not to pretend to find a bad show a good one. But to pretend that a good show—as I tried to make clear I thought yours was— is for me a great one. The premise being that in an age of routine exaggeration, where "super-star" means someone who has appeared in two profitable movies in a row, anything less than an ecstatic review of a stage play will be taken by the public to mean that they can pass *that* one up, thank God.

P, it is just not a game I would feel right about playing. It isn't that I consider it uncool for a theater critic—or reviewer, or whatever we are—to rave about a show that really excites him. Not only is this honest, it's fun— to jump astride your exuberance and watch the article write itself. Later, there's the knowledge of how many others shared your pleasure in the show, and the satisfaction in feeling you helped introduce it to some of them. Believe me, P, it is a joy to go ape in the paper.

Except when you're faking it. Then you feel a little like a whore. First reason: Ridiculous as it may seem to the creative people we write about, we parasitic critics are as jealous of the integrity of the work we turn out as they are of theirs. To ask us to habitually amphetamize our copy so as to turn on the dullest reader is analogous to asking the director of a Molière comedy to stage it like a noisy slapstick farce, because that way nobody will fall asleep.

Not only would the director be insulted, he would reply that this is just the approach to Molière that does put people to sleep. And that leads me to my second reason for not hyping my copy any more than I feel the occasion warrants.

Ultimately, I don't think it helps. It seems to me that the tradition of the all-stops-out review, when at least a couple of stops should have been left in, has helped to decrease—not increase—the theater's permanent congregation. It has led to overexpectation on the part of the audience going into a show and disappointment on the way out, a sequence which repeated often enough leads people to conclude that theater just isn't for them. It has led to the hit-flop syndrome that groups like yours have worked so hard to eradicate: The attitude that if we can get tickets to it before March it can't be any good, so let's go to the movies. Oversell breeds skepticism, and I think that's what's happened in New York. I don't want it to happen here.

I don't blame you, P, for seeing my role as that of a drumbeater for good shows, and for finding my reluctance to bang my drum just a bit harder than I felt your work merited as a little ungenerous. But, you see, I feel that the theater critic's function isn't to sell shows, even good ones. I don't sneer at the shopping-service aspects of the job (and the advantage to the producer of keeping it an honest shopping service ought to be evident). But I don't think these can be allowed to corrupt its basic function, which is to teach, or let's say, remind people about the theater as a general artistic enterprise. That it's there; that it has something to give us that we can't get on television; that your pleasure in it deepens the more you see what it's all about; that one of the best ways to do that is to try in very specific terms about the show you saw last night, for instance. . . .

Which audience does pro football need the most, the Beautiful People who drop into the Super Bowl, or the fans who go every week? The theater critic is trying to develop similar fans for the theater, people who really know and really care, people who don't need critics because they can make their own distinctions. You don't do that by pretending the distinctions aren't there.

You do it by trying to know what you are talking about and trying to say it as lucidly as you can: Which includes your tone of voice. I'm conscious of how often my work falls short of being satisfactory in either regard, but that will continue to be the attempt.

Very noble, you say. Meanwhile, we go broke. Well, I'm with you, P—it's a problem. What I think you should study while you're out here is what I consider to be the very healthy relationship that obtains between groups like Civic Light Opera and Center Theatre Group-Mark Taper Forum and their audiences: groups who have, for better or worse, found a constituency and managed to please them quite independently of what the critics said. As a theater editor I'll continue to do all I can to get you together with the public that might form a similar constituency for you; but as a critic I'm afraid I'll still have to say on occasion, yes—but. Good luck with the new show.

Sullivan's remark "oversell breeds skepticism, and I think that's what's happened in New York" is particularly relevant.

I'd like Sullivan to speak now on the critical judgment of playwrights versus the plays themselves.

After having been told for years that we critics are killing the theater by expecting too much of it, it is interesting to consider the possibility that we're killing it by settling for too little.

Stanley Kauffman puts forth the argument in a recent issue of the *New Republic*. Kauffman, a member of the trade himself, writes that too many American drama critics have become "Sunshine Boys," professional yea-sayers who greet every halfway talented new playwright as if he were the Messiah who would raise the theater from the dead.

"The result," Kauffman says, "is almost always a painful graph. A new playwright of small talent is hailed as a big talent, gets an inflated reputation and then, with future work, gets deflated. [He] never was as good as he was said to be. . . . But he is put in the false position of having disappointed the very critics who overpraised him to begin with, of having 'fallen off,' they say, when it was they who put him up where he should never have been. . . ."

The work of a young writer—unless he is a genius or an idiot—is rarely all of a piece. The pattern that his first couple of plays makes does not necessarily tell all we need to know about him as an artist. If it is wrong to overpraise a new writer on the strength of one successful work, it is equally wrong to predict, as Kauffman does, that a Jason Miller or a Howard Sackler (*The Great White Hope*) will never again write an even halfway-good play. An overconfident critic might have said the same of Shakespeare after *Titus Andronicus*. The evidence just wasn't in.

Perhaps what we should all do, sunshine boys and groundfog boys, is write more about plays and less about playwrights; to assess what happened on the stage last night and forget about canonizing or condemning the author until we've seen a really representative sample of his work. Until this happens young playwrights would be well advised to follow the old rule in professional sports: "Never believe your press clippings." Especially the ones you've helped plant yourself.

The eclectic Clive Barnes and overreactive Martin Gottfried are too often guilty of overpraising flawed first plays. Two or three years ago, Barnes' enthusiastic reviews sent playgoers scurrying to every loft, basement, church, garage and rabbit hole in New York. Disappointment was so general that Barnes' enthusiasm in the new faraway area—probably well intentioned—no longer has much meaning. Gottfried's diatribes delivered noisily against or for a playwright, as distinguished from the particular play at hand, are constantly guilty of judgment by comparison. On the other hand, to quote Sullivan: "One good play . . . doesn't make a man a playwright—and one bad play doesn't prove he's not one."

Regarding shows en route to Broadway:

. . . I do think it's time the American theater realized that Los Angeles isn't Out of Town anymore.

Neither, in my opinion, are Washington or San Francisco or Mankato, Minn. But I live here, in the Entertainment Capital of the World. And I am getting tired of half-finished entertainments supposedly on their way to fame and fortune in New York if only we will help their creators decide what's wrong with them.

It's especially annoying when you're aware that the real point of certain "pre-Broadway" tours isn't so much the Broadway engagement (which doesn't always come true) but all that lovely money to be made on the road first. Producer Harry Rigby, for example, has just announced that he doesn't care what the *New York Times* critic says about his revival of *Good News,* because by that time it will have cleaned up across the country. It is not unreasonable to assume that some such thinking is behind the *Lorelei* tour, which started in February and will end next January.

Anything wrong with that? Not a thing. It's sound business. It assumes, correctly, that there's an appetite for theater out there. It further assumes, realistically, that bad New York notices—just one bad one in the *Times*— can hurt a show's chances on the road as well as The Street. So take your case to the country first.

Only make sure—this is my point—that it's the best case you've got. I'm positive that nobody connected with *Gigi* or *Lorelei* or *GWTW* ever came right out and said at a production meeting, "Well, we'll open it this way and fix it later." But the lick-and-a-promise attitude was nevertheless implicit in all three shows. The week before *Gigi* closed at the Dorothy Chandler Pavilion, Daniel Massey was still walking through the title number like a floor walker looking for the elevators. *Lorelei's* libretto after all those months on the road is as tangled as Lorelei's checkbook. And *GWTW,* starting with that ludicrous backwards-chugging choo-choo train, was practically all I'll-think-about-it-tomorrow.

One can argue that regional audiences are still getting good value because (in *Lorelei's* case) after all it is Carol Channing up there, and imagine how much you would have to pay on Broadway to see her. All right, imagine. Broadway musicals these days generally have a Saturday night top of $15, for which price one expects quality. But is the Shubert's top—$12.50— that much less of a strain on the pocketbook? How many plotholes and flat gags does the missing $2.50 buy a producer? And what about Theater Guild subscribers who pay more for their tickets, prorated, than the walk-in public does, because without their money in advance the Shubert couldn't float a season at all? How much are they saving?

Again, what I'm scoring isn't any particular show, but an unspoken attitude backstage and in the counting houses that nothing really matters until your show hits Broadway. This is dated, dangerous thinking. The Los Angeles audience, if I read it right, is less and less impressed with Broadway, with what's been there and what's going there. We hear that Richard Chamberlain's *Cyrano de Bergerac* may be going to New York. That's nice, we say: But how good is it now? (Very.)

We're pragmatists. If your show gives us a full evening in the theater— and for some people *Lorelei* has done just that—we'll buy it. If it doesn't we do not take comfort in the possibility that it might be better, later, in somebody else's theater. We love experimental drama—we've just had a month of it at the Mark Taper Forum—but not at $12.50 a ticket. Subsidy isn't our bag anymore. We're getting choosy. Just like New York.

Now for the reviews; touring companies Broadway-bound first. *Good News:* "The discomfort index at *Good News* is very high. If you are into old movie stars, it gives you a chance to see Alice Faye and John Payne in the flesh. If you are into theater history it shows you the kind of pea-brained musical comedy that Oscar Hammerstein didn't want to write any more. . . .

"Heaven. But as it worked out, heaven forbid, starting with Miss Faye.

"The years have been as kind to this nice lady as she has been to them. She still has those dreamy eyes and that drowsy voice—when you can hear it. But she is essentially a film performer and her ten months with *Good News* have not taught her about the stage.

"She dances a little, sings quite a lot and has a respectable number of lines to say (even some jokes), and it all comes out small and covered. Not only do we get very little sense of her; she gets very little sense of us. One result is that she rushes, as if feeling that we've had enough of something that we've only just begun to enjoy (as in the "I Wanna Be Bad" number, which comes out very blurry). . . .

"Payne is more animated and more audible. Unlike his co-star, he seems to be enjoying himself. But his presence, while more mellow, isn't any more intense than in the old days. Rather than a football coach he suggests an agreeable golf pro.

"Watching this pleasant man and this pleasant woman is like watching your neighbors get up and dance at their silver wedding anniversary party—good old Edna and Joe. On the other hand Edna and Joe didn't charge admission.

"*Good News* is not all vanilla. In fact the rest of the show has a strangely sour taste, a suggestion that the 1920s were a sweaty and boorish decade, all elbows and chewing gum.

"The show is nominally set in the mid-30s, in honor of Miss

Faye's having pulled us through the Depression. But the spirit and sound of the show (and sometimes even the look—Donald Brooks' costumes for the boys in particular) is 1927. And the backward view is one of veiled contempt rather than *Nanette's* wry affection.

"The boys are either sissies or lunkheads, the girls either snobs or Dumb Doras—none of this so pointed that it gives the show a real edge, merely enough to take out the charm. The young cast has a kind of wind-up drive but nobody really smiles. Saddler's 'Varsity Drag' number is the ugliest thing—under Tharon Musser's greenish lighting—that I've ever seen in a supposedly cheerful musical.

"You have heard of affectionate satire. This is the unaffectionate kind, without the guts to come out and declare its purposes. America's good-time musical gave this reviewer the worst time he has had in the theater since Judith Anderson played Hamlet, and the embarrassment is by no means limited to Miss Faye.

"Among the better people in the supporting cast are Stubby Kaye as the team's trainer, and Marti Rolph as a nice girl. Everyone else gets A only for energy. In the spirit of the evening, Oenslager's sets are flimsy and vapid, Brooks' costumes graceless without being fun. *Good News* is a pain."

This notice is thoughtful and precise, adverse without being malicious. It was even kind to the stars, inexperienced in stage musicals, who were being (hopefully) exploited by the unwise producer.

Now observe Sullivan with a touring play *after* Broadway: *A Moon for the Misbegotten*. Here I quote a section in praise of Colleen Dewhurst and its analysis of the role she played.

"The play's central image is that of Josie cradling Jamie through the night, a strong woman lending her wholeness to a broken man. O'Neill prepares it so realistically and leads away from it so humorously (Josie's complaint in the morning that her bones will never be the same) that the image doesn't seem strained or pretentious. It does, though, have great size. Without becoming any less herself Josie becomes Jamie's mother as well—which is why Miss Dewhurst can forgive Robards without seeming to humor him. Beyond that she is the Virgin Mother that the O'Neill brothers stopped praying to early, but never really stopped believing in. And beyond that a much older goddess, the Mother Earth that bears a child, that feeds him and that finally covers him up. Concentric moons, and Miss Dewhurst contains them all without fuss.

"As O'Neill wanted, this Josie is sturdy enough to do a man's work, without being a brute animal. She has spirit, pride, a light foot, a rough tongue, a laugh that comes from deep inside and a heart that opens at the sight of another's pain rather than contracting. Goodness and strength so secure that they can be shared; the beauty of an honest mug on a healthy body. There is nothing dainty about this Josie but, as O'Neill writes, she is all woman.

"She and Robards sitting on those steps together, he spent from delivering his dirty little secret, she brimming with repose for him, can't be far from what the playwright intended. It is a great theater moment and the afterglow of consummation lasts for the rest of the play. . . ."

This review is rich in imagery, spelling out the writer's experience in terms of play and performer. The two here are inseparable. Sullivan imbues the reader with enthusiasm through his graphic picture.

San Francisco's American Conservatory Theatre (ACT) visited Los Angeles with two plays. Sullivan wrote about them and supported his views with sound reasoning.

"The Taming of the Shrew and *The Cherry Orchard.* No more revealing test of a repertory company's strengths and weaknesses can be imagined than these two 'comedies,' the first so close to farce, the second so close to tragedy. The American Conservatory Theatre's recent production of *Shrew* at the Claremont Colleges showed us everything that is right about ACT. And its *Cherry Orchard* showed everything that is wrong.

"Right or wrong, we are going to have to see this company more often than once every six years. (They last came down from San Francisco in 1968.) They have energy, clarity, versatility and the homogeneous quality that a real rep company acquires—nothing like the unevenness that marked the background playing in the Mark Taper Forum's *Hamlet* or the Ahmanson's *Richard II.* As instruments they ring true.

"And their leader, William Ball, who directed both plays, is a man with a definite vision of the theater and the ability to get that vision up on stage. For Ball, theater exists not so much to illumine as to astonish, a philosophy that sometimes serves the play he is working on and sometimes does not. It serves *Shrew* magnificently.

"This is Ball's homage, not just to *commedia dell'arte,* the production's point of departure (stage-within-a-stage, masked players, etc.), but to all funny theater *shtick* from the Greeks to Mister Magoo. Ball's Padua is a dodge-'em course where everybody barges into everybody and bounces right off, being equipped with rubber bumpers. But lightly, lightly; so that the fun, never insisted on, doesn't pall. Ball is an acutely musical director (sometimes I think his real home is opera) and this was Mozart applied to slapstick

comedy. You will recall from his letters that Mozart always liked
a practical joke.

"But deft ensemble playing isn't enough for a great *Shrew*. You
also need a couple of stars to play Petruchio and Kate. Not necessarily name stars, but actors with an air of the champion (one of
Ball's favorite words) about them. If they seem likable and young
as well, two qualities lacking in the Burtons' strenuous characterization in the film, you are in business.

"Ball's stars, Marc Singer and Fredi Olster, were superbly cast.
They made Petruchio and Kate two fiery young thoroughbreds
commanded by nature to mate and be fruitful; but not before completing an elaborate courting dance that had the outward semblance
of a fight. They followed these instructions with so much zest and
so little malice that *Shrew* lost its usual sickish connotations of
sexism and sadism and became an innocently merry play again, as
likable as a Hepburn-Tracy romp and as funny as Tarzan and Jane.

"For all its boisterousness this *Shrew* demonstrated Ball's taste a
good deal better than did the quieter *Cherry Orchard* which was both
vulgar and empty. The vulgarity included turning the maid, Dun-
yasha, into Judy Canova and the clerk, Yepihodov, into the Mad
Hatter—two grotesque examples of Ball's need for superficial stage
pep, no matter what it does to the text. Granted that there is humor
in these characters, to pursue it this hard flattens them into gross
cartoons. A *commedia Shrew* is fun. A *commedia Cherry Orchard* is
dumb.

"A small but telling example of the production's hollowness was
Varya's call to Anya at the second-act curtain. This wasn't an older
sister trying to get a younger sister into the house because it was
getting dark. It was a director trying to get an audience to feel misty
and Chekhovian by vocal means alone—theatricalism where reality
would be three times as 'evocative.' The gesture with which the old
servant Firz covers up his face at the end of the production was
equally stylish and wrong—a man playing a death scene rather
than a man falling asleep.

"Such touches brought some surface life to this *Cherry Orchard*
and the acting was competent, though vocally underprojected. Elizabeth Huddle as Madame Ranevskaya was, indeed, superior to
ACT's original Ranevskaya, Sada Thompson, when it came to conveying the character's artistocracy. (Miss Huddle stepped in at the
last minute for Miss Thompson's replacement, Nancy Wickwire,
when Miss Wickwire fell ill: happy the company with that kind of
depth.) Yet the acting remained acting. Rarely did we feel ourselves
in the presence of people we could recognize and identify with (as
happened in the National Theatre of Great Britain's filmed *Three*

Sisters, which certainly didn't lack external style). Cold Chekhov isn't Chekhov at all.

"What ACT continues to need is a strong Method-oriented director (by which I don't mean a mumbles and T-shirt type: Let's throw away that cartoon) to balance Ball's galvanism and mastery of theater effect. Also the rehearsal time that's necessary for deeper work to sink in. The potential for a great company is here, once ACT learns to go under as well as over the top.

"Meanwhile, it remains the best classical company on the West Coast and, on a good night, such as *Shrew,* the best in the country."

Praise and displeasure, each clearly reasoned, and warmth for the company. Any reviewer could have a field day with a Chekhov production he disliked, but Sullivan is respectful and rational. He has done no harm to a company that has sincere and serious intent. Perhaps he has even been helpful.

On occasion Sullivan investigates Broadway, and his report in the *Los Angeles Times* has encouraged producers to form West Coast companys. In this case, Hal Prince *did* send another company to Los Angeles and then to other cities.

Here is a tiny portion of Dan Sullivan's report dealing with source material versus adaptation:

"Bergman fans will probably leave the show grumbling that Hugh Wheeler's book thins the people in the film into musical comedy stereotypes: I heard a couple of lobby comments to that effect at the weekend preview I attended.

"But if you don't know the film, the impression is quite the reverse: that these are rather more complicated people than we usually meet in musicals and that Wheeler and Sondheim have sketched them lightly but with sensitivity."

The following excerpts are about two contemporary plays: Rod Serling's *Storm in Summer* and Ray Bradbury's *Leviathan '99.* In these sections, Sullivan has to create his own guidelines. These are new theater pieces, home-produced.

"San Diego: There were some honest snuffles in the audience as the old Jew and the young black boy said goodby in the last act of Rod Serling's *Storm in Summer* at San Diego's Off-Broadway Theater on Wednesday night, and you had to respect the reaction. But not the material that provoked it.

"A paradox: Serling has long been an advocate of 'maturity' in TV drama, yet given a medium where real maturity is possible—the stage—he reverts to *Abie's Irish Rose,* as retold for the Hallmark Hall of Fame. Freedom, it would appear, can be as inhibiting to a writer not used to it as censorship."

This point seems simple enough but it is surprising how many creative people are unable to make an effective shift from one medium to another.

"Bradbury's intention is to translate Melville's *Moby Dick* into science-fiction terms, turning the white whale into a malevolent white comet and Captain Ahab into a rocket-man crazily trying to track it down.

"Bradbury has explained that he's been haunted by *Moby Dick* ever since he wrote the screenplay for John Huston's film. He has also said that his new play is an attempt to bring poetry back to the theater, which could certainly use more of it.

"But Bradbury has not explained what he thinks is to be gained by setting this particular legend in deep space, and this, for me, is *Leviathan's* chief problem. Its parallels are clever and its language has a certain ring. But its chief effect is that of a strained update of a statement that needs no updating—and in an awkward medium for the statement, at that."

The questions Sullivan raises and answers seem obvious. Without having seen the show, one can easily comprehend the author's self-made plight. Again, this review is clear and constructive, not mean but unfavorable.

To conclude this section devoted to Dan Sullivan's reviews, I should like to reproduce an entire notice about a new and experimental theater group, the ProVisional Theater.

"Colleges and universities, looking for theater groups to present on their community-artists series, don't often enough look in their own backyards. UCLA broke that shortsighted tradition over the weekend by bringing the ProVisional Theater to Schoenberg Hall for three performances of its new work-in-progress, *America Piece, Part I.*

"The evening left some viewers elated, some bored and some (including this writer) half-and-half. The one response it didn't bring was, isn't that nice. Clearly, UCLA hadn't chosen the ProVisional just to be charitable to some deserving locals. Like it or not, this was major league ball.

"It is, in fact, obvious after about ten minutes of *America Piece* that the ProVisional has become as chiseled and as musical an experimental theater ensemble as the Open Theater used to be, but with a character of its own.

"There are eight actors, five men and three women. At Friday night's performance, each seemed alive to the fingertips, both as an individual and as a member of the group. Their moves were articulated and focused, as in dance. Their voices had throw and clarity.

Even when *America Piece* seemed murky conceptually, they gave it a physical line that was a pleasure to follow.

"Besides having a clean cutting edge, the group has a genuine sense of fun, an even rarer quality in vanguard art, perhaps, than in the establishment kind. *America Piece* at its best combines the bump of slapstick comedy with the wince of psychiatric satire, as if Mack Sennett had come with a button-down mind.

"The subject, at first, is neuroses—the kind that nice people have. Alienation, fragmentation, excessive guilt, inability to connect. Each player is the carrier of a particular hangup, which he acts out solo and then with the group, in twos or threes or eights.

"What is being represented here is not, of course, funny; not unless you really dig pain. But the representation is superbly so, a gallery of fabulous fun freaks among whom you may see yourself.

"There is Candace Laughlin's Worrier, her world a mine field set to go off in five minutes. There is Norbert Weisser's Self-Punisher, who keeps giving himself karate chops to the head. There is Michael Dawdy's Fragmented One, drifting like a radio dial looking for a station. There is Ricky Manoff's Leaner, coming about like a loose sail in a typhoon.

"These are funny alone and funnier together. An example is a section where Miss Laughlin and Miss Manoff bump into each other on the invisible line they both inhabit—you will have gathered that *America Piece* is not a realistic play—and are too scared to do anything but babble.

"Dawdy's foot ends up in Miss Laughlin's hands, in this section. His motive I can't remember; his placement is beautiful.

"So is nearly everything in the first half of the piece. The tone is playful and free. The stage patterns are witty (we can assume that director Steve Kent had a lot to do with that). The playing is precise. And, for all the abstractions of the piece, an idea comes through: something about the shyness of most people at really close range, a fact that we are none of us certain what we are doing as we pretend. Americans are 'The Lonely Crowd.'

"Up to this point *America Piece* is working. It is working without preciousness or self-congratulation. It is clear and it is funny without being trivial. But little by little it begins to . . . become just the kind of portentous ritual drama that it had seemed such an interesting departure from.

"Now the images, still clean and well-executed, take on an allegorical quality. Now we seem to be in the middle of an epic. Our actors travel; build; destroy; dream—all a little aimlessly. At the end, they are a grim band marching, in excruciatingly slow motion, off stage. Their shoulders push down the junk structures they have built. But not, it would seem, on purpose. Their move to the wings is the point.

"Empty stage. Lights out. Obviously a heavy statement has been made. If you know the ProVisional Theater you might guess that it's about the repression mechanism of capitalist society. But one is confused.

"For example, where are the capitalists? If *America Piece* intends to be a truly comprehensive statement of the American experience, it should offer a wider variety of character types than it does. It should represent the outward-reaching acquisitive urge as well as the inward-looking self-protective one.

The hardest character in the play as it stands is Bill Hunt's Cynic, and he takes one step back for every two forward. It is not the way the oil barons moved.

"The victims are over-represented, the exploitation is indeed the theme that *America Piece* explores. But, truthfully, it was difficult after a point to say what the theme was.

"Our actors had various adventures, but one wasn't clear as to how much responsibility they bore for them, or even as to whether we were to think of the piece as being concerned with historic process at all. Perhaps it is simply a fantasia on the American character, as seen by the ProVisional and its librettist, Don Opper.

"At any rate, the latter half of the piece seems much too dogged for an evening which starts out so joyously rooted in the theater moment. To connect the two halves of the meeting, to make it truly one, is the next job for this work-in-progress.

"Meanwhile, to repeat, the ProVisional establishes itself with this work as one of the most accomplished performing ensembles we have—'we' meaning the United States, not merely Los Angeles. One thing the city could do about that is to let the group perform as well as rehearse in its clean, well-lighted theater behind Chatterton's bookstore on N. Vermont Ave. Mayor Bradley?"

As this review was written in October 1974, it is doubtful that many people—especially those of us residing on the East Coast—have seen the ProVisional Theater. But Sullivan's review tells us exactly what it is like.

It is obvious that Sullivan likes this group but his sympathies do not prevent his spelling out his reservations, which are reasonably supported. Sullivan also ends this review with an appeal to the city of Los Angeles on behalf of the company.

Sullivan's civic-mindedness is real and often causes him some of the discomforts experienced in the past by Claudia Cassidy in Chicago. His point of view in regard to the Los Angeles Civic Light Opera Company is contemporary and he inveighs against the opera's older policies, created for and perpetuated by its subscribers who overwhelmingly belong to the older generation.

But Sullivan is astute: he does not employ double standards of reviewing and he does not subscribe to any one single school of theater. What he wants is vital theater, and like Cassidy, he will not accept a hand-me-down from Broadway for Los Angeles.

8

Et Resurrexit

THIS IS NO PAEAN TO MEDIOCRITY, nor is it an appeal for lowering standards—few of which in fact exist. It is however a plea to those who write reviews to consider for a moment what is actually there. To perceive *first*, to assess its overall effect and finally, (perhaps almost parenthetically) to nit-pick. This is a plea that will eventually become a warning.

Not to digress. Recently I attended a performance of *Götterdämmerung*. The Brünnhilde was *not* Birgit Nilsson, the superstar whose voice has seemed indestructible for a long time and whose artistry in the Wagnerian repertory has been everything one might dream of. As a generation, we have been spoiled because Nilsson followed on the heels of Flagstad. (Scandinavia has been bountiful.) Before Flagstad, there were some fine artists like Frida Leider, Florence Easton, Gertrude Kappel, Marjorie Lawrence, Maria Müller, Nanny Larsen-Todsen, and others, but none of them—despite high artistry —was quite the astonishing equal vocally of Flagstad or Nilsson.

Before attending *Götterdämmerung*, I heard a good many moans from people who had heard the newcomer and had sneered: they had no patience with her; she simply was not Nilsson!

This reminds me of the English drama critic Ivor Brown, who wrote: "Let us not rush to the ancestor-worship that sees no talent alive and genius unparagoned in every muse that comes down to us in the essayists of long ago." And earlier in the same piece Brown said, "As yet there are no heirs apparent."

What *I* mean is somewhat what Brown meant but also something infinitely simpler. The Brünnhilde I heard was a superior artist with a voice that often rose to the occasion and sometimes did not quite make it. Nevertheless, she looked *svelte* and young. She acted simply and appealingly. She often—if not invariably—sang well. Her diction was impeccable. I felt satisfied and the audience gave her a rousing (and standing) ovation. True, her voice was not as large or as perfectly produced as Nilsson's. But Nilsson has served for more than fifteen years, and *Götterdämmerung* has been around exactly ninety-nine years, and I *did* go to hear the opera. And I did hear it. As it was conducted at a reasonable pace and with appropriate style, and as the singers were excellent and persuasive, I had a very good evening. If *our* Brünnhilde was not Nilsson or Flagstad, neitser were *they* the legendary Lilli Lehmann, Johanna Gadski Nordica, or Fremstad.

In the theater of Broadway today, this also very much applies, but with a difference: the "Nilssons" are the shows themselves. Gone (thankfully) are the days when, for example, David Belasco could produce gaudy melodrama such as *The Heart of Maryland* (1895), with Mrs. Leslie Carter, that ran 240 performances (an enormous hit at that time); *The Music Master* (1904), with David Warfield, Minnie Dupree and Jane Cowl—a newcomer—that ran 288 performances; *The Girl of the Golden West* (1905), with Blanche Bates, James Kirkwood, Robert Hilliard and Frank Keenan, that ran 224 performances; and *The Rose of the Rancho* (1906), with Frances Starr, that played 240 performances. Also long gone are the musical peccadillos of the old clowns such as Weber and Fields who produced and starred in such vehicles as *Whirl-I-Gig* (1899), with David Warfield and Lillian Russell, running 264 performances; and *Fiddle-Dee-Dee* (1900), with Lillian Russell, Fay Templeton, De Wolf Hopper, and themselves, that rang up 262 performances. These shows, incidentally, had music by one of the Richard Rodgers of his day —John Stromberg.

During this truly representative hysteria, "serious" theater also came but went more or less quickly: Mrs. Leslie Carter in *Zaza*—42 performances in 1900; Richard Mansfield in *Henry V* (1900)—54 performances. The Henry Irving–Ellen Terry Repertory (1899) played three weeks in *Robespierre*, *The Amber Heart*, *Nance Oldfield*, *The Merchant of Venice*, *The Bells* and *Waterloo*. In 1904 Sothern and Marlowe played four weeks in three of Shakespeare's plays. Arnold Daly presented stars in five plays by George Bernard Shaw; they had a combined run of eight weeks. Olga Nethersole did nine plays in three weeks. The Sarah Bernhardt Repertory did six plays in a month (1896), while the Eleanora Duse Repertory in the same year presented five plays in about two months.

Today there are no stars except in some films, television, or in recording. Few real stars are willing to tie themselves down to continuous performances over a protracted period of time. The play, then, is in truth the thing. While that is hardly a new fact, of late a new dynamic has been introduced: critical approval is not invariably meaningful, and lately it has been significantly apparent that hits and considerable runs have become possible in the face of poor daily reviews. Perhaps even one year ago this would have been impossible. But there have been some extenuating circumstances in each of these cases.

First and foremost, the audience's ability to relate and to enjoy has been at the heart of the matter. I refer specifically to three healthy shows that were generally unblessed at birth: *Shenandoah, The Wiz,* and *The Ritz.*

Clive Barnes in the *Times* cannot be faulted for his review of *Shenandoah,* which is very near the truth as this writer sees it. However there is enough emphasis on things Barnes considers to be wrong with it to discourage attendance or to make the potential or indecisive theatergoer pause before taking the plunge. A portion of Barnes' review follows:

"The traditional American musical, full of high principles and strong ballads, simple truth and simpler sentiments, seems to have passed out of favor in recent seasons. Well, *Shenandoah,* which opened at the Alvin Theatre last night, is an attempt to bring it back into style. In some respects it succeeds, such as the fine cast, with the superlative acting and singing of John Cullum in the leading role, and in other respects it is less fortunate. But the aspirations are brave and the results, despite a distressing sentimentality, remain lusty.

"The story is a strong one and unusually ambitious for a musical. . . .

"The music and lyrics are altogether smoother in execution, although markedly less ambitious in concept. There are a few lovely ballads here, all beautifully sung; a touching little number called 'Violets and Silverbells' and a roistering song for the Anderson sons, 'Next to Lovin', I Like Fightin',' which recalls the masculine bounce of that film musical *Seven Brides for Seven Brothers,* and might well have been intended to.

"Neither the staging by Philip Rose nor the choreography by Robert Tucker is unduly distinguished, and the scenery by C. Murawski appears modest, drab and unimaginative. The overall look of the show is poor—it seems as though it came all too hot-foot from Connecticut, without really stopping on the way in to get gussied up for Broadway. This was a mistake.

"John Cullum has had many Broadway chances, including the starring role in *On a Clear Day You Can See Forever,* but no role has extended him so well and to such splendid advantage. He is an actor-singer of the quality of Richard Kiley, and *Shenandoah* shows it all. He can even make partially convincing some maudlin conversations with the grave of his wife, and the warmth, tone and characterization of his voice are exemplary.

"The five elder Anderson boys prove bright and attractive, and the two girls, Penelope Milford and Donna Theodore, were both fetching and sang with spirit.

"The youngest son, Joseph Shapiro, was cute, as was his little black buddy, Chip Ford.

"*Shenandoah* will please most those who like musicals a little serious and a trifle old-fashioned. But it is nice to have a show around that not only dares to be tuneful but is even willing to throw in a morsel of moral uplift along with the country-style jokes. So even if some people may find the sweetness of that southern molasses somewhat cloying (it even has a wet-eye ending) a lot of people will have a good time. It is a very likable musical."

In the omitted sections of this notice, there is a reference to the film: "I must admit here that my memory of the original screenplay suggests that it was richer and more interesting than the present book. Films cover a broader canvas."

This review offers perfect examples of an on-the-surface favorable critique peppered with qualifications that are by no means unjustified. Nevertheless, if Mr. Barnes' true intention was to lead audiences to the Alvin Theatre, he did not altogether succeed.

"*Shenandoah* is an attempt to bring it back [the traditional American musical] into style."

"In some respects it succeeds."

" . . . in other respects [other than cast and star] it is less fortunate."

"despite a distressing sentimentality."

" . . .[the songs are] markedly less ambitious in concept."

"Neither the staging . . . nor the choreography . . . is unduly distinguished, and the scenery appears modest, drab and unimaginative. The overall look of the show is poor."

"He [Cullum] can even make partially convincing some maudlin conversations with the grave of his wife."

"*Shenandoah* will please most those who like musicals a little serious and a trifle old-fashioned."

" . . . sweetness somewhat cloying."

Barnes' qualifications cannot be argued because they are understandable. But what is unfortunate for this or any other show that the reviewer has a mixed reaction to is that there is so much against it that what is left in the reader's mind is a sense of suspicion: this show is—well, I don't know.

The reviews in the two other New York dailies were out-and-out pans. The following are the first and final two paragraphs in Douglas Watt's notice in the *Daily News:*

"Offhand, I'd say that the Civil War isn't a very profitable topic for a Broadway musical. And *Shenandoah,* which made an at-best genial impression but more often a gloomy one last night at the Alvin, does nothing to alter this opinion. . . .

"Philip Rose, who also serves as co-producer and (with lyricist Udell) as co-librettist, has staged *Shenandoah* neatly but as if he were composing a series of scenes for museum showing. C. Murawski's skeletal scenery gives the show a nice, clean look, and the costumes by Pearl Somner and Winn Morton are adequate but uninspired like most everything else about the show, including Don Walker's orchestrations and Robert Tucker's dances.

"Did I mention that there's also a token black? Well, he's a teenager, a slave who gets freed, and I must say Chip Ford, who plays him, shows remarkable restraint. For not only does he have to call the daughter 'missy'; he must also keep addressing his fishing pal, that youngest of the Anderson boys who gets captured, by the term 'boy.' There's a clever switch."

The *Post's* Martin Gottfried was equally unfavorable:

"*Shenandoah* is as corny as Kansas and Iowa and *Oklahoma!* would wish it had never invented fake farmland musicals if it saw the one that opened last night at the Alvin Theatre. With all its homespun wisdom and sentimental Americana, *Shenandoah* should be sold at Disneyland souvenir shops. As musical theater it is contemporary enough to be recorded at 78 rpm.

"The show is based on the 1965 James Stewart movie of the same name—one I don't remember though it had to have a better second act. The first act of the musical version begins promisingly enough with a stretch of interesting music that unfortunately isn't elastic. What follows is a series of pop songs that occasionally respect the story's Civil War setting. More often Gary Geld, the composer, wrote any style song, even country rock, for any or no reason at all. . . .

"John Cullum plays the sexless stud at center stage—it is hard to remember him moving—but his singing voice is one of the most beautiful in the theater. The others in the company come and go like pegs on a board, moved about by Philip Rose (the director) according to the minimal needs of the crude book written by James Lee Barrett with the assistance of Rose and Peter Udell. Udell is also responsible for the lyrics and it is hard to say whether their vacant content deserved their sloppy technique.

"I would like to think that *Shenandoah* was a cynical attempt to commercialize Americana. Condescension isn't much, but it's better than delivering this nonsense seriously and amateurishly. Heaven help them. I think the show's makers were sincere."

While there is no question about the hostile intentions of this notice, one still has to question the meaning of "interesting music that unfortunately isn't elastic," and to point out Gottfried's oft-repeated "cynical attempt to commercialize Americana."

The show was very well received at its summer tryout at the Goodspeed Opera House in East Haddam by Walter Kerr of the *Times* and Boston's Kevin Kelly *(Evening Globe)*, while Boston's Elliot Norton *(Herald-American)* called it "a mistake."

However, like all musicals, *Shenandoah* was both expensive to produce and to operate.

The New York dailies would normally have succeeded in padlocking the Alvin Theatre at the end of the show's first week. There was no star (in the Streisand sense) and little else found unflawed that could act as a magnet.

However, the Kander–Ebb musical *Chicago* scheduled to open at about the same time as *Shenandoah* was postponed after a single day of rehearsal due to the serious illness of Bob Fosse, its director. The theater parties that had been booked for it were transferred to *Shenandoah*—pure serendipity.

Audiences, in the main, liked the show. Many people found this or that same frailty mentioned by this or that reviewer, but they were generally more involved in the show as a whole, and there was an overall acceptance.

Then, other reviews—normally too late for practical support—were published, and the daily reviewers were outvoiced and outnumbered.

Billboard asked, then answered: "Are these concepts considered to be old-fashioned and square? Perhaps. But the story unfolds so beautifully, embraced by songs that at once deal with these 'old-fashioned' values in a contemporary way, that they carry out 'traditional theater' to the fullest."

In *Newsday* George Oppenheimer began: "There has come to the Alvin Theater *Shenandoah*, one of the best musicals that I have seen since the days of the Rodgers and Hammerstein classics."

In *Cue* Marilyn Stasio began and ended: "For people who like a lot of MUSIC in their MUSICal theatre, this new folk-tale MUSICal is a MUSICal treat. The luscious score packs in more than a dozen richly melodic songs—sweet ballads, frisky novelty numbers, even a hymn and a lullaby. The work of Gary Geld and Peter Udell, it has a Rodgers-and-Hammerstein flavor that has long been missing from our popular musical theater. . . .

"Not since 1776 have we had a musical play so clearly expressive of our current national yearning for firm values and immutable beliefs, for a lost golden age when we were mighty, true, and pure. The show's problem, and ours, is the falseness of the dream. Charlie Anderson is a lovely dream, but an unattainable ideal. It is not as a man, but as a symbol of our wistful and impossible longings for a hero, that he moves us."

Walter Kerr in the Sunday *New York Times* concluded (after much cogent reasoning): "Whatever its occasional faults (narrative, mainly), it is all of a piece; it belongs to itself. Innocence, in the theater, is hard to come by, harder to believe in. It is also a quality difficult to tap in ourselves; few of us possess much, worn as we are. Put worn materials and worn eyes together and *Shenandoah* may elude you. Seeing it, don't *think* too soon. Let it make the first move; it knows where it's going and just possibly where it's come from."

Jack Kroll in *Newsweek* said it another way: "The easy mistake is to look at *Shenandoah* as pure corn with its stubborn, pioneer father who talks to his wife at her graveside, its clean-cut, thigh-slapping sons, its daughters out of Currier and Ives, its idealistic young men in blue and gray who go out to die for cause and country. But *Shenandoah* is not corn; it has been put together by gifted and intelligent people who have an idea. They know that underneath any age's turmoil and disillusions (which are themselves illusions) it is only a renewal of simplicity that can heal psychic wounds and bring confidence and savor to human living. So they have tried to make a show out of simple, clear, strong blocks of pure human feeling.

"And they've succeeded to a remarkable degree. Producer-director Philip Rose has given the show a chronicle-like structure, moving ahead in set-piece scenes, which build a real cumulative power. Composer Gary Geld and lyricist Peter Udell, whose score for *Purlie* was one of the best (and most underrated) in recent years, have worked carefully to hit a different emotional target in each number, from hymns to lullabies to country tunes to love-songs to elegiac meditations. Choreographer Robert Tucker aims for archetypal movement rather than dazzling originality. The cast projects a true and touching sincerity, resonant with many layers of feeling —Donna Theodore and Penelope Milford as the girls, Ted Agress and Joel Higgins as the eldest sons and especially John Cullum, who has the eagle look of a D.W. Griffith hero and probably the best singing voice on the American musical stage.

"So why am I split on *Shenandoah*? Because the creation of emotional and moral simplicities is the hardest of tasks on stage as in life itself. Time and again at *Shenandoah* I felt my heart being moved, and my brain resisted, saying such seduction was too easy. I think that tension itself is what this deceptive, often noble theater work is about. Our culture on all levels badly needs an esthetics of virtue, as our society needs virtue itself in the places of power. But to achieve this requires an intellectual toughness that *Shenandoah* just misses."

The last sentence hardly compliments the show but what precedes it is strong and helpful.

William A. Raidy of the *Long Island Press* concluded: "It is a lovely show to be cherished by all."

Edwin Wilson in the *Wall Street Journal* concluded: "In spite of yourself, you get a catch in the throat when sorrow strikes the stalwart family and you get a lift when songs reach their climax. For those who don't care for the mod version of anything, but rather, like to hear music sung the way it used to be sung and to shed a tear or two, *Shenandoah* is calling."

Of course John Simon fabricated for *New York* Magazine: "It's all so cornshuckingly, fingerlickingly, hornswogglingly folksy that any stomach unturned by it can be sold as shoe leather."

There were a few other pros and a few cons. But through the reprieve given *Shenandoah* by the re-routed theater parties, the show lived to be assisted by the later critics during which time its nightly audience (in the main) stayed to cheer. Now in its second year and with no sign of folding, *Shenandoah* has survived the New York daily press to find its audience and to thrive. "Feeling" was the key that was largely overlooked or unrecognized by our dailies. And feeling in some form—empathy—is of first importance in the relationship between stage and audience.

A second recent example of similarly cool local daily reception and ultimate success in spite of it can be found in Terrence McNally's *The Ritz*.

Clive Barnes in the *Times* says in his second paragraph that the play "is not at all about homosexuality, but it is set in a gay steambath."

After relating the events of what he considers to be a nonplot play, Barnes writes:

"One does not wish to knock a play this amusing. It started at the Yale Repertory Theatre, where is was called *The Tubs,* and does in this new version give a lot of naughtily innocent fun to its audience. It has been produced by Adela Holzer, and it is not all that unlike Mrs. Holzer's other current Broadway offering, Murray Schisgal's *All Over Town.* Where Mr. Schisgal's talent is more for absurdity of character, Mr. McNally's aims at absurdity of situation. Both are bizarre, and very slightly egg-headed, addle-pated farces. But is Mr. McNally really fulfilling his norm? We are grateful for the jokes and the chases, the snide remarks, and those beautifully sly inuendoes that he can use with such blue-eyed innocence.

"But lurking beneath Mr. McNally's sunnyside-up raunchiness, there is, one suspects, something darker, deeper and more serious. He has a psyche that could do with a little more probing.

"Robert Drivas has directed the play at just the right pace—he ought to take part in a run-off sprint championship with Dustin Hoffman, the director of the Schisgal farce—and the scenery by Lawrence King and Michael H. Yeargan (they are credited with the costumes too, but anyone can do towels) is most glamorous. It looks like Jean Genet's fantasy of heaven.

"The playing has the kind of sheen to it that lights up Broadway. As the tawdry cabaret queen of queens, who almost speaks English, can nearly sing, and will tear out the eye of Cyclops for a main chance, Rita Moreno is pure beauty. She has the best part—even when she needs subtitles her lines are funny—and she goes to it like a spitfire in heat. I adored her. . . .

"In summation, the straights (and I presume we are still in a majority) will find this a hilarious tourist trip, and few people— even gay-libbers or the Mafia—will be offended. I laughed a lot and who should ask for anything more?"

Not bad!

I don't quite understand Douglas Watt's headline in the *Daily News,* BEING GAY IS HARD WORK IN *The Ritz,* since the play, described accurately by Barnes, "is not at all about homosexuality." However, Watt disliked it intensely and his opening paragraph delineates that dislike graphically.

"When a real live girl is the most entertaining feature in a gay bathhouse, it's time for the boys to disband. Even the mighty efforts of the sinuous and supercharged Rita Moreno, one of Broadway's most expert comediennes, aren't enough to save Terrence McNally's farce, *The Ritz*, which opened last night at the Longacre."

Martin Gottfried in the *New York Post* began his review with Lesson Number One in playwrighting for the edification of the author, Terrence McNally, and then made no secret of his finding nothing in the play.

Variety's Hobe Morrison began: "Superlatives are in order for *The Ritz*, last Monday night's arrival at the Longacre Theatre. It's a wildly wacky, uproariously funny comedy by Terrence McNally on a subject some people may find distasteful. An opening night Broadway audience hasn't laughed as hard in years."

Jack Kroll in *Newsweek* says little that is critical (in a brief review) but concludes: "Among the funny performances—Jack Weston as the fugitive, F. Murray Abraham as a super-gay—the funniest is by beautiful, stiletto-sharp Rita Moreno as a shlock performer trying to move from show-biz fairyland to the big time. Miss Moreno —literally—gives off sparks."

Again, the audiences reacted volubly, screaming with laughter. The play as a work of art leaves much to be desired but then so do many other things that *merely* amuse. *The Ritz* is certainly flawed as a play, but it manages the difficult task of generating enormous fun—irresponsible, frivolous, harum-scarum.

Such notices would make betting in the show's favor grossly unfair. However—and this is again part of what appears to be a new trend—*The Ritz*, now in its second year, seems to be going along healthily. Most audiences simply enjoy it. And Mrs. Adela Holzer, its producer, is reputed to be extremely wealthy.

The last of these escapes is *The Wiz*—a smash hit which opened January 6, 1975—for which no single ticket is available at the box office for about six weeks!

Barnes in *The New York Times*: "Criticism is not objective. This does not mean that a critic cannot see qualities in a work that does not evoke much personal response in himself. A case in point is *The Wiz*, a black musical that opened last night at the Majestic Theater. It has obvious vitality and a very evident and gorgeous sense of style. I found myself unmoved for too much of the evening, but I was respectfully unmoved, not insultingly unmoved. There is a high and mighty difference. . . .

"Unfortunately, with the blaring, relentless rhythms of Mr. Smalls' music and the visually arresting but rather tiring scenic spectacle, the total result is a little cold. This is not helped by a somewhat charmless book by William F. Brown.

"It is eventually the story, or more correctly the treatment of the story, that I found tiresome. A fairy tale, to work, has to have magic. We have to give ourselves up to it, to suspend our cynical disbeliefs and, to some extent, identify with the characters. To me, this proved impossible in *The Wiz*.

"When so much is individually good it is difficult to justify a personal sense of disappointment. Perhaps it is, at least for me, that fantasy is enthralling only when it is rooted in experience. Also the stylistic unity of the show, which may prove very exciting to many Broadway theatergoers is, of course, familiar to me from years of going to the ballet and the opera, so its originality is diluted. There are many things to enjoy in *The Wiz*, but, with apologies, this critic noticed them without actually enjoying them."

This review is direct, supported, personal and unfavorable.

Douglas Watt of the *Daily News* wrote, in part: "Though neither the book nor the songs, and particularly the songs, do a great deal for *The Wiz*, which opened last night at the Majestic, this all-black version of L. Frank Baum's children's classic *The Wizard of Oz* is so enormously good-natured, spectacular looking and slickly done that it is hard to resist.

"Geoffrey Holder, who directed the book, has designed acres of fantastic costumes, and their magnificence, together with Tom H. John's fanciful scenery, make *The Wiz* the most stylish Broadway musical since *Pippin*.

"Then, in a uniformly engaging cast, there are a Cowardly Lion and Wicked Witch of the West so delightful as to make you momentarily cast aside memories of Bert Lahr and Margaret Hamilton in the thirty-six-year-old movie (the first stage musical came thirty-six years before the film).

"Mabel King, the Big Mama of a Wicked Witch, appears only in the first scene of the second act, being quickly disposed of by Dorothy and her friends, but she has a fine chance to badmouth her way into a shout song, 'No Bad News,' that is one of songwriter Charlie Smalls' more effective pieces. . . .

"The music palls and the book is spotty, but *The Wiz* is a sight to behold and its people are wonderful."

If one examines this notice and most of what is here omitted, it is really a warm review. But here is where accent leads the reader astray. Any review that begins "Though neither the book nor the songs . . . do a great deal for *The Wiz*." and ends "The music palls, and the book is spotty . . ." is almost certain to create the feeling that the critic has composed a pan piece which *this* review certainly is not.

Martin Gottfried in the *New York Post* wrote: "Consider all the foolish things inherent in the very idea of a new, musical, all-black *Wizard of Oz*, it would have been amazing if anything about it worked at all. Imagine, then, that up until the moments before the first act ended, the show is practically fabulous. Instead of sitting smugly unsurprised at a disaster, we're left with deep disappointment that the second act fell apart. *The Wiz* is half of something when it might have been something and a half.

"What was foolish about the idea? To begin with, an all-black anything never had any business anywhere. (How about an all-Jewish *Oklahoma!* or *My Fair Lady* cast with short Irishmen?) It reminds you of *Carmen Jones* and *The Hot Mikado*—a minstrel show with black skin instead of burnt cork. Let white audiences watch the darkies sing and dance. And then there is the classic movie to contend with, and its classic songs. . . .

"It is great fun and circusy and driving right up toward that intermission when, of all things, the curtain comes down on book rather than music.

"That didn't have the look of knowledge. Neither did what was going on before, but that had been working—on sheer energy as it turned out. Sooner or later, if you really don't know what you're doing, your machine is going to fall apart and that's what happened to *The Wiz*. Too bad. It was great fun while it lasted."

A half-rave.

After these daily notices, matters were shaky at the Majestic box office. No stars, a musical trying to operate against a classic image, and with expensive on-going weekly operational costs.

Tom Topor writing in the *New York Post* tells the complete history of near-closing to smash hit:

"*The Wiz*, a black, soul version of L. Frank Baum's 1900 classic, *The Wonderful Wizard of Oz*, is Broadway's hot musical: standing-room-only for the last three weeks, eight Tony nominations, nearly $500,000 in the till for future performances and nothing but riches in sight.

"And yet when *The Wiz* opened in January, there was no hint of this. Quite the contrary.

"During its out-of-town tryout, the show lost about $300,000 and its original director.

"The management, growing more panicky by the minute, shipped out a series of would-be replacement directors to take over but they all refused. Finally, it turned to Geoffrey Holder, who had designed the costumes and had been with the show since its conception in 1972, and asked him to take over.

"In its first week of previews here, *The Wiz* took in $35,887; in its second week, a little more than $40,000. There was no advance, there were no theater parties, there were no stars.

"The closing notice was posted opening night. The three important daily reviews were only so-so.

"The first week of regular performances drew a mere $53,000 —$20,000 less than break-even. Under the usual rules, that should have been the end.

"But *The Wiz* was not conceived, financed or executed under the usual rules.

"The sole sponsor of the show is Twentieth-Century-Fox, the movie company. Fox put up $780,000 for the show and by opening night, all that, plus another $280,000 was gone.

"Ken Harper, who produced the show and who sold Fox the idea, asked the company for survival money: All he had to offer was the out-of-town record (though the show lost money, it built everywhere it played) and faith.

"Fox, which invested to begin with because of what the company saw as a multi-media bonanza (show, movie, records, toys, T-shirts, and so on), agreed to throw in another $150,000 to keep the show alive and promote it. . . ."

After the shaky beginning, *Time, The Christian Science Monitor, Newsday, Woman's Wear Daily,* and especially *Newsweek*—quoted as follows—wrote happily in favor of *The Wiz*.

"American blacks have been moving down a yellow brick road (badly in need of repair) for a long time, looking for Oz or the Emerald City or some other dream deferred, so the idea of an all-black version of *The Wizard of Oz* makes perfect sense. And happily *The Wiz* is more than that; it's also perfect nonsense and one of the most cyclonic blasts of high energy to hit Broadway in a long time. Only a wicked witch or a pooped-out drama critic could remain unmoved by *The Wiz's* blazing high spirits, its piping-hot servings of soul and its sly sagacity about the pleasures and perils of fantasy.

"Unlike most recent big-time musicals, which carefully parcel out their meager rations of pleasure, *The Wiz* is a show that doesn't quit, for which director Geoffrey Holder deserves great credit. The rhythm-and-blues score by Charlie Smalls (who also wrote the lyrics) has drive, wit and theatricality. Tom H. John's settings also have real wit: his Emerald City is a kind of utopian cocktail lounge, a cool green art-nouveau grotto studded with green-glowing stones, like traffic lights telling fantasy to Go! Holder has also designed sensational costumes: the tornado that whirls Dorothy from her Kansas home to Munchkin Land is whipped up by black-clad dancers led by a tall Tornado Queen whose plumed headdress gradually wraps the stage in an infinity of twisting wind. This and all of choreographer George Faison's dances are exciting, funny and jumping with character.

"William F. Brown's book absorbs L. Frank Baum's classic into the black experience with good-humored cleverness. Some will say *The Wiz* exploits that experience with its flip references to drugs, sex and such matters, but in our culture of interlocking exploitations how refreshing to see it done with warmth and flair. When the Good Witch informs Dorothy, 'I have a magic act, I do tricks,' the funky Munchkins comment, 'Does she ever!' At one point Faison's dancers become a field of poppies who turn on the Cowardly Lion with a blast of poppy dust. When the Mice Squad comes on to scatter these horticultural pushers, the crestfallen lion comments: 'How come you never find a mouse when you need one?'

"The biggest fun of *The Wiz* is encountering its parade of delightful characters. Clarice Taylor is beautifully tacky as the trick-doing witch. As the Scarecrow, eighteen-year-old Hinton Battle never stops dancing in his search for brains. The Tinman is played by Tiger Haynes in a pointedly trashy armor of garbage-can torso, beer-can legs and skillet hat. Ted Ross struts and cringes with equally high style as the Cowardly Lion.

"The Wiz himself is played by Andre De Shields as the apotheosis of all ghetto con artists, a shyster preacher, pimp and politician whose crowning satiric nuance is a touch of the epicene ('Where did you get such a marvelous pair of silver pumps?' he gushes to Dorothy). As the Wicked Witch, Mabel King shouts a hilarious gospel of evil. The majestically beautiful Dee Dee Bridgewater counters this with her pure jazz singing as the Good Witch Glinda. Big-voiced fifteen-year-old Stephanie Mills is a down-home Dorothy. If talent, hard work and true energy mean anything, *The Wiz* will find a big audience of all ages and colors."

It has.

Not every production—some possessing this or that meritorious aspect—can boast of the happy sailing these three shows are enjoying in the face of predictable doom.

O'Neill's recently celebrated *A Moon for the Misbegotten* first appeared on our stage in 1957 starring Wendy Hiller. Most of the men on the aisle were kind to the performers but faulted the play, which lasted sixty-eight performances. Seventeen years later with a different cast and director, the same play was extolled. Remember that the play that had previously been faulted had not been altered; nevertheless, the first judgment now appears to have been a mistaken one.

My own (with Moe Septee) production of Romberg's *The Desert Song* came to New York following a wonderfully received tour in Philadelphia, Baltimore, Chicago, and Washington, the night following Labor Day 1973. If the decision had been mine to bring it to New York or close it, it would not have been brought in, but it came to Broadway where, after three weeks, it closed after losing additional money.

Most of the reviewers were kind. Some of them found the quality that it had. What was argued by some was that it was played for "camp." It was not.

Naturally *The Desert Song* was faulted by comparison with *No, No, Nanette,* and *Irene* but no one (even those reviewers who liked it) mentioned two of its virtues: that this was a bona fide revival and that it had a fine singing ensemble of thirty-two voices —something Broadway has not heard in almost a century.

No, No, Nanette was entirely rewritten—a fact that helped enormously to make it acceptable. *Irene* bore little resemblance in book or score to its original. Both productions boasted stars.

The Desert Song had superb singers and was not rewritten. The presentation marked an effort to present it as nearly as possible as it might have been presented in 1926. The scenery was not elaborate, nor was it in the original production if one is to judge by photographs.

The London production in 1927 boasted a singing ensemble of eighty-eight. In New York this alone would have cost about $25,000 weekly! Nobody seemed to have remembered that the last large singing ensemble heard on Broadway was in *Oklahoma!* in which there were sixteen, or half as many singers. Since *Oklahoma!* that number diminished until in *West Side Story* there were no singers, and in *Company* there was no ensemble—singers or dancers.

The star of *No, No, Nanette* was Ruby Keeler who, despite audience astonishment that she could even *walk,* could not sing, dance, or act. The star of *Irene* was adorable Debbie Reynolds. The female star of *The Desert Song* was Chris Callan, who could sing demanding songs very well, and looked well.

However, it was obviously a mistake to do a straight and honest revival, with capable young performers rather than stars with reputations regardless of limitations, and the essential singing ensemble of thirty-two lusty voices was faulted by—guess who—for containing ugly girls!

And yet—no double critical standards? In May 1975, Victor Herbert's *Naughty Marietta* (1910) was well revived by the dedicated William Mount-Burke, and Equity Library Theatre presented Rudolf Friml's *The Three Musketeers.* The former was reviewed in *The*

New York Times by Raymond Ericson and the latter in the same paper by Howard Thompson. *Naughty Marietta* boasts an abundance of still-popular songs; *The Three Musketeers* contains only one song that we remember, "We Are the Musketeers." Neither production had an orchestra; the singing ensembles were necessarily limited. The librettos—and especially the comedy sequences of both—leave something to be desired now as they did then.

Both *Times* reviews were splendid; neither show or production was faulted. In fact, Thompson's review of *The Three Musketeers* begins:

"The bracing effect of *The Three Musketeers* is so marvelous in its revival at the Equity Library Theatre . . . that you wonder why the 1929 Ziegfeld musical hasn't been dusted off long before."

Mel Gussow, who reviewed *The Desert Song* for the *Times*, suggested that it might have been better done either pared down for off-Broadway or greatly enlarged in the Busby Berkeley manner. The fact that it was done exactly as written was obviously not acceptable. The fact that it played *on* Broadway and with an orchestra were strikes against it. Somehow—or so it seems—something is amiss. . . .

Perhaps something new is in the wind. *Shenandoah, The Ritz* and *The Wiz* are alive, Tony Award winners, and well in spite of a damaging daily press. In the past such things have happened, although infrequently. Almost invariably it has been possible only because money has been available to buy time—time to pay staggering weekly bills for continuing performances—to buy advertising, to bring in audiences by many and devious routes in the hope that word-of-mouth would eventually convince audiences to *buy* their tickets, allowing the show to pay its own way. David Merrick has had the money and has known how to spend it profitably. *Shenandoah* got the audience and the money because of *Chicago's* delay, and those interim audiences and the money they brought in extended the life of the show until the better magazine and Sunday write-ups appeared. *The Ritz's* producer was able to furnish the necessary extra capital. *The Wiz* had a single wealthy investor (20th Century-Fox) who believed that, with time, the show could repay the investment, and the faith.

Each of these shows had some likable quality that audiences could and did indeed enjoy despite debatable shortcomings. Nothing more.

Under such circumstances—that is, having something sufficiently appealing—shows ought always to be able to find their audiences. In these three instances, something important has been proven.

9

Conclusion

A POSITIVE RESPONSE, whether favorable or not, is the easiest to express. It requires no thinking, and the reporter has little difficulty spilling out his gut reaction. An uncontrolled adverse reaction is usually activated by anger. How simple it is to complain to a waiter that food is not hot or that service is poor. Reasoning need not play any part in communicating such a feeling. In the same way, joyous expostulation at a sudden burst of fireworks or sight of a roseate sunrise is also a natural response, easily voiced.

The reviewer and the critic, on the other hand, have a greater obligation to their readers, to the theater, and even to themselves to *think* about what they say and how they say it. As human beings, their reactions are personal, but what they relay through their public journals should be tempered, enlarged and reasoned—a rational, meaningful interpretation.

While considering what is to be expressed, it would seem desirable to take into account not only the work under scrutiny but also the many kinds of theatergoers, some sizable segment of whom might conceivably enjoy something that the reviewer found too "anything" for his own taste.

Nearly everyone expressing himself is necessarily conscious of some personal ego-problem that colors his feeling, thinking and judgment. He has a responsibility to avoid as far as possible its intrusion into what he writes since his public expression will, in all likelihood, control the decisions many others will make.

Each of us is aware of many types of theater—good and bad—that we would avoid, or many others that we might go to any lengths to experience. But some of us, like the night-after-night reviewers, have been subjected to many more performances than the average ticket-buyer. We have become more satiated and less tolerant. We have seen nearly everything on the face of the earth in some form or other. Most people have not, or if they have, they are less aware than we of the geneses, similarities, repetitions, and so on.

Because we, and the reviewers, have become less patient with the oft-repeated product, is this sufficient reason for curtailing the life of a production and, by so doing, depriving a segment of the public of some accountable pleasure, while simultaneously depriving a group of theater workers of their livelihoods?

I think the answer must be "no."

Certainly there are shows of such low quality that they could interest no one. Among them, *Via Galactica, Dude, Status Quo Vadis, The Secret Affairs of Mildred Wild, Ambassador, Billy,* and too many others that are disgracefully devoid of any idea, style, distinction, or honest attempt at going somewhere new and fresh. As productions, they were misjudgments and each met its deserved fate quickly.

Of course producers who select poor properties and proceed to devote one or two years of their lives in money-raising, casting, rehearsing and getting productions onto the stage, are at fault for not having had better taste. While this is pathetic and even reprehensible, it cannot in one fell swoop be accredited to greed. But consider some of the disasters and near-disasters like *Seascape, J.B., God's Favorite, Box-Mao-Box, Out Cry, Anyone Can Whistle, Flowers,* and many others. No one responsible for them could have nourished dreams of owning Mediterranean yachts. These productions had to have been sincerely motivated. Of course, it is possible that no one expected to *lose* money, but neither could they have harbored delusions of wealth.

The critical reception of these and similar shows in no way should have produced anger or ridicule. Wasn't it sufficient that the producers found that their shows failed to work? And often in the theater—because of the inherent difficulty in meshing together many elements—no one, no one can be sure until it has been assembled and put before an audience whether or not it will work.

Therefore the high-dudgeon reception is iniquitous and demonstrates more than anything else that the reviewer guilty of such an attitude is ignorant of the theater and is a profoundly tasteless member of the human race.

On the other hand, a reviewer may honestly be miffed by the poverty of some show, but then the question to himself should be: Does it provide for some people an electric star performance (Carol Channing in *Lorelei*), something stimulating and adventurous (*Anyone Can Whistle*), a brave, lyrical, and exciting concept (*Seascape*), a hilarious evening (*Grease*)? Is it then not the reviewer's duty to discover this very real fact—for it is a fact—and to focus his article on those qualities which might find a sympathetic audience response? (Remember: A reviewer is not a critic.)

Just naming these four shows at random reveals a truth. An audience interested in *Seascape* might conceivably like *Anyone Can Whistle*. *Grease's* large audience would definitely not like these first two but might enjoy *Lorelei*. The possible combinations of taste and revulsion are endless. A reviewer who cancels out any one of them is guilty of depriving a segment of the public of something that might be appealing, and of plundering the theater.

And there are many other shows, flawed, reminiscent of better ones from the past, that *we* saw and recall, which many other people, younger, less experienced, geographically less fortunately located, did not see and might now be interested in seeing if given the opportunity.

It must also be remembered that the reviewers are on hand at (nearly) every opening performance. Those of us vitally interested in theater are there at the same time or very shortly afterward. But the majority of potential theatergoers are in less of a hurry to attend a show, even though they may want to and even plan on going. Theatergoing is not their *raison d'être*. If the reviewers have panned it, they will never get there; they will lose the desire and the show will close.

Eric Bentley wrote: "Today there are dozens of publics separated by differences of interest as well as levels of taste, intelligence and education."

Some of these publics would enjoy many things in the theater that neither I nor the reviewers would dream of recommending. Nevertheless, a way must be found that would, unhampered, *allow* them to find and experience whatever interests them.

The fact of our ages, of our geographical backgrounds, and of our natural predilections should never be far from our (or the reviewers') consciousness when we issue bulletins about what we have seen.

Consider age first. Let me speak for myself. When I attended the

New York premiere of *Mame*, I was irritated by the screams of laughter and the applause that of late always accompanies laughter, at the sight of one of the principal's singing a song while swinging, seated, in a crescent moon. Why should people behave as though they had never seen such a thing? Why? Because they never had seen such a thing! I saw Beatrice Lillie do it in *At Home Abroad* (1935). I conducted *Goldilocks* (1958) when Elaine Stritch did much the same thing. I know from illustrated books on theater that the device was employed many times even before I was born. The reception it got in *Mame* angered me until I realized that not nearly everyone was as old as I. Or some had just never seen it before, and when they saw it at *Mame* it made them laugh.

This aspect of age-and-criticism should be remembered when reviewers are tempted to think of something as "old hat" even when in truth it *is* "old hat." What about those oncoming and even current millions to whom it is "new hat"? Is denigration or annihilation excusable under such circumstances?

Next: geographical background. An Englishman might have ample personal reason to resent a threadbare play about members of the British royal family. An American from the Deep South might react against a play laid in his part of the world because it or the studied inflections of the actors might seem inauthentic and therefore phony. Place-of-birth accidents unconsciously breed political and ethnic prejudices. Inaccurate representations of home and related conditions can engender disbelief in the expatriot observer. Reactions due to prejudice are often uncontrollable and yet readers of reviews written by human beings subject to these particular motor responses are unjustly misled.

The third "regulator" of reaction—nonthinking, first class—relates to natural predilection. Martin Gottfried in writing about Henry Fonda in *Clarence Darrow* illustrates this point perfectly: "If I told you that the name of the play was *Clarence Darrow* and that it was a one-man show starring Henry Fonda, would you really have to go to the Helen Hayes Theatre or even read this review to find out what it is like? That's what it is like."

I might have felt similarly in advance but on being taken to a performance, I felt quite otherwise. When I attended *Rodgers and Hart*, I forced myself to accompany a friend whose invitation I had earlier accepted and later regretted. Here, my reasons for not wanting to go were clearly personal: I knew all of the songs, had conducted recordings of many of them, conducted performances of some of the shows, and, in any event, *knew* them intimately. What, then, could I find to enjoy while being trapped for an entire evening of these wonderful "familiars"?

To my surprise, the small, unpretentious, swift-moving, energetic, youthful evening provided many unalloyed pleasures and I left the theater afterward in a state of simple euphoria.

Had I been committed to writing about these shows, I would have felt it my duty to see them through, trying hard to eschew these preconceived and personal prejudices. Then I would have—had I disliked them—been most guarded about the wording of my review, remembering that my earlier feelings could not have failed to have had some effect on my reaction and realizing also that few if any other people could have shared my very special reasons for not having wanted to attend.

This brings up the question of the critical language, which by word, placement, and accent controls the effect of what is handed down as judgment.

Throughout this book, the reader has observed the use of identical adjectives to describe both the promising and the accomplished. Certainly this practice is incontrovertibly wrong. There is no need to elaborate on it again.

"Placement" and "accent" have also been illustrated, but the following excerpts will emphasize the point I am trying to make.

Barnes, *The New York Times:* "Here is an old-fashioned, well-made play that is well made in a new way for new times. It is an evening of unadulterated fun—all right then, adulterated fun."

Gottfried, *New York Post:* ". . . play is by no means high theater, but then it doesn't mean to be. It is, however, exactly what it does mean to be and that is the first test of any play.

"The premise is admittedly gimmicky. . . . The solution might have been more imaginative."

Watt, *New York Daily News:* ". . . slender, implausible but occasionally diverting play. . . . This is all utter nonsense, of course . . . plays on his audience with comfortable jokes and situations, so that you begin to look for the telephone to ring before it actually does . . . may be a year ahead of television, but probably no more than that. . . ."

Beaufort, *Christian Science Monitor:* "Some of the running gags seem overcalculated, and the author is hard-pressed on occasion to give one more twist to a limited two-character situation."

Sharp, *Women's Wear Daily:* "The humor in the first act is sharper than in the second, perhaps because the first act deals with old sexual jokes that haven't been fossilized by the movies and television shows of the 1950s."

Kalem, *Time* Magazine: "It is the kind of theatrical fare that fiftyish middle-class marrieds have been starved for on Broadway in recent seasons, and they are likely to queue up for tickets in avid droves."

Hewes, *Saturday Review:* "Their expertness and concentration hold the audience so surely that we believe them even when we don't believe the play, which is, come to think of it, most of the time."

With the exception of Watt's notice in the *Daily News* these excerpts are hidden within rave notices for one of New York's most solid recent hits, *Same Time, Next Year,* which opened March 13, 1975. My feeling is that all the reviewers except Watt genuinely enjoyed it. (I did not.) But all reviews included some conscionable fault-finding in their pieces. Nevertheless, these were not *accented.* What *was* accented included:

Barnes, *The New York Times* (opening paragraph): "Do not put off till tomorrow what you can do today. Get tickets for *Same Time, Next Year.* It is the funniest comedy about love and adultery to come Broadway's way in years. If that were not enough, it is also touching—it has two superbly poised performances by Ellen Burstyn and Charles Grodin. . . ."

Barnes, *The New York Times* (last paragraph): "If Mr. Slade knows how to flatter and massage an audience, so do his actors. This is an enchanting evening."

Gottfried, *New York Post* (opening paragraph): "It is a pleasure to announce the arrival, last night, of a brand new, bouncing and altogether lovable comedy at the Brooks Atkinson Theater. *Same Time, Next Year* is a very funny romantic play—genuinely funny and genuinely romantic. It is also honest and true and heartfelt—a really rewarding entertainment."

Gottfried, *New York Post* (last paragraph): "Still, Slade's writing, Saks' direction and Burstyn–Grodin playing are too funny and too filled with humanity to be shot down by minor awkwardnesses of structure. The work is too good. This season at last has the really funny comedy it has been waiting for, and in the bargain has been given feelings that really touch the heart. For *Same Time, Next Year* is simply about why we need a lifetime to grow up, only to find out that we haven't grown at all."

Kalem, *Time* Magazine (last paragraph): "Rarely have a man and a woman on a stage mixed the honey of love and the glue of marriage so deftly that both are bonded in sweetness and surety."

Beaufort, *Christian Science Monitor:* "But these are quibbles of a kind which a delighted first-night audience happily overlooked."

Sharp, *Women's Wear Daily* (opening paragraph): "Bernard Slade's
new comedy at the Brooks Atkinson Theater proves that good old
jokes—like good old songs—seem to improve with the years. The
old jokes in *Same Time, Next Year* encompass unexpected labor
pains, impotence and sexual hypocrisy. In the hands of lesser actors,
these good old jokes could seem like schtick; in the hands of Ellen
Burstyn and Charles Grodin, the comedy glistens."

Jack Kroll, *Newsweek* Magazine: "You'll never see froth better produced, and in fact you'll never hear better, funnier, more sincere
froth than Slade's. When commercial work is this good it needs no
apology and takes its rightful place in our jam-packed mass culture.
Billions of my cells enjoyed *The Misanthrope* and millions of my
other cells enjoyed *Same Time, Next Year.*

Same Time, Next Year is a tremendous hit. It will be a hit film.
It will tour forever. There will never be a season without it at community and high school theaters. It appeals to capacity audiences
that scream the house down. It has humor and pathos, and it relates to all people, particularly to married couples who, depending
upon fidelity or secret, guilty profligacy, will enjoy it loudest.

Although I thought it sometimes amusing, it also seemed obvious, patent, and synthetic. Nevertheless, recognizing the fact that
it is capable of bringing unmitigated joy to most other people, I
would have fought (had it been necessary) for the general public's
rights to have it succeed.

On the other hand, it is the *critic's* job to discover and spell out
the truth of what every theater-piece contains, to reason and substantiate. The reviewer affects today's theater and its public; the
critic maintains a running document for serious students of the
theater and for the world of the future.

The theater reviewer is unique among his colleagues who report
on the other arts. The music reviewer generally pronounces judgment after the fact: the concert, opera, or recital is past. The reviewer's poor opinion of the event has little effect upon last night's
audience. In some cases—the opera or the symphony orchestra—
there will be one or two repeat performances, but most of these
are sold by subscription in advance. A favorable verdict may help
to sell a few remaining tickets but the previously bought ones cannot be refunded.

The art reviewer writes about material objects—paintings, sculp-
ture, lithographs, etc.—which are completed and will not be altered; the objects will survive a poor review and continue to survive.
Their sale may be restricted, but with physical survival, sales are

always possible and future opinions can drastically alter the entire situation.

The book reviewer writes about publications which cannot—presto! change-o!—become unpublished. A poor review may greatly curtail sales and a good one will certainly stimulate them, but, again, if a work is more worthy of praise at some later time, it can be reactivated.

Books and objets d'art can also be studied in advance and thoughtfully written about against no pressing deadline.

The theater reviewer is unique among all the rest. The public has been conditioned to "morning-after" judgment. There is no time for mature consideration. Likewise, time for survival of the object—the play or musical—is nil. If the writers on the three daily papers—the writer on *The New York Times* in particular—are displeased or even indifferent, the production will cease to exist. The book, the picture, remain physically alive: no further money is needed to sustain them. Only the theater piece is perishable. It can seldom live on in the face of censure because it alone requires the continuing work of performers, technicians and a place in which all of these can function. These require money. In the face of poor reviews, it is seldom to be found, or seldom can be found for a long enough time to allow the work to become self-sustaining; the actors disband, the scenery is destroyed.

The reviewer can correctly contend that a producer's choice of a poor work must be held responsible for the disastrous reception, but there are too many other works that are merely imperfect or fragile that should and would perhaps find interested audiences, given sufficent reprieve from immediate slaughter.

The theater reviewers did not create themselves nor did they usurp their power. They have been ever-present. But today in a very special way they have been created by the producers of Broadway. They have had their fame, hence their power, bestowed on them.

In 1900, there were thirteen daily newspapers in New York, each carrying dramatic opinions. In 1910, there were twelve. The year 1920 again boasted thirteen reviews; 1930, twelve. At this writing, there are only three daily papers in Manhattan.

When there were a dozen or more opinions, there were about seventy-seven theaters operating simultaneously in the Broadway area. Production and operating costs were low and the price of tickets correspondingly low. The number of theatergoers was large and, as theatergoing was not costly, they saw many shows. (There was no danger in the streets and no television at home.) Audiences were largely immune to newspaper opinion since the cost of tickets did not constitute a major investment, and the plethora of verdicts was seldom of a single mind.

Thus as the number of daily newspapers, and therefore the number of reviewers, diminished, although complemented at a later time by television and radio opinions, responsibility and power grew and were concentrated in the few.

The reviewing power is due not only to the greater concentration in the fewer journalists and gentlemen of the airways, plus the investment-size price of tickets but also to the producers who scream with pain when their presentations are not thought well of. The producers did thrust power into the hands of the reviewers by advertising their favorable words, phrases, sentences and often entire criticisms. In an effort to enhance their own productions, the entrepreneurs made the critics famous.

Los Angeles' Dan Sullivan sent me the theater ad-page for the *Morning Telegraph* (New York) of Sunday September 11, 1910. No advertisement is more than one column in width, none larger than two inches. Although (according to Burns Mantle's *Best Plays* series) there were twenty shows running at that time and eleven others scheduled to open before the end of the month, there were only twenty-one ads. (Remember, this was a Sunday paper.) Of these twenty-one ads, only five carried critical quotations and only *one* named the reviewer instead of his newspaper.

Despite the sharp theater shrinkage, on Labor Day 1974, when the new season was not yet underway, there were fifteen Broadway shows in the small ABC ads and seven off-Broadway shows. There were ten larger ads (Broadway) all with quotes, and eight off-Broadway proclamations also decorated with encomiums. All of them credited the reviewers by name.

In another way, producers—aided and abetted by press agents— have also created a state of emergency in their *need* for reviews immediately following their Broadway openings. It is quite understandable that, like any other gambler, the producer who has invested his last available cent in a new show, itches to see the spots on the dice the moment they stop rolling; he has won or lost— possibly everything. But even in this analogy, there is a difference. In the dice game, if he has lost (unless he is a compulsive gambler), no more money is required. In the case of his theatrical investment, *much* more money is required—and immediately—if the producer is to continue operating the show he has already paid for. If the daily reviews are all raves, he will embark on an expensive advertising campaign (again adding to the fame of the reviewers) to make certain that every prospective ticket-buyer is made aware of his treasure. If the reviews are mixed, he will weigh his chances at transforming an indecisive quantity into a known one—again through expensive advertising. If the reviewers have unanimously disliked the show, the producer will deliberate on the show's chances at being pulled out of the mire. If he decides to try to keep it running, he will need enough capital to pay its weekly expenses for at least two or three weeks *plus* perhaps an even greater outlay for advertising, hoping that word-of-mouth and perhaps some favorable later-arriving weekly notices can be used effectively in building the show to the point where it will sustain itself.

All of these possibilities—and they *seem* to be the only ones—are contingent upon morning-after reviews; these will tend to indicate the appropriate course of action. Something immediate must happen. In truth, delay is very costly since the outlay for continuing operation is very real and very dear.

And so, under these conditions—the importance of the verdict from the daily press, cost of operation, and, overhanging both, the immediacy—the daily reviews are panted for.

For centuries the theater—on or off-Broadway, in New York or Detroit—has been a commercial business. In the United States, it survives on that basis, or, failing, it ceases to exist. But "commercial" is not necessarily a dirty word and it has been known to produce art.

Despite the producer's "need" of a morning-after review, there are times when he and the theater would be better off without it.

A newspaper strike in 1953 provides one example of what happens when a show opens to no immediate reviews. (Of course, the nonappearance of reviews because no newspapers are being published is hardly synonymous with a show's opening being ignored.) However, the absence of newspapers was the sole cause of *Kismet*'s not being criticized the morning following its opening.

Nothing could have been more beneficial for *Kismet* than the strike. The songs, adapted from some of Borodin's loveliest tunes, plus Alfred Drake, heard and seen at his very best, were far and away better than anything else in the show. The product as a whole was gaudy, old-fashioned, dreary, and foolish.

But neither the producer nor press agent was to be defeated by the prospect of no reviews. To fill in the gap, they were able to persuade such musical authorities as Miss Helen Hayes (a dear lady and the only one of several luminaries I recall specifically) to appear on television immediately after the premiere to speak about the show. I recall Miss Hayes—all charm and enthusiasm. She *adored* *Kismet* and Alfred Drake and the scenery and the costumes and the music and the dances and just everything. (I believe that the other luminaries were equally friendly.) The following several days found endless lines at the box office clamoring for tickets.

When newspapers resumed publication, opinions were varied and predictable. Brooks Atkinson (*The New York Times*) and Walter Kerr (*New York Herald-Tribune*), the two superior judges, were less than excited.

Brooks Atkinson: "*Kismet* has not been written. It has been assembled from a structure of spare parts . . . the assembly method is no substitute for creation . . . the rich massiveness of *Kismet* is stupefying. . . . It is a display of wealth, but it is not a work of art. . . . The lyrics comprise some of the most fearful poetry of our time. . . . *Kismet* . . . adheres strictly to the commonplace . . . a cumbersome show."

Walter Kerr: ". . . strictly commercial entertainment . . . about the only thing this song-and-dance *Kismet* hasn't got is any particular integrity. . . . It's the sort of show that would sell its soul for a joke. . . . Robert Wright and George Forrest have been fairly conscience-less . . . collegiate wit."

Robert Coleman (*Daily Mirror*): "Alfred Drake . . . an inspired idea. . . . Richard Kiley and Joan Diener . . . are outstanding . . . lavish settings and costumes . . . sprightly and enchanting choreography. . . . Albert Marre has staged the book with skill. . . . The Wright-Forrest arrangements are certain to put Borodin on the Hit Parade at long last."

John McClain (*Journal-American*): ". . . lavish, tuneful and terrific . . . maidens expensively under-clad . . . enormous sets . . . fabulous effects . . . book . . . brilliantly souped-up . . . there is an adroit and melodious [*sic!*] performance by Doretta Morrow."

Richard Watts Jr. (*New York Post*): ". . . has a frankly old-fashioned amalgamation of stateliness and sex . . . none of the numbers struck me as exactly inspired. . . . Mr. Drake's musical-comedy heroes are pretty much alike. . . . Joan Diener . . . makes physical allure irresistibly absurd. . . . Heavy and literal in its romantic magnificence."

William Hawkins (*New York World-Telegram*): "The biggest and brightest of magic carpets, may not be subtle or original, but nobody intended it to be."

John Chapman (*Daily News*): ". . . hesitant as to humor. . . . [Wright and Forrest] often mistake big long words and involved rhymes for wit . . . best scenery west of Rockefeller Center. . . . I do wish Alfred

Drake could have one big song number with a lot of sock in it—for instance, something titled 'My Heart Belongs In Baghdaddy.' "

Meanwhile, however, a great many people enjoyed *Kismet,* and a large cast and orchestra were employed for seventy-three weeks in the show's initial run. Is that sinful?

On the other hand, nearly *all* the reviewers loved *Man of La Mancha* and so did the vast majority of people who saw it. (I did not like it although I tested and retested my own judgment by seeing it four times.) Had the reviewers felt as I did, and said so, it is doubtful that *Man of La Mancha* would have had any run. I am perfectly content—feeling otherwise about its qualities—that it did enjoy a long run.

However, by delaying a bad review, a show like *Kismet* has some possibility of a word-of-mouth build. The daily reviewer will not have killed it at birth. There were a great many other people who liked *Abie's Irish Rose, Hello, Dolly!* and others that were not first-rate. *Abie* succeeded at a time when continuation in the face of a bad press was infinitely less costly. *Dolly* polled so many votes for its star and director that any consideration of the show's quality took a back seat, and the public overwhelmingly did the rest. They could not have exercised discernment but they thoroughly enjoyed it. Walter Kerr in the Sunday *Times* has recently (June 1, 1975) pointed out an interesting and related fact:

"What I think I like best about *A Chorus Line* is the fact that it's a hit that was made by the public (and at the Public Theater, just to add to the felicity). Long before any reviewers, who must normally function as huff-and-puff artists blowing laggard theatergoers stage-wards, were permitted to come near the entertainment, word had got about: something was brewing in one of Joseph Papp's downtown houses, the previews going on were as exciting as any opening night could hope to be, ticket buyers were lining up at the Lafayette Street box office terrified that they might not be able to see the show before they were told to. *A Chorus Line* was selling out before any sales pitch had been made by anybody, a theatrical event had gained momentum on word-of-mouth alone.

"What, being a reviewer, do I like about that? For one thing, it fits, very snugly, my own ideal but rarely realized notion of what the audience-reviewer relationship ought to be. It ought to be a conversation about something *both* had seen, not a preemptory command to get going or keep out. I realize, of course, that no one who wishes to write about the theater can possibly wait until absolutely everybody's beat him to it; but if the audience has already claimed the show as its own, if there's a consensus in the air that suggests more and more spectators are determined to attend no matter what *anybody* says, then the reviewer is relieved of his burden of functioning as a shopping service and is free to chat, to compare notes —the audience having already proclaimed its own freedom.

"That's part of it. The other is the evidence that the audience has acquired *energy* again. In the theater's dull periods, audiences are notoriously, somewhat understandably, sluggish and need prodding. When they really want to go to the theater, though, want to go badly enough to do some potluck experimenting of their own, things are obviously looking up. Theater's become a lure rather than an obligation once more, a magnet instead of a maybe. And that in turn suggests that the recent Broadway upsurge is no temporary phenomenon, no accident. The groundswell may have greater proportions than we'd quite dared to hope."

The weeks of previews Kerr has reference to (four or five) were made possible by the Public Theater's subscribers and the Shubert Foundation which paid the losses that were incurred. Because of the small size of the theater it wasn't possible to break even even when the house was sold out.

These weeks of playing prior to the reviews provided the show's creative people with invaluable time for studying the show, evaluating the audiences' reactions to it and general editing and revising. Usually this is possible only when a show plays several weeks prior to Broadway in Boston, Philadelphia, and other cities. However, I have long advocated the New York preview system in preference to travelling about, since more time is then available for rehearsal, the out-of-town review may confuse the creative people, and the audience reaction elsewhere will differ from that of a New York audience.

In the case of *A Chorus Line*, from the time of its first public preview, it was an excellent if imperfect show. With changes—and there were many—it got better each week. The audience reaction was consistent and its enthusiasm was so widespread that opening night became a time of enormous apprehension.

The reviews were marvelous. But even had they been otherwise, the message that preview audiences had already broadcast was so strong and so well known that it is doubtful that *A Chorus Line* could have really flopped.

Perhaps the preview is one way around the reviewers but it would of course only work when the show is as well thought of in advance of its opening as *A Chorus Line* was. However, what is wrong with the present system has nothing to do with the reviewers telling people *what* to see but rather with their making what they do not favor sound too dreary to interest anyone.

The reviewer should be the enlightened servant of both public and theater, and as impersonal as possible. (Should anyone *care* about any one else's self-expression?) When his review is personal, we are reminded of Molière's *The Misanthrope:*

> He scolds at all the latest books and plays,
> Thinking that wit must never stop to praise,
> That finding fault's a sign of intellect,
> That all appreciation is abject,
> And that by damning everything in sight
> One shows oneself in a distinguished light.*

Whether they like it or not, the reviewers occupy the position of judge, a billet bestowed upon them by masochistic producers, then strengthened by the reliance of necessarily economy-minded play-goers. And it is the tone and accent of the review rather than its precise content that will determine the playgoers' decision.

Immortal judgment in depth is in the hands of the critics, who will affect posterity more than the ticket-buyers. The critic will preserve a sense of taste through careful analysis; the reviewer should direct people to whatever kind of theater each may enjoy.

*Translated by Richard Wilbur (New York: Harcourt, Brace & World, Inc., 1954–1956).

Index

Aarons, Alex, 181
Abbott, George, 56, 59, 71
Abel, Walter, 71
Abélard and Héloïse, 186
Abie's Irish Rose, 285, 317
Abraham, F. Murray, 299
Absence of a Cello, 247–8
Absurd Person Singular, 34
Adams, Polly, 116, 143
Adelson, Leonard, 181
Agate, James, 94
Ages of Man, The, 49
Agress, Ted, 297
Aïda, 4–5
Ailey, Alvin, 6
Albee, Edward, 10, 60, 74–5, 108, 191, 209–10, 213–15, 260–1, 270–1
Alexander, Ronald, 235–6
All About Eve, 136
All American, 262
All Over, 191, 213–16
All Over Town, 135, 298
Allan, Gene, 19
Ambassador, 307
Amber Heart, The, 291
America Hurrah, 29, 80
America Piece, 286–8
American Graffiti, 120
American Mercury, 96
American Millionaire, An, 193
American Shakespeare Festival, 193
And Miss Reardon Drinks a Little, 17
Anderson, Maxwell, 99
Andrews Sisters, 193
Anouilh, Jean, 106, 108, 165, 172
Antony and Cleopatra, 46
Anyone Can Whistle, 307, 308

Applause, 136
Aranha, Ray, 5, 31, 201
Archer, William, 94
Archers, The, 95
Ari, 6, 30–2
Arlen, Harold, 11, 96, 99
Aronson, Boris, 9, 11, 33, 129–30, 172, 266
As You Like It, 70, 75, 175–7
Astaire, Adele and Fred, 181
At Home Abroad, 309
Atkinson, Brooks, 1, 2, 97–101, 228, 316
Aubrey, John, 138, 139
Auliss Joseph G., 134
Awake and Sing, 78, 111, 147
Ayckbourn, Alan, 34

Baba Goya, 160
Babe, Thomas, 218–19
Bad Habits, 135, 199
Bach, Johann Sebastian, 51
Bach, Karl Phillip Emanuel, 50–1
Baker, Paul, 246, 248–9
Baker, Word, 211
Baker Street, 52
Balfour, Eva, 71
Ball, William, 283–5
Ballard, Kay, 181
Ballentine, E. J., 71
Bankhead, Tallulah, 152n, 153
Barber of Seville, The, 68
Barcelo, Randy, 26
Barefoot in the Park, 105, 134, 242
Barkentin, Marjorie, 164
Barnes, Clive, 1–30, 47–8, 68, 75, 85, 88, 114, 175–6, 197–8, 201n, 260, 276, 279–80, 292–4, 298–300, 310–11

Barrett, James Lee, 295
Barrie, Barbara, 33
Barry, Philip, 99, 100
Basic Training of Pavlo Hummel, The, 111, 114
Bates, Blanche, 291
Battle, Hinton, 221, 303
Battle of the Angels, 229, 258–9
Baum, L. Frank, 221, 268, 300, 301, 303
Bay, Howard, 230
Bean, Orson, 234, 242
Beard, The, 223
Beatles, 36, 169
Beaton, Cecil, 66, 67
Beatty, Talley, 32
Beaufort, John, 126–32, 310–11
Beck, Toni, 246
Beckett, Samuel, 5, 19, 128–30, 148, 151, 163, 208–9, 271
Bedford, Brian, 219
Beerbohm, Max, 94
Beethoven, Ludwig van, 10
Beggar's Opera, The, 89, 184, 222
Behrman, S. N., 99
Belasco, David, 74, 291
Bells, The, 291
Bells Are Ringing, The, 233
Ben-Ami, Jacob, 152
Benchley, Robert, 98
Bennett, Constance, 231
Bennett, Michael, 10, 11, 33, 53, 73, 134, 136, 221
Bentley, Eric, 97, 152n, 308
Bergman, Ingmar, 136, 138, 266, 285
Bergman, Sandahl, 38
Berkeley, Busby, 305
Berkvist, Robert, 222
Berlin, Irving, 11, 99
Bernhardt, Sarah, 96, 155, 187–8, 292
Bernstein, Leonard, 12, 36, 53, 71, 72, 96, 99, 222, 256–7
Berrigan, Daniel, 202
Best Plays, 192, 314
Bettis, Valerie, 164
Big Time Buck White, 78
Billboard, 295
Billy, 5, 18–19, 307
Billy Noname, 5–6
Birch, Patricia, 52, 112
Black Comedy, 45, 160
Black Crook, The, 56
Black, David, 19
Black Sunlight, 4
Black Terror, The, 31, 32
Blitzstein, Marc, 11, 56, 204, 205
Bloom, Claire, 191
Bloomgarden, Kermit, 230
BMI Musical Theatre Workshops, 67
Bolger, Ray, 262
Book of Job, The, 175

Boom Boom Room, 155–6, 193, 223
Booth, Shirley, 153
Boris Godunov, 151
Borodin, Mikhail, 315, 316
Boston Evening Globe, 295
Boston Evening Transcript, 97
Boston Globe-Traveler, 245
Boston Herald-American, 232, 295
Boston Post, 232
Boston Sunday Herald Advertiser, 232
Boucicault, Dion, 69, 70, 95, 116, 131, 132, 143–4 177, 178, 267
Bovasso, Julie, 156, 273
Box-Mao-Box, 60, 74–5, 307
Bradbury, Ray, 285–6
Brandon, Johnny, 5
Bread, 223
Brecht, Bertolt, 196, 204, 205, 273
Breeze from the Gulf, A, 19, 37
Brent, Romney, 71
Bridgewater, Dee Dee, 221, 303
Brief Lives, 49, 138, 139
Brigadoon, 67
Brittan, Robert, 67, 68, 254–5
Broadway Journal, 95
Broadway's Beautiful Losers, 216
Brook, Peter, 160, 195, 211–13
Brooklyn Eagle, 95
Brooks, Donald, 140, 282
Brooks, Mel, 262
Brown, Ivor, 94, 290–1
Brown, John Mason, 98
Brown, Lew, 140
Brown, Pamela, 71
Brown, William F., 221, 268, 299, 303
Browning, Susan, 33
Brustein, Robert, 197
Brynner, Yul, 133
Buka, Donald, 248
Bullshot Crummond, 218
Burch, Ramsey, 252
Burrows, Abe, 71, 262
Burstyn, Ellen, 311, 312
Bury, John, 191
Buttrio Square, 58

Cabaret, 7, 17, 53, 75, 80–1
Caesar and Cleopatra, 46
Cahn, Sammy, 197
Caldwell, Zoë, 185–6
Callan, Chris, 304
Camelot, 67
Camillo, Marvin Felix, 162
Can-Can, 246
Candida, 231
Candide, 36–7, 52–4, 74–5, 178, 222, 256
Capek, Karel, 99
Capote, Truman, 18
Carmines, Al, 13–15, 25

Carney, Art, 240
Carnival, 261–2
Carousel, 17, 53, 75, 110, 244
Carr, Benjamin, 95
Carr, Jay, 263–75
Carroll, Leo G., 71
Carter, Mrs. Leslie, 291
Cassidy, Claudia, 227–32, 246, 276, 288–9
Cat on a Hot Tin Roof, 78, 177–8
Cater, John, 143
Center Theater Group, 137, 277, 279
Ceremonies in Dark Old Men, 265
Chairs, The, 165
Chaliapin, Feodor, 151
Chalmers, Thomas, 71
Chamberlain, Richard, 281
Champion, Gower, 34
Changing Room, The, 117, 162–3, 169–171, 190, 269–70
Channing, Carol, 72, 120, 181–2, 280, 308
Chaplin, Sydney, 233
Chapman, John, 316–17
Charley's Aunt, 59, 74
Chekhov, Anton, 117, 126–7, 163, 171–172, 194, 285
Chemin de Fer, 195, 223
Cherry Orchard, The, 163, 283–4
Chicago, 71–3, 75, 295, 305
Chicago Lyric Opera, 227, 231
Chicago Symphony Orchestra, 227, 231
Chicago Tribune, 227–9
Children of the Wind, 181
Chorus Line, A, xiv, 73, 75–6, 93, 317–18
Christian Science Monitor, The, 126, 302, 310, 311
Civic Light Opera (Los Angeles), 57, 276, 279, 288–9
Civilization and Its Discontents, 161
Clarence Darrow, 47, 49, 309
Clark, Bobby, 71, 78
Clary, Robert, 230
Cleveland *Plain Dealer*, 133
Cleveland *Press*, 133
Clockwork Orange, A, 119
Clurman, Harold, 77, 97, 146–54, 225, 271
Cocteau, Jean, 152
Coe, Fred, 68
Coe, Richard, 68, 253–62
Cogan, David J., 127
Colby, Barbara, 217
Cole, Kay, 169
Coleman, Cy, 42, 105, 316
Colette, 185–6
Colum, Padraic, 164
Comden, Betty, 233
Come Back, Little Sheba, 186, 196
Comedy of Errors, The, 69

Company, 8–11, 13, 32–3, 53, 57, 75, 167, 173, 304
Connection, The, 206–8, 211
Conrad, Joseph, 140–1
Conried, Hans, 247–8
Consul, The, 101
Contractor, The, 116–17, 169–71, 222
Cook, Peter, 194
Coover, Robert, 223
Corbin, Clayton, 231
Coward, Noël, 13–15, 100, 140, 173
Cowl, Jane, 291
Cradle Will Rock, The, 56
Craig, Michael, 83
Crawford, Bill, 231
Critic, The, 94
Crowley, Mart, 37
Crucible, The, 61
Cry for Us All, 7, 17
Cue, 147, 216, 296
Cullum, John, 292–3, 295, 297
Cyrano de Bergerac, 40, 281

Daily Variety 132, 135–7
Dale, Jim, 220
Dallas Morning News, 245
Dallas Symphony, 246
Daly, Arnold, 291
D'Amboise, Jacques, 6
Dame aux Camellias, La, 187
Dames at Sea, 16
Daniels, William, 209
Dante, Ron, 19
Dariou, Joe, 88
Darling of the Day, 109–10
Darling of the Gods, The, 74
David, Mack, 181
Davidson, Gordon, 202
Davila, Diana, 133
Davis, Al, 4
Davis, Bette, 230
Dawdy, Michael 287
Dear World, 5, 7
Death of a Salesman, 54, 62–3, 264–5
de Havilland, Olivia, 231
Dekker, Thomas, 70
Derwent, Clarence, 71
Desert Song, The, 31, 63, 70, 304, 305
De Shields, André, 221, 303
De Sylva, Buddy, 140
Detroit News, The, 263
Devils, The, 254
Dewhurst, Colleen, 47, 48, 50, 106, 131, 215, 282–3
Dexter, John, 46, 123, 160, 162, 269
Dhery, Robert, 230
Diener, Joan, 133, 316
Different Drummer, A, 248–9
Digges, Dudley, 71
Divine Pastime, The, 147–8, 153

Doll's House, A, 17, 78, 191, 217
Donneybrook, 261–2
Don't Bother Me, I Can't Cope, 27–8
Dotrice, Roy, 49, 138, 139
Douglas, Margaret, 71
Drake, Alfred, 29, 37, 38, 66, 67, 315–17
Drama Review, 14, 185, 189
Dramatists Guild Quarterly, 2, 8n, 11, 21, 22
Drivas, Robert, 37, 298
Driver, Donald, 42–3
DuBarry Was a Lady, 44
Duchartre, Pierre Louis, 91
Dude, 13, 307
Dunlap, William, 95
Dupree, Minnie, 291
Duse, Eleanora, 96, 155, 187–9, 292
Dynamite Tonight, 60

Eagle Has Two Heads, The, 152–3
Easton, Florence, 290
Eck, Marsha L., 181
Edward, My Son, 152, 231
Edwards, Ben, 47
Edwards, Bill, 135–7
Elder, Lonnie III, 265
Elektra, 68
Eliot, T. S., 200, 214
Ellis, Mary, 99
Emperor Jones, The, 246–7
Endgame, 208
Engel, Lehman, 70, 304, 309
Entertainer, The, 129
Epstein, Julius, 22
Equus, 5, 21n, 45–7, 75, 122–3, 160–2, 182–3, 198–200, 269
Era of the Cutie Closes, The, 92–3
Ericson, Raymond, 305
Esmond, Jill, 100
Esterman, Laura, 134
Exodus, 6
Eyre, Ronald, 116, 131, 143

F. Jasmine Addams, 5, 15
Fabray, Nanette, 136
Faison, George, 222, 268, 303
Fantasticks, The, 137, 211
Farentino, James, 40–1
Farther Off from Heaven, 252
Fashion, 52, 75, 95
Faye, Alice, 139, 281–2
Feingold, Michael, 144
Fellini, Federico, 105
Feydeau, Georges, 75, 135, 190, 195
Fiddle-Dee-Dee, 291
Fiddler on the Roof, xii, 17, 53, 57, 72, 75
Field, Betty, 215
Field, Ronald, 53
Fields, Dorothy, 42, 105, 153

Fig Leaves Are Falling, The, 8
Filippo, Eduardo de, 180
Find Your Way Home, 179
First Breeze of Summer, The, 216–17
Firth, Peter, 161, 220
Five Finger Exercise, 45
Flagstad, Kirsten, 290–1
Flanagan, Fionnuala, 164–5
Flanders, Ed, 106, 131
Flatt, Ernest O., 193
Flaxman, John, 18
Flemyng, Robert, 71
Flowers, 141–2, 180, 307
Follies, 7, 17, 53, 57, 167–8, 173
Fonda, Henry, 47, 49, 309
Ford, Chip, 293, 294
Ford, Paul, 242
Ford, Ruth, 37
Fornes, Maria Irene, 13
Forrest, George, 316
Forty Carats, 18
Fosse, Bob, 15, 29, 58, 59, 71–5, 105, 262, 295
Fourberies de Scapin, Les, 179
Franklin, J. E., 28
Freedley, Vinton, 181
Freibus, Florida, 248
Fremstad, Olive, 291
Freud, Sigmund, 161
Fried, Donald, 201
Friedman, Gary William, 112
Friml, Rudolf, 13–15, 304
Front Page, 18
Fry, Christopher, 129
Fuller, Penny, 231
Fuller, Rosalind, 71
Funke, Lewis, 1
Funny Face, 181
Funny Girl, 237–40, 243
Funny Thing Happened on the Way to the Forum, A, 241–2, 261–2
Funzapoppin, 231
Furth, George, 9, 13, 32

Gardenia, Vincent, 134, 221
Garland, Patrick, 139
Gay, John, 89, 222
Gaynes, George, 38
Gelber, Jack, 206, 211, 223
Geld, Gary, 294, 296
Genet, Jean, 141–2, 162, 271–4, 298
Gennaro, Peter, 6, 167
Gentlemen Prefer Blondes, 120, 181
George M!, 16
Georgy, 5, 8, 20, 58
Gershwin, George, 11, 13–15, 52, 98–100
Gibson, B. G., 169
Gielgud, John, 49, 71, 215
Gigi, 16, 29, 37–9, 66, 67, 74, 120, 280
Gilbert and Sullivan, 14

Giles, David, 195
Gilford, Jack, 81
Gill, Brendan, 146, 173–84
Gillette, Anita, 262
Gingerbread Lady, The, 23–4, 186
Gingold, Hermione, 173
Giraudoux, Jean, 99, 150–2
Girl Crazy, 100
Girl of the Golden West, The, 4, 68, 291
Gish, Dorothy, 71
Glass Menagerie, The, 124–5, 229, 250
God's Favorite, 69, 74, 118–19, 134, 174–5, 221, 307
Godspell, 8, 17
Going, John, 19
Going Through Changes, 55–6
Goldbergs, The, 181
Goldilocks, 309
Goldsmith, Oliver, 94, 144
Good Evening, 194
Good News, 135, 139–40, 280–2
Good Woman of Setzuan, The, 196
Gordon, Ruth, 238, 259
Götterdämmerung, 190, 290–1
Gottfried, Martin, 21n, 23, 38–9, 42, 44–76, 95, 102, 123–4, 131, 176, 194, 199, 200, 218, 254, 259, 267, 279–80, 294–5, 299, 301, 309–11
Grande de Coca Cola, El, 218
Granger, Michael, 217
Grant, Micki, 27, 28
Grass Harp, The, 18
Grease, 120, 308
Great God Brown, The, 99
Great MacDaddy, The, 30, 32, 85, 86
Great White Hope, The, 279
Green, Adolph, 233
Green, Stanley, 110
Greene, Graham, 86
Grey, Joel, 81
Grimes, Tammy, 243–4
Grodin, Charles, 311, 312
Grossman, Larry, 8
Guare, John, 104
Gussow, Mel, 1, 305
Guthrie, Tyrone, 190
Guys and Dolls, 75, 110, 245
Gypsy, 75, 78, 178, 191

Hackaday, Hal, 8
Hail the Conquering Hero, 261–2
Hair, 8, 11–13, 57, 111
Hall, Peter, 83, 160
Hamilton, Margaret, 300
Hamlet, 49, 69, 97, 283
Hamlisch, Marvin, 75
Hammerstein, Oscar, 99, 110, 232, 281
Hampden, Walter, 71, 97
Handke, Peter, 158, 159

Haney, Carol, 52
Hansberry, Lorraine, 67, 68, 127, 254–5
Happy End, 205
Happy Time, The, 109
Harburg, E. Y., 110
Hardy, Joseph, 38
Harper, Ken, 302
Harper's New Monthly Magazine, 96
Harrigan, Edward, 96
Harris, Julie, 220
Harris, Rosemary, 40–1
Harrison, Paul Carter, 30, 86
Harrison, Rex, 174, 220
Hart, Lorenz, 12n, 99, 173
Hart, Moss, 71, 100, 104, 236
Harvey, Dyane, 86
Hastings, Harold, 33
Hasty Heart, The, 22
Hawkins, Trish, 186
Hawkins, William, 316
Haworth, Jill, 80
Hayes, Helen, 315
Haynes, Tiger, 221, 303
Hazlitt, William, 54, 89, 94, 184
Heart of Maryland, The, 74, 291
Hedda Gabler, 17, 191
Heimat, 187
Hellman, Lillian, 61, 62, 75, 99, 230
Hello, Dolly!, xiv, 259, 317
Heming, Violet, 71
Henderson, Ray, 140
Henning, Doug, 66
Henry V, 291
Henry, Sweet Henry, 5, 8, 15, 16, 58
Her First Roman, 5, 16
Herbert, Victor, 304
Here Today, 102
Here's Love, 241
Herlie, Eileen, 152, 262
Herman, Jerry, 52
Herrmann, Alexander, 66
Hewes, Henry, 203–16, 271, 311
Heyman, Barton, 217
Higgins, Joel, 297
High Spirits, 242–4
Hiller, Wendy, 303
Hilliard, Robert, 291
Hofmannsthal, Hugo von, 89
Hogan's Goat, 5
Holder, Geoffrey, 221, 268, 300–2
Holiday, 223
Holm, Ian, 83
Holt, Will, 112
Holzer, Adela, 135, 298–9
Home, 170, 171, 195–6
Home Sweet Homer, 133
Homecoming, The, 78, 81–4, 109, 160
Hooray! It's a Glorious Day, 60
Hope Is the Thing with Feathers, 231
Hopkins, Anthony, 46, 161

Hopkins, John, 179
Hopper, De Wolf, 291
Horizon, 91
Hot L Baltimore, The, 222
Hot Mikado, The, 301
Hotel Universe, 100
Houdini, Harry, 66
House of Flowers, 60
Housman, A. E., 168
How the Other Half Loves, 18
How to Succeed in Business Without Really Trying, 242, 262
How Now Dow Jones, 5, 16
Howard, Sidney, 99
Howells, William Dean, 96
Howland, Beth, 33
Huddle, Elizabeth, 284
Hughes, Langston, 127
Hughes, Tom, 246
Hunt, Bill, 288
Hurwit, Lawrence, 48
Husmann, Ron, 262
Huston, John, 286

I Can Get It for You Wholesale, 237
Ibsen, Henrik, 10, 54, 78, 190
Iceman Cometh, The, 48, 106, 193, 223
In Praise of Love, 20, 118, 174, 220
In Search of Theater, 152n
Inadmissible Evidence, 205–6
Indians, 7, 78
Inge, William, 61, 99, 196, 252
Inherit the Wind, 250–1
Inquest, 201–2
Ionesco, Eugène, 5, 83, 160, 165
Irene, 72, 121–2, 166–7, 304
Irving, George S., 167
Irving, Henry, 96, 291
Italie, Jean-Claude van, 79

J.B., 129–30, 134, 259, 307
Jackson, Anne, 107, 172
Jacob, Sally, 212
James, Henry, 95–6
Jenkins, Gordon, 137
Jennie, 241
Jessel, Patricia, 231
Jesus Christ Superstar, 15, 17, 25–6, 268–9
Jew of Malta, 91
Joffrey, Howard, 6
John, Tom H., 300, 302
Johns, Glynis, 173
Jonah, 68
Jones, Dean, 10, 32, 33
Jones, Margo, 190, 246, 249–53
Jones, Robert Edmond, 71
Jones, Tom, 211
Joseph, Stephen M., 112
Journey of Snow White, The, 13, 14

Joyce, James, 163–4
Jubilee, 98
Jumpers, 157–8, 219

Kafka, Franz, 263
Kahn, Madeline, 156, 186
Kalem, T. E., 123, 146, 154, 155, 168–73, 311
Kanin, Garson, 238
Kappel, Gertrude, 290
Karnilova, Maria, 29, 37, 38, 134, 221
Kaspar, 158–9
Katselas, Milton, 209–10
Kauffman, Stanley, 1, 279
Kaufman, George S., 100, 104
Kay, Hershy, 53, 54
Kaye, Stubby, 282
Kazan, Elia, 130, 259
Keeler, Ruby, 304
Keenan, Frank, 291
Keiser, Kris, 4
Kellar, Harry, 66
Kelly, Kevin, 245, 295
Kelly, Patsy, 121, 167
Kemp, Lindsay, 141–2, 180
Kent, Steve, 287
Kern, Jerome, 11, 71, 98
Kerr, Larry, 10
Kerr, Walter, 1, 2, 30, 77–93, 149, 295–6, 316–18
Kid Champion, 219
Kidd, Michael, 233–4
Kiley, Richard, 293, 316
King and I, The, 68, 75, 110, 241
King, Lawrence, 31, 298
King Lear, 10, 49, 206, 259–60
King, Mabel, 221, 300, 303
Kingsley, Sidney, 61, 99
Kirkwood, James, 291
Kiser, Terry, 134
Kismet, 79, 315–17
Kiss Me Kate, 67, 245
Klotz, Florence, 266
Knickerbocker, R. C., 248
Kober, Arthur, 102
Kopit, Arthur, 7, 78
Kosinski, Jerzy, 160
Krapp, Herbert J., 181
Krapp's Last Tape, 208–9
Kroll, Jack, 146, 154–68, 173, 271, 296–7, 299, 312
Kubelik, Rafael, 227

Lahr, Bert, 44, 69, 83, 300
Lahr, John, 144
Laing, R. D., 161
LaNoire, Rosetta, 134
Lansbury, Angela, 72, 178
Larsen-Todsen, Nanny, 290
Last of the Red-Hot Lovers, The, 24

LaTour, Nick, 134
Laughlin, Candace, 287
Launzi, 97
Laurents, Arthur, 61, 178, 256–7
Lawrence, Carol, 233
Lawrence, D. H., 70, 161
Lawrence, Gertrude, 100
Lawrence, Jerome, 250–1
Lawrence, Marjorie, 290
Lee, Leslie, 216–17
Lee, Ming Cho, 20
Lee, Robert E., 250–1
Lehman, Richard B., 227
Lehmann, Lilli, 291
Leider, Frida, 290
Leigh, Mitch, 60, 88, 133
Leighton, Margaret, 229
Lennon, John, 36
Lenny, 19, 268
Lenya, Lotte, 81
Lerman, Leo, 146
Lerner, Alan Jay, 38, 66, 67, 71, 232
Lester, Edwin, 38, 67
Leviathan '99, 285–6
Levin, Ira, 39, 40
Lewis, Emory, 216
Life and Times of Joseph Stalin, The, 217–18
Lillie, Beatrice, 243–4, 309
Lithgow, George, 170
Little Me, 261
Little Night Music, A, 57, 75, 136–7, 167–8, 172–3, 245, 266–7
Lives of Eminent Men, 139
Livingston, Jerry, 181
Livingston, Robert H., 112
Liza, 195
Lloyd, Bernard, 143
Loesser, Frank, 71, 110
Loewe, Frederick, 38, 66, 67, 71, 232
Logan, Joshua, 71, 262
London Assurance, 69, 95, 115–16, 131–2, 142–4, 177, 267–8
London Chronicle, 94
London Observer, 147
London Sunday Times, 118
Long Day's Journey into Night, 23
Long Island Press, 297
Look to the Lilies, 5, 20
Loot, 7
Loquasto, Santo, 217
Lord, Pauline, 97–8
Lorelei, 72, 120, 181–2, 193, 280–1, 308
Los Angeles Times, 275, 285
Love for Love, 70–1
Ludlum, Charles, 142
Lunt, Lynn and Alfred, 155

Macbeth, 10, 14, 49, 86, 190
Macbird, 60

McCarthy, Joseph, 61
McCartney, Paul, 36
McClain, John, 316
McClure, Michael, 223
McCowen, Alec, 46
McDermott, Eugene, 252
MacDermott, Galt, 104
McDevitt, Ruth, 247–8
McFarlin Auditorium, Dallas, 247
McGhee, William, 247
McGill, Everett, 161
Mack and Mabel, 34
McKay, Scott, 37, 231
McKechnie, Donna, 33
Mackey, W. W., 5, 133
McKinney, Gene, 248–9
MacLeish, Archibald, 129–30, 134, 259
McNally, Terrence, 297–9
Mademoiselle, 146
Madwoman of Chaillot, The, 150–1
Maggie Flynn, 5, 8, 15, 18, 58
Magic Show, The, 63–6
Maharis, George, 209
Mahler, Gustav, 14
Mallonee, George, 263–4
Mame, 309
Man of La Mancha, 17, 60, 88–9, 317
Man Who Came to Dinner, The, 84
Mann, Theodore, 193
Manoff, Ricky, 287
Mansfield, Richard, 291
Mantle, Burns, 192, 314
Marat/Sade, 160
Marlowe, Christopher, xiv, 91
Marlowe, Edward H., 291
Marre, Albert, 88, 133, 316
Marriage of Figaro, The, 68, 190
Martin, John, 189
Martin, Mary, 72, 78, 241–2
Mary, Mary, 242
Mary Stuart, 46
Massey, Daniel, 38, 280
Matchmaker, The, 259
Matthau, Walter, 240
Maulinier, Thierry, 127
Maxwell, Roberta, 161
Me Nobody Knows, The, 111–12
Mead, Shepherd, 262
Medea, 263
Medoff, Mark, 119–20, 265–6
Melville, Herman, 18, 286
Member of the Wedding, A, 147, 173–4
Mencken, Henry L., 96, 97
Mendelssohn, Felix, 15
Menotti, Gian-Carlo, 101
Merchant, Vivien, 82
Merchant of Venice, The, 91, 107–8, 149–50, 291
Meredith, Burgess, 164
Merman, Ethel, 44, 78, 178

Merrick, David, 123, 305
Merrill, Bob, 15, 136, 237
Merry Wives of Windsor, The, 78
Messel, Oliver, 38
Metcalfe, Mark, 193
Midsummer Night's Dream, A, 17, 190, 211–13, 266
Mielziner, Jo, 20
Mighty Man Is He, A, 102
Milford, Penelope, 293, 297
Milk and Honey, 262
Miller, Arthur, 54, 61–3, 75, 99, 265
Miller, Jason, 279
Mills, Stephanie, 221–2, 303
Milner, Ron, 4, 85–6
Minnelli, Liza, 195
Minnie's Boys, 5, 8, 15, 19, 58, 185
Misanthrope, The, 94, 312, 319
Mitchell, Ruth, 136
Moby Dick, 286
Mod Donna, 19–20
Moise and the World of Reason, 124
Molière, 49, 50, 75, 94, 96, 178–9, 184, 190, 278, 319
Molly, 58, 180–1
Molnar, Ferenc, 99
Montevecchi, Liliano, 230
Moon for the Misbegotten, A, 22–3, 47–8, 50, 74, 104–6, 130–1, 166, 282–3, 303
Moonchildren, 160, 222
Moore, Charles, 5
Moore, Dudley, 194
Moore, Robert, 24
Moore, Victor, 78
Moorehead, Agnes, 38
Moreno, Rita, 298–9
Morley, Robert, 152
Morning, Noon and Night, 18
Morning Telegraph, 314
Morrison, Adrienne, 71
Morrison, Hobe, 133–5, 137, 299
Morrow, Doretta, 316
Morton, Winn, 294
Moses, Gilbert, 268
Moss, Lawrence John, 134
Most Happy Fella, The, 75
Mostel, Zero, xii, 4, 164–5
Moths, The, 18
Mount-Burke, William, 304
Mowatt, Anna Cora, 95
Mozart, W. A., 14, 68, 190
Mr. President, 261
Müller, Maria, 290
Murawski, C., 292, 294
Murderer Among Us, A, 60
Murray, Brian, 172
Music Man, The, 241
Music Master, The, 291
Musser, Tharon, 130, 134, 282

My Fair Lady, 16, 39, 66, 67, 75, 149, 198, 241, 245, 256, 301
My Fat Friend, 194
My Heart's in the Highlands, 90
My Romance, 11
My Sister, My Sister, 5, 31, 32, 201
Myers, Michaele, 248
Myers, Pamela, 33

Nance Oldfield, 291
Naomi Court, 50, 192
Napier, John, 161
Nathan, George Jean, 96–7
Nation, The, 146, 147, 154
National Health, The, 34–5, 190
National Observer, 126
Naughty Marietta, 304–5
Neeley, Ted, 169
Nelson, Kenneth, 234–5
Nemiroff, Robert, 67–8, 255
Nethersole, Olga, 291–2
Never Too Late, 242
Neville-Andrews, John, 218
New Republic, The, 147, 279
New York, 9, 10, 147, 173–4, 184, 190, 297
New York Daily Mirror, 316
New York Daily News, 26–7, 47–8, 77, 126, 294, 298, 300, 310–11, 316
New York Herald-Tribune, 77, 102, 316
New York Journal-American, 316
New York Post, 47–8, 50, 71, 77, 102, 123, 294, 299, 301, 310–11, 316
New York Shakespeare Festival, 19, 31, 104, 222–3
New York Times, The, 1–3, 8, 20–1, 26–7, 47–8, 68, 77, 85, 93, 97–8, 189–90, 203, 222, 275, 280, 292, 295–6, 298–9, 304–5, 310–11, 313, 316–17
New York Times Book Review, The, 124
New York *World-Telegram*, 316
New Yorker, The, 98, 146–7, 173, 174, 183
Newsday, 102, 103, 138–44, 296, 302
Newsweek, 146, 154, 155, 190, 296, 299, 302, 312
Newley, Anthony, 234–5
Newman, Phyllis, 234
Nicholls, Allan, 169
Nichols, Mike, 172, 240
Nichols, Peter, 35, 190
Night of the Auk, 257–8
Night of the Iguana, The, 229–30
Nights of Cabiria, 105
Nilsson, Birgit, 290–1
No, No, Nanette, 16, 17, 66, 70, 121, 167, 203, 304
No Sad Songs for Me, 220
Nobody Loves an Albatross, 235–7

Nordica, Johanna Gadski, 291
Norman Conquests, The, 198
Norton, Elliot, 232–45, 295
Nourish the Beast, 223

Oates, Joyce Carol, 223
Oboler, Arch, 257–8
Odd Couple, The, 105, 134, 240
Odets, Clifford, 54, 61, 98, 99, 111, 264
Odyssey, 133
Oenslager, Donald, 282
Of Thee I Sing, 100
Oh! Calcutta, 250
O'Horgan, Tom, 25, 169, 268–9
Oklahoma!, 67, 75, 110, 241, 245, 301, 304
Oliver!, 241, 261
Oliver, Edith, 146, 184
Olivier, Lawrence, 4, 100, 129
Olsen and Johnson, 230, 231
Olster, Fredi, 284
Oman, Julia Trevelyan, 138
On the Town, 16, 96
Once in a Lifetime, 100, 236
110 in the Shade, 241
O'Neill, Eugene, 4, 10, 22–3, 47–8, 96, 99, 100, 105–6, 130–1, 156, 166, 246–7, 282–3, 303·
O'Neill Henry, 71
Operation Sidewinder, 111–13
Oppenheimer, George, 102, 103, 109–114, 138, 296
Opper, Don, 288
Orpheus Descending, 258–9
Osborne, John, 129, 170, 205–6
O'Sullivan Maureen, 242
Othello, 193, 249
Our Lady of the Flowers, 141–2
Out Cry, 75, 108, 123–6, 307
Over Here!, 29–30, 167, 193

Pacific Overtures, xi
Paint Your Wagon, 67
Pajama Game, The, 16, 56–9, 74
Pal Joey, 63
Papp, Joseph, 104, 155, 162, 223, 317
Parker, H. T., 97
Parry, William, 169
Passionate Playgoer, The, 102
Patrick, John, 22
Payne, John, 281
Pecorone, Il, 91
Pène du Bois, Raoul, 191
Pepper, Stephen, xiii
Perkinson, Coleridge-Taylor, 30
Peters, Bernadette, 34
Phillips, Margaret, 231
Piñero, Miguel, 162
Pinter, Harold, 5, 10, 50, 75, 78, 81, 83, 109, 153, 160, 170

Pippin, 8, 15, 17, 29, 57, 72, 73, 300
Pirandello, Luigi, 99
Plaza Suite, 134
Plume de ma Tante, La, 230
Plummer, Christopher, 40
Poe, Edgar Allan, 95
Poitier, Sidney, 127
Pope, Thomas, 91
Porgy and Bess, 98
Porter, Cole, 11, 44, 98, 99, 173
Preston, Robert, 34, 235–6
Price, Vincent, 110
Priddy, Nancy, 248
Prime of Miss Jean Brodie, The, 186
Prince, Harold, 9, 13, 33, 52, 136–7, 167, 168, 173, 267, 285
Private Lives, 100, 140
Prodigal Sister, The, 27–9
Promenade, 13–15, 20
Promises, Promises, 16, 78
Puccini, Giacomo, 4, 13–15, 68
Purlie Victorious, 28, 247, 296
Pygmalion, 245

Quick, Eldon, 248
Quintero, José, 47, 50

Rabe, David, 113–14, 155–6, 160
Rabb, Ellis, 40–1
Raidy, William, 271, 297
Raisin, 67–8, 74, 190, 254
Raisin in the Sun, A, 68, 127–8, 254
Ralston, Tari, 33
Randolph, Robert, 32, 105, 191
Rattigan, Terence, 118, 162, 174, 220
Ravel, Maurice, 37
Red Gloves, 152
Red, White and Maddox, 15
Reed, Alaina, 169
Reed, Florence, 97
Rees, Roger, 143
Reilly, Charles Nelson, 134, 221
Reiner, Fritz, 227, 231
Respectful Prostitute, The, 231
Return of Peter Grimm, The, 74
Revere, Anne, 231
Reynolds, Debbie, 72, 121, 167, 304
Rice, Tim, 269
Richard II, 193, 283
Richards, Lloyd, 127
Richardson, Ralph, 193
Richardson, Tony, 129
Rigby, Harry, 280
Rigg, Diana, 186
Rimers of Eldritch, The, 60
Ritchard, Cyril, 71
Ritman, William, 134
Ritz, The, 292, 297–9, 305
River Niger, The, 6, 30, 32, 85–7, 137
Rivera, Chita, 73

Robards, Jason, 48, 50, 106, 131, 166, 282–3

Robbins, Jerome, 58–9, 72–3, 96, 238, 256–7

Roberta, 98

Robespierre, 291

Rocket to the Moon, 264

Rodgers and Hart, 309–10

Rodgers, Richard, 11, 68, 71, 99, 110, 232

Rodgers, Rod, 28

Rodgers, Shev, 133

Rogers, Paul, 83

Rolph, Marti, 282

Romantiques, Les, 211

Romberg, Sigmund, 11, 12, 304

Rome, Harold, 11, 99

Romeo and Juliet, 60, 257

Room Service, 20

Roosevelt, Karyl, 124

Rose, George, 194

Rose, Philip, 127, 292, 294–6

Rose of the Rancho, The, 291

Rosencrantz and Guildenstern Are Dead, 157

Rosenfield, John, 245–53, 263

Rosenkavalier, Der, 70, 266

Ross, Ted, 221, 303

Rossini, Gioacchini, 29, 37, 68

Rostand, Edmond, 40, 211

Roth, Ann, 41

Routledge, Patricia, 110

Royal Hunt of the Sun, The, 45, 160

Royal Shakespeare Company, 83, 116, 143, 211, 267

"Rumble, The," 257

Russell, Lillian, 291

Sackler, Howard, 279

Saint Joan, 137, 254

Saint-Subber, 38

Saks, Gene, 237, 311

Salvation, 19, 78

Same Time, Next Year, xi, 43–4, 311–312

Sapper (H. C. McNeile), 218

Sardou, Victorien, 155

Saroyan, William, 90, 99

Sartre, Jean Paul, 130, 190, 271–2

Saturday Night, 60

Saturday Review, 98, 147, 203, 204, 311

Saturday Review, The (England), 187

Saturday Sunday Monday, 22, 29, 179–180

Sawyer, Michael, 50

Scapino, 178–9

Schapiro, Herb, 112

Schiller, Johann von, 46

Schisgal, Murray, 135, 298

Schmidt, Harvey, 211

School for Scandal, The, 95

Schulz, Michael A., 112

Schwartz, Arthur, 11, 99, 153

Scofield, Paul, 259–60

Score, 186

Screens, The, 271–5

Seagull, The, 10

Seascape, 108, 260–1, 270–1, 307, 308

Secret Affairs of Mildred Wild, The, 307

Seesaw, 41–2, 136

Segal, Erich, 133

Seidelman, Arthur A., 111

Semi-Detached, 60

Septee, Moe, 304

Serling, Rod, 285

Seven Brides for Seven Brothers, 292

1776, 15, 20, 296

Sextet, 29, 48–9

Sgt. Pepper, 168–9

Shaffer, Peter, 45, 122–3, 160–2, 182–3, 199

Shakespeare, William, 50, 60, 70, 75, 91–2, 95–6, 104, 107–8, 111, 139, 144–5, 149, 163, 176–7, 190, 206, 212–13, 220, 257, 266, 279, 291

Shanghai Gesture, The, 97

Shapiro, Joseph, 293

Shapiro, Mel, 104

Sharp, Chris, 310, 312

Shaw, George Bernard, 94, 99, 155, 187–9, 198, 231, 245, 254, 271, 291

Shaw, Irwin, 61, 98, 99

She Loves Me, 52, 242

Shenandoah, 155, 292–7, 305

Shepard, Sam, 112–13, 223

Sheridan, Richard Brinsley, 94–5, 144

Sherin, Edwin, 160

Sherlock Holmes, 21n, 143

Sherry!, 84, 104

Sherwood, Robert E., 99

Shevelove, Burt, 70

Shoemaker's Holiday, 69

Short Eyes, 162, 194, 197

Show Boat, 98

Shumlin, Herman, 250

Siegfried, 152

Silvers, Phil, 18

Simmons, Jean, 266

Simon, John, 10, 76, 174, 184–6, 189–203, 260, 297

Simon, Neil, 23–4, 34, 69, 74, 75, 84–5, 105, 118, 134, 136, 145, 174–5, 220–1, 240, 277

Sinden, Donald, 115–16, 131–2, 143, 220, 267

Singer, Marc, 284

Sirens, The, 54–5

6 Rms, 44

Skin of Our Teeth, The, 128, 261

Skinner, Cornelia Otis, 71
Slade, Bernard, 311–12
Slight Ache, A, 83
Smalls, Charlie, 221, 268, 299–300, 302
Smiles of a Summer Night, 136, 168, 266
Smith, Art, 257
Smith, Catherine Lee, 133
Smith, Euan, 143
Smith, Maggie, 140
Smith, Oliver, 38, 66, 67, 229
Smith, Walt, 6, 31
Somner, Pearl, 294
Sondheim, Stephen, 9, 10, 12, 13, 32–3, 71–2, 99, 136–7, 167–8, 172–173, 256–7, 266, 285
Sophie, 261
Sophocles, 63
Sorcerer's Apprentice, The, 15
Sothern, Julia, 291
Sound of Music, The, 18, 241
South Pacific, 110, 241
Spriggs, Elizabeth, 143
Standing, Lionel, 140
Stapleton, Maureen, 24, 186
Star-Spangled Girl, 84–5
Starr, Frances, 291
Stasio, Marilyn, 216–24, 296
Status Quo Vadis, 42–3, 307
Stehli, Edgar, 71
Stennett, Michael, 144
Sterling, Jan, 196
Sternhagen, Frances, 161
Stevens, Connie, 84
Stewart, Lesley, 234
Sticks and Bones, 113–14, 155, 160
Stigwood, Robert, 269
Stockhausen, Karlheinz, 15
Stone, Peter, 135–6
Stop the World, I Want to Get Off, 234–5, 241–2, 261
Stoppard, Tom, 156–8, 219–20
Storey, David, 5, 75, 117, 162–3, 169–71, 190, 195, 222, 269
Storm in Summer, 285
Stowe, Harriet Beecher, 95
Strange Interlude, 96, 99–100
Strauss, Richard, 68, 70, 89
Streetcar Named Desire, A, 40, 124, 125, 148
Streisand, Barbara, 72, 237–40
Strike, Maurice, 59
Stritch, Elaine, 33, 309
Stromberg, John, 291
Student Prince, The, 63, 98
Styne, Jule, 11, 99, 110, 136, 237–240
Subways Are for Sleeping, 232–4
Sudermann, Hermann, 187
Sugar, 135–6
Sullavan, Margaret, 220
Sullivan, Dan, 1, 275–89, 314

Summer and Smoke, 231, 249–50
Sunshine Boys, The, 136
Sweet Charity, 42, 57, 78, 104–6
Swenson, Swen, 164
Sydney, Basil, 99

Tagg, Alan, 144
Taming of the Shrew, The, 99, 283–5
Tandy, Jessica, 215
Taubman, Howard, 1
Taylor, Clarice, 221, 303
Taylor, Laurette, 149, 151
Taylor, Robert Lewis, 262
Tempest, The, 193
Templeton, Fay, 291
Ter-Arutunian, Rouben, 191, 215
Terry, Ellen, 96, 291
Tesich, Steven, 160, 223
Thacker, Russ, 133
That Championship Season, 222
Theater Divided, A, 63
Theatre Arts Magazine, 98, 227–8
Theodore, Donna, 293, 297
Theodore, Lee Becker, 52–3
They Knew What They Wanted, 97
Thomas, Dylan, 118
Thompson, Howard, 305
Thompson, Sada, 284
Thoreau, Henry, 12, 13
Three Musketeers, The, 304–5
Three Sisters, The, 126–7, 163, 284–285
Thurston, Howard, 66
Tillinger, John, 193
Time, 123, 146, 154, 168, 190, 302, 311
Time of Your Life, The, 89–90
Titus Andronicus, 279
To Bury a Cousin, 60
Toller, Ernst, 99
Tooth of Crime, The, 223
Topor, Tom, 301
Topper, 102
Tovarich, 261
Toys in the Attic, 230–1
Tragedy and Comedy, 91
Tree Grows in Brooklyn, A, 153
Trial, The, 263-4
Trial of the Catonsville Nine, The, 202
Tubs, The, 298
Tucker, Robert, 292, 294, 297
Tumarin, Boris, 126
Tune, Tommy, 41, 136
Tunick, Jonathan, 33
Twentieth-Century-Fox, 302, 305
Two by Two, 186
Two for the Seesaw, 41, 136
Two Gentlemen of Verona, 19, 29, 104

Udell, Peter, 294–6
Ullmann, Liv, 217
Ulysses in Nighttown, 163–5

Uncle Tom's Cabin, 95
Uncle Vanya, 163, 171–2
Uris, Leon, 6, 7, 31
Ustinov, Peter, 135

Variety, 132–5, 137, 299
Verdon, Gwen, 73, 78, 105
Veronica's Room, 39–40, 181
Vertes, Marcel, 230
Via Galactica, 307
Victor, Lucia, 32
Victory, 140–1
Vidnovic, Martin, 133
Viet Rock, 60
View from the Bridge, A, 61
View from the Sixties, A, 102
Village Voice, The, 144–5
Visit, The, 191, 223
Volanakis, Minos, 273

Wagner, Richard, 10, 14, 190
Wagner, Robin, 26
Waiting for Godot, 19, 69, 128–9, 151, 208
Walken, Christopher, 219
Walker, David, 144
Walker, Don, 58, 294
Walker, Joseph A., 6, 30, 87, 137
Wall Street Journal, The, 115, 126, 297
Wallach, Allan, 138–44
Wallach, Eli, 107, 165–6, 172
Wallach, Ira, 247–8
Waltz of the Toreadors, The, 106–7, 147, 165, 172
War Against Mrs. Hadley, The, 102
Ward, Douglas Turner, 87
Warfield, David, 291
Warner, Neil, 60
Washington Post, 68, 253
Wasserman, Dale, 88
Waterloo, 291
Waterston, Sam, 217
Watson, Dr. Jack, xiii
Watt, Douglas, 26–44, 47–8, 176, 294, 298–300, 310–11
Watts, Richard, Jr., 47–8, 102–8, 114, 123, 316
Weaver, Fritz, 262
Webb, Virginia Dancy, 35
Weber, Andrew, 269
Weber and Fields, 291
Weidner, Paul, 31
Weill, Kurt, 11, 13–15, 81, 204, 205
Weisser, Norbert, 287
Weller, Michael, 160
Welles, Orson, 69
Wesley, Richard, 31, 55–6
West Side Story, 11, 16n, 17, 53, 63, 72–3, 75, 233, 241, 255–7, 261, 304
Weston, Jack, 299

What the Wine-Sellers Buy, 4, 30, 32, 85–6
Wheeler, Harold, 221
Wheeler, Hugh, 136, 285
When You Comin' Back, Red Ryder?, 119–20, 222, 265–6
Where's Charley?, 134–5
Whirl-I-Gig, 291
Whispers on the Wind, 137
White, Diz, 218
White, Onna, 6, 38, 66, 67
Whiting, John, 254
Whitman, Walt, 95
Who's Afraid of Virginia Wolf?, 5, 241, 261
Who's Who in Hell, 135, 174
Why Hanna's Skirt Won't Stay Down, 19
Wickwire, Nancy, 284
Widowing of Mrs. Holroyd, The, 70
Wild and Wonderful, 29
Wilder, Gene, 135
Wilder, Thornton, 259, 261, 274
Williams, Clifford, 176
Williams, Dick A., 4
Williams, Heathcote, 222
Williams, Tennessee, 10, 50, 61, 62, 75, 78, 99, 108, 123–5, 178, 201, 210, 229–30, 249–50, 258
Williamson, Nicol, 172
Wilson, Andrew, 142
Wilson, Edwin, 115–26, 297
Wilson, Robert, 142, 217–18
Winters, Shelley, 185
Wiz, The, 155, 221–2, 268, 292, 299–303, 305
Woldin, Judd, 67, 68, 254–5
Wolfe, Karin, 38
Wolfit, Donald, 260
Women's Wear Daily, 47–8, 52, 54–6, 59–60, 63, 66–7, 302, 310, 312
Wood Demon, The, 194–5
Wood, John, 220
Wood, Peggy, 71
Woollcott, Alexander, 97, 228
Wonderful World of Oz, The, 221
Words and Music, 197
World of Musical Comedy, The, 110
Wright, Robert, 316

Yeargan, Michael H., 298
"Yesterday," 36, 98
Youmans, Vincent, 17
Young, Loretta, 96–7
Young, Stark, 97–8
Your Own Thing, 78, 111

Zaltzberg, Charlotte, 255
Zaza, 291
Zoo Story, The, 209–10, 266
Zorba, 17, 53, 57